International Law and the Global South

Perspectives from the Rest of the World

This book series aims to promote a complex vision of contemporary legal developments from the perspective of emerging or developing countries and/or authors integrating these elements into their approach. While focusing on today's law and international economic law in particular, it brings together contributions from, or influenced by, other social sciences disciplines. Written in both technical and non-technical language and addressing topics of contemporary importance to a general audience, the series will be of interest to legal researchers as well as non-lawyers. In referring to the "rest of the world", the book series puts forward new and alternative visions of today's law not only from emerging and developing countries, but also from authors who deliberately integrate this perspective into their thinking. The series approach is not only comparative, post-colonial or critical, but also truly universal in the sense that it places a plurality of well-informed visions at its center.

The Series

Provides a truly global coverage of the world in reflecting cutting-edge developments and thinking in law and international law

Focuses on the transformations of international and comparative law with an emphasis on international economic law (investment, trade and development)

Welcomes contributions on comparative and/or domestic legal evolutions

Nitish Monebhurrun • Carolina Olarte-Bácares •
Marco A. Velasquez-Ruiz
Editors

International Investment Law and Arbitration from a Latin American Perspective

Springer

Editors
Nitish Monebhurrun
University Centre of Brasilia
Brasilia, Brazil

Carolina Olarte-Bácares
University of Javeriana
Bogotá, Colombia

Marco A. Velasquez-Ruiz
University of Javeriana
Bogotá, Colombia

ISSN 2510-1420 ISSN 2510-1439 (electronic)
International Law and the Global South
ISBN 978-3-031-49381-2 ISBN 978-3-031-49382-9 (eBook)
https://doi.org/10.1007/978-3-031-49382-9

This Springer imprint is published by the registered company Springer Nature Switzerland AG
The registered company address is: Gewerbestrasse 11, 6330 Cham, Switzerland

Preface

The book brings to light how Latin American States have traditionally stood before the field of International Investment Law and Arbitration. It delves into their posture of resistance to critically examine how their perspective has gradually changed and how they have adapted their investment agreements so as not to leave their position as players in the field of International Investment Law. Many Latin American States have appeared as defendants before international investment tribunals and some of these, like Venezuela, Bolivia, or Ecuador, have denounced their international investment agreements.[1] At the time Ecuador and Venezuela denounced the Washington Convention which instituted the International Center for the Settlement of Investment Disputes—in 2009 for Ecuador and in 2012 for Venezuela—these States ranked high as defendants in the list of investor-State arbitration cases.[2] In reaction to this, in 2013, Ecuador instituted a Commission for the Auditing of the Treaties on the Reciprocal Protection of Investments and the International Investment Arbitration System [*Comisión para la Auditoría Integral Ciudadana de los Tratados de Protección Recíproca de Inversiones y del Sistema de Arbitraje Internacional en Materia de Inversiones (Caitisa)*].[3] In one of its reports, the

[1]Tanzi A., Asteriti A., Polanco Lazo R. and Turrini P., Introduction, in, Tanzi A. *et al.* (2016), International Investment Law in Latin America/Derecho Internacional de las Inversiones en América Latina, Leiden, BRILL, 1; Polanco Lazo R., Two Worlds Apart: The Changing Features of International Investment Agreements in Latin America, in, Tanzi A. *et al.* (2016), International Investment Law in Latin America/Derecho Internacional de las Inversiones en América Latina, Leiden, BRILL, 76; Álvarez Zárate J.M.; Zenkiewicz M., Introducción, in, Álvarez Zárate J.M.; Zenkiewicz M. (eds.) (2021), Derecho Internacional de las inversiones. Desarrollo actual de normas y principios, Bogota, Universidad Externado de Colombia, 23–24; Luque Mácias M.J. (2021), Re-Politicising International Investment Law in Latin America Through the Duty to Regulate Paradigm, Cham, Springer, 90–91.

[2]UNCTAD (2011), Latest Developments in Investor-State Dispute Settlement, IIA Issue notes, no. 1, 12.

[3]CAITISA (2013), Un exceso de los BITs es ceder espacio de solución de conflictos al exterior [available at: https://caitisa.org/].

Commission stated that there was no evidence that the investment agreements signed by Ecuador had brought more investments to the State.[4] The report critically denounced that the investment agreements signed by Ecuador lacked legitimacy because they were not submitted to a debate before the legislative power.[5] Still, it is noteworthy that Ecuador has rejoined the ICSID Convention in 2021.[6]

With a posture of its own, Brazil has long been a fervent objector to the whole system of international investment law which it however joined as from 2015 by proposing a new type of investment agreement which excludes investor-State arbitration as well as classical provisions like the fair and equitable treatment, full protection and security or indirect expropriation.[7] Often deeming the law field as imbalanced,[8] many Latin American States have looked for alternatives to continue providing legal protection to foreign investors while protecting their right to regulate local matters of public concern.[9] Some interesting investment agreement models or domestic law adaptations have consequently flourished and have arrested the attention of those studying or working with international investment law.

According to the UNCTAD's 2022 World Investment Report, foreign direct investment (FDI)—including greenfield investments[10]—flows have increased by 56% in Latin America and the Caribbean in 2022, leading to a partial recovery after the COVID-19 harshest years.[11] The increase in FDI for South America for the same period is as high as 74%.[12] There was an increase of FDI in Bolivia in 2022 after a wave of divestment in 2020.[13] Additionally, capital exportation from Latin America rose, namely due to Brazilian and Chilean multinational companies.[14] Latin America is therefore still on the map when it comes to international investments and

[4] CAITISA (2020), Boletines: Caitisa entregó informe final de los BITs al Ejecutivo [available at: https://caitisa.org/boletines/].

[5] Ibid.

[6] IISD (2021), Investment Treaty News: Ecuador Rejoins the ICSID Convention [available at: https://www.iisd.org/itn/en/2021/10/07/ecuador-rejoins-the-icsid-convention/].

[7] On this question, see the chapter authored by Nitish Monebhurrun and Leonardo Vieira Arruda Achtschin [Dispute Prevention Methods in the Brazilian Agreements on Cooperation and Facilitation of Investments (CFIAs)] in this book.

[8] Álvarez Zárate J. M.; Zenkiewicz M., Introducción, in, Álvarez Zárate J. M.; Zenkiewicz M. (eds.) (2021), Derecho Internacional de las inversiones. Desarrollo actual de normas y principios, Bogota, Universidad Externado de Colombia, 23.

[9] See generally: Luque Mácias M. J. (2021), Re-Politicising International Investment Law in Latin America Through the Duty to Regulate Paradigm, Cham, Springer, 285p.

[10] UNCTAD (2022), World Investment Report 2022 (Chapter 1: Global Investments Trends and Prospects), UNCTAD/WIR/2022, 36.

[11] Ibid. p. 7.

[12] Ibid. p. 15.

[13] Ibid. p. 18.

[14] Ibid. p. 21.

notwithstanding a traditional form of resistance[15] it remains on the map of international investment law. Some recent investment—or investment-related—agreements signed by Latin American States include, for instance: the Venezuela/Colombia Bilateral Investment Agreement (03/02/2023); the Uruguay/Turkey Bilateral Investment Agreement (23/04/2022); the Pacific Alliance/Singapore Free Trade Agreement (26/01/2022); the Chile/Paraguay Free Trade Agreement (01/12/2021); the Colombia/Spain Bilateral Investment Treaty (16/09/2021); the Central America/ United Kingdom Economic Association Agreement (18/07/2019); the Chile/Ecuador Economic Complementation Agreement (13/08/2020); the Brazil/India Agreement on Cooperation and Facilitation of Investments (25/01/2020); the Hong Kong, China/Mexico Bilateral Investment Treaty (23/01/2020); the Intra-Mercosur Cooperation and Facilitation Investment (07/04/2017).

The main objective of this book is to critically discuss how Latin American States have accepted, resisted, or adapted themselves to international investment law and arbitration. Accordingly, the general connection between these States and international investment law will be explained in the **introduction**. The latter will examine the general trends as per which Latin American States have offered a legal protection to foreign investments. The **first chapter** will enter the merits of where international investment law and arbitration stand in some Latin American States whereby the experience of Brazil, Chile, Argentina, Venezuela, and Uruguay will be discussed. The **second chapter** will explain the trends in international investment law and arbitration in Latin America. These trends are namely related to dispute settlement and governance, to the connection between investment law and human rights and finally to regionalization. In this chapter, the experience of States like Brazil, Colombia, Peru, and Mexico will be perused.

Brasilia, Brazil
Bogotá, Colombia

Nitish Monebhurrun
Carolina Olarte-Bácares
Marco A. Velasquez-Ruiz

[15] Polanco Lazo R., Two Worlds Apart: The Changing Features of International Investment Agreements in Latin America, in, Tanzi A. *et al.* (2016), International Investment Law in Latin America/Derecho Internacional de las Inversiones en América Latina, Leiden, BRILL, 69.

Acknowledgement

This book's royalties will be given to ASOCAB (a Colombian peasant association victim of forced displacement from the Hacienda Las Pavas) to support their agricultural projects in the process of claiming their right to return to their land. Part of the research undertaken for this book received the support of the Research Foundation of the Federal District, Brazil (FAP/DF).

Contents

List of Contributors

Leonardo Vieira Arruda Achtschin University Center of Brasilia, Brasilia, Brazil

João Paulo Santos Borba University Center of Brasilia, Brasilia, Brazil

Ana María Aranda Castillo Pontificia Universidad Javeriana, Bogota, Colombia

Rafael Ramos Codeço Ministry of Economy, Brasilia, Brazil

Ana Rachel Freitas da Silva Office of the Attorney General, Ministry of Economy, Brasilia, Brazil

Pablo Nilo Donoso Investment Arbitration Unit of the Vice-Ministry of International Economic Affairs, Santiago, Chile

Ivette S. Esis Villarroel University Finnis Terrae, Santiago, Chile

Virdzhiniya Petrova Georgieva Universidad Nacional Autonóma de México (UNAM), Mexico City, Mexico

Salvador Herencia-Carrasco University of Ottawa, Ottawa, ON, Canada

Nitish Monebhurrun University Center of Brasilia, Brasilia, Brazil

Carolina Olarte-Bácares Pontificia Universidad Javeriana, Bogota, Colombia

Juan P. Pontón-Serra Universidad del Rosario, Bogota, Colombia

Enrique Prieto-Rios Faculty of Law, Universidad del Rosario, Bogota, Colombia

Gustavo Ferreira Ribeiro University Center of Brasilia, Brasilia, Brazil

Christian G. Sommer National University of Córdoba, Córdoba, Argentina
Catholic University of Córdoba, Córdoba, Argentina

Marco A. Velasquez-Ruiz Pontificia Universidad Javeriana, Bogota, Colombia

Magdalena Bas Vilizzio University of Monterrey, Monterrey, Mexico

Introduction—Legal Protection Offered to Foreign Investment in Latin America: Context and General Trends

Marco A. Velasquez-Ruiz, Carolina Olarte-Bácares, and Ana María Aranda Castillo

1 Introduction

This chapter presents a general historical and political-economy portrait of the legal protection that has been offered to foreign investment in Latin America, particularly through of the systematic conclusion of international investment agreements (hereafter IIAs)[1] by the countries of the region. This picture aims to illustrate the factors and circumstances under which said safeguarding has entered into tension with the protection of public interests within the realm of investor-state arbitration (hereafter ISA).

The chapter starts by considering Latin America beyond its territorial nature or administrative configuration. Instead, the region is portrayed as a historical product: a political, social, and economic reality, crucial for the consolidation of the global project known as *modernity*.[2] The corresponding diagnosis speaks about the fact that the process of consolidation of Latin American states has been marked by a series of events that account for their *instability*. The latter condition is defined as an essential and permanent friction between the states' expectation to adjust to the global model in which they are registered as members of the international community, and the satisfaction of the general interests of their population by virtue of their

[1] For the purposes of this chapter, the term "international investment agreements" encompasses both bilateral investment treaties and free trade agreements that include specific investment chapters.

[2] The project of modernity is supposed to represent rationalism, technocentrism, the standardization of knowledge and production, a belief in linear progress and in universal, absolute truths. See Meiksins (1997), pp. 539–560.

M. A. Velasquez-Ruiz (✉) · C. Olarte-Bácares · A. M. A. Castillo
Pontificia Universidad Javeriana, Bogotá, Colombia
e-mail: velasquez.m@javeriana.edu.co; c.olarte@javeriana.edu.co; aranda_a@javeriana.edu.co

N. Monebhurrun et al. (eds.), *International Investment Law and Arbitration from a Latin American Perspective*, International Law and the Global South,
https://doi.org/10.1007/978-3-031-49382-9_1

constitutional orders. Instability is thus traced back in several phenomena that have characterized the region's progression: *violence, inequality, and external intervention.*

Henceforth, the chapter turns to pose a brief historical account of the legal protection that has been offered to foreign investment in the region. This tale suggests that such phenomenon should be traced back to the very emergence of Latin American states, denoting that since the latter were consciously erected as fundamental elements for the consolidation of the *liberal market-economy democracy* global model, foreign investors/investments have permanently counted with effective mechanisms to safeguard their rights and economic expectations. In particular, they have had the possibility to access judicial and non-judicial schemes to claim compensation for damages that, in a great number of cases, are related to the exertion of public regulatory powers to achieve the general interest.

Finally, the chapter advances on an analysis of investor-state arbitration in Latin America. First, it provides some insights on the process through which Latin American states decided to implement a policy of systematic conclusion of IIAs, and consequently faced setbacks to adjust their domestic legal orders to the global investment protection system under development. Thereafter, it presents a series of statistics around the occurrence of investor-state arbitration in Latin America and provides an analysis as to their link with the particularities of the region. This examination aims to identify trends from the standpoint of (1) the countries that have assumed the greatest load of litigation of this kind, and the contextual reasons for such tendency; (2) the type of foreign investors or investments that have suited sovereign states before investor-state arbitration tribunals; (3) the type of public interests and social actors that, on the occasion of their tension with the interests of foreign investors/investments, have been under discussion through investor-state arbitration; and (4) the main outcomes of the cases.

2 Context: A Young Unstable Region

What is nowadays known as *Latin America* must be understood as one of the most relevant components of the political/social/economic project known as *modernity*. The territory corresponding to Latin America was subjected for more than three centuries to the domination of various European powers (Spain, Portugal, and France, among others). Yet, on the occasion of the flow of liberal ideas framed within The Enlightenment, the decay of colonial administrations, and the empowerment of local Creole elites, between the end of the eighteenth century and the beginning of the nineteenth century emancipatory processes were unleashed, thus leading to the formation of nation-states.[3]

[3] See generally Simon (2021).

The new republics inherited the political division under which the colonial establishment maintained control and authority over populations, lands, and natural resources. The latter elements were necessary to consolidate the former as government entities and thus be recognized by the international community as free and equal members. This is, fit in the standards of law and international relations of the time in order to join the club of sovereign peoples considered as civilized.[4]

From the standpoint of the international community[5] of the time, mainly formed by European countries and the United States, Latin America was considered a strategic location for the consolidation of *liberal market-economy democracy*, the model considered adequate to guide global destinies. From a political economy point of view, the region turned to be identified as a privileged enclave to meet two associated objectives. On the one hand, accessing to land, natural resources, and work, production factors necessary to feed the increasingly prosperous industrialization process that was taking place at the Global North. On the other hand, locating surplus capital generated by the aforementioned process, so as to continue generating wealth under a transnational dynamic.

On the other hand, the nascent Latin American states—and correspondingly the elites that had won independence and that therefore had decision-making capacity over said territories—considered that it was essential to consolidate as members of the international community to advance towards regional stability. Predominantly, they aimed at deterring either an attempt of European reconquest or the invasion of other external powers. But it was also considered important to access the expertise, technologies, and capital that could boost the novel states to function, from the perspective of the global model, as *engines of civilization* or mechanisms of development.

Considering the latter context, it must be pointed out that the consolidation of Latin American States and the corresponding development of their national projects has been marked by a series of events that account for their *instability*. Such condition is shaped by a tension between their willingness to adjust to the global model in which they are registered, on the one hand, and the fact that they must comply with the satisfaction of the general interests of their population by virtue of their constitutional orders, on the other. Throughout their history and on the way to consolidate their national projects, the Latin American states have faced destabilizing phenomena generally associated with *violence, inequality, and external intervention*. Although each context own particular features, these situations are common in the region and reflect the gap between the action (political, social, economic) of the states as constituted authority and the crystallization of the collective aspirations of the national societies that they are supposed to represent.

---

[4] See generally Anghie (2012); Tzouvala (2021).

[5] The concept "international community" is here used to resemble the set of political entities with sovereign characteristics that, under the aspiration of identifying and managing common interests, conduct practices and conclude agreements to guarantee the stable accomplishment of such shared position.

2.1 Violence

Violence is here considered as a broad concept that intends to include a great variety of situations. Following Johan Galtung's structuralist vision, the former implies that human beings are being influenced so that their actual somatic and mental realizations are below their potential realizations.[6] Hence violence is regarded from a holistic perspective according to which there are factors affecting, positively or negatively, an individual's effective possibility to sustain a life under basic wellbeing conditions. Consequently, it has both personal and structural manifestations, which are interconnected.[7]

Whereas Latin American emancipation implied the conduction of wide-range military actions to take authority from the European colonizing powers, the use of force to access and manage power continued over the republican life of the new states. Political discrepancies among socioeconomic elites led to innumerable civil wars all around the region, which imperiled the states' capacity to address their constitutional mandates and directly impacted peoples' personhood and property.

In addition, the explosion of socioeconomic crises in Latin American countries at the onset of the twentieth century propelled local violence. The emergence and consolidation of movements with a popular and communitarian extraction—unionized workers, women, the peasantry, and indigenous peoples, among others—that questioned the established order and demanded the production of structural changes, led to dynamics of repression exerted by public authorities.[8]

Within the context of the international struggle between ideological models—labelled by historical accounts as the Cold War—, in the second half of the twentieth century popular animosity and discontent went further on in Latin America, with the rising of diverse insurgent movements. The latter interrogated structural inequalities and power abuse by public authorities, and consequently aimed at overturning official governments. With the exception of Cuba, where the insurgency had success in taking out power from the establishment, revolution intents turned into long and degraded internal armed conflicts. The latter eventually included the participation of paramilitary forces and produced millions of victims with varied associated affectations. On the other hand, violence also crystallized in the surge of despotic regimes in various countries of the region, some of which greatly influenced by the military, which exerted repressive action on the population.

Finally, violence in Latin America has recently expanded on the occasion of the increase of common criminality, mainly in urban areas, where the complex socioeconomic conditions under which the population lives have produced the emergence

---

[6] See generally Galtung (1969), pp. 167–191.

[7] Violence is directly connected with inequality insofar it builds into the structure and shows up as unequal power and consequently as unequal life chances.

[8] A salient outcome of this phenomenon was the success of a revolutionary movement in Mexico that advance on the nationalization of key industries such as petroleum, land, and the railroads, thus affecting foreign interests that had been placed all over the Region. See Meyer (2010).

of organizations and gangs. In the same way, the spreading out of illicit economies such as drug trafficking or illegal mining has fueled the growth of armed structures that are involved in these businesses.

2.2 *Inequality*

Inequality is here regarded as the presence of socioeconomic discrepancies people, and concretizes in status, rights, and opportunities.[9] High inequality increases poverty and reduces the impact of economic development on poverty reduction.[10] Likewise, it has been shown how excessive inequality could erode social cohesion, lead to political polarization, and ultimately lower economic growth.[11]

Regardless of particular variations from case to case, Latin American countries have maintained a scheme of great inequality among their population. Since the outset of the new republics in the nineteenth century onwards, control over decision-making, economic resources, and information has been concentrated in particular sectors of the population, which generally coincide with the elites that undertook the emancipatory project. According to a 2004 study conducted by the World Bank,

> Latin American inequality is pervasive, characterizing every aspect of life, including access to education, health and public services; access to land and other assets; the functioning of credit and formal labor markets; and attainment of political voice and influence. Inequality is also resilient; in its modern form, high inequality is rooted in exclusionary institutions that have been perpetuated ever since colonial times and that have survived different political and economic regimes, from interventionist and import substitution strategies to more market-oriented policies. Significant racial and ethnic differences also continue to persist even today.

As a result, the richest decile of the population of Latin America earn 48% of the total income, while the poorest 10% of the population earn only 1.6% of the income.[12]

[9] United Nations, Concepts of Inequality Development Strategy and Policy Analysis Unit w Development Policy and Analysis Division Department of Economic and Social Affairs (2015), https://www.un.org/en/development/desa/policy/wess/wess_dev_issues/dsp_policy_01.pdf (last visited Jun 16, 2021).

[10] Adams (2003); Busso and Messina (2020), https://publications.iadb.org/publications/english/document/The-Inequality-Crisis-Latin-America-and-the-Caribbean-at-the-Crossroads.pdf (last visited Jun 16, 2021).

[11] See generally Rodrick (1999), pp. 385–412; Berg (2011).

[12] See De Ferranti (2004).

2.3 External Intervention

Although from a formal point of view Latin American states achieved their independence and recognition as sovereign nations at the beginning of the nineteenth century, the region's history has been marked by external interventions. These interferences have been conducted by states with high levels of development, and therefore with political and economic capacities to influence decision-making at the internal level. The dynamics of external intervention in Latin America have occurred under two scenarios. On the one hand, destabilization of national governments that have assumed a certain type of political ideology contrary to the vision of external influencing power. And on the other hand, specific incidence in political and economic decision-making to favor the interests of the influencing external power.

Following the work of Edward Said on imperialism, this scheme encompasses a relationship characterized by one state influencing the political sovereignty of another political society and can be evidenced in the existence of effective economic, social, or cultural dependency.[13] In this line, J. A. Hobson have pointed out that throughout their process of consolidation, industrialized nations found themselves jeopardized by issues associated to the profitable disposal of their economic resources. On the one hand, production exceeded the growth of consumption so new markets were required. On the other hand, the capital surplus consequence of massive industrialization had to be exported in order not to lose its cost-effectiveness. Furthermore, additional raw materials were needed to satisfy the internal demand. With these issues in mind, such nations had to look for a privileged position at sites out of their direct territorial domain to obtain what was needed to both maintain internal industrial production and generate wealth.[14]

3 Brief Historical Account of the Legal Protection Offered to Foreign Investment in Latin America

3.1 Emergence of Latin American States and Friendship, Commerce, and Navigation Treaties

The legal protection offered to foreign investment can be traced back to the very emergence of Latin American states. This denotes that since Latin America was consciously erected as a fundamental element of the eco-socio-political global project behind modernity, foreign investors/investments have permanently counted with effective mechanisms to safeguard their rights and economic expectations.

[13] See Said (1994).

[14] See generally Hobson (1975). (Originally published by James Pott and Co., at New York, in 1902).

In the first half of the nineteenth century, the region's administrative division—determined by four centuries of European presence—went from being a colonial enclave to becoming a series of independent political units in need of recognition by and interaction with the international community. Struggles for independence left the region highly indebted and henceforth marked the way in which the nascent republics would relate to the industrialized states.[15] Indeed, the importation of the ideal of freedom through the Creole elites was not only reflected in the ideological bases of independence, but also formed part of the legal imaginaries of the region. Therefore, the legal culture that took shape in Latin American countries reveals the way in which the elites were identified with the legal patterns coming from Europe and the United States.[16] Furthermore, the recognition required to be accepted within the international scene was necessarily related to the acceptance of those precepts.

Friendship, commerce, and navigation treaties (FCNTs) were the first international legal mechanisms used to offer protection to foreign investment in Latin America and may be considered as a primitive form of IIAs. FCNTs were one of the most familiar instruments to exert diplomatic relations in the outset of the nineteenth century, and under the context of the region's emancipation, they performed a decisive role in the consolidation of the new republics' sovereignty vis à vis the international community of states. Not only they supported the emerging republics, but also sought opposing the possible reestablishment of a monarchy in the continent and obtaining access to a new market.[17] As their object was fixing the ground-rules governing day-to-day intercourse between countries, nations secured reciprocal respect for their normal interests abroad, according to agreed rules of law.[18]

The language and clauses incorporated in FCNTs were not that of investment protection, but rather a broad approach to the reciprocal protection of foreigners and their private property. The guarantees and rights stipulated in this type of treaties were presented by the developed countries as the way in which a friendly treatment could be ensured with the new States, in which basic legal and economic principles such as respect for private property or free trade, were the base of the relationship.[19] Kate Miles assimilates this process of internationalization of private welfare, through the FCNTs, with a form of imposition of mandatory compliance for developing countries—in this case of Latin America—that allowed extraterritorial legal control over their nationals on the detriment of local legal forms.[20]

From the perspective of the industrialized states, FCNTs were a fundamental tool to facilitate the expansion of trade and for the assurance of a system based on the internationalization of capital. Thus it was considered that since this capital had to be

[15] See Bulmer-Thomas (1994).

[16] See Anghie (2012).

[17] See Lorca (2010), p. 515.

[18] See Walker (1957), pp. 805–824.

[19] Ibídem.

[20] See Miles (2013).

protected from the violent and unstable contexts of non-European nations, their safeguards were decisive for these countries to agree for a successful association with the new states.[21] In this regard and following Sornarajah,[22] it can be affirmed that FCNTs were used on Latin American states as a tool to expand the influence of European and US powers for at least three reasons. Firstly, the need to be granted the international community membership to consolidate both legal and political status; secondly, the evidence of power imbalance in the bargaining between the corresponding parties; and thirdly, the perception of threat as to the use of force by industrialized countries on the occasion of affectations to foreign persons and property. Ultimately, as this international legal model was extrapolated to regulate regional relations, a great number of FCNTs were concluded between the emerging Latin American republics.

3.2 Gunboat Diplomacy and the Calvo Doctrine

The change in the political administration of the Latin American territory had a direct effect on the arrival of foreigners. Without the mobility restrictions imposed by the colonial former powers, paths were opened for the migration of the population from Europe in search of new life alternatives. To the same extent, Latin America represented an economic opportunity for the industrialized states. Hence through their citizens, the former countries sought to both gain access to scarce production factors and generate wealth through the development of businesses of various kinds, mostly related to infrastructure and the extraction of natural resources.

In addition to the law-making process that was crystallized in the early version of the FCNTs, industrialized countries progressively established a supplementary norm to go further on the stabilization of their political and economic expectations at peripheral states, including those of Latin America: the international minimum standard of treatment.[23] This behavioral benchmark was developed to establish a global practice that had to be observed by the international community of states, especially by capital importing countries, with regards to their relationship with foreign persons and property. States receiving capital had thus to consider this minimum standard even when it exceeded the guarantees and rights granted by national laws.[24] Hence, failure to comply with these standards of treatment could entail the international responsibility of the host state, and consequently a response of the foreigner's home State.[25] Such response often translated in the direct intervention of the home state on behalf of its nationals, a practice known as *diplomatic*

[21] *ibidem.*

[22] See Sornarajah (2021).

[23] See Borchard (1940), p. 445.

[24] See Sornarajah (2021).

[25] See Anghie (2004).

protection. The latter entailed the use of the diverse means available—diplomatic, economic, and even belligerent—to safeguard the rights and interests that could have arisen out of the wrongful conduct, and consequently the normative breach.[26] Henceforth, diplomatic protection implied an effective means to take actions against another state on behalf of its national whose rights and interests have been injured by that state.[27]

No few cases that took place under the context of Latin American states breaching either the minimum standard of treatment or affecting the rights and expectations of foreign persons and property in the nineteenth century included the use of force by home states. Such historical phenomenon was then accounted as *gunboat diplomacy* and entailed a forceful means to settle the disputes. When this occurred, the home state's military might be deployed to ensure that the threat of war was a sufficient encouragement to obtain a compensation tailored to the needs of the affected person, either directly or by means of a *claims commission,* which was the most common international dispute settlement scenario of the time. It is noteworthy that the implementation of diplomatic protection, whether as political protest or through use of force, implied that the local reasons or perspectives surrounding the nature and extent of the dispute between the host State and the foreigner were not extensively considered.[28] This was problematic to the extent that the system was unaware of certain contexts of political and economic instability, or even the fact that the behavior of foreigners could have implied a breach of domestic law. Nineteenth century's Latin America was the scenario of multiple cases of the exertion of gunboat diplomacy. For instance, the arrival of French and British troops in Veracruz, Mexico, on January 7, 1862, to ensure the negotiation of the repayment of debt bonds that were in hands of citizens of such countries. Other examples can be found in the shipping of naval fleets down the *Río de la Plata* between Paraguay and Argentina to ensure the "prompt, adequate and effective" compensation of the seizure of some assets owned by the Paraguay Navigation Company in 1864, and the bombing of Caracas, Venezuela, in 1903, perpetrated by Great Britain and Germany to oblige the Latin American country to accept the jurisdiction of arbitration commissions for the resolution of controversies with investors original from those states.[29]

Throughout the nineteenth and early twentieth centuries, Latin American states suffered great impacts from the particular exertion of diplomatic protection by industrialized states. Yet, a number of local initiatives began to emerge in response to the corresponding condition of dependency. Such initiatives based on the realization of a rule of national treatment as opposed to the international treatment

[26] See Miles (2013).

[27] See John Dugard, Diplomatic protection Oxford Public International Law, https://opil.ouplaw.com/view/10.1093/law:epil/9780199231690/law-9780199231690-e1028 (last visited Aug 19, 2021).

[28] See Olarte-Bácares (2015).

[29] See Miles (2013).

standard and came to be known as the *Calvo Doctrine* in honor of its initial proponent, the Argentine jurist Carlos Calvo.[30] The Doctrine aimed at guaranteeing that foreigners were treated accordingly to the treatment offered to local citizens. In addition, it appealed for the alien actors to resort to local judicial mechanisms for the resolution of disputes that could arise with the host State, instead of advancing on international claims through diplomatic protection.[31]

Although this Doctrine was greatly defended by Latin American countries throughout the nineteenth century, such account had relative success since the advocates of the international standard did not consider it sufficient for the safeguarding of private property in the contexts of instability and violence of the region.[32] Still, many countries in the region eventually achieved its contractual incorporation—by means of the so-called Calvo clause—, by virtue of which private contractors waived their rights to diplomatic protection on behalf of local judicial remedies in the event of an arising dispute.[33] All in all, the ultimate achievement associated with this doctrine would be earned well into the twentieth century, when it was embodied in the Charter of the Organization of American States, in spite of the reluctance manifested by the United States.[34]

3.3 Revolutions and Social Unrest: The Rise of Foreign Investors Disputes

After a century of modest national projects consolidation, partly by the conditions of instability and violence that permeated the region, Latin American states welcomed the twentieth century with a great incidence of foreign intervention at different levels. As mentioned, at that time the intervening States rejected the doctrine of national treatment, as it was considered insufficient for the protection of the interests of their nationals as per the reining political, social, and economic conditions in the region. For instance, while Venezuela was overcoming a long civil war founded on social imbalances, British and German nationals affected by the outcomes of the associated military actions started particular claims against such state that ended up in the abovementioned 1903 Caracas incident.

As in the latter anecdote, the turbulent context that Latin America experienced during the outset of the twentieth century propelled the massive emergence of emergence of disputes of all kinds with foreign investors. The main orientation of

---

[30]Carlos Calvo, Derecho internacional teórico y práctico de Europa y América, vol. I, Paris, D'Amyot, Durand y Pedone-Lauriel, y Carlos Calvo, Derecho internacional teórico y práctico de Europa y América, vol. II, Paris, D'Amyot, Durand y Pedone-Lauriel, 1868.

[31]See Olarte-Bácares (2015).

[32]See Anghie (2012).

[33]García-Amador (1958), p. 60.

[34]Charter of the Organization of American States (1951), art. 2b and 16.

these disputes was the protection of the rights and interests of foreigners that were affected by the various sociopolitical processes that were taking place in most states of the region. Perhaps the most telling process of these affirmations occurs with the Mexican Revolution that took place from 1910 to 1920. The implementation of profound changes in the country's constitutional model, including an in-depth social-oriented agrarian reform, inevitably affected several foreign interests.[35] In addition, the aim to regain control over certain natural resources whose extraction had been trusted to persons and companies—particularly US nationals—led to the occurrence of expropriations so as to transfer their effective control to the state.[36] In response, the Mexican state argued that since such process had a social justification, it was not accurate to speak about expropriations but of nationalization for the public benefit of the Mexican people. These allegations were deeply rejected by the United States by means of the instrumentalization of what was then identified as the *Hull Formula.* This normative guideline, alleged to have an international customary nature, was accounted as a mandate to orient any type of taking of property to consider a "prompt, adequate and effective" compensation for the affected parties, notwithstanding the justifications beyond the measure.[37] The region was again facing the discussion of the internationalization of private property protection against the consideration of a regional regard of justice and welfare.

This pattern of socioeconomic transformations in the region continued—for instance the revolutionary movements that took place in Bolivia (1952) and Cuba (1959)—, thus producing an indefectible influence on the increase of disputes of this kind against Latin American countries, especially from the perspective of United States persons and their property. In the meantime, attempts to place the Calvo Doctrine at the center of the international dialogue as a legitimate approach to foreign investment protection were held by several states of the region. But it was not until 1933, at the Montevideo Conference, that the United States adopted the Convention on the Rights and Duties of the States, in which a basic version of the Calvo Doctrine was incorporated into the normative sphere of the states' regulatory space.[38]

3.4 *The Introduction of Latin America into the Global Investment Protection System*

Although the aftermath of the Second World War represented the overcome of serious menaces to international peace and security through the rising of the modern international community scheme around the United Nations, political turbulence

[35] See Miles (2013).

[36] See Sornarajah (2021).

[37] See Miles (2013).

[38] Scott (2000).

maintained as a global trend. While under the realm of Cold War decolonization processes became frequent in Africa and Asia, Latin America experienced violent transitions from democracies to military regimes and the spread of popular insurgent movements. Under such context, the protection of foreign persons and property was included as a fundamental element for the erection of a global economic system, incarnated in international institutions with transnational reach and commonly known as "Bretton Woods".[39] Therein, capital-owning and exporting countries assumed the responsibility of channeling the protection of private property through the development of international legal instruments arranged for this purpose. For such purpose, it was also necessary to consolidate a particular legal imaginary that would allow the development of the idea that foreign investment was essential to achieve the economic growth objectives of developing countries. Although this process took a large part of the twentieth century through different regulatory proposals, it would materialize in the Convention on the Settlement of Disputes relating to Investments between States and Nationals of other States, by which the International Center for Settlement of Investment Disputes (ICSID) was created in 1966.[40]

The need for the creation of a center with the characteristics of ICSID was presented as a reaction to the appearance of realistic legal visions that ensured that private property was not a natural right (as it had been defended until then), but that it came from the power of the State to grant it.[41] From this perspective, and hand in hand with the claims for a New International Economic Order, private property ceased to be seen as an exclusive privilege of the person who owns it and the perspective according to which property has certain social functions to meet began to be more commonly accepted. For a long time, Latin American countries, based on these perceptions of property rights, as well as on the will to develop autonomously through the implementation of industrialization by import substitution and the closed regionalism of the Economic Commission for Latin America and the Caribe (ECLAC),[42] refused to join ICSID.

However, after the debt crisis in the early 1980s in Latin America, the new global consensus that was established proposed the rewriting of the world economy around some basic liberal principles: free enterprise, protection of private property as a natural right and the minimum intervention of the State in economic affairs, among others. What became known as the Washington Consensus together with the collapse of the Soviet Union meant that foreign investment regained importance in the region.[43] Furthermore, the structural adjustments imposed in the region with the objective of negotiating the debts that had caused the crisis, determined that the implementation of these basic liberal principles was mandatory within the regional

[39] See Gold (1984), pp. 799–852.

[40] See Studies in International and Comparative Law (2021). Perrone (2021).

[41] *ibidem.*

[42] See Bielschowsky (2009).

[43] See Perrone (2021).

development models.[44] With this, the Latin American countries, previously skeptical of the signing of the ICSID Convention, acceded to its jurisdiction by adhering to this international center, but also by signing a series of IIAs that will open the door to the modern investment protection system.

4 Analysis of Investor State Arbitration in Latin America

Although certain Latin American countries were part of the global BITs project laboratory,[45] most of the states of the region started concluding international legal instruments of that kind between the end of the decade of 1980 and the outset of the decade of 1990.[46] This is explained by the release of the *structural adjustment program*. This program, designed by the World Bank and the International Monetary Fund under the mandate of enabling the consecution of stable and open economic relations around the world,[47] visualized Latin America as one of its main targets.[48] Under widespread conditions of a capitalist production crisis and an associated fiscal crisis in the region, the program sought to promote the conduct of profound regulatory reforms at the domestic level as a *condictio sine qua non* for the provision of loans, urgently required to deal with economic turmoil.[49] Hence, one of the recommendations suggested by the global economic institutions was to both internationalize and liberalize Latin American economies by means of the systematic conclusion of BITs, to facilitate the transnational movement of capitals and thus attracting FDI.[50] Both these instruments and the free trade agreements that started to be negotiated in the 1990s within the region included specific provisions around the settlement of investment disputes through investor-state arbitration.

This section intends to present a series of statistics (Table 1) around the occurrence of investor-state arbitration in Latin America and provide an analysis as to their link with the particularities of the region. This will help to identify trends from the standpoint of (1) the countries that have assumed the greatest load of litigation of this kind, and the contextual reasons for such tendency; (2) the type of foreign investors or investments that have suited sovereign states before investor-state arbitration

[44] See Bulmer-Thomas (1994).

[45] Ecuador with Germany (1965) and Switzerland (1968); Costa Rica with Switzerland (1965); El Salvador with France (1978); Panama with Switzerland (1983).

[46] As Sornarajah stresses out, although they started to be negotiated as early as 1959, there was a massive proliferation of bilateral investment treaties in the 1990s. See Sornarajah (2021).

[47] Williamson (2004), pp. 195–206; Ocampo (2004), pp. 293–314.

[48] On the global governance role of the Bretton Woods institutions, see generally Stone and Wright (2007); Gigli (1997), pp. 1–27.

[49] See Bajpai (1990), pp. 791–794.

[50] For instance, see OECD Report presented at the Council meeting at Ministerial level which took place in May 1995 (DAFFE/CMIT/CIME (95)13/FINAL, 5 May 1995). Retrieved from http://www.oecd.org/daf/mai/htm/cmitcime95.htm.

Table 1 Number of cases in which Latin American countries acted as respondents

Sued country	Number of cases
Argentina	56
Venezuela	49
Perú	34
México	31
Colombia	16
Ecuador	14
Costa Rica	12
Bolivia	5
Chile	5
El Salvador	4
Uruguay	3
Total	**229**

Source: Own elaboration based on ICSID data

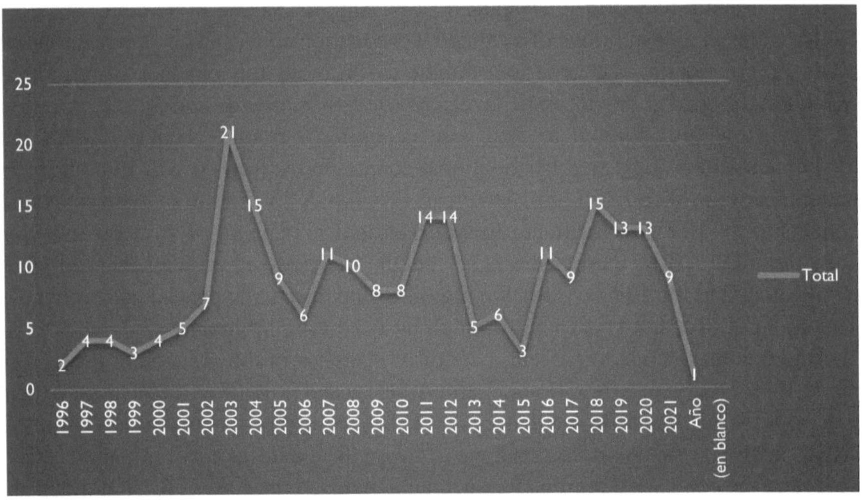

Fig. 1 Cases by year. Source: Own elaboration based on the ICSID case database

tribunals; (3) the type of public interests and social actors that, on the occasion of their tension with the interests of foreign investors/investments, have been under discussion through investor-state arbitration; and (4) the main outcomes of the cases.

As of July 2021, 229 investor-state arbitration cases opened at ICSID have involved the selected Latin American states as respondents (Fig. 1). Of those cases, 156 have been concluded (68%) and 73 are still in progress (32%).

The countries with the greatest number of claims are Argentina (56), Venezuela (49), Peru (34), and Mexico (31). While the Latin American states that first entered into international investment agreements were Ecuador (1965), Costa Rica (1965), Panama (1982), Bolivia (1987), and Uruguay (1987), the case of the

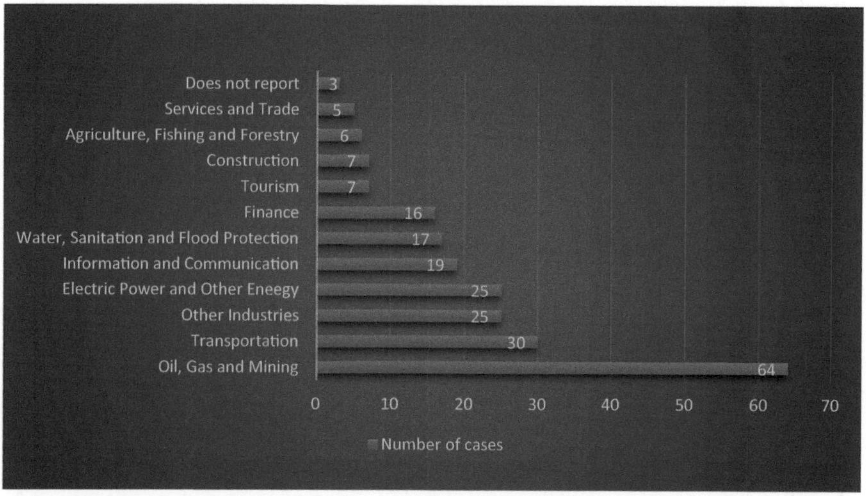

Fig. 2 Economic sectors related with the investor-state disputes. Source: Own elaboration based on ICSID database

abovementioned states is that of having implemented a policy of systematic conclusion of BITs and FTAs under the context of global economic liberalization.

Hereafter, the occurrence of investment lawsuits leading to formal claims has had three peaks. The first milestone took place between 2002 a 2003 and is mainly identified with the Argentinian economic crisis and the corresponding state measures that were taken to reestablish public stability and confidence, as well as the Mexican irruption into the NAFTA integration scheme with USA and Canada. The second peak went from 2010 to 2013, when 23 case were held against Venezuela on the occasion of a wave on nationalizations of foreign-owned companies, supported by the left-oriented government of Hugo Chaves. Finally, a later pinnacle happened between 2017 and 2019, and was principally related to cases carried out against Colombia (8 cases) and Peru (8 cases). These cases are related with the consolidation of constitutional orders cognizant of human rights and the environment, and the consequent crystallization of jurisdictions that have assumed an active role in the protection of the public interest *vis à vis* the safeguarding of private rights and expectations.

An account of the type of foreign investor/investment involved in the arbitration claims against Latin American states shows that the extractive industry (oil, gas, and mining) is the main economic sector around which the cases gravitate (64). This trend is explained by the region's abundance of natural resources, the corresponding scope of the national development policies, and the conflict that is often generated by the superposition between the undertaking of these activities and the safeguarding of socio-environmental public interests. Successively, the sectors with the greatest incidence on the investor-state arbitration dynamic are transportation (30), energy (25), telecommunications (19), water sanitation (17), finance (17), infrastructure (7), and tourism (7) (Fig. 2).

Table 2 Precedence of the investor-state arbitration claimants

Country	Cases
United States	66
Spain	37
Netherlands	25
Canada	19
France	16
United Kingdom of Great Britain and Northern Ireland	10
Peru	8
Switzerland	8
Chile	7
Italy	7
Luxembourg	7
Germany	6
Barbados	5
Argentina	4
Panama	4
Colombia	3
Portugal	3
Venezuela	2
Uruguay	2
Singapore	2
Belgium	1
Mexico	1
Malaysia	1
Austria	1
Costa Rica	1
India	1
China	1
Total	**248**[a]

Source: Own elaboration based on ICSID data
[a] The total does not coincide with the number of cases against the countries of the region because in some cases the claimants are from multiple nationalities

Table 2 depicts the origin of the investment-state arbitration cases held on the 11 Latin American states object of analysis, from the point of view of the nationality of the claimants and based on the international investment agreements correspondingly invoked. The numbers reveal that the investors/investments responsible of activating the jurisdiction of arbitration tribunals in the region are mainly based in United States (66), Spain (37), Netherlands (25), Canada (19), France (16), United Kingdom (10) (Table 2). The presence of the United States in the top of the list is explained by the traditional influence exerted on the economic models and political decisions of several countries of the region, as well as by the geographic and commercial proximity with Mexico. In the case of Spain, the great number of claims are related with the massive establishment of economic actors from such jurisdiction

Table 3 Public interests in tension with investment

Public interest in tension with investment	Frequency
Fiscal and/or financial sustainability	56
Proper provision of public service	42
Monetary policy	37
Environment	33
Natural resources	33
Human rights	30
National industry	29
Justice	30
Water	22
Free competition	23
Efficiency in public procurement	21
No particular reference	18
Coercive jurisdiction	15
Sovereignty	12
Public order	10
Vital minimum	7
Food sovereignty and security	6
Regulatory power	6
Social security	4
Prior consultation	4
Cultural and/or archeological heritage	3
Territorial planning	2
Social function of property	1
Public health	1
Total	**445**

Source: Own elaboration through the Reading of different sources provided by ICSID, Italaw, Investment Policy Hub, and newspaper articles

in Latin America, provided the historical ties existent. On the other hand, Canada and the European states are recognized capital-exporting enclaves that have several interests in the region, especially within the extractive industry.

The data introduced in Table 3 draws attention on the public interests that have been discussed in the ICSID arbitral awards associated with the 11 Latin American states here considered. They correspond to regulatory measures that entered into tension with the protection offered to foreign investors/investments by means of the international investment agreements concluded by the countries of the region, and consequently are considered the root of the affectations alleged by the claimants (Table 3).

Apart from the general references made to the states' regulatory capacity,[51] fiscal and financial sustainability appears to be the public interest mostly discussed within

[51] Sovereignty (12), public order (10), and regulatory power (6), for a total of 28 references.

the arbitration cases under analysis.[52] This is mainly explained by the number of cases emerged on the occasion of the Argentinian crisis in the early 2000s, where the country enacted the Emergency Law. Such normative instrument stipulated a series of measures intended to stabilize the economy, including deep fiscal, monetary, and financial reforms that eventually affected foreign investors. The latter considered that the mandatory conversion of bank deposits to the national currency amounted to the indirect expropriation of their assets in the country.

Next, territory-oriented interests subject of public regulation appear to be the most disputed aspect within investor-state arbitration on Latin America. In this regard, the topics particularly discussed (environment, access and use of natural resources, water, territorial planning, and property[53]) reflect the fact that the region has performed as a pantry of factors of production, thus boosting the consolidation of the global economic model. Within such dynamic, the concept and extent of nature is an element under permanent tension as to its aptitude to be extracted in order to generate wealth versus the public demands of conservation and sustainability.

As illustrated, recounting the history of the formation of Latin American states allows us to understand how, in light of permanent and similar dynamics of instability in the region, there is a deep tension between the protection of rights and economic expectations of foreign investment and the safeguarding of general public interests. From this point of view, it was observed that the protection of private property and foreign persons has always had protection mechanisms and access to compensation. However, it was the progressive development of international legal instruments and international arbitration schemes that managed to consolidate a transnational legal safeguard scheme based on the idea of predictability and legitimate expectations.

Henceforth, human rights appear to be a relevant point of reference around which debates concerning the rights and expectations of foreign investors/investments in Latin America gravitate. The particular topics (human rights, vital minimum, food sovereignty and security, social security, prior consultation to ethnic groups, cultural and/or archeological heritage, and public health[54]) reflect the existence of profound socioeconomic inequalities within the countries of the region. Correspondingly, there seems to be a progressive recognition by the governments of the need to advance on the integral safeguarding of their citizens and the associated historical misbalances, in spite of the eventual affectation of acquired rights and legitimate expectations.

Finally, it is important to mention the categories *justice, provision of public services, protection of national industry, public procurement,* and *free competition,*

[52]Fiscal and financial sustainability (56), and monetary policy (37), for a total of 93 references.

[53]Environment (33), natural resources (33), water (22), territorial planning (2), and social function of property (1), for a total of 91 references.

[54]Human rights (30), vital minimum (7), food sovereignty and security (6), social security (4), prior consultation (4), cultural and/or archeological heritage (3), and public health (1), for a total of 55 references.

as supplementary public interests that have been subject of discussion in the context of investor-state arbitration in Latin America.[55] They give an account of the complexities that the countries of the region must face to implement regulation linked to the management of the economy and the standardization of market relations, as well as around the consolidation of a business environment grounded on legal certainty and accountability.

Associated to the public interests under tension within the realm of ISDS arbitration, the cases concerning Latin American states have included a number of actor whose involvement in international legal disputes has not been common. Yet, both the particularities of the disputes and the diverse multicultural nature of the population located in the region led to the need of considering their particular rights and interests so as to evaluate the extent of the tensions generated between the assuring of international business stability and the achievement of public interests. Hence, of the 229 cases under study, 16 involved peasants; 13 addressed the situation of indigenous communities; 31 discussed the situation of workers; and 2 dealt with traditional miners.

Investment arbitration tribunals tend to ignore the situation of these actors, and their particular interests, as determining elements to establish whether states are responsible for violating legal provisions of investment treaties, therefore affecting foreign investors. However, their inclusion in the discussions carried out in the realm of the cases reveals that the adoption of policies to attract foreign investment based on offering competitive advantages to those who are established to carry out an economic activity has direct effects on the rights and interests of the population. Thus, within the framework of the constitutional regimes of the Latin American states, there is a gap between economic policy-making and the guarantee of subjective rights.

5 Concluding Remarks

This chapter aimed to presents a general historical and political-economy portrait of the legal protection that has been offered to foreign investment in Latin America, particularly through of the systematic conclusion of international investment agreements (hereafter IIAs)[56] by the countries of the region.

As illustrated, recounting the history of the formation of Latin American states allowed to understand how, in light of permanent and similar dynamics of instability in the region, there is a deep tension between the protection of rights and economic

[55]Provision of public services (42), Justice (30), national industry (29), free competition (23), public procurement (21).

[56]For the purposes of this chapter, the term "international investment agreements" encompasses both bilateral investment treaties and free trade agreements that include specific investment chapters.

expectations of foreign investment and the safeguarding of general public interests. From this point of view, it was observed that the protection of foreign private property and persons has always had effective claims mechanisms and access to compensation. However, it was the progressive development and implementation of international legal instruments and investment arbitration schemes that managed to consolidate a transnational legal safeguard scheme based on the ideas of predictability and legitimate expectations.

Taking the above into account, the current trends in international investment arbitration show that Latin America is one of the regions with the highest amount of litigation of this type, and that cases are configured in the field of access and use of land and natural resources. Therefore, there is a high incidence of lawsuits from companies in the extractive and infrastructure industries. Notwithstanding the foregoing, the financial sector has also had a great impact on this type of legal conflict. The tensions with the protection of public interests related to human rights, the environment and certain population groups such as indigenous communities are evident and reflect the need to advance in the search for solutions to these types of problems.

References

A Multilateral Agreement on Investment Report by the Committee on International Investment and Multinational Enterprises (CIME)/and the Committee on Capital Movements and Invisible Transactions (CMIT, CMITCIME report 1995 - multilateral agreement on investment. https://www.oecd.org/daf/mai/htm/cmitcime95.htm (last visited Aug 19, 2021)

Adams RH (2003) Economic growth, inequality, and poverty: findings from a new data set. Policy Research Working Paper No. 2972

Anghie A (2004) Imperialism, sovereignty, and the making of international law. Cambridge University Press

Anghie A (2012) Imperialism, sovereignty and the making of international law

Bajpai N (1990) World bank's structural adjustment lending: conflicting objectives. Econ Polit Wkly 25:791–794

Berg AG (2011) Inequality and unsustainable growth: two sides of the same coin? IMF Discussion Note SDN/11/08

Bielschowsky R (2009) Sesenta años de la CEPAL: estructuralismo y neoestructuralismo. Revista de la CEPAL 97

Borchard E (1940) The minimum standard of treatment of aliens. Mich Law Rev 38(4):445

Bulmer-Thomas V (1994) La historia de América Latina desde la Independencia

Busso M, Messina J (2020) The inequality crisis: Latin America and the Caribbean at the Crossroads. https://publications.iadb.org/publications/english/document/The-Inequality-Crisis-Latin-America-and-the-Caribbean-at-the-Crossroads.pdf (last visited Jun 16, 2021)

De Ferranti DM (2004) Inequality in Latin America: breaking with history?

Dugard J, Diplomatic protection Oxford Public International Law. https://opil.ouplaw.com/view/10.1093/law:epil/9780199231690/law-9780199231690-e1028 (last visited Aug 19, 2021)

Galtung J (1969) Violence, peace, and peace research. J Peace Res 6:167–191

García-Amador FV (1958) Third Report on International Responsibility - A/CN.4/111. Annuaire de la Commission du droit international 2:60

Gigli JM (1997) Neoliberalismo y Ajuste Estructural en América Latina. Revista del Centro de Estudios Internacionales para el Desarrollo 1:1–27
Gold J (1984) Public international law in the international monetary system. Southwest Law J 38: 799–852
Hobson JA (1975) Imperialism: a study
Lorca AB (2010) Universal international law: nineteenth-century histories of imposition and appropriation. Harv Int Law J 51:515
Meiksins E (1997) Modernity, postmodernity, or capitalism. Rev Int Polit Econ 4:539–560
Meyer L (2010) México para los mexicanos. La Revolución y sus adversarios
Miles K (2013) The origins of international investment law: empire, environment and the safeguarding of capital
OAS (1951) Charter of the Organization of American States
Ocampo JA (2004) Beyond the Washington consensus: what do we mean? J Post Keynes Econ 27: 293–314
Olarte-Bácares C (2015) La articulación del Derechos Internacional de las Inversiones y de los Derechos Humanos: el caso de América Latina
Perrone NM (2021) Investment treaties and the legal imagination: how foreign investors play by their own rules
Rodrick D (1999) Where did all the growth go? External shocks, social conflict, and growth collapses. J Econ Growth 4:385–412
Said EW (1994) Culture and imperialism
Scott J (2000) The international conferences of American states, 1889-1928 : a collection of the conventions, recommendations, resolutions, reports, and motions adopted by the first six International Conferences of the American States, and documents relating to the organization of the conferences
Simon J (2021) The ideology of Creole revolution. Imperialism and independence in American and Latin American political thought
Sornarajah M (2021) International law on foreign investment
Stone D, Wright C (eds) (2007) The World Bank and governance: a decade of reform and reaction
Tzouvala N (2021) Capitalism as civilisation: a history of international law. Cambridge Studies in International and Comparative Law
United Nations (2015) Concepts of Inequality Development Strategy and Policy Analysis Unit w Development Policy and Analysis Division Department of Economic and Social Affairs. https://www.un.org/en/development/desa/policy/wess/wess_dev_issues/dsp_policy_01.pdf (last visited Jun 16, 2021)
Walker H (1957) Modern treaties of friendship, commerce and navigation. Minn Law Rev 42:805–824
Williamson J (2004) The strange history of the Washington consensus. J Post Keynes Econ 27:195–206

Marco A. Velasquez-Ruiz graduated at the Pontificia Universidad Javeriana, Bogotá and completed a Masters in International Law at the Graduate Institute of International and Development Studies. and a PhD in Law at the Osgoode Hall Law School, Toronto, Canada. He has worked as Researcher at the PENSAR Institute and as Law Professor at the Pontificia Universidad Javeriana. Also, he has performed as consultant in projects on human rights, forced migration, public policy, development, and extractive industries in Colombia. Between 2018 and 2020, he was an adjunct magistrate at the Colombian Special Jurisdiction for Peace. Currently, he is a Foreign Relations Counsellor at the Embassy of Colombia before the Netherlands.

Carolina Olarte-Bácares is an associate Professor, Pontificia Universidad Javeriana. Ambassador of Colombia to the Kingdom of The Netherlands. Agent of Colombia before the International Court of Justice, Member of the Permanent Court of Arbitration. Former Dean Law School,

Pontificia Universidad Javeriana, Bogota, Colombia. Ph.D. in International Law University Paris 1 Panthéon-Sorbonne, Master of research in international law, Robert Schuman University, Strasbourg. Lawyer, Pontificia Universidad Javeriana, Law School, Bogota. Independent Consultant in international law, investment arbitration, human rights, and business and human rights, and external consultant for diplomatic representations in Colombia on matters related to diplomatic privileges and immunities. Founding member of the Colombian Academy of International Law (ACCOLDI), Board Member of the Global Business and Human Rights Scholars Association, and the Latin American Business and Human Rights Academy and Co-Chair of the International Law Association (ILA) Committee on Business and Human Rights.

Ana María Aranda Castillo Researcher, Pontificia Universidad Javeriana, Colombia.

Part I
International Investment Law in Latin America: Where Do We Stand?

Brazilian CFIA: Evolution Towards the Traditional?

Ana Rachel Freitas da Silva and Rafael Ramos Codeço

1 Introduction

Brazil enjoys a peculiar position in international investment policymaking. The country has never ratified any of the Bilateral Investment Treaties (BIT) signed in the 1990s; neither is part of the ICSID Convention.[1] BITs containing traditional protection clauses found a tough resistance in the legislative branch leading the executive to withdraw them without approval.[2] Despite that, it has been ranked among the 10 top destinations of investments worldwide.[3] The discussions in the legislative highlighted two main concerns regarding the compatibility of the BITs with the Brazilian Constitution: BITs' provision ensuring effective, prompt, and adequate compensation,[4] in contrast with the constitutional provision that provides for the payments with bonds in expropriations for agrarian reform; and the privilege

[1] Kalicki and Medeiros (2007), pp. 57–86.

[2] Lemos and Campello (2013) described a conflictive process during the legislative approval proceedings in Brazil. They mentioned the divergences at the committee level concerning constitutional clauses and the changes that disfigured the bills at the floor level, which forced the treaties to come back to the discussion while the opposition gained powers. They blame the dubious position of the executive branch in pushing the agreements.

[3] In the last available edition of UNCTAD's World Investment Report, Brazil was listed as the 9th top destination of FDI inflows worldwide in the biennium 2018/2019. UNCTAD (2020), p. 12. Reports from the previous years also confirmed Brazil as an important FDI recipient and can be found on the webpage of the organization.

[4] Article 5 of the Brazil-Finland BIT.

A. R. F. da Silva (✉)
Office of the Attorney General of the National Treasure, Ministry of Finance, Brasilia, Brazil

R. R. Codeço
Ministry of Development, Industry, Foreign Trade and Services, Brasilia, Brazil
e-mail: 630039@alumni.soas.ac.uk

N. Monebhurrun et al. (eds.), *International Investment Law and Arbitration from a Latin American Perspective*, International Law and the Global South,
https://doi.org/10.1007/978-3-031-49382-9_2

given to international investors—not available to nationals—to use arbitration against the State.[5]

After its self-exclusion from the international investment regime until the 2010s, and, at a moment when many countries adopted a critical approach on international investment agreements (IIAs), Brazil heightened its interests in actively participating in the regime.[6] Through its Cooperation and Facilitation Investment Agreement Model (CFIA), Brazil started implementing a new approach to international investment law highly focused on cooperation and investment facilitation. The title of the agreement is self-explanatory. The text embodies many provisions on facilitation, cooperation, and promotion of investments, setting aside traditional protection clauses such as fair and equitable treatment, indirect expropriation, and investor-state arbitration.

The CFIA model was developed within the specific mandate of supporting the internationalization of Brazilian companies in a period when Brazil has become a major source of outward FDI, most of which concentrated in South America. According to statistics from 2011, the main destinations for Brazilian investment projects were: Argentina (46.7%); Chile (26.7%); Uruguay (20.0%) and Colombia (6.7%).[7] Moreover, at that time, Brazil was engaged in the development of South-South relations, and Brazilian authorities have identified promising investment opportunities in Africa,[8] mainly in the extractive, energy, engineering, and construction sectors.

Accordingly, CFIA model reflected the preferences of Brazilian MNEs going abroad, which privileged institutional cooperation and facilitation based on three pillars: (i) risk mitigation/framework for the treatment of investors, (ii) institutional governance, and (iii) agendas for cooperation and investment facilitation.[9] During the last six years, CFIA has been consolidated as an alternative to the traditional BITs.[10] By early 2021, 15 agreements have been signed, and two of them are already in force.[11] The viability of the model lies not only in its capacity to address investors' difficulties but in its ability to balance the concerns of capital exporters and capital importers.

---

[5] Azevedo (2001).

[6] Muniz et al. (2017), p. 404.

[7] Iglesias and Costa (2012).

[8] Veiga and Rios (2014).

[9] Godinho (2014).

[10] Schill and Vidigal (2018).

[11] This analysis will consider the Cooperation and Facilitation of Investment Agreements signed with Mozambique, Angola, Malawi, Mexico, Colombia, Chile, Ethiopia, Suriname, Guyana, Morocco, India, United Arab Emirates, Ecuador, as well as Brazil-Peru Economic and Trade Expansion Agreement and Intra-MERCOSUR Cooperation and Facilitation Investment Protocol. The texts of all of these agreements are available at UNCTAD Investment Policy Hub webpage at: https://investmentpolicy.unctad.org/international-investment-agreements/countries/27/brazil?type=bits.

As the current Administration envisages enhancing economic integration with developed countries, Brazil might face certain demand for additional provisions on investment protection and might need to review certain aspects of CFIA model while exploring alternatives to incorporate new elements of investment protection.

This article aims to discuss the CFIA from an evolutionary perspective. This means to assess the changes already incorporated in the CFIA Model since its conception back in the 2010s and the transformations following the negotiations with several developing countries—resulting in an evolutionary process comprised of three generations. It also analyses the challenges to the CFIA *status quo* posed by the intended negotiations with developed countries. There is no doubt that the CFIA Model, as it stands now, is closer to a traditional BIT than the first agreements signed back in 2015. The movement towards developed countries can deepen this process.

First, we will address some of the most innovative provisions of the Brazilian model.[12] The second session will discuss how the model has been evolving and how can it be further challenged by the negotiation with developed countries, with a special focus on six potential innovations that can trigger further discussions about the future of the CFIA: definition of investment, minimum standard of treatment, investor's responsibilities, expropriation, dispute settlement and performance requirements.

2 Innovative Provisions in CFIA

Initially, it is important to have in mind that there are 15 CFIAs signed, which we are grouping under the denomination of "CFIA model" or "Brazilian model" and are a slightly heterogeneous group of texts with some differences that were gradually incorporated along six years of negotiations. Some of the differences resulted from Brazils' counterparts' demands, while others were certain "improvements" incorporated into the model. From a historical perspective, CFIA's can be divided into three generations.

The first three CFIAs signed with African countries: Angola, Mozambique, and Malawi belong to the first generation. They are smaller, simpler, and closer to a cooperation agreement. The second generation consists of CFIAs with Latin American countries, such as Mexico, Colombia, Chile, and Peru, and those with Ethiopia, Morocco, and Suriname. These agreements are more complex, especially the dispute settlement session. Brazilian model 2015 encompasses all the main characteristics of the second generation.[13]

A third generation arose after the negotiations with India. Although the treaty was signed recently, negotiations dated back to 2016. India-Brazil CFIA is seen as "a

[12] Idem.

[13] Brazil Model BIT 2015. Available at: <https://investmentpolicy.unctad.org/international-investment-agreements/treaty-files/4786/download>.

remarkable sophistication of each of the two positions on investment agreements".[14] In the third generation of CFIAs, the provision entitled "treatment" resembles the traditional international minimum standard of treatment, including a reference to customary law. The language on investor's obligation is also more emphatic than the previous "best efforts" Corporate and Social Responsibility (CSR) clauses.[15] CFIAs with Guyana, India, United Arab Emirates, Ecuador, and MERCOSUR Protocol follow these new trends. We can also speculate about a fourth generation after the negotiations with developed countries, where CFIA could get even closer to a traditional BIT—after incorporating new provisions traditionally demanded by these countries.

CFIAs seek a greater balance between investment protection and the host state's development agenda by bringing new wording to traditional clauses such as National Treatment and Most Favored Nation Treatment while excluding others like fair and equitable treatment and indirect expropriation. It also introduces new clauses in the realm of IIA policymaking aimed at safeguarding State's right to regulate and encourage investor's responsible conduct. CFIA's provisions on prevention and resolution of disputes are another innovation, though not properly new, but certainly a departure from the investor-state arbitration scheme, widespread in traditional BITs. Although arbitration between States is much older than investor-State arbitration, CFIA dispute settlement can also be taken as a novelty because of the role of the Institutional Arrangements (Joint Committees and Ombudsperson) in preventing disputes.

This section firstly addresses CFIA's "traditional clauses with new wording". Then, it continues the analysis of CFIA's new clauses and concludes with some comments on dispute settlement provisions.

2.1 *Traditional Clauses with New Wording*

CFIA's Definitions of "investment" and "investor" are not that different from the traditional BITS. One of the orientations given by CAMEX in a template of 2014 was the limited scope of protection for direct investment.[16] These concerns are manifested when the language defines investment as "a direct investment" and may be repetitive as they exclude "portfolio investment" from the treaty's scope. (See, for example, CFIA Brazil Suriname, art. 1). Some CFIAs, together with the qualificative "direct", define this type of investment as the one which allows the investor to exercise control or significant degree of influence over the management.[17]

[14] Moraes and Cavalcante (2021).

[15] We will discuss this topic in the following session.

[16] Morosini and Badin (2015).

[17] Brazil Model BIT 2015.

Some CFIAs from first and second generations relied on a traditional asset-based definition of an investment.[18] CFIA signed with India changed this definition to an enterprise-based one.[19] It also includes some elements of Salini test in the definition[20] which is also another formula to guarantee the protection of direct investment.

The definition of investor also follows the approach of traditional BITs. It is worth mentioning that the text uses a rule of incorporation[21] to determine the nationality of an enterprise but does not contain a 'denial of benefits' type-of-provision that can exclude juridical entities that do not have substantive business activities in the home country.[22]

It also considers a "permanent resident" as an investor. This enlarges the scope of the agreement to investors from a third country or even to Brazilian nationals because citizens with dual nationality are not excluded from the definition. Considering that CFIA does not encompass ISDS, an investor—either national, dual national, or permanent resident—would need the Home State sponsorship to challenge a measure from the Host State. If diplomatic protection rules apply to State-to-State arbitration (SSDS) related to damages suffered by an investor, there may be some difficulties to harmonize the nationality requirement with the more extensive definition of investor found in the CFIAs.[23] However, we believe that general rules of diplomatic protection are not applicable when the agreement has specific provisions. This also occurs in relation to exhaustion of local remedies.[24]

Expropriation. CFIA's provision on expropriation with Angola is closer to a traditional BIT. There is no specific limitation to direct expropriation—as provided for in other CFIAs—nor reference to domestic law standards.[25] On the other hand, the expropriation clause in the CFIA with Malawi limits the protection only to the circumstances of direct expropriation and refers to domestic law as the applicable

---

[18] Article 1.3 of Brazil-Guyana CFIA, for example, defines investment as "any kind of asset invested by investors (. . .)".

[19] According to article 2.4., "investment means an enterprise, including a participation therein (. . .) The following assets of the enterprise, among others are covered under this Treaty (. . .)".

[20] The **Salini test** defines an **investment** as having four elements: (1) a. contribution of money or assets; (2) a certain duration; (3) an element of risk; and (4) a contribution to the economic development of the host state. (*Salini Costruttori S.p.A. and Italstrade S.p.A. v. Kingdom of Morocco*, ICSID Case No. ARB/00/4, Decision on Jurisdiction of 31 July 2001, para 52. Available at: https://www.italaw.com/cases/958.

[21] Article 1 of CFIA Brazil-UEA, for example, defines investor as "a national, permanent resident or enterprise of a Party that has made an investment in the territory of the other Party" and enterprise as "any entity constituted or organized under applicable law, whether or not for profit, whether privately owned or State-owned, directly or indirectly, including any corporation, trust, partnership, sole proprietorship, joint venture and entities without legal personality".

[22] Muniz et al. (2017).

[23] See article UN ILC. Draft Articles on Diplomatic Protection with commentaries (2006). Report of the International Law Commission on the work of its fifty-eight session. Available at: https://legal.un.org/ilc/texts/instruments/english/commentaries/9_8_2006.pdf.

[24] Silva (2019b), pp. 11–13.

[25] Art. 9.

law to determine the State act that consists of an expropriation.[26] The CFIAs signed with Mozambique and Mexico are located somewhere between the former and circumscribe the possibilities of expropriation to those provided in the national law of the Parties,[27] implying that indirect expropriation is allowed if the national legislation of one Party admits so. The expropriation clause in the Colombia CFIA returns to the criteria of Angola's treaty but does not exclude indirect expropriation from the scope of the agreement nor mention domestic law. Some CFIAs from the second generation included a welcomed clarification restricting the reach of the protection against expropriation to the contours of the[28] Brazilian constitutional regime regarding expropriation for agrarian reform.[29] This clarification is essential to assure the consistency between the Brazilian Constitution and the CFIA that can be helpful for the legislative referendum since this incompatibility was one of the arguments against the BITs that were rejected in the 1990s.[30]

Most favored nation (MFN) and national treatment (NT) clauses follow the recommendations of best practices manual.[31] adopting the qualificative "in like circumstances" while excluding from the scope of MFN, procedural provisions, and regional agreements.

Treatment clauses are the ones that experienced significant changes. CFIAs from third-generation provide the basis for comparison as the language is more similar to traditional Fair and Equitable Treatment (FET) Clauses,[32] although they also vary considerably. The absence of a FET clause was considered a differential in the CFIA.[33] However, the last agreements are closer to a typical FET clause containing a reference to "the applicable rules of international law as recognized by each of the Parties" and include a list of measures that could be inconsistent with the treaty. Finally, the Treatment provisions in the third generation CFIAs contain an interpretative-explanatory paragraph aimed at avoiding the use of the standards of

---

[26] Art. 8.2.

[27] Art. 8.2.

[28] Art. 7.2.5 of Brazil-Chile CFIA, 7.2.5 of Brazil-Ethiopia CFIA and art 7.5 of Brazil-Suriname CFIA.

[29] See, for example, footnote no. 1 in Brazil-Guyana CFIA: "For the avoidance of doubt, where any of the Parties is the expropriating Party, compensation for the expropriation of property may be provided in the form of debt bonds, in accordance with its laws and regulations, and nothing in this Agreement shall give rise to the interpretation that such form of compensation is inconsistent with this Agreement".

[30] Check footnotes no. 3 and 5.

[31] Nikiema (2017).

[32] "The obligation to provide "fair and equitable treatment" is often stated, together with other standards, as part of the protection due to foreign direct investment by host countries. It is an "absolute", "non-contingent" standard of treatment." These terms are vague, determined by reference to specific circumstances (OECD 2004).

[33] UNCTAD IIA Mapping Project, for example, identified 125 out of 2575 mapped treaties without a FET clause. Brazilian CFIAs are in this list. More details can be access in the organization website at: https://investmentpolicy.unctad.org/international-investment-agreements/iia-mapping#section-38.

"fair and equitable treatment" and "full protection and security" in investment dispute settlement.[34] The following section better illustrates the challenges to deepen CFIA's provisions on treatment.

2.2 *New Clauses*

As mentioned above, the Brazilian model has three main pillars: (i) institutional governance, conducted by national focal points and joint committees; (ii) risk mitigation and dispute prevention, also carried out by these two institutions; and (iii) agendas on cooperation and facilitation of investments.[35] CFIA's second pillar highlights a model that emphasizes dispute prevention over dispute resolution.[36] The Institutional Governance and Dispute Prevention activities, carried out by the Ombudsperson and the Joint Committee, certainly constitute the most innovative provision in the CFIA. The provisions within the realm of institutional governance aim to establish Ombudspersons that would be responsible for assisting and providing guidance to foreign investors during all phases of the investment cycle. This is crucial for the CFIA model as it materializes an on-demand type of support for foreign investors, capable of reducing uncertainty and providing helpful information for companies seeking to invest in markets where it would not be willing to in the absence of such support. Yet, the creation of an Ombudsperson for investments is likely to become an essential point of information to improve laws and regulations, steer regulatory reforms, and improve the investment climate in the host country.[37] The **Joint Committee** (JC) is equally important to ensure the success of the agreement. It provides an instance for the Parties to oversee the outcomes as well as the difficulties faced by their respective investors and to propose solutions to enhance mutual investments. It is also the key element in the dispute prevention scheme as the agreement provides for a mandatory preliminary phase before the arbitration between the States takes place.[38] As the treaty allows only arbitration between States, and there is no automatic jurisdiction to decide about damages, there are strong incentives to reach a mutual agreement at this stage and do not escalate the complaint to a dispute that might be lengthy and costly to resolve.

The 2015 CFIA Model provides for **three different levels of dispute resolution mechanisms.** It starts with the Ombudsperson and the Joint Committee's joint action to assess suggestions and complaints from the other Party to recommend actions to improve the investment environment and prevent disputes. The second level provides for consultations and negotiations between the parties and the Joint Committee

[34] Article 4 of Brazil-UAE CFIA.

[35] Godinho (2014).

[36] Monebhurrun (2017).

[37] Oliveira (2020).

[38] Art. 23.2 of Brazil Model BIT 2015.

and only evolve to arbitration (third and final level) if the dispute is not resolved upon the lapse of the timeframe established therein or in case of non-participation of one of the Parties.

Regarding dispute resolution, it is worth mentioning that many IIAs do have provisions on SSDS. However, the reach of their SSDS proceedings is generally much stricter in comparison with those of the CFIA, being limited to the treaty interpretation and do not address a specific grievance.[39] The primary influence for the CFIA's SSDS is the WTO Dispute Settlement Understanding (DSU), even though CFIA's Dispute Settlement purpose is closer to diplomatic protection. First of all, CFIAs signed after 2015 mention 'affected investors' (in the plural form), suggesting that this procedure can address concerns that affect a variety of investors,[40] similarly to the DSU rulings, which affect every individual that fall under the circumstance that come to be ruled as inconsistent with the WTO agreements. The resemblance can also be noticed in the objective of the arbitration, which is "to determine the conformity [...] of a measure that a Party claims not to be in conformity with the Agreement".[41] When the model was first conceived, Brazilian policymakers did not envisage compensation as the primary remedy. The option for bringing the measure to conformity instead of providing for compensation reinforces Brazil's decision not to grant investors access to arbitration. Although a pro-arbitration movement can be seen in Brazil,[42] this scenario may not change soon.

Investors do not have standing before an international arbitral tribunal. The agreements are strictly formulated when they say that investors depend upon the sponsorship of their Home State (nationals or permanent residents). The aggrieved investor should persuade its Home State that it has suffered damage or impairment. Under this arrangement, it would be expected that only robust claims would proceed to arbitration, thus avoiding frivolous claims. This is because Brazilian policymakers were convinced that excessive litigation resulting from traditional BITs harms the business environment and the effort to attract and maintain investments in

[39] See, e.g., EU – Singapore Investment Protection Agreement. Section B applies to divergences concerning "the interpretation and application of the provisions of this Agreement." (art. 3.25), while section A applies to the resolution of disputes between Investors and Parties. Available at: <https://investmentpolicy.unctad.org/international-investment-agreements/treaty-files/5714/download>.

[40] Muniz et al. (2017).

[41] Article 25.2 of the Brazil-Guyana CFIA.

[42] Enactment of the Arbitration Act together with further legislative developments and a less resistant position of Brazilian judiciary helped arbitration to flourish in Brazil (Giusti and Catarucci 2019). Besides, it is worth mentioning that changes in the Arbitration Act, in 2015, authorize Public Administration to engage in arbitration. (Law no. 13.129, of 2015).

developing countries, as well as the regulatory capacity of the State to pursue legitimate policy interests.[43]

Because of that, dispute prevention would become a preferred regulatory alternative, either for attraction or retention of FDI. By focusing on dispute prevention, the host government will have the major responsibility of helping to resolve disputes amicably and make ISDS less critical for national companies investing abroad and foreign investors investing in the country. Therefore, a significant inspiration for establishing a Dispute Prevention Mechanism under Brazilian CFIA was to provide apparatuses of institutional cooperation to achieve early settlement of potential grievances. To accomplish this objective, CFIA commitments encourage Parties to act before damages have been done. In this manner, the host country would anticipate possible causes of investment arbitration by taking necessary action much earlier.[44] A recent study by OECD on the "Drivers of Divestment Decisions of Multinational Enterprises"[45] has found that IIAs do not appear to impact divestment decisions significantly and concluded that other host country factors that embody the business environment are significantly relevant to discourage divestments by multinational enterprises. Other recent empirical research[46] has found a positive correlation between ISDS disputes and divestment decisions, concluding that following an ISDS case, the firms directly involved in a dispute are more likely to divest in the country where the dispute occurs. Even though CFIA's formulation has preceded the abovementioned studies, it was built upon similar assumptions.

Such an argument has proven very influential in the IIA policymaking. In the discussions taking place at the UNCITRAL Working Group III (WG III), the only concrete outline of a permanent mechanism for resolving international investment disputes devotes a whole section arguing in favor of the convenience of settling disputes peacefully. It defends the establishment of mechanisms for institutional support to encourage early settlements of grievances before it escalates to a dispute in the prospective International Court System envisaged by the European Union in substitution to the ISDS.[47] Another significant influence that CFIA contributed to the IIA policymaking is the negotiations to discuss a multilateral framework on Investment Facilitation at the WTO. WTO mandate aims at setting up a more transparent, efficient, and investment-friendly business climate by simplifying, speeding up, and coordinating processes regarding foreign investments,[48] a set of objectives largely inspired by CFIA's main pillars. Although some of these measures existed in

[43] Submission from the Government of Brazil to the UNCITRAL Working Group III on Possible reform of investor-State dispute settlement (ISDS). Document A/CN.9/WG.III/WP.171. June, 2019.

[44] Idem.

[45] OECD (2019).

[46] Blake and Moschieri (2017).

[47] Submission from the European Union and its Member States to the UNCITRAL Working Group III on Possible reform of investor-State dispute settlement (ISDS). Document A/CN.9/WG.III/WP.159/Add.1. January, 2019.

[48] WTO (2020).

previous treaties, CFIA represents a paradigmatic shift towards Investment Facilitation as it managed to bring all these provisions together, an experience that enables Brazil to assume leadership in the negotiations at the WTO.[49]

CFIAs also embrace concerns regarding investor responsibilities, including CSR provisions (Cooperation and Facilitation Investment Agreement between the Federative Republic of Brazil and the United Arab Emirates [Brazil-UAE CFIA] 2019, Art. 15), the commitment to fighting against corruption and illegality (Brazil-UAE CFIA 2019, Art. 16), as well as the emphasis on investor obligations to comply with national laws (Brazil-UAE CFIA 2019, Art. 14). Although the commitments are, in substance, classical, their presence in an international investment instrument is a remarkable innovation.[50]

3 CFIA: A Model Under Construction

Much has changed since the first conceptual principles that framed the CFIA model back in the 2010s. Since then, CFIA has incorporated several of the negotiating practices of Brazil's IIA counterparts. Nonetheless, most of the CFIA provisions are still far from those provided for in traditional BITs. However, they are closer than they were in the first versions of the CFIA model, indicating a trend of convergence with traditional international treaty practice. This subsection turns to explore the most remarkable evolution on some provisions and the perspectives for the future of the CFIA considering Brazil's intent to reproach developed countries as envisaged by the Administration inaugurated in 2020.

BITs, like most other treaties, are a product of the time when they are negotiated and are influenced by specific economic and geopolitical contexts. In this sense, the investigation of recent developments in the domain of International Investment Law is of fundamental importance for Brazilian policymakers to perceive the new trends and perspectives of IIA. If new evolutions on CFIA are to follow international trends, any further protection to be incorporated in its framework might entail the highest level of explanatory detail as to avoid broad, vague, and controversial provisions in order to reach an adequate balance between the rights of investors and States, as recommended by influential documents such as the Reform Package for International Investment Regime (UNCTAD 2018) and the International Investment Agreements Reform Accelerator (UNCTAD 2020). It means that any additional element of investment protection must be accompanied by provisions aimed at clarifying and restricting the circumstances under which the protection must apply to reduce the level of uncertainty of the provision. Moreover, additional protections must be qualified by exceptions for public policies or national security reasons to safeguard adequate regulatory space.

---

[49] Ramos Codeço and Freitas da Silva (2020).

[50] Monebhurrun (2015).

As stated above, CFIA's primary policy objective was to support the internationalization of Brazilian companies, especially in South America and Africa. As Brazil reframes its foreign policy towards closer economic ties with developed countries, CFIA's provisions will be further challenged to incorporate new elements for investment protection. It is also reasonable to expect that further protection elements that CFIA will include might follow a trend of popularity as observed in other recent IIAs and the expectations of Brazil's current trade partners regarding provisions on investment protection.

Taking this into account, we will discuss the changes already incorporated in the CFIA framework as well as the challenges posed to the current language vis-à-vis the negotiations with developed countries regarding the following provisions: (i) arbitration of damages suffered by an investor; through SSDS or ISDS; (ii) strengthening of investor's obligations and CSR clauses; (iii) inclusion of indirect expropriation; (iv) rapprochement of the treatment to foreigners according to international standards, including fair and equitable treatment; and (v) expansion of the definition of investment to encompass portfolio investments. We also comment on prohibited performance requirements, a provision currently absent in the CFIA Model but defended by developed countries.

3.1 *Arbitration of Damages Suffered by an Investor Through SSDS or ISDS*

CFIA dispute settlement scheme was originally conceived to bring the measure into conformity with commitments stated therein. Some CFIAs, however, provide for the possibility of compensation for damages. Such novelty is observed since the CFIA negotiated with Mexico (art. 19.2) and was (unevenly) repeated in the agreements with Colombia (art. 23.14), Ethiopia (art. 24.11), Suriname (art. 25.13), the United Arab Emirates (art. 25.13) and Ecuador (art. 25.13). Such alternative scheme allows Parties, through a specific agreement, to request arbitrators to establish compensation for damages.

This is a welcomed modification in the CFIA original framework as the compensation may be the best alternative to the Host State in circumstances where the revision of the measure is undesirable or unfeasible. Nevertheless, the possibility of compensation is severely restricted by certain circumstances.[51] Such restriction has been criticized, especially because investors are not lawfully entitled to diplomatic protection. Neither International Customary Law nor CFIA impose any obligation

[51] A claim for compensation is not possible for disputes which have been previously resolved and where *res judicata* applies. In case of pending procedures in national courts or national arbitration, the claim for compensation under CFIA can only be initiated after the withdrawal of the former procedures. (See, e.g., art. 23. 14 (b) of Brazil-Colombia CFIA).

on a State to grant diplomatic protection to a national,[52] a circumstance prone for creating political preferences regarding a possibility that should be open to all investors, not counting the extra layer of bureaucracy and slowness to a case.

Since the ILC Draft Articles on Diplomatic Protection (2006) requires exhaustion of local remedies as a condition for the State to sponsor a case, some commentators have been arguing that such requirement would apply to Parties seeking to resort to arbitration under CFIA.[53] However, as CFIA brings specific rules regarding SSDS proceedings without including such a requirement, we understand that contracting Parties have implicitly abdicated the customary international law regarding the exhaustion of local remedies as provided in the ILC Draft Articles on Diplomatic Protection. Anyway, there are merits in the requirement of exhaustion or, at least, the need to submit the case to local courts. Such condition seeks to safeguard the state sovereignty, empowering domestic legal systems and preventing them from being circumvented by requiring individuals to seek redress for any harm allegedly caused by a State within its domestic legal system before pursuing international proceedings against that State.[54] However, as CFIAs provided for a previous submission of the controversy to the Joint Committee, it is expected that the claim will be mature if and when an arbitration takes place.

Another obstacle for the investor to pursue "arbitration of damages" is the provision aimed at avoiding double recovery, which links the SSDS procedure in international arbitration to the dispute between the investor and the Host State in domestic courts.[55] However, it may be difficult, in practice, to limit an investor's right to seek a legal remedy since there is no obligation for the State to sponsor the claim under an SSDS tribunal. Although investors have no right to diplomatic protection and, consequently, no right to receive a compensation,[56] CFIA provides a legal basis to ensure the transfer of the damages to the aggrieved investor.[57]

---

[52] ICJ. Barcelona Traction, Light and Power Company Limited. Second Phase Judgement, ICJ Reports, 1970, p. 3, p. 4.

[53] Monebhurrun (2019).

[54] Brauch (2017).

[55] See, for example, art. 25. 13. b of Brazil-UAE CFIA: "This paragraph shall not be applied to a dispute concerning a particular investor which has been previously resolved and where protection of *res judicata* applies. Suppose an investor had submitted claims regarding the measure at issue in the Joint Committee to local courts or an arbitration tribunal of the Host State. In that case, the arbitration to examine damages could only initiate after the withdrawal of such claims by the investor in local courts or an arbitration tribunal of the Host State. If after the establishment of the arbitration, the existence of claims in local courts or arbitral tribunals over the contested measure is made known to the arbitrators or the Parties, the arbitration will be suspended".

[56] De Nanteuril (2017), p. 20.

[57] If the arbitration award provides monetary compensation, the Party receiving such compensation shall transfer to the holders of the rights of the investment in question after deducting the costs of the dispute under the internal procedures of each Party. The Party to whom restitution was granted may request the Arbitral Tribunal to order the transfer of the compensation directly to the holders of rights of the affected investment and the payment of costs to whoever has assumed them (art 25. 13. c of Brazil-UAE CFIA).

Despite being frequently criticized for not providing for strong protection of investors and their investments, CFIA manages to find an alternative to balance investor's rights and obligations in terms of dispute settlement. While the shift from "bringing the measure into conformity" to "compensation for damages" seems to be consolidated in the CFIA framework, a further change towards adopting ISDS mechanisms is unlikely due to the deep uncertainties regarding the future of the ISDS, where even the usual proponents of the system have been hesitating in adopting such a scheme on their IIAs recently negotiated.[58] Therefore, Brazil might not move away from the CFIA's current approach of privileging dispute prevention and state-to-state dispute settlement.

3.2 *Strengthening Investor's Obligations and CSR Clauses*

Another remarkable shift observed in the CFIA relates to provisions establishing investors' responsibilities. After negotiations with India, CFIA model incorporated a provision found in India's BIT model from 2015 establishing the obligation of investors to comply with domestic law.[59] Brazil-Morocco CFIA, in its article 4, provides for a similar language when dealing with the admission of investment.[60] Such an obligation may seem obvious, but it can spark debates when an investor who does not follow their responsibilities seeks protection.[61] An alternative to fixing such incompatibility could be a clear language requiring the arbitrators to consider the investor's behavior when deciding upon some case.

As previously discussed, the main policy objective envisaged by the CSR provisions is to qualify investments and multiply the benefits for the sustainable development of the local community and the State that receives them through the adoption of a high degree of socially responsible business practices. To achieve this, CSR provisions encourage high standards of social, environmental, and corporate responsibility on investors and their investments.

Under the current CFIA model, the CSR provisions are not subject to dispute settlement. It marks a change *vis-a-vis* four of the oldest CFIAs signed in 2015 (Angola, Mozambique, Malawi, and Mexico) which allow the dispute settlement regarding CSR provisions. Since the CFIA signed with Colombia in 2015, such matters came to be excluded from the scope of the dispute settlement. At first sight, it may appear a dubious movement the fact that CFIA incorporated mandatory obligations for investors to comply with national law at the same time as CSR

[58] Sachetim and Codeço (2019).

[59] Model Text for the Indian Bilateral Investment Treaty, 2015. Available at: https://investmentpolicy.unctad.org/international-investment-agreements/treaty-files/3560/download., art. 11.

[60] Brazil-Morocco CFIA, art. 4.

[61] Silva (2019a).

obligations were excluded from the reach of Dispute Settlement. However, this shift is positive and is motivated by sound reasoning. First, the controversies that may arise from CSR provisions would relate to the responsibilities of investors in handling those provisions, and the breach of such responsibilities would be strange to a dispute between States[62] since investors are not claimants nor counterclaimants in SSDS proceedings.

On the other hand, CSR commitments are a mechanism foreseen to strike a more balanced relation between investors and states. Hence, excluding the CSR commitments from the reach of Dispute Settlement could, arguably, put the thumb on the scale to the detriment of host States. However, the CSR provision has always been a best-endeavor clause based on voluntary principles since the first CFIA. Thus, the enforcement of commitments that are not mandatory may be innocuous.[63] Art. 25.3 of the Brazil Guyana CFIA that prevents the CSR provisions of being "subject to arbitration" does not exclude its interpretative function.[64] Besides, once the State of nationality is required to sponsor an investor's claim and, consequently, to defend the investor's behavior, it is expected that this combination can add incentives against litigation since home States would probably avoid sponsoring investors' misconduct.

3.3 Inclusion of Indirect Expropriation

Indirect expropriation provisions are among the most popular investment protection clauses in IIAs and might be subject to demand in Brazil's future negotiations. Modern treaty practice recommends restricting the broadness and the vagueness of traditional IE clauses (UNCTAD reform accelerator, 2020), widely known to allow international arbitration to determine the payment of damages for legitimate regulatory acts by states. This can be achieved by excluding certain types of state regulation from the definition of indirect expropriation; and explicitly listing the factors intended to assist the courts in interpreting an indirect expropriation claim to reduce uncertainty about the State's right to regulate (UNCTAD reform accelerator, 2020).

Nevertheless, the compatibility between IE and Brazilian legal order would still challenge Brazilian negotiators since some protections provided under IE provisions do not find correspondence in Brazilian legal order, resulting in more favorable

---

[62] ILC understood that the clean hands doctrine and other related illegality doctrines should not be raised in Diplomatic Protection cases. See Sixth report on diplomatic protection, by Mr. John Dugard, Special Rapporteur. DOCUMENT A/CN.4/546. See Sixth report on diplomatic protection, by Mr. John Dugard, Special Rapporteur. DOCUMENT A/CN.4/546.

[63] Silva and Ribeiro (2018).

[64] Monebhurrun (2019).

treatment to foreign investors than to national investors.[65] Such an asymmetric treatment between national and foreign investors is not a singularity of Brazil since the degree of protection against indirect expropriation under domestic laws varies significantly across countries[66] and might challenge policymakers to turn IIA's provisions compatible with domestic law. In some cases, this asymmetry is settled through interpretative notes stating that any provision shall not grant more favorable treatment to foreign investors with respect to national investors.[67]

Besides restricting the reach of the provision as to avoid conflicts with its legal order, Brazil might explore the avenues through which IE can fit in. For example, IE resonates well with art. 37, § 6 of the Brazilian Constitution, which attributes liability for damages to public legal entities and private legal entities rendering public services. What is more, Brazilian case law already protects the private property against state acts that result in a restriction that diminishes its economic value and precludes the possibility of returning the property to the individual.[68] Therefore, there is ground to incorporate indirect expropriation within the CFIA. The main challenge for this type of provision to fit into the Brazilian legal order is to circumscribe its hypothesis and to limit its reach to the circumstances already available to national investors.

While IE provisions commonly found in traditional BITs envisage to provide greater predictability to the business environment and to give investors reasonable guarantees that the regulatory framework will remain stable and will protect their investments against undue government interferences, the corresponding jurisprudence shows a large number of examples in which national capacity to coordinate investments and pursue legitimate policy objectives has been reduced due to the foreign investment protections conferred by IIAs,[69] resulting in that one major shortcoming of investment treaties has been the curtailment of countries' policy space, which is constantly challenged by investors—a situation occurring most frequently in developing countries.[70]

Therefore, Brazilian policymakers might take a cautious approach on IE to avoid unintended consequences on curtailing State's policy space and restricting their freedom to develop policies that they judge as more appropriate for their

[65] Rights and privileges granted to foreigners not extended to nationals may be argued as being in confront with the principle of equality as stated in article 5 of Brazilian Constitution, verbis: "all persons are equal before the law, without any distinction whatsoever, Brazilians and foreigners residing in the country being ensured of inviolability of the right to life, to liberty, to equality, to security, and to property." (Brazil Federal Constitution (1988). Available at: http://english.tse.jus.br/arquivos/federal-constitution).

[66] OECD Policy Framework for Investment, 2015.

[67] https://www.iisd.org/itn/en/2020/12/19/are-interpretative-declarations-appropriate-instruments-to-avoid-uncertainty-the-cases-of-the-colombia-france-bit-and-the-colombia-israel-fta-carolina-olarte-bacares-enrique-prieto-rios-juan-ponton-se/.

[68] Zavaschi (2004).

[69] Tienhaara (2017).

[70] Pauwelyn (2014).

developmental needs. Sometimes, it is not the content of an IE clause that frightens policymakers, but who would interpret it and how it would be interpreted. As international arbitrators do not have the responsibility of judging a treaty provision in harmony with the national legal order, CFIA language that would provide for protection against IE has to confine its reach into the strict contours of the Brazilian legislation.

3.4 Rapprochement of the Treatment to Foreigners to International Standards, Including Fair and Equitable Treatment

CFIAs have always avoided mentioning the expressions related to minimum standards of treatment (MST) according to customary international law (CIL), and, in some cases, expressly excluded the terms Fair and Equitable Treatment and Full Protection and Security.[71] The CFIAs negotiated with Angola, Mozambique, and Malawi did not mention any commitment regarding treatment besides non-discrimination. The group of CFIAs known as "the second generation" apply specific standards of treatment according to the laws and regulations of the host state.[72] The most recent CFIAs, e.g., those negotiated with Guiana, United Arab Emirates, and India, provides for more detailed clauses, based on the applicable rules of international law as recognized by each of the Parties and their respective national law, ensuring protection against denial of justice, breach of due process, targeted discrimination, manifestly abusive treatment, and discrimination in ensuring enforcement of the law and provision of public security.[73] Yet, some of the CFIAs from the second and third generation expressly exclude the application of the standards of fair and equitable treatment and full protection and security as a ground for any dispute settlement procedure.[74]

Investment protection entailed by MST are deemed problematic since it can give rise to a lack of predictability in the application of the standard, especially the minimalist treaty language making reference to unqualified formulations of Fair and Equitable Treatment or Full Protection and Security, or broad and vague terms such as "investors' legitimate expectations".[75] The reference to the CIL in the MST provision adds another layer of difficulty to harmonize the provision with the Brazilian legal order since it detaches the protection standards stated therein from domestic legislation and practices. Some standards under the CIL may provide for far greater protection to foreign investors when it comes to the imputation of

[71] UAE art. 4.3 e no PCFI (preamble and art. 4.3), Suriname 4.3.

[72] See Colombia (article 4), Ethiopia (article 4), Chile (article 4), Suriname (art. 4).

[73] See Guiana (art. 4), United Arab Emirates (art. 4), and India (Art. 4).

[74] PCFI (art. 4), Suriname (art. 4), Guiana (art. 4), United Arab Emirates (art. 4).

[75] Bonnitcha et al. (2017).

responsibility to the State. As a consequence, even a non-discriminatory measure enacted by Brazil could constitute a violation of the MST.

State actions enumerated in recent IIAs as to configure violation of MST include denial of justice, a fundamental breach of due process of law, manifest arbitrariness, abusive treatment, and failure to provide physical security to investors and covered investments.[76] Some of them do not seem to pose any incongruences with Brazilian legal order, such as denial of justice and breach of due process of law, which are principles with constitutional status in Brazil[77] and are even included in some CFIAs.[78] Other provisions entail a greater deal of subjectivity, such as manifest arbitrariness—which requires an assessment as to judge whether a measure is not rationally connected to a legitimate policy objective.[79] It can be problematic because the scrutiny of public policies by international arbitration could challenge principles with constitutional statuses such as national independence (art 4.i) and national sovereignty (art 1.i).

Likewise, the protection against "failure to provide physical security" could trigger an inconsistency with Brazilian national law since the concept may imply the idea that investors have the right not to suffer any damage,[80] while national law merely provides for the duty of due diligence for the State to promote a peaceful environment and deter physical violence when it occurs.[81] This kind of provision would be acceptable if accompanied by a clarification that the standard requires merely a non-discriminatory duty of due diligence and does not create absolute liability for the State to deter physical violence.

Moreover, incorporating MST to the CFIA might require the qualification of the standards through an exhaustive list of state actions that would constitute a violation of the protection to be more precise and predictable in its implementation and subsequent interpretation. By doing so, Brazilian policymakers would be able to modulate the compatibility of the provision with the whole national legal order. Regarding the reference to the customary international law, the circumscription of the concept to the meanings "as recognized by Brazil and its national laws" would suffice. Indeed, this has been adopted in the CFIAs with India, Guiana, and United Arab Emirates (article 4.1).

There have been extensive discussions regarding the differences between the standards of international minimum standard of treatment (IMST) and the fair and equitable treatment (FET) clauses.[82] Since Brazil has never signed a BIT encompassing FET nor has taken part in an arbitration dealing with FET-related claims, Brazilian policymakers would better adopt a language that prevents

[76]UNCTAD (2020).

[77]Brazilian Constitution, article 5°, XXXV and LIV.

[78]See CFIAs Colombia (article 4), United Arab Emirates (article 4), India (article 4), among others.

[79]Stone (2012).

[80]Mantilla Blanco (2019).

[81]See article. 144 of Brazil Federal Constitution.

[82]See OECD (2004).

standards developed in ISDS tribunals from being used in future arbitration encompassing IMST. It is the rationale behind the "for greater certainty" language excluding the terms FET and FPS from the coverage of some agreements.[83] As far as the "treatment clause" includes other elements from traditional BITs, it is worth maintaining this clarification as it is.

3.5 *Expansion of the Definition of Investment to Include Some Types of Portfolio Investment*

The Brazilian mandate for IIA's negotiation, as previously approved by CAMEX, limits the scope of protection under the agreement only to "productive investments".[84] Accordingly, CFIA's text explicitly excludes portfolio investments from its coverage. Besides, CFIA's traditional definition of investment that primarily reflects the criteria of the Salini Test by requiring a commitment of capital that enables the investor to exercise a significant degree of influence, with the objective of establishing a lasting interest, the expectation of gain and the assumption of risks.[85] This stance came from the perception that portfolio investments, due to their speculative nature and detachment from job creation, technology inflows, and increasing production capabilities; would not trigger positive economic impacts and would imply vulnerabilities associated with speculative capital flows creating harmful effects on the balance of payments.

Portfolio investments are usually defined as freely circulating instruments, with no specific term of duration, not necessarily involving participation in management or even entry into the jurisdiction where the assets are put to productive use.[86] Although CFIA does not establish the criteria for defining neither the duration of the investment to characterize it as "lasting interest" nor the degree of commitment of capital to characterize it as "significant influence", it is implied that CFIA's definition relies on widely accepted conventions that define the thresholds to meet those requirements, such as the OECD Detailed Benchmark Definition of Foreign Direct Investment,[87] and the IMF's Balance of Payments and International Investment Position Manual.[88]

Nonetheless, modern arrangements through which FDI is operationalized blur the lines that distinguish portfolio investment from direct investment. Arguably, such a murky separation could create an element of uncertainty concerning certain investments that, although could fall under portfolio investment's usual definition, would

[83] See Guiana (art. 4), United Arab Emirates (art. 4), and India (Art. 4).

[84] Morosini and Badin (2015).

[85] See footnote 20.

[86] Sornarajah (2009).

[87] See OECD (2008).

[88] See IMF (2009).

meet CFIAs criteria of exercising a significant degree of influence with the objective of establishing a lasting interest. This uncertainty could include investments made through Collective Investment Institutions (CII), such as mutual funds, feeder/master funds, hedge funds, and distressed funds, as well as sovereign wealth funds, and pension funds.

The advocators of the coverage of portfolio investments in IIAs claim that the abovementioned entities commit a large amount of capital that genuinely contributes to productive investments,[89] e.g., equity investments carried out by Pension Funds that, remarkably, finance infrastructure projects.[90] In the late 2010s, Pension Fund Assets in OECD countries reached USD 32 trillion,[91] a minor part of which would be enough to fill the investment gap of infrastructure in Brazil.[92] The same argument would apply to sovereign wealth funds (SWF). However, since SWFs are state-owned funds, their coverage by the CFIA would require adjustments to include States in the definition of investor.

However, the need for change in the CFIA language to cover such types of investment is debatable. Modern reporting standards state that an investment should be regarded as FDI if the applicable voting power threshold is met, regardless of the person conducting the investment or the instrument used to acquire it.[93] What is more, the inclusion of portfolio in CFIA's coverage could spark unintended consequences and unnecessary shortcomings in several areas of policymaking.

In the domain of macroeconomic management, it would diminish financial regulators' leverage over Brazil's capital account and include some risks associated with capital mobility. It could occur because CFIA contains commitments regarding capital mobility ensuring free transfer of funds related to covered investments and its contributions to capital, profits, and dividends. The same provision regulating "transfers" ensures the right to adopt temporary restrictive measures for transfer in case of a balance of payments crisis. Nonetheless, the protection of portfolio investments would restrict financial authorities' leverage over the capital account in ordinary circumstances where Brazil would need a tighter grip on the capital controls for other public policies' objectives. Even under the current *status quo,* this issue is already sensitive as investors have long been using creative legal mechanisms to disguise portfolio investment as FDI in order to avoid capital controls and other restrictions.[94] The flexibilization of the language regarding portfolio could worsen this scenario.

On top of that, the protection of portfolio investments deserves several ethical considerations. First and foremost is the lack of rationale for protecting investments of such nature. The underlying factor for IIAs' to protect investors is to provide stability by ensuring *ex-ante* that the regulatory *status quo* will not change drastically

---

[89] See IISD (2012).

[90] See Della Croce (2011).

[91] See OECD (2020).

[92] See ABDIB (2020).

[93] See OECD (2008).

[94] See OECD (1996).

to prejudice the conditions of management relevant to conduct business activities. Therefore, such protection can only be justifiable for those investments that entail long-term and steady relationships with the host state's economy. Portfolio investments lack nexus for protection because their focus is primarily on earnings resulting from the acquisition and sales of shares and other securities without expecting to control or influence the management of the assets underlying these investments.[95]

Besides that, portfolio investments do not require the same level of protection as direct investments since they can easily reduce their country-specific risk by diversifying their investment in different countries. Moreover, portfolio investors inherently have less sunk costs that would require them to continue to hold their investments for a longer-term and possess a higher ability to recover the value of their investments and withdraw them from the host country.[96] All of this would contradict the need for protection in case a State acts contrary to their interests.

There are also essential concerns regarding regulatory chill given the risk of portfolio investors suing governments for legitimate State acts that they deem inappropriate and causing a loss in their asset's value. Such a hypothesis is very feasible given the record of claims involving indirect expropriation, where investors seek compensation following a government action that allegedly diminished the economic value of an investment. It is reasonable to assume that the possibilities of attributing asset losses to State legitimate action are way more likely in portfolio investments, given that short-term investments are inherently more volatile.[97]

Therefore, including portfolio investments in CFIA coverage is inappropriate as it lacks the rationale between the protection and investors' activities. Moreover, it would also expose the Brazilian State to international arbitration for demands on the grounds of fluctuations in the values of assets inherently volatile and, thus, should not serve to judge the validity of State actions.

3.6 Inclusion of Discipline on Prohibited Performance Requirements

Performance requirements constitute an option for inward-related investment promotion provisions (host-country measures) designed to link State actions to specific developmental results to condition the host country's incentives on the sustainable development impact of the investment. Measures aimed at enforcing performance requirements normally impose specific operational undertakings upon investors and their investments to serve specific national goals of the Host State, such as

[95] See OECD (2008).

[96] See IISD (2012).

[97] See IISD (2012).

maximizing the beneficial impacts and increasing the generation of value-added to FDI, as well as diversifying and expanding the State's industrial base.[98]

Prohibited performance requirements (PPR) in IIA's arose as a remedy for trade concerns in developed countries/net FDI exporters since outward FDI generates significant demand for home-state exporters of goods and services to their foreign subsidiaries. Consequently, trade-distorting performance requirements were seen as a threat to home states manufacturing base, and its prohibition became an important part of developed countries' trade policy.[99] As Brazil approaches developed countries, the demand to include disciplines on PPRs will undoubtedly be in high demand.

PPRs became popular in IIAs during the 70s and were incorporated in the WTO's framework through the Agreement on Trade-Related Investment Measures (TRIMS), which provides an illustrative list of performance requirements inconsistent with WTO's obligations of national treatment and eliminates quantitative restrictions. Whereas PPRs found in IIAs negotiated right after the TRIMS consist in incorporating the TRIMS' prohibitions, modern IIAs usually expand PPRs in order to prohibit other measures such as technology transfer and even data localization requirements concerning digital trade.[100]

Recent IIAs normally enumerate the prohibited investment measures in an exhaustive list that builds on and expands the hypothesis stipulated in the TRIMS' illustrative list. The exhaustive list approach has the advantage of providing more transparency as well as legal certainty as to allow policymakers to design development policies without incurring forbidden investment measures inadvertently, as Brazil's recent programs concerning tax incentives to the information and communication technology (ICT) and automotive sectors[101] that came to be ruled as inconsistent with the TRIMS.[102]

On the other hand, by expanding the list of PPRs, CFIA may enact prohibitions in addition to those that Brazil is already obliged to follow given the tendency of new treaties to cover performance requirements on services and expand the PPRs provided by TRIMS (UNCTAD 2018; Collins 2019), incurring in further curtailment of policy space. Unlike other investment protection provisions, the inclusion of PPRs in CFIA's framework requires more than a mere assessment of the compatibility between the provision and the national legal order. If it is to be meaningful and provide for protections in addition to those already established at TRIMS, it will

---

[98] UNCTAD (2018).

[99] Savoie (2020).

[100] Collins (2019).

[101] The tax incentives in the ICT sector were carried out by the Informatics programme, the programme of Incentives for the Semiconductors Sector (PADIS), the programme of Support for the Technological Development of the Industry of Digital TV Equipment (PATVD), and the programme for Digital Inclusion (Digital Inclusion); whereas the tax incentives in the automotive sector we given through the Programme of Incentive to the Technological Innovation and Densification of the Automotive Supply Chain (INOVAR-AUTO).

[102] WTO (2018).

necessarily imply further curtailment of policy space that may be essential for formulating development policies related to FDI.

Further commitments on PPRs deserve all considerations regarding the permanent reduction of the State's capacity to formulate industrial policies. Especially, the timing for deepening such a discipline on CFIA's framework can sound anachronic and inappropriate given the rise of State involvement in the economy in the face of a post-COVID-19 pandemic where many states are reviewing their industrial policies and considering the necessary measures to ensure adequate domestic manufacturing capacity for which additional PPRs would undoubtedly be a constraint.

4 Conclusion

In a moment of rising skepticism regarding traditional investment treaty practice, Brazil managed to create an innovative and welcoming approach towards IIA rulemaking. CFIA model has constantly been evolving and incorporating new clauses as Brazil expands its network of investment agreements. The current scenario might require further changes in the CFIA framework as Brazil intends to negotiate with developed countries.

The concern of Brazilian policymakers with the modernization of the CFIA model should not be restricted to the capacity of enticing developed countries to negotiate nor the ability to attract FDI, but also to increase the potential of FDI to contribute to sustainable development. While data and case studies suggest divergent conclusions on the effects of FDI for different economies, the logical conclusion is that FDI could be beneficial for sustainable development, but it will always depend on how it is conducted.[103]

The recent developments in Brazil's internal political scenario suggest an approximation to negotiating practices of developed countries to strengthen CFIA's elements of investment protection. The success of forthcoming negotiations and implementation of CFIAs incorporating traditional IIAs provisions will depend on the stability of internal politics and the will of the Brazilian legislative. Now, likewise in the 90s, it might be possible that the Congress would reject CFIAs with protection clauses similar to those of traditional IIAs, despite the Executive Branch's effort to reproach developed countries' negotiating practices. Besides the intent to negotiate investment agreements and other economic integration instruments with developed countries, there are no other convincing reasons for any radical change in the Brazilian policy on the protection of FDI.[104]

Regardless of the future improvements, CFIA's Dispute Settlement scheme might maintain the same structure, by privileging dispute prevention and resorting to State-to-State proceedings as long there is no clear trend in IIA policymaking towards

[103] Cohen (2007).

[104] Andrade and Oliveira (2013), p. 106.

ISDS, SSDS, or the establishment of an International Court System as articulated by some countries in the UNCITRAL Working Group III.

CFIA's institutional arrangements to facilitate investments and implement the agendas for further investment cooperation between the Parties might remain the model's core. Such arrangements are very recent and were not properly tested to assert their effectiveness since only two CFIAs (Angola and Mexico) came into force. Therefore, the practical results of the governance structure are yet to be seen. Moreover, Brazil has invested plenty of efforts to establish and adequately structure its Direct Investment Ombudsman. Brazilian policymakers keep a high expectation on the results it might achieve from the improvement of the investment environment, leading to higher attraction and retention of FDI. Brazil bets that a couple therapy, as we can understand the dispute prevention system, would prevent a divorce.[105]

References

ABDIB (2020) Investimento em Infraestrutura no Brasil é menos da metade do necessário. https://www.abdib.org.br/2020/12/01/abdib-investimento-em-infraestrutura-no-brasil-e-menos-da-metade-do-necessario/

Andrade GFA, Oliveira GHJ (2013) Chapter 5: investment treaties, foreign investment and Brazilian law: the magic of reality. In: Levy DA, de Borja Mercereau AG et al (eds) Investment protection in Brazil. Kluwer Law International, pp 71–106

Azevedo DB (2001) Os acordos para a promoção e a proteção de investimentos assinados pelo Brasil. Câmara dos Deputados, Brasília: May/2001. Available at: <https://www2.camara.leg.br/atividade-legislativa/estudos-e-notas-tecnicas/publicacoes-da-consultoria-legislativa/arquivos-pdf/pdf/102080.pdf>

Blake DJ, Moschieri C (2017) Policy risk, strategic decisions and contagion effects: firm-specific considerations. Strateg Manag J 38(3):732–750

Bonnitcha J, Skovgaard Poulsen LN, Waibel M (2017) The political economy of the investment treaty regime. Oxford University Press

Brauch MD (2017) IISD best practices series: exhaustion of local remedies in international investment law. International Institute for Sustainable Development

Brazil. Submission from the Government of Brazil to the UNCITRAL Working Group III on Possible reform of investor-State dispute settlement (ISDS). Document A/CN.9/WG.III/WP.171. June, 2019

Cohen S (2007) Multinational corporations and foreign direct investment: avoiding simplicity, embracing complexity. Oxford University Press, Oxford

Collins D (2019) Performance requirement prohibitions in international investment law. In: Chaisse J, Choukroune L, Jusoh S (eds) Handbook of international investment law and policy. Springer, Singapore. https://doi.org/10.1007/978-981-13-5744-2_3-1

De Nanteuril A (2017) Droit international de l'investissement. Pédone, Paris

Della Croce R (2011) Pension funds investment in infrastructure: policy actions. OECD Working Papers on Finance, Insurance and Private Pensions, No. 13, OECD Publishing. https://doi.org/10.1787/5kg272f9bnmx-en

Giusti G, Catarucci DD (2019) Brazil. In: The international arbitration review, 10th edn. Derbshyre, pp 106–114

[105] Silva (2019b).

Godinho D (2014) The Brazilian experience with IIAs. In: UNCTAD, World Investment Forum 2014: investing in sustainable development. IIA Conference. Geneva, Switzerland, 16 October. At https://worldinvestmentforum.unctad.org/wp-content/uploads/2014/10/Godinho.pdf
Iglesias and Costa (2012) Mapa do investimento brasileiro na América do Sul e no México: análise das informações do IndexInvest Brasil. Breves CINDES 63. Centro de Estudos de Integração e Desenvolvimento. Available at: https://www.cindesbrasil.org/site/index.php?option=com_jdownloads&Itemid=62&view=finish&cid=625&catid=4
IISD (2012) Integrating sustainable development into international investment agreements: a guide for developing countries. https://www.iisd.org/system/files/meterial/6th_annual_forum_commonwealth_guide.pdf
IMF (2009) Balance of Payments and International Investment Position Manual. Sixth Edition (BPM6). https://www.imf.org/external/pubs/ft/bop/2007/pdf/bpm6.pdf
Kalicki J, Medeiros S (2007) Fair, equitable and ambiguous: what is fair and equitable treatment in international investment law? ICSID Rev Foreign Invest Law J 2(1):24–54. https://doi.org/10.1093/icsidreview/22.1.24
Lemos LB, Campello D (2013) The non-ratification of bilateral investment treaties in Brazil: a story of conflict in a land of cooperation (April 1, 2013). Available at SSRN: https://ssrn.com/abstract=2243120 or https://doi.org/10.2139/ssrn.2243120
Mantilla Blanco S (2019) 'Protection and security' clauses in investment treaties: a typology. In: Full protection and security in international investment law. European yearbook of international economic law, vol 8. Springer, Cham. https://doi.org/10.1007/978-3-030-24838-3_14
Monebhurrun N (2015) Crônicas de direito internacional dos investimentos. Revista de Direito Internacional, Brasília 12(1):32–38
Monebhurrun N (2017) Novelty in international investment law: the Brazilian Agreement on cooperation and facilitation of investments as a different international investment agreement model. J Int Dispute Settlement 8(1):79–100
Monebhurrun N (2019) O mecanismo de resolução de disputas nos novos Acordos de Cooperação e de Facilitação dos Investimentos do Brasil. In: Carlos Esplugues Mota (org) Inversiones extranjeras y arbitraje de inversión em Latinoamérica: realidad presente y futura. Tirant Lo Blanch, Valencia
Moraes HC, Cavalcante PM (2021) The Brazil-India Investment Cooperation and Facilitation Treaty: giving concrete meaning to the "right to regulate" in investment treaty-making. ICSID Rev, forthcoming
Morosini F, Badin MRS (2015) The Brazilian Agreement on Cooperation and Facilitation of Investments (ACFI): a new formula for international investment agreements? Invest Treaty News 6(3):3–5
Muniz JP et al (2017) The New Brazilian BIT on cooperation and facilitation of investments: a new approach in times of chance. ICSID Rev Foreign Invest Law J 32(2):404–417
Nikiema S (Feb 2017) The most-favored nation clause in investment treaties. IISD Best Practices Series. Available at: https://www.iisd.org/system/files/publications/mfn-most-favoured-nation-clause-best-practices-en.pdf
OECD (1996) Detailed benchmark definition of foreign direct investment, 3rd edn (BD3). OECD, Paris. https://www.oecd.org/daf/inv/investment-policy/2090148.pdf
OECD (2004) Fair and equitable treatment standard in international investment law, OECD Working Papers on International Investment, 2004/03. OECD Publishing. https://doi.org/10.1787/675702255435
OECD (2008) Benchmark Definition of Foreign Direct Investment. Fourth edition. https://www.oecd.org/daf/inv/investmentstatisticsandanalysis/40193734.pdf
OECD (2019) Drivers of divestment decisions of multinational enterprises - a cross-country firm-level perspective. OECD Working Papers on International Investment. https://www.oecd-ilibrary.org/docserver/5a376df4-en.pdf?expires=1604426564&id=id&accname=guest&checksum=6A93DD61D6F418C64F935FC6FFB97C47

OECD (2020) Pension funds in figures. https://www.oecd.org/pensions/Pension-Funds-in-Figures-2020.pdf
Oliveira R (2020) The useful institution of an investment ombudsperson. Policy Paper, Columbia Center on Sustainable Investment, New York. At https://academiccommons.columbia.edu/doi/10.7916/d8-psm1-jk77
Pauwelyn J (2014) At the edge of chaos?: Foreign investment law as a complex adaptive system, how it emerged and how it can be reformed. ICSID Rev 29(2):372–418
Ramos Codeço R, Freitas da Silva AR (2020) Multilateral framework of investment facilitation at WTO: initiatives and perspectives from the global South (November 19, 2020). Contexto Internacional May/Aug 2021 (Forthcoming). Available at SSRN: https://ssrn.com/abstract=3849689 or https://doi.org/10.2139/ssrn.3849689
Sachetim H, Codeço R (2019) The investor-state dispute settlement system amidst crisis, collapse, and reform. Arbitr Brief 6(1):20–59
Savoie PO (2020) Performance requirement prohibitions in international investment law. Par Alexandre Genest. Leiden: Brill, 2019. 274+ iv pages. Can Yearb Int Law/Annuaire canadien de droit international 57:667–679
Schill SW, Vidigal G (2018) Cutting the Gordian Knot: Investment Dispute Settlement à la Carte. RTA Exchange, Geneva International Centre for Trade and Sustainable Development
Silva ARF (2019a) A Arguição de Ilegalidade na Arbitragem Investidor-Estado. Editora Processo, Rio de Janeiro
Silva ARF (2019b) A evolução da solução de controvérsias nos ACFIS. Revista de Direito Internacional, Brasília 16(2):7–13
Silva ARF, Ribeiro GF (2018) A Arguição de Ilegalidade na Arbitragem Investidor-Estado: Construindo a Argumentação Jurídica Que Permita o Exame da Conduta do Investidor. Revista Brasileira de Arbitragem 15(57):23–44
Sornarajah M (2009) Portfolio investments and the definition of investment. ICSID Rev 24(2): 516–520. https://doi.org/10.1093/icsidreview/24.2.516
Stone J (2012) Arbitrariness, the fair and equitable treatment standard, and the international law of investment. Leiden J Int Law 25(1):77–107. https://doi.org/10.1017/S0922156511000598
Tienhaara K (2017) Investor–state dispute settlement. In: Drahos P (ed) Regulatory theory: foundations and applications. ANU Press. At: http://www.jstor.org/stable/j.ctt1q1crtm.51
UNCTAD (2018) UNCTAD's reform package for the international investment regime. United Nations Publications, New York, p 65
UNCTAD (2020) World Investment Report 2020: international production beyond the pandemic. United Nations Publications, New York, p 12
Veiga and Rios (2014) Os investimentos brasileiros na África: características, tendências e agenda de política. Textos Cindes 39. Centro de Estudos de Integração e Desenvolvimento. Available at: https://www.cindesbrasil.org/site/index.php?option=com_jdownloads&Itemid=7&view=finish&cid=883&catid=7
WTO (2018) Brazil – certain measures concerning taxation and charges. Reports of the Appellate Body. WT/DS472/AB/R and WT/DS497/AB/R. https://docs.wto.org/dol2fe/Pages/SS/directdoc.aspx?filename=q:/WT/DS/472ABR.pdf&Open=True
WTO (2020) Structured discussions on investment facilitation for development move into negotiating mode. https://www.wto.org/english/news_e/news20_e/infac_25sep20_e.htm
Zavaschi T (2004) Possession protection in Brazilian Constitution and in the New Civil Code. Direito e Democracia 5(1)

Ana Rachel Freitas da Silva Coordinator of Financial Operations in the Office of the Attorney General in the Ministry of Finance, Brazil. She holds an MSc and a Doctorate in International Law from Centro Universitário de Brasília (UniCEUB).

Rafael Ramos Codeço is Head of Department of the Consumer Goods Industry at the Ministry of Development, Industry, Foreign Trade and Services, Brazil. He holds a master's degree in Globalization and Development from SOAS University of London.

International Investment Law in Chile: Recent Developments in Times of Reform

Pablo Nilo Donoso

1 Introduction

Chile has been an attractive destination for foreign investment over the years. Its commitment to fostering international economic relations is reflected in a web of bilateral investment treaties ("**BITs**") and free trade agreements ("**FTAs**") with numerous countries around the world. These treaties have vested foreign investors with legal protections and incentives to invest in various sectors of the economy.

However, in the last decade, international investment law has undergone significant scrutiny and debate, leading to a series of reforms aimed at striking a balance between attracting foreign capital and safeguarding the state's right to regulate.

This article delves into the recent developments in Chile's international investment law landscape in light of the ongoing reforms. The first part provides a general overview of Chile's international trade policy. Then, it explains the change of paradigm in the State's international investment practice that translated in a suspension of negotiations of bilateral investment agreements. Finally, it presents a summary of the main investment provisions negotiated by Chile in its latest free trade agreements.

The second section introduces Chile's participation in multilateral forums, where discussions on the modernization and reform of the investor-State dispute settlement mechanism are currently being held.

The third section presents a summary of Chile's cases in investor-State arbitration, as well as the steps that have been taken for the institutionalization of its defense in international investment arbitration proceedings. This section also analyzes dispute prevention actions carried out by the Program for the Defense of the State in

The original version of the chapter has been revised. A correction to this chapter can be found at https://doi.org/10.1007/978-3-031-49382-9_12

Note from the ed.: at the time of this publication, Mr. Nilo Donoso is no longer affiliated to the Republic of Chile's Defense Program in International Investment Arbitration or its superseding agencies. The opinions and assertions expressed herein are those of the author and do not necessarily reflect the current official policy or position of the Republic of Chile.

P. Nilo Donoso (✉)
Investment Arbitration Unit of the Vice-Ministry of International Economic Affairs, Santiago, Chile

N. Monebhurrun et al. (eds.), *International Investment Law and Arbitration from a Latin American Perspective*, International Law and the Global South,
https://doi.org/10.1007/978-3-031-49382-9_3

International Investment Arbitration (also "the Program"), and it ends by highlighting the threats currently faced by the State, and the amicable consultations under international investment agreements that are being held by the State.

Finally, the fourth section presents conclusions about Chile's most relevant developments in the field of investment arbitration, and it offers final thoughts about the current historic moment that the country is experiencing after a constitutional convention was elected in May 2021.

2 International Investment Regime: Context and Evolution

2.1 Chile's International Trade Policy: Liberalization Towards Free Trade

In 1990, Chile started its transition to democracy and began recovering from decades of international isolation. The first steps comprised of the negotiation of bilateral trade agreements with neighboring countries,[1] the promotion of international investment through BITs, and a unilateral tariff reduction for imported goods.[2]

In the early '90s, Chile's authorities recognized that the country's path towards economic development was intrinsically linked to its openness to foreign markets.[3] In 1994, Chile joined the Asia-Pacific Economic Cooperation forum, and in 1997 Chile's first Free Trade Agreement ("**FTA**")[4] entered into force, advancing a model that would become the cornerstone of the country's foreign economic policy. As of June 2021, Chile has ratified 30 trade agreements,[5] becoming one of the most open economies in the world by connecting through preferential access to 65 economies,

[1] Agreement of Economic Complementation ("**ACE**") N° 16 with Argentina (1991), ACE N° 22 with Bolivia (1993), and ACE N° 38 with Peru (1998).

[2] *See* Law 19.589 of 14th November 1998, providing for tariff rates reduction and introducing amendment to other tax and economic regulations.

[3] *See* letter 004948 of 18th October 1993, from President Patricio Aylwin Azócar to President William J. Clinton. Available at: https://archivospublicos.uahurtado.cl/.

[4] *See* Free Trade Agreement between the Government of Canada and the Government of the Republic of Chile, which entered into force on 5th July 1997.

[5] Chile has entered into commercial agreements with the following countries (in chronological order): Bolivia (April 1993), Venezuela (July 1993), Mercosur (October 1996), Canada (July 1997), Mexico (July 1999), Central America (February 2002), European Union (February 2003), South Korea (April 2004), European Free Trade Association (December 2004), Unites States of America (January 2004), P4 (Brunei Darussalam, Chile, New Zealand, Singapore) (November 2006), China (October 2006), India (August 2007), Japan (September 2007), Cuba (June 2008), Panama (March 2008), Peru (March 2009), Australia (March 2009), Colombia (May 2009), Ecuador (January 2010), Turkey (March 2011), Malaysia (April 2012), Vietnam (January 2014), Hong Kong (November 2014), Thailand (November 2015), Pacific Alliance (Chile, Colombia, Peru and Mexico) (May 2016), Uruguay (December 2018), Indonesia (August 2019), Argentina (May 2019), and United Kingdom (January 2021).

representing more than 88% of the world's Gross Domestic Product.[6] These FTA networks provide access to Chilean goods and services to a market of more than 5 billion people.[7] As a consequence, today, 57% of Chile's economy depends on international trade.[8]

Over the last twenty years, Chile has made a consistent effort to provide its population with greater access to the benefits of free trade agreements. In the last decade, the State has opened a permanent dialogue with civil society to incorporate a more inclusive and sustainable approach to future international negotiations.

2.2 *Change of Paradigm in Investment Negotiations*

In 2003, after more than a decade negotiating BITs with several States, Chile established a moratorium on new and current BIT negotiations[9] while it evaluated the functionality of those treaties within the framework of FTAs. Official messages to missions abroad and foreign embassies in Chile[10] further explained the rationale behind the moratorium by stating that BITs negotiated during the '90s:

> [D]id not contain properly circumscribed obligations for the State, providing room for excessively broad interpretations by international arbitral tribunals [. . .] these obligations could only make sense in the broader context of a wider commercial integration encompassing multiple disciplines. [...] Chile's policy regarding investment protection favors the negotiation of such provisions in the framework of comprehensive trade integration processes, as it is the case of investment chapters in Free Trade Agreements. Through those instruments, the State seeks to establish a framework of protection for investors by providing a series of guarantees under current international legal standards, while safeguarding the regulatory powers of the State. If such rights are not respected, investors are given access to independent international tribunals, through duly developed procedural rules. These rules provide legal certainty, both to the investor and the host State.

Another diplomatic note addressed to the Embassy of Morocco[11] in 2016 highlighted the following:

> [T]he Chilean government has been consistent in seeking to grant a high degree of protection and legal certainty to foreign capital while safeguarding the regulatory powers of the State to achieve its legitimate economic and social objectives.

---

[6] *See* information provided by the Vice-Ministry of International Economic Affairs of Chile at https://www.subrei.gob.cl/ [last visit: 12th of June 2021].

[7] Ibid.

[8] Vice-Ministry of International Economic Affairs (2019), p. 8.

[9] Official Message N° 725 of May 30th, 2003, from the General Directorate of International Economic Affairs to all Embassies of Chile, missions, and general consulates.

[10] Official Message N° 871 of General Directorate of International Economic Affairs to the Chilean Embassy in South Africa, September 2nd, 2016.

[11] *Note Verbale* N° 6862 from the Ministry of Foreign Affairs to the Embassy of the Kingdom of Morocco in Chile, December 30th, 2015.

> Notwithstanding, in recent years, the Agreements for the Promotion and Reciprocal Protection of Investments have been questioned as to their effectiveness in attracting foreign investment and by the multiplicity of disputes that foreign investors have brought against host States, especially before the International Center for the Settlement of Investment Disputes (ICSID).
>
> Given the above, the Chilean Government decided, more than a decade ago and through a broad technical and political agreement, to apply a moratorium on the negotiation, updating or renegotiation of this type of international instruments.

Nevertheless, before the 2003 moratorium, Chile had already ratified 40 BITs[12] granting legal protection to foreign investors from contracting parties, as well as an investor-State dispute settlement regime that provided an independent forum to solve investment disputes presented against the State.

2.3 *New Paradigm: Investment Chapters in Free Trade Agreements*

Since the moratorium, Chile has negotiated investment chapters in Free Trade Agreements with 11 economies.[13] The main differences between Chile's first generation's BITs and the investment chapters negotiated in the context of FTAs relate to several characteristics:

1. First generation's BITs do not guarantee the access of foreign investment to the territory of the other party in a specific sector since that access is subject to the current legislation in the host country. The FTA model that Chile has followed

[12] Chile has signed BITs with the following countries (in chronological order): Spain (March 1994), France (July 1994), Norway (September 1994), Argentina (January 1995), Italy (February 1995), Venezuela (May 1995), China (August 1995), Malaysia (August 1995), Denmark (November 1995), Sweden (December 1995), Ecuador (February 1995), Finland (May 1996), Croatia (June 1996), Czech Republic (October 1996), United Kingdom (April 1997), Romania (July 1997), Philippines (August 1997), Ukraine (August 1997), Paraguay (December 1997), Portugal (February 1998), Uruguay (April 1999), Germany (May 1999), Bolivia (July 1999), BLEU (Belgium-Luxembourg Economic Union) (August 1999), South Korea (September 1999), Australia (November 1999), El Salvador (November 1999), Panama (December 1999), Poland (January 2000), Costa Rica (June 2000), Cuba (September 2000), Austria (October 2000), Nicaragua (January 2001), Peru (August 2001), Guatemala (December 2001), Honduras (January 2002), Dominican Republic (May 2002), Greece (October 2002). It is worth mentioning that the following agreements were terminated and replaced by more comprehensive investment chapters in FTAs: Argentina, China, Australia, Peru, and South Korea. The BITs with Bolivia and Ecuador were subject to denunciation (in May 2013 and May 2017, respectively) but were not replaced by subsequent investment agreements. The BIT with Uruguay was replaced by a modern investment agreement that entered into force in March 2012.

[13] Chile has entered into FTAs with the following countries (in chronological order): Canada (July 1997), Mexico (July 1999), United States of America (January 2004), South Korea (April 2004), Japan (September 2007), Peru (March 2009), Australia (March 2009), Colombia (May 2009), China (April 2014), Pacific Alliance (May 2016), Argentina (May 2019).

(the NAFTA approach) guarantees the access of foreign investment to each party's territory with exceptions provided in the lists of sectoral reservations. An essential element of access and liberalization of investment flows is the listing of existing non-conforming measures.[14] These measures are contained in annexes to the Investment Chapters and correspond to laws and regulations that are in contradiction with provisions such as national treatment, most favored nation treatment, performance requirements, and senior managers and boards of directors. Additionally, standstill and ratchet clauses are incorporated, which means that Chile and its trading partners should list all existent barriers and refrain from introducing any new restrictions. As a corollary, any future market liberalization is automatically incorporated into the FTAs.

2. First generation's BITs do not usually include denial of benefits clauses, whereas FTAs tend to include denial of benefits clauses that preclude certain investors from using the investment chapter's advantages. For instance, if a company is owned or controlled by an investor of the denying Party, and it has no substantial business activities in the territory of the Party under whose law is constituted, it is not allowed to enjoy the protections provided by the FTA.
3. FTAs involve the integration of a greater number of disciplines than those covered by first generation's BITs, such as the general prohibition on applying performance requirements to foreign investments[15] or requiring a certain nationality for the members of the board of directors of a company.
4. Substantive provisions in FTAs are better defined and offer greater certainty on the extent of the States' obligations, providing further clarity to arbitral tribunals when interpreting the respective agreement's standards. For example:
   a. National Treatment and Most-Favored-Nation Treatment provisions in first generation's BITs are in certain instances vaguely defined and do not take into consideration the more recent developments in international arbitration. For example, arbitral tribunals have evolved to recognize that the non-discrimination standard must be accorded to investments of the other Party when they are in like circumstances and with respect to specific stages of the investment, such as the establishment, acquisition, expansion, management, conduct, operation, and sale or other disposition of investments.
   b. Additionally, Most-Favored Nation obligations in FTAs specifically limit the "treatment" that can be imported through the clause by excluding international

[14] "A non-conforming measure is any law, regulation, procedure, requirement or practice, which violates certain articles of the investment agreement. For example, a law prohibiting an investor of another member country to own a factory does not conform with the article on national treatment". *See* Foreign Trade Information System, Dictionary of Trade Terms at http://www.sice.oas.org/dictionary/in_e.asp [last visit: 13th of June 2021].

[15] By limiting the possibility to impose or enforce certain requirements (such as exportation levels, percentage of domestic content, preference to local goods or services, or technology transfers) in connection with the establishment, acquisition, expansion, management, conduct, or operation of an investment.

dispute resolution procedures or mechanisms, to avoid expansive interpretations of the standard.

c. First generation's BITs normally refer to the obligation to extend fair and equitable treatment ("**FET**") without defining its content or specifying its elements, whereas FTAs normally link the standard to the customary international law minimum standard of treatment, thus facilitating arbitral tribunals' interpretations by explicitly providing a high bar for the breach of the standard.
d. FTAs also specify the obligations comprised in the FET standard, normally listing the obligation not to deny justice in criminal, civil, or administrative adjudicatory proceedings in accordance with the principle of due process.
e. More recently, FTAs have provided greater certainty to the scope of fair and equitable treatment, by denying the possibility to bring claims against states when they adopt or maintain measures necessary to secure compliance with laws and regulations to protect human, animal or plant life or health, or necessary for the conservation of living or non-living exhaustible natural resources.
f. The rules on expropriation are clearer and more specific in FTAs, defining the concept of indirect expropriation and providing explicit criteria to determine whether a measure can be categorized as expropriatory, namely the impact of the measure on the investment, the extent to which the measure interferes with distinct, reasonable investment-backed expectations and the character of the measure. Finally, Chile's FTAs clarify that even in the case of a non-discriminatory measure that cannot be reasonably regarded as adopted and applied in good faith (mainly due to its severity), when designed and applied to protect legitimate public welfare objectives, such as health, safety, and the environment, it cannot amount to an indirect expropriation.

5. With respect to procedural rules, the investor-state dispute settlement mechanism contained in FTAs is more sophisticated and developed than the provisions included in first generation's BITs, providing further assurances for the state and a more balanced approach regarding the rights of the State and those of the investor. For example, the most recent investment chapters that Chile has negotiated[16] contain clauses with clear rules governing ISDS proceedings, such as:

    a. Status of limitations to present claims
    b. Consolidation of claims
    c. Clear rules for mediation
    d. Specific conditions to submit claims to arbitration, such as waivers to initiate or continue disputes before local courts or tribunals
    e. Regulations for third-party funding
    f. Precise rules on appointment of arbitrators
    g. Regulation of non-disputing party submissions

[16] See, for example, the modernized investment chapter of the Chile-Canada FTA, that entered into force on February 5th, 2019.

h. Rules on transparency
i. Regulations for preliminary objections
j. Clear indication of the governing law stating, inter alia, that interpretations provided by the FTA Commission on the provisions of the agreement are binding on the tribunal
k. Provisions relating to the appointments of experts by the tribunal
l. Regulations on interim measures of protection of disputing parties' rights
m. Specifications of the essential content of final awards, limiting it to monetary damages and restitution in property
n. Rules on the enforcement of awards

3 Chile's Participation in Multilateral Forums to Reform the Investor-State Arbitration System and Modernize Its Rules

3.1 United Nations Commission on International Trade Law

At its forty-eighth session in 2015, the United Nations Commission on International Trade Law (**"UNCITRAL"**) noted that the current circumstances around investor-State arbitration "posed a number of challenges, and proposals for reform had been formulated by a number of organizations. In that context, the Commission was informed that the Secretariat was conducting a study on whether the United Nations Convention on Transparency in Treaty-based Investor-State Arbitration could provide a useful model for possible reforms in the field of investor-State arbitration [. . .] In so doing, the Secretariat was requested to conduct broad consultations, and to take into consideration the views of all States and other stakeholders, including on how this project might interact with other initiatives in this area and on the format and processes that could be used".[17]

The responses to the consultation process highlighted the fact that the Investor-State Dispute Settlement System presented specific particularities differentiating it from traditional mechanisms since it allowed foreign investors to bring claims directly against States, without the need of resorting to diplomatic protection, thus serving as an avenue for the de-politicization of investment disputes.

Delegations agreed that the system presented a variety of flaws that needed to be corrected to increase its legitimacy[18] and in July 2017, UNCITRAL mandated the

[17] A/CN.9/917 (2017), Possible future work in the field of dispute settlement: Reforms of investor-State dispute settlement (ISDS) paras. 1 and 5.

[18] Discussions on the perception of lack of legitimacy were held in the Working Group III, concluding that main criticism to ISDS related to the use of arbitration to resolve disputes between states and foreign investors instead of using domestic adjudicatory systems, thus creating asymmetries when offering such a system only to certain kind of individuals. Additionally, it has

Working Group III to advance the potential reform of the ISDS system[19] through a government-led process, focusing "on the procedural aspects of dispute settlement rather than on the substantive provisions."[20] The mandate consisted of the following phases:

1. Identify and consider concerns regarding investor-State dispute settlement;
2. Consider whether reform would be desirable in light of any identified concerns; and
3. If the Working Group were to conclude that reform was desirable, develop any relevant solutions to be recommended to the Commission.

During 2017 and 2018, three main concerns were identified:

1. Lack of coherence and consistency[21] in arbitral decisions rendered by tribunals in ISDS cases;
2. Lack or apparent lack in adjudicators' independence and impartiality;[22]
3. Duration and costs of ISDS proceedings.[23]

been stated that "much of the criticism of ISDS has its roots in concerns about the democratic accountability and legitimacy of the dispute resolution process. Critics do not accept or recognize the power of individual arbitrators to decide on an ISDS case. Further, party-appointment may be contrasted unfavorably with the appointment of judges in domestic courts through processes designed to ensure integrity in upholding the rule of law and to provide public scrutiny of judicial decision-making. Finally, while states themselves have established and consented to the current ISDS regime and confirmed its legitimacy under international law, this legitimacy as such may not be accepted by their constituencies." (A/CN.9/WG.III/WP.142 (2017), Possible reform of investor-State dispute settlement (ISDS), para. 47, in relation to a Paper prepared by the Geneva Center for International Dispute Settlement, titled "Can the Mauritius Convention serve as a model for the reform of investor-State arbitration in connection with the introduction of a permanent investment tribunal or an appeal mechanism? Analysis and roadmap", para. 23.

[19] A/72/17, Report of the United Nations Commission on International Trade Law Fiftieth session, para. 264.

[20] A/CN.9/930/Rev.1, Report of Working Group III (Investor-State Dispute Settlement Reform) on the work of its thirty-fourth session - Part I, para. 20.

[21] A/CN.9/935, Report of Working Group III (Investor-State Dispute Settlement Reform) on the work of its thirty-fifth session, paras. 20 and ff.

[22] Ibid. paras. 47 and ff.

[23] A/CN.9/930/Rev.1, Report of Working Group III (Investor-State Dispute Settlement Reform) on the work of its thirty-fourth session - Part I, para 34 and ff; A/CN.9/964, Report of of Working Group III (Investor-State Dispute Settlement Reform) on the work of its thirty-sixth session, para. 109 and ff. *See also* Note by the Secretariat A/CN.9/WG.III/WP.153, Possible reform of ISDS - Cost and duration.

Additionally, there was consensus that other concerns, such as lack of transparency,[24] frivolous claims[25] and issues of third-party funding,[26] should be considered as they also had an impact on the overall functioning of ISDS.

After completing both the first and second phases between 2017 and 2018, the Working Group has begun to discuss the different reform options, assessing their feasibility, the degree of support among member states, and the prioritization with which the reform options should be examined.

In this third phase of the reform process, Chile has been an active voice and in joint efforts with other member states, it has produced two working papers that have been presented to the UNCITRAL Secretariat.[27] Additionally, together with Colombia, Mexico and Peru, Chile expressed during the 38th session of the Working Group, its interest to prioritize: (1) the establishment of a Code of Conduct with provisions regulating ethics that are binding on arbitrators and adjudicators; (2) the establishment of a multilateral instrument that allows reform, modernization and unification of certain procedural aspects already included in recent international investment agreements; (3) the institution of stricter regulations of Third-Party Funding in ISDS; and (4) the strengthening of dispute prevention measures, as well as the analysis of alternative dispute resolution mechanisms.

As of June 2021, the Secretariat is preparing a Workplan establishing the time allocated to discuss and implement each reform option. During this process, Chile has committed to advance towards the implementation of a Multilateral Investment Reform Agreement ("**MIRA**") that would allow States to modernize their old existing Bilateral Investment Treaties through model clauses. Such an instrument would provide flexibility to States in terms of reform options that they may consider most align with their interests and concerns. The rationale behind the creation of the MIRA responds to the fact that not all States face the same concerns or are able to

---

[24] A/CN.9/935, (Investor-State Dispute Settlement Reform) on the work of its thirty-fifth session, para. 76 and ff.

[25] A/CN.9/WG.III/WP.142, Possible reform of investor-State dispute settlement (ISDS), para 29; A/CN.9/1004, Report of Working Group III (Investor-State Dispute Settlement Reform) on the work of its thirty-eighth session, paras. 24, 82; A/CN.9/964, Report of Working Group III (Investor-State Dispute Settlement Reform) on the work of its thirty-sixth session, para. 110 and ff.; A/CN.9/930/Rev.1, Report of Working Group III (Investor-State Dispute Settlement Reform) on the work of its thirty-fourth session - Part I, para. 46; A/CN.9/930/Add.1/Rev.1, Report of Working Group III (Investor-State Dispute Settlement Reform) on the work of its thirty-fourth session - Part II, para. 1.

[26] A/CN.9/930/Rev.1, Report of Working Group III (Investor-State Dispute Settlement Reform) on the work of its thirty-fourth session - Part I, paras. 57, 64, 69; A/CN.9/935, Report of Working Group III (Investor-State Dispute Settlement Reform) on the work of its thirty-fifth session, paras 44, 89–92; A/CN.9/964, Report of Working Group III (Investor-State Dispute Settlement Reform) on the work of its thirty-sixth session, paras. 120 and 134; A/CN.9/970, Report of Working Group III (Investor-State Dispute Settlement Reform) on the work of its thirty-seventh session, paras. 17 and ff; A/CN.9/1004, Report of Working Group III (Investor-State Dispute Settlement Reform) on the work of its thirty-eighth session, paras. 79 and ff.

[27] A/CN.9/WG.III/WP.163 - Submission from the Governments of Chile, Israel, and Japan; and A/CN.9/WG.III/WP.182 - Submission from the Governments of Chile, Israel, Japan, Mexico and Peru.

implement the same solutions at the same time. Hence, the MIRA ensures the widest possible participation of States in the reform process, while providing a flexible framework in implementing the solutions developed by the Working Group.

Along these lines, Working Paper 182 presented by Chile, Israel, Japan, Mexico, and Peru (and formally supported by Australia and the United States) proposes to offer States a range of reform options that would allow advancing multilaterally with the procedural reforms contained in the Working Group's mandate. Additionally, Chile considers that an instrument that focuses on reforming procedural elements would allow solutions to begin to be implemented in the short to medium term, leaving time for those reforms that are considered structural and require more debate, and therefore require more time for analysis.

Moreover, Chile considers that a multilateral investment treaty on procedural issues could be an efficient and effective way to modernize first-generation treaties and ensure a homogeneous implementation of best practices that have been developed in investment arbitration decisions, while achieving greater uniformity of procedural rules and, thus, greater consistency and coherence of the international investment regime.

Different ways of implementation of such instruments have been discussed. In June 2016, before the reform process commenced at the Working Group, the University of Geneva and the Center for International Dispute Settlement prepared a research paper[28] that sought "to analyze whether the Mauritius Convention on Transparency could provide a useful model for broader reform of the investor-State arbitration framework". Based on that model, if both the respondent host State and the investor's home State are part of an international investment treaty ("**IIA**") and are also parties of the multilateral convention, the latter would provide the possibility to modify the existent IIA.

Even though the research paper explored the idea of "replacing or supplementing the existing investor-State arbitration regime in international investment agreements"[29] to avoid the renegotiation of ISDS provisions in instruments that are already in force, one of its main objectives was to discuss the possibility of advancing a permanent investment tribunal and/or an appeal mechanism. Hence, the proposed Convention was considered to be "the instrument by which the Parties to international investment agreements express their consent to submit disputes arising under their existing IIAs to the ITI [International Tribunal for Investments]/AM [Appeal Mechanism]."[30]

Chile considers that there are several procedural amendments that would increase the legitimacy of the ISDS system in the short term,[31] while not requiring a complete

[28] Kaufman-Kohler and Potesta (2016).

[29] Ibid. p. 4.

[30] Ibid. p. 4.

[31] *See* A/CN.9/WG.III/WP.182 (2019), Possible reform of investor-State dispute settlement (ISDS) Submission from the Governments of Chile, Israel, Japan, Mexico and Peru, where examples of provisions that have already been incorporated in international agreements are presented as possible

institutional reform of the current investment regime, including the creation of a permanent tribunal. Among UNCITRAL member States, there is no consensus on this proposal[32] and there are serious concerns about its compatibility with the current system, the additional costs of having a permanent body, and the consequences it may have on the autonomy of the disputing parties.

Another alternative suggested for the implementation of the MIRA is based on Colombia's proposal to "replicate the OECD model followed during the negotiation of the Multilateral Convention to Implement Tax Treaty Related Measures to Prevent Base Erosion and Profit Shifting – MLI",[33] which could "lead to a rapid and plausible multilateral outcome to implement the solutions envisaged by Working Group III given the high degree of flexibility provided".[34] This is recognized in the MLI by allowing "ample scope and flexibility for countries to decide, progressively, according to their own interests".[35] This model requires two parties to an IIA to identify the alternatives in the proposed multilateral treaty that would most satisfy their interest of reform. The multilateral treaty would contain different minimum standards serving as options to the treaty parties. When a provision in the original bilateral treaty does not reflect the minimum standard, the parties to that treaty have the flexibility to opt out of that provision and replace it by the MLI provisions.

In the current stage of the reform process a detailed work plan defining the allocated time for working group sessions and intersessional work has been presented to delegations by the Secretariat. Member States have presented their opinions about its feasibility and the necessity to prioritize certain reforms over others.

In that sense, Chile has produced two sets of comments to the work plan, highlighting the need to begin the discussions on the MIRA as early as possible since Chile's position is that the form and architecture of the multilateral instrument will certainly provide the basis of its content. As Chile presented in its first set of comments "it should be clear that we may fail to jointly 'deliver' if we don't identify and address questions relating to the Treaty's structure, legal implications, and interpretations, at an early stage [. . .][given that] it is extremely complex to start laying bricks in a house without first having developed the architecture: the risk of doing so is considerable, as the construction could collapse because it does not have a solid foundation."[36] In that sense, "being able to agree on a common set of

---

solutions to the identified concerns pertaining to arbitrators and decision makers, costs and duration, and lack of consistency, coherence predictability and correctness of arbitral decisions by ISDS tribunals.

[32] *See* Investment Arbitration Reporter (2021).

[33] A/CN.9/WG.III/WP.173 (2019), Possible reform of investor-State dispute settlement (ISDS), Submission from the Government of Colombia, para. 4.

[34] Ibid para. 32.

[35] Ibid para. 16.

[36] Comments to the Work Plan submitted by Chile in January 2021.

procedural rules at a multilateral level, may, at the end, have the most chances of providing predictability and certainty to the system and thus reform ISDS."

During the last meeting of the Working Group (4–5 May 2021), delegations commented on the second version of the Work Plan presented by the Secretariat and the Chair of the Working Group. The proposal envisaged finalizing negotiations for ISDS reform in 2025, with four working group sessions between 2022 and 2024 (representing an increase of two sessions per year compared to the current pattern). The identified reform solutions that were proposed to be analyzed simultaneously encompassed the following topics:

1. Alternative Dispute Resolution Mechanisms and Dispute Prevention,
2. Selection and Appointment of Arbitrators,
3. Code of Conduct for Arbitrators and Adjudicators,
4. Reform of ISDS Procedural Rules (including frivolous claims, multiple proceedings, reflective loss, counterclaims, security for costs, third party funding and treaty interpretation),
5. Discussions of the institution of a Multilateral Advisory Centre,
6. Appellate Mechanism,
7. Multilateral Permanent Investment Court, and
8. Multilateral Instrument to Implement Reforms.

Some member States presented their concerns regarding the feasibility of the work plan. Given that many delegations, specifically those from developing countries, lack resources to attend the required four formal meetings and informal discussions, the proposed plan represents a major challenge. Therefore, some delegations considered the plan to be overambitious and unrealistic, with the consensus leaning towards one additional working group session per year from 2022 to 2025 instead of two. This reduction of annual sessions translated into a one-year extension in the reform process, thus projecting the end of the work plan to 2026. Additionally, some delegations requested the inclusion of certain topics in the work plan, such as damages in ISDS (its calculation methods and the relevance of establishing limitations)[37] and the exhaustion of local remedies, which were added by the Secretariat in a revised work plan.

The final version of the work plan implementing the comments of different delegations will be presented to member States before the next session of the Working Group, which will take place in November 2021.

[37] In this sense, during the fortieth session, Chile mentioned that it could be relevant to link the calculation of damages as a possible ground for appeal, for instance when an award in damages exceeds a specific percentage of each country's Gross Domestic Product.

3.2 *ICSID Rules and Regulations Amendment Process*

3.2.1 Context

The International Centre for Settlement of Investment Disputes is in the process of amending its rules and regulations. The ICSID Convention, a multilateral treaty that Chile entered into in 1992, that creates the International Centre for Settlement of Investment Disputes, is not subject to revision. Since its adoption, there have been four rounds of amendments to the rules. The last process of this nature culminated in 2006, with the adoption of the currently-applicable arbitration and conciliation rules. Taking into account that in the last fifteen years, the practice of investment arbitration before ICSID has evolved considerably with the emergence of new trends (such as Third-Party Funding), a revision of its rules became necessary. An extensive review has provided insights of such developments revealing the need to incorporate new concepts and tools into the current amendment process. The objective of the process is to modernize the ICSID Rules based on the experience obtained through casework, taking into consideration the need to reduce the costs and duration of the proceedings. Additionally, the adoption of mediation rules and a new chapter on expedited arbitration are being proposed.

The ICSID Secretariat has prepared four working documents for the process of amending its rules and regulations, incorporating the observations and comments of the various member states, organizations, and practitioners in a transparent and inclusive manner.

In addition, the ICSID and UNCITRAL Secretariats are collaborating in the preparation of a Code of Conduct for Adjudicators in Investor-State Dispute Settlement proceedings. Chile presented its last comments during a join session held by both Secretariats on the 7th and 10th of June 2021.

3.2.2 Comments by the Republic of Chile on the ICSID Working Papers

Chile has individually presented three different sets of comments in the context of the amendments to the ICSID Rules and Regulations that commenced in 2016, and it has been actively involved in the process.[38] Comments to Working Paper 1 and 2[39] were presented in June 2019, comments to Working Paper 3[40] in December 2019 and comments to Working Paper 4[41] in July 2020.

Additionally, in June 2019, Chile submitted joint comments with Colombia, Costa Rica, Mexico, and Peru, highlighting its objectives in the amendment process, such as achieving a more balanced approach between the rights and obligations of States and investors, and reducing the costs and duration of arbitration proceedings

[38] Investment Arbitration Reporter (2020).

[39] Rule Amendment Project (2019).

[40] Comments on Working Paper # 3 (2019).

[41] Compendium of Comments for Working Paper # 4 (2020).

to move towards a more efficient ISDS system, with due consideration of maintaining legal certainty and procedural fairness between disputing parties.

Specific comments regarding the timing of preliminary objections or the option of submitting memorials before the first tribunal session were among the concerns that were emphasized in the joint document. Other concerns expressed related to the possibility of considering the request for arbitration as claimant's memorial on the merits. The joint submission discussed additional considerations relating to the notice of third-party funding, bifurcation, transparency in relation to publications of awards and decisions on annulment, submissions and participation of non-disputing treaty parties, security for costs, content of the award (to emphasize the need to adequately sustain tribunal's decisions), as well as expedited arbitration.

In February 2020, Chile submitted a joint proposal in relation to Rule 2 (related to the content of a request of arbitration), together with Australia, Canada, Colombia, Costa Rica, Korea, Mexico, Peru, and Singapore. Additionally, a joint proposal from the same States and Israel was submitted in relation to Rules 14 (Notice of Third-Party Funding), 28 (waiver of rights to object non-compliance), 41 (Manifest Lack of Legal Merit, as an objection to claims), 51 (Decision on costs, referring to circumstances that the tribunal shall consider when allocating costs of the proceeding), and 52 (Security for costs, especially with respect to the evidence of Third-Party Funding as an element to consider for requesting such guarantee).

3.2.3 Comments by the Republic of Chile on the Code of Conduct

A draft Code of Conduct for Adjudicators in investor-State dispute settlement was first presented at the 35th session of UNCITRAL Working Group III.[42] After receiving comments from Member States, both ICSID and UNCITRAL's Secretariats were requested to prepare a draft Code at the 38th session of the Working Group in October 2019. The UNCITRAL Secretariat presented a note which served as background for the preparation of an initial draft.[43] In May 2020, this proposal crystalized in the first draft of the Code, which addressed fundamental ethical concerns identified by the delegations, in particular "the lack or apparent lack of independence and impartiality of ISDS tribunal members."[44] In this context, it became highly relevant to incorporate rules that would allow the homogenization of the standards to challenge arbitrators and adjudicators. Therefore, one of the objectives of the Code would be to establish a general benchmark for assessing the independence and impartiality of arbitrators to avoid conflicts of interest.

The draft Code presents several innovations to address longstanding ethical issues identified by stakeholders as a basis for ISDS critique, such as double hatting,

[42] A/CN.9/935 (2018), Report of Working Group III (Investor-State Dispute Settlement Reform) on the work of its thirty-fifth session, para 64.

[43] A/CN.9/WG.III/WP.167 (2019), Background information on a code of conduct.

[44] A/CN.9/935 (2018), Report of Working Group III (Investor-State Dispute Settlement Reform) on the work of its thirty-fifth session op cit. para. 51.

multiple appointments, and issue conflict. It attempts to strike an appropriate balance to achieve relevant objectives that could inform the rules, ensuring that any decision remains fact driven. Its main purposes relate to the need to put parties on a level playing field by closing the information gap, so everyone has access to the same facts.

Several activities have been organized by both Secretariats to present the Code of Conduct to member States[45] and delegations have had the opportunity to submit their comments to the draft articles.[46] Given that one of the main concerns presented in the Working Group referred to the lack or apparent lack of independence and impartiality of adjudicators, the Code of Conduct enjoys a high degree of acceptance among UNCITRAL member States and there was consensus in prioritizing its discussions in the work plan.

The draft Code is a remarkable achievement that allows a tangible basis for discussion, since it puts together what is moral and adequate in a particular setting, reflecting questions from different cultures with regard to relevant issues such as confidentiality, to reach further consensus. The broad concept of adjudicators presented by the drafters ensures the applicability of the provisions to a wide range of decision-makers, from arbitrators to prospective judges in permanent tribunals or appeal mechanisms, and it also extends its duties (such as independence and impartiality) to arbitrators' assistants. Chile has contributed to expanding the scope of application by adding language that avoids limitations regarding the arbitrator's method of appointment.

With regards to the availability that adjudicators require to ensure complete participation in the cases and render their decisions in a timely manner, Chile has suggested including further obligations under the duty of diligence, such as "performing a comprehensive and thorough review of the full record of the case and evidence adduced by the Parties; and to participate constructively in hearings and deliberations."[47] In the same vein, Chile has proposed to limit adjudicators' ability to accept subsequent obligations that would prevent them from complying with their duties in pending ISDS proceedings.

Additionally, Chile has promoted a broader concept of the obligation to disclose information by recommending a permanent duty to disclose all publications on an ongoing basis for the duration of the proceedings, seeking a balanced approach that does not prevent academic discussions from flourishing. At the same time, the country has proposed stricter rules limiting multiple roles, including a ban on multiple roles in ISDS proceedings throughout their entire duration, as well as for proceedings arising out of the same treaty or any other international agreement.

---

[45] Webinars of 18 November 2020 – The draft code of conduct for adjudicators in ISDS; 3–4 March 2021 – The draft Code of Conduct, as well as follow-up sessions in French and Spanish on 8th March 2021; and additional webinars on 7th and 10th March 2021 on the draft Code of Conduct - Version Two.

[46] Chile presented its comments in November 2020.

[47] See comments of the Republic of Chile to Article 8.

Regarding double hatting, Chile believes that its limitation should be extended not only to the oncurrent roles of arbitrator and counsel, but also to the roles held by an arbitrator, counsel, and legal expert when procedures take place simultaneously, even if they are submitted under different international agreements.

Accordingly, Chile is conscious that a potential ban on multiple roles could have a negative impact on gender and regional diversity, as well as on the generational renewal of arbitrators. Therefore, to find a balanced solution, Chile has explored a pragmatic compromise that could allow the transition from one role to another. In that sense, it has considered proposing a waiver benefitting younger lawyers from diverse backgrounds to integrate the pool of arbitrators, thus allowing them to act as counsel and arbitrators for a certain period of time.

Regarding the enforcement of the Code's obligations, member states are still defining an appropriate way to deter conduct contravening its principles. In that respect, Chile has commented that monetary, disciplinary, or reputational sanctions should be considered depending on how the language of those provisions advances in the following iterations.[48] Challenges to arbitrators are still one of the natural options to avoid conflicts of interest,[49] notwithstanding the fact that other avenues linked to reputational sanctions should be explored, such as the issuance by independent bodies of publications presenting compiled information about individuals that have been involved in such conflicts.

4 Chile's Experience in ISDS Proceedings

Only six ISDS claims have been submitted against Chile in its history (the most recent was registered by ICSID on May 17th, 2021[50]). Five of the cases were filed under the auspices of the ICSID system and one before the Permanent Court of

[48] See comments of the Republic of Chile to Article 12.

[49] On the importance of challenges, see for instance, the decision on annulment on the Eiser case of June 11th, 2020 (*Eiser Infrastructure Limited and Energía Solar Luxembourg S.à r.l. v. Kingdom of Spain*, ICSID Case No. ARB/13/36), where the Committee annulled the Award "in its entirety for improper constitution of the Tribunal and for 'serious' departure from a fundamental rule of procedure. The Applicant was compelled to go through these annulment proceedings because it was deprived of the opportunity to challenge Dr. Alexandrov, and consequently, deprived of the benefit and protection of an independent and impartial tribunal" (para. 270). It is worth mentioning that "Dr. Alexandrov's non-disclosure resulted in the Parties' pleading, and the Tribunal deliberating, without any knowledge of Dr. Alexandrov's and/or Sidley Austin's relationship with Mr. Lapuerta and/or the Brattle Group" (para. 245) [both were Claimants' experts in the Eiser case, have worked previously with Dr. Alexandrov in at least nine cases, and were at the same time working with Dr. Alexandrov in another case in which he was claimant's counsel]. Therefore, the Committee concluded that "to an independent third party observer, based on an objective assessment of all the facts, it would be manifestly apparent that Dr. Alexandrov lacked impartiality" (para. 240).

[50] *Interconexión Eléctrica S.A. E.S.P. v. Republic of Chile* (ICSID Case No. ARB/21/27).

Arbitration under UNCITRAL Rules. These numbers place Chile as the least litigious country in the Pacific Alliance and one of the States with the fewest claims in Latin America.

However, Chile holds the unfortunate record of having the longest case in ICSID history,[51] which after 22 years of proceedings terminated in a favorable result for the State in 2020.

The following subsections will present an overview of Chile's ISDS cases.

4.1 Victor Pey Casado and President Allende Foundation v. Republic of Chile *(ICSID Case No. ARB/98/2)*

In 1997, Mr. Víctor Pey Casado, a Chilean-Spanish national, and *Fundación Presidente Allende* filed a claim before ICSID alleging the Republic of Chile's violation of the Agreement for the Promotion and Protection of Investments signed between Chile and Spain (Chile-Spain BIT). The dispute arose from the issuance of Decree N° 165 of 1975, which dissolved the companies "*Consorcio Publicitario y Periodístico S.A.*" ("CPP") and "*Empresa Periodística Clarín Ltda*", both responsible for the edition of *El Clarín* (a newspaper associated with the political views of President Salvador Allende's government). Additionally, Decree N° 165 materialized the confiscation of the companies' assets more than 20 years before the entry into force of the Chile-Spain BIT.

Claimants argued that such actions amounted to an unlawful expropriation under Article 5 of the BIT and presented claims arguing discrimination (Art. 3) and violation of fair and equitable treatment (Art. 4). For these breaches, they initially sought US$515 million in compensation, which they later increased to US$797 million.

In its defense, Chile argued, *inter alia*, that the Tribunal lacked jurisdiction *ratione materiae* (claimants had no investment that qualified as such under the ICSID Convention and the BIT since Mr. Pey never owned CPP shares), jurisdiction *ratione personae* (Mr. Pey did not meet the requirement of not being a national of the same State against which he had brought the claim, as the ICSID Convention and the BIT require), and jurisdiction *ratione temporis* (the dispute arose before the treaty's entry into force). On the merits of the case, Chile also argued that the State could not be held liable for breaching the provisions of the BIT invoked by claimants, given that the obligations allegedly breached were not in force at the time that the alleged international wrongful act was committed, *i.e.* in 1975. Since the expropriation was an instantaneous act that occurred prior to the entry into force of the BIT, it was not within the scope of the treaty's substantive obligations. Regarding those acts that took place after the entry into force of the treaty (which claimants claimed as

[51] *Victor Pey Casado and President Allende Foundation v. Republic of Chile*, ICSID Case No. ARB/98/2.

constituting new violations), Chile argued that they were merely consequences of an expropriation that has already concluded but were not wrongful acts in and of themselves.

In 2008, after more than ten years of proceedings, the arbitral tribunal issued a first award dismissing the central claim of expropriation because it considered that the confiscation was not a continuing wrongful act (*fait illicite continu*) nor a composite violation and therefore had occurred as a *fait accompli* before the BIT entered into force. However, it found that the State had failed to comply with its obligation to accord claimants fair and equitable treatment, including the obligation to refrain from any denial of justice. The tribunal's reasoning was based on a decision by the Ministry of National Assets to compensate third parties for the confiscation of *El Clarín* in 2000[52] (that excluded Mr. Pey, because he deliberately decided not to seek compensation under Law 19.568).[53] Additionally, the tribunal elaborated its denial of justice conclusion based on the absence of a decision by Chilean Tribunals on the claim regarding the restitution of a printing press initiated by Mr. Pey in 1995. The Tribunal ordered the State to compensate claimants for US$ 10,132,690, including costs and expenses incurred by Mr. Pey and *Fundación Presidente Allende*, and a percentage of the procedural costs.

In 2009, the State filed a request for annulment of the 2008 award, which was partially accepted by an ad-hoc committee in a 2012 decision. This ruling annulled the compensation section of the award, after considering that the first tribunal did not adequately substantiate its decision on the amount of compensation awarded to claimants[54] and maintained the validity of the remaining sections.

[52] Decision 43 of 28th April 2000, of the Ministry of National Assets.

[53] Law 19.568 of 23rd July 1998, which provided restitution or indemnification for property confiscated and acquired by the state through certain legal or administrative acts.

[54] As "parties never pleaded the damages claims arising from the breaches of Article 4 of the BIT [...] Chile was deprived of the right to present its arguments on the standard applicable to the calculation of damages [which] was a critical component of the Award and [...] materially prejudiced Chile" (see First Annulment Decision at paras. 262 and 269). Additionally, the First Annulment Committee noted that "the Tribunal went beyond the standard it established, *i.e.*, placing the Claimants in the position they would have been but for the breaches of the BIT, because in fact it left them far better off 'by granting them over US$ 10 million rather than the US$ 2 million they were asking for in Chile'." (See First Annulment Decision at para. 269). This conclusion resulted from a contradictory reasoning from the first award, as the Committee emphasized: "In paragraph 688 of the Award, the Tribunal expressly stated that an evaluation of the damages allegedly suffered by the Claimants as a result of the expropriation was irrelevant and that all the allegations, discussion and evidence related to such damages could not be considered by the Tribunal [...] because the expropriation in 1975 had occurred prior to the entry into force of the BIT and was thus outside the temporal scope of the BIT [...] however, the Tribunal then proceeded to determine the calculation of the Claimants' damages on the basis of the evaluation made by the Chilean Ministry of National Assets in accordance with Decision No. 43 for the purpose of compensating the persons it considered to be the owners of El Clarín for the expropriation of the newspaper." (See First Annulment Decision at paras. 283–284).

In 2013, claimants (including Ms. Pey Grebe, Mr. Pey's daughter) presented a resubmission request under Article 52(6) of the ICSID Convention,[55] in an attempt to revisit the sections of the award that were annulled in 2012. This process concluded in Chile's favor with the issuance of a second award in 2016, where a new arbitral tribunal determined that Chile owed nothing to claimants as they failed to prove damages resulting from the breach of the fair and equitable treatment standard. In 2017, the claimants filed a request for annulment of the 2016 award, which was dismissed by a second ad-hoc Committee in 2020, imposing on claimants the obligation to reimburse the State the costs of the arbitration which amounted to US$ 182,202.79.

4.2 MTD Equity Sdn. Bhd. and MTD Chile S.A. v. Republic of Chile *(ICSID Case No. ARB/01/7)*

In 2001, two Malaysian companies, *MTD Equity Sdn. Bhd* and *MTD Chile S.A.*, initiated proceedings against the Republic of Chile before ICSID, claiming the alleged violation of the Investment Promotion and Protection Agreement signed between Chile and Malaysia (Chile-Malaysia BIT). The dispute was related to the development of a real estate project and arose from the decision of the former Foreign Investment Committee to approve the transfer of funds from MTD to Chile for the implementation of that project, even though the land procured for the construction was legally designed for forestry and livestock use, thus making the project impracticable.

MTD requested compensation of US$ 28,523,916, claiming the breach by the State of certain obligations contained in the Chile-Malaysia BIT, specifically, the infringement of its obligation not to expropriate without complying with the requirements of the treaty (Article 4 of the BIT) and its obligation to grant fair and equitable treatment to investment according to the Chile-Croatia and Chile-Denmark BITs, to which the Malaysian claimants had access through the Most-Favored-Nation Treatment set out in Article 3 of the Chile-Malaysia BIT.

In May 2004, after three years of proceedings, the Arbitral Tribunal rendered its award ordering Chile to compensate MTD US$ 5,871,332 after considering that the State had violated its obligation to grant fair and equitable treatment when frustrating MTD's legitimate expectations through the authorization of an investment that was not feasible under Chilean urban policy. However, it considered that Claimants should bear 50% of the inflicted damages, because several of their own business decisions increased the risk to which they were exposed. On May 25, 2004, Chile filed a request for annulment that was later dismissed by an ICSID ad-hoc Committee in March 2007.

[55] Article 52(6): If the award is annulled the dispute shall, at the request of either party, be submitted to a new Tribunal constituted in accordance with Section 2 of this Chapter [Chapter IV of the ICSID Convention].

4.3 Sociedad Anónima Eduardo Vieira v. Republic of Chile (ICSID Case No. ARB/04/7)

In 2003, Sociedad Anónima Eduardo Vieira ("**Vieira**") submitted a claim against the Republic of Chile before ICSID for considering that certain actions of the State violated the fair and equitable treatment (Art. 4.1), national treatment (Art. 4.1), most favored nation treatment (Art. 4.2) and expropriation (Art. 5) provisions of the Agreement for the Promotion and Protection of Investments between Chile and Spain (Chile-Spain BIT).

The dispute related to a fishing permit granted in 1989 by Resolution 291 of the Undersecretariat of Fisheries of the Ministry of Economy ("**SUBPESCA**"). This Resolution authorized CONCAR, a company owned by Vieira, to carry out fishing activities only in internal waters located south of the 47th parallel. Following this first decision, CONCAR initiated a series of appeals and requests to expand its fishing permit to external waters. After several appeals, in 1999, Chile's Comptroller General ordered to SUBPESCA to extend the Company's fishing rights. However, such an extension became futile because in the meantime and following the criteria established by Law 19.713 of January 2001, SUBPESCA decided that CONCAR did not qualify for the allocation of fishing quotas in those waters.

After almost four years of arbitration proceedings, the Arbitral Tribunal issued its award on August 21, 2007 deciding, by a majority, that it did not have jurisdiction over Vieira's claims, since the central facts of the dispute occurred before March 29, 1994, the date on which the Chile-Spain BIT entered into force. Vieira filed a request for annulment, which was rejected by a decision of the ICSID ad hoc Committee on December 10, 2010.

4.4 **"President Allende" Foundation, Victor Pey Casado, Coral Pey Grebe v. Republic of Chile** *(PCA Case No. 2017-30)*

In April 2017 and while the second annulment proceeding before ICSID was still pending, Mr. Víctor Pey Casado, Ms. Coral Pey Grebe, and *Fundación Presidente Allende* initiated a second case under the Chile-Spain BIT. This time claimants opted to bring their case to the Permanent Court of Arbitration and substantiate it under the UNCITRAL rules.

The dispute was based on the same factual background that ICSID tribunals and ad-hoc committees had heard since 1998. It related to the confiscation of *Consorcio Publicitario y Periodístico S.A.* and *Empresa Periodística Clarín Limitada,* and the same provisions of the Chile-Spain BIT were invoked. Claimants stated that certain facts and claims were not subject to the original dispute or had not been decided by previous ICSID tribunals.

After more than two years of arbitration proceedings, the Arbitral Tribunal issued an award deciding that it lacked jurisdiction to hear any of Claimant's claims and ordered Claimants to reimburse Chile all costs of the arbitration (EUR 350,000) and 80% of Chile's legal representation costs (US$ 1,536,631.94 and CLP 29,273,572.8).[56]

4.5 Carlos Rios and Francisco Javier Rios v. Republic of Chile *(ICSID Case No. ARB/17/16)*

In 2017, Colombian nationals Francisco and Carlos Ríos Velilla, controlling shareholders of bus companies Alsacia and Express (public transportation operators in Santiago), initiated ICSID proceedings against Chile, claiming that certain actions and omissions by the State regarding the implementation of the concession contracts in the framework of the *Transantiago* reform of 2011 violated Articles 9. 2 (National Treatment), 9.4 (Minimum Standard of Fair and Equitable Treatment and Full Protection and Security) and 9.10 (Expropriation) of the Chile-Colombia Free Trade Agreement ("**FTA**"). On this basis, claimants requested US$ 354 million.

After an arbitration procedure of almost four years, in January 2021, the Arbitral Tribunal issued an award dismissing Claimants' claims in their entirety. The Tribunal concluded that it lacked jurisdiction to hear several claims, as Claimants had not complied with the statute of limitations clause of the FTA (Art. 9.18.1, which limits the possibility to submit a claim to arbitration after 39 months from the date claimants had knowledge or should have had knowledge of the alleged violations and the damages). With respect to the claims that fell within the Tribunal's jurisdiction, it found that Chile had not been responsible for the Companies' economic losses, concluding that Chile's conduct did not violate its obligations under the FTA. Consequently, the Tribunal ordered Claimants to bear their legal costs plus 100% of the costs of the proceedings (US$ 680,000) and 40% of the costs incurred by the State in its defense, ordering to reimburse the Republic of Chile more than US$ 2.6 million.

4.6 Interconexión Eléctrica S.A. E.S.P. v. Republic of Chile *(ICSID Case No. ARB/21/27)*

On April 7th, 2020, *Interconexión Eléctrica S.A. E.S.P* ("ISA"), *Interchile S.A.* and *ISA Inversiones Chile Limitada* notified Chile their intention to submit a dispute to arbitration and invited the State to start amicable consultations according to Article 9.15 of the Chile-Colombia FTA. From June 2020 to January 2021, amicable consultations were held between Chile and the companies. ISA is a 60% State-

[56] Award of 28th of November 2019, para. 347.

owned enterprise that operates among others, the electric transmission industry in Chile.

On April 2021, ISA on its behalf and on behalf of *Interchile S.A.* and *ISA Inversiones Ltda.* presented a request for arbitration against Chile before ICSID under the Chile-Colombia FTA. The request for the institution of arbitration proceedings was registered on May 17th, 2021. The dispute relates to the construction of an electric transmission line called "*Nueva Línea Cardones-Polpaico*" (the "Project"), which consists of three sections and entered into operation in May 2019. The Company presented delays of 135 and 499 days for the completion of sections 2 and 3 of the Project, respectively. After the conclusion of two administrative proceedings, in which Claimants had the opportunity to present evidence and arguments, the Ministry of Energy determined, based on the applicable regulations, that there was no exoneration of liability (such as *force majeure* or unforeseeable circumstances, among others) that would justify the total delays. Consequently, and under Chilean legislation, Interchile was subject to penalties for such delays which materialized in the collection of guaranteed bonds and the application of fines between March 2019 and February 2020.

5 Institutionalization of Chile's Defense

5.1 Current Practice

5.1.1 Institutionalization Under Supreme Decree 125 of 2016

Since 2017, the defense and representation of the State in negotiations, amicable consultations, and international arbitration has been developed within the institutional framework established under Supreme Decree 125 of the Ministry of Foreign Affairs, enacted in December 2016 ("**Decree 125**"). This legal instrument created the Interministerial Committee for the Defense of the State in International Investment Disputes (the "**Committee**"), a multisectoral entity that seeks to respond in a coordinated and effective manner to investment claims.

The Committee is permanently integrated with the Minister of Foreign Affairs and the Minister of Finance. Additionally, for the Committee is integrated with the relevant Ministry or agency of the specific sector involved in the respective dispute. To date, the Committee has met twenty-five times, which is a clear sign of the active role that it plays in the disputes and potential disputes' decision-making process.

In general terms, Decree 125 confers on the Vice-Ministry of International Economic Affairs the mandate to coordinate international investment dispute proceedings arising out of IIAs.

In fulfilling its mandate, the Committee proposes actions, guidelines and other specific measures for the coordination, defense, and representation of the State and is therefore responsible for, *inter alia,* (a) determining the suitability of carrying out negotiations with natural or legal persons that submit notices of intent to initiate arbitration or amicable consultations under international investment agreements, (b) establishing the courses of action and mechanisms for conducting the consultation processes, (c) approving the defense strategies of the State during the development of the arbitration processes, (d) approving the appointment of arbitrators, (e) selecting external counsel representation as well as experts and witnesses for each case, and (f) defining communication strategies taking into consideration the public interest of each dispute.

In operational terms, Decree 125 designated the former General Directorate of International Economic Affairs (legal predecessor of the current Vice-Ministry of International Economic Affairs) as the Technical Secretariat of the Committee. In practice, the Technical Secretariat's responsibilities fall under the Program for the Defense of the State in Investment Arbitration, based on the Vice-Ministry of International Economic Affairs. The main tasks of the Technical Secretariat refer to the handling of friendly consultations and arbitrations initiated against Chile and include, among others:

- To coordinate the operation of the Committee in each dispute, which involves (i) summoning all entities involved in each case; (ii) proposing coordination procedures for each dispute; and (iii) defining the negotiation agenda, including objectives and deadlines;
- To collect, centralize and analyze background information relevant for the dispute, keeping the Interministerial Committee constantly informed;
- To identify the elements of each dispute that may be part of a negotiated solution during amicable consultation proceedings or negotiations;
- To coordinate amicable consultations and negotiations that stem from international dispute settlement mechanisms;
- To propose precise actions and guidelines for the representation and defense of the State in each phase of the arbitration proceedings. Among others, the Technical Secretariat has overseen and supervised the State's external legal advisors, ensuring the adequate implementation of the defense strategy defined by the Committee. In general terms, the Technical Secretariat actively participates in the preparation of written submissions before international investment tribunals, as well as in the preparation of witnesses and experts for hearings, among other necessary measures to carry out the adequate representation of the State.

5.1.2 Ministry of Foreign Affairs' "Modernization Law"

In 2018, Law 21.080 was enacted to modernize the legal framework of the Ministry of Foreign Affairs. Among other innovations, it stipulates that the Minister of Foreign Affairs shall be empowered to establish, by presidential decree, a specialized advisory unit to safeguard Chile's interests in international proceedings.[57]

[57] At the time of writing, a unit of this nature has not yet been created. In 2018, the President of the Republic summoned a group of experts to define the general characteristics that such a unit shall

As of June 2021, such a unit has not yet been established. However, the defense duties and capacities related to investment disputes established in the "modernization law" have mandated the Vice-Ministry of International Economic Affairs with different functions, such as overseeing the compliance, application, and execution of international economic agreements.[58] Additionally, that law confers the Vice-Ministry of International Economic Affairs the role of coordinating the rights and interests of Chile in disputes involving the State in international economic affairs,[59] as well as the responsibility for the prevention of disputes that may arise within the framework of those agreements.[60]

Accordingly, under Law 21.080 and Supreme Decree 125 the Program for the Defense of the State in International Investment Arbitration (the "Program") has carried out the mandate of the Vice-Ministry of International Economic Affairs with regards to the defense of the State in ISDS. This legal framework has enabled the State to respond efficiently and effectively to claims arising out of the ISDS mechanisms incorporated in Chile's international treaties.

In fulfilling its mandate, the Program has developed specific procedures to respond to amicable consultation requests under international investment treaties. The current practice has helped to institutionalize such proceedings, establishing clear steps to follow when a dispute arises. Accordingly, in an interpretation of Chile's General Comptroller Authority requested by the Program for the Defense of the State in International Arbitration,[61] it was confirmed that the Minister of Foreign Affairs has the power to sign transactional agreements on behalf of the State within amicable consultations processes. This is an important step towards the institutionalization of a robust dispute prevention mechanism, since providing such powers to the Ministry of Foreign Affairs will allow it to efficiently settle potential disputes.

5.2 *State Practice in Dispute Management/Prevention: The State's Response to Amicable Consultations' Requests*

Once a notice of dispute requesting the initiation of consultations under an international investment agreement is received by the Program for the Defense of the State in International Investment Arbitration, it proceeds to inform the Ministry of Finance (in its role of a permanent member of the Interministerial Committee) of the

have. In their report, there was general acceptance about the convenience of concentrating in one sole entity the defense of the diverse interests of Chile in the international arena, specifically those litigious disputes involving: territorial claims, investment arbitration under investment agreements, and international human rights disputes.

[58] Law 21.080, Art. 28 N° 7.

[59] Law 21.080 Art. 28 N° 8.

[60] Law 21.080 Art. 28 N° 7.

[61] *See* Chile's General Comptroller Authority's opinion E106514N21 of 19th May 2021.

existence of such a notice. Simultaneously, the Program conducts a preliminary analysis assessing the potential risk of the alleged breaches contained in the respective notice. Within a timeframe that usually does not exceed one week, the Vice-Minister of International Economic Affairs acknowledges receipt of the request for consultations and invites applicants to address all future communications to the Defense Program. In that communication, claimants are usually summoned to a preliminary meeting with the Program. The purposes of this first preliminary meeting are:

- To allow the Defense Program to explain the characteristics of the process that would be carried out if the State decides to initiate a consultation process under the respective International Investment Agreement, as well as to inform applicants about the role of the Interministerial Committee, and the coordination work that the Defense Program undertakes; and
- To allow applicants to present the merits of their claims, explaining the State measures that they consider to be in breach of Chile's international obligations and how they deem that the challenged measures could give rise to an investment dispute under the invoked Treaty. This information will then be presented to the Interministerial Committee, which will determine whether or not to accept the request to initiate a consultation process

These preliminary informative meetings will be held as many times as it is considered necessary to understand the claims and the applicants' purpose in starting a consultation process (normally between one to two meetings are held for this purpose).

Following the preliminary meeting(s), the Interministerial Committee is summoned to a formal session, where the content of the claims and requests made by the claimant are presented by the Program. Normally, during this meeting, the members of the Committee will decide whether to accept the request to start a consultation process.

If amicable consultations are approved, the Interministerial Committee will establish a technical table, led by the Defense Program and integrated by representatives of the ministries that constitute the Committee for the specific dispute. The technical table will act as a counterpart of applicants during the amicable negotiations.

To safeguard the confidentiality of negotiations, the Interministerial Committee will propose a draft of a Confidentiality Agreement that will also establish the framework of the negotiations in a manner that is conducive to the resolution of the conflict. After the Agreement is concluded, it will serve the double purpose of safeguarding the privacy of communications between the parties while ensuring that, if consultations are unsuccessful, any potential concession made in the process may not be brought into play to support the position of any of the parties in an eventual arbitration. In addition, the Confidentiality Agreement establishes an express reservation of rights in relation to the potential dispute, adding that nothing in the Agreement should be interpreted as a waiver or limitation of the State's rights under Chilean or international law, nor as an implicit or explicit recognition of any right, quality or power of the entity or natural person requesting the consultations.

Upon approval of the course of action by the Interministerial Committee, a first formal consultation meeting shall be convened. Prior to that meeting, applicants shall inform the names and association of the representatives that will participate in the coming sessions, designating a counterpart to exchange communications effectively. Meetings will be held as often as deemed necessary to attempt to find a solution, considering that the Interministerial Committee shall provide the guidelines and directives for any position or course of action to be taken by the technical table on behalf of the State.

5.3 *Dispute Prevention*

It has been widely accepted by the literature that effective dispute prevention mechanisms are a powerful tool to avoid the costs and duration associated with international litigation.[62] In that sense, the Defense Program has committed substantial efforts to prevent disputes by establishing internal protocols and practices aiming to create consciousness and awareness among public officials of the content of the State's obligations in international investment agreements.

5.3.1 Identification of Sectors and Grievances with the Potential to Become Investment Disputes

In order to prevent disputes effectively, it is fundamental to recognize the main sectors where foreign direct investment is concentrated. Once those industries are categorized, a narrowing-down exercise is required to establish a registry identifying specific investors and their investments to closely monitor situations that could become potential disputes in each specific sector.

---

[62] See, for instance, Valderrama (2018), pp. 114–118. In this sense, see also UNCTAD (2010), concluding that "it is unquestionable that a multiplication of investment disputes can only result in a negative impact on a country's economic development. This is because the occurrence of multiple investment disputes in a country will portray a negative image on this country's investment climate, potentially reducing the inflow of FDI that the country is seeking to attract in line with its development objectives. Furthermore, one could assert that, in the long run, the balance between the costs incurred as a result of ISDS cases and the capital inflows received through major investment projects, possibly as a result of the conclusion of IIAs [International Investment Agreements], may not remain positive in many States. Indeed, the high amounts of compensation awarded to investors and the costs involved in the defence of ISDS cases are taking a toll on the budget of States. These funds could be better spent on economic development projects and the improvement of human capital in developing countries. An appropriate preventative action by the host State, preferably with the support of the treaty partner to an IIA, would have very positive implications in this Context", pp. 101–102.

Given the existence of different mechanisms to bring foreign capital into the country, there is no centralized registry of foreign investors. The Defense Program has explored ways to create a common and centralized registry, but, considering the different legal regimes governing investments in the country and the scattered nature of capital flows, such a project will require a high-level mandate to establish a technical group composed of diverse entities to efficiently undertake this task.

The Defense Program has held meetings with the investment promotion agency (InvestChile), the Central Bank, the Sustainable Project Management Office, the National Productivity Commission, the Ministry of Finance, and certain chambers of commerce to gather information on the investment flows that each one of those entities has in their registries. Those meetings have been valuable to understand the dispersion of the information and were helpful to reflect on an adequate framework to move towards the creation of a centralized registry. Unfortunately, the current contingencies and the immediate solutions required to address them have forced the State to postpone the creation of such a repository.

In order to tackle this situation and as a supplementary assessment of the current risks associated with foreign investment projects, the Defense Program contacted all Chilean embassies abroad,[63] as well as all ministries[64] to request prompt information on grievances that could potentially develop into investment disputes. This has been useful to establish focal points in different State's Secretariats and to create a permanent and continuous obligation to address all information related to potential disputes to the Defense Program, which has been a fundamental tool to react in an efficient and timely manner to avoid international litigation.

5.3.2 Capacity Building on the International Obligations of the State Among Government Officials

The Defense Program has worked on the implementation of training for government officials of entities that are in frequent contact with foreign investors so that they:

- are aware that their actions and statements may compromise the international responsibility of the State;
- develop basic responses that they should take into consideration when dealing with foreign investors to avoid compromising the international responsibility of the State;
- maintain direct communication with the Defense Program from the moment that a grievance is presented in order to prevent it from becoming an international

[63] Official Message N° 196 from Vice Ministry of International Economic Affairs to all Embassies, General Consulates, and Official missions before International Organizations, requesting prompt information regarding potential concerns that could lead to investor-State disputes, 2 October 2019.

[64] Communication from the Ministry of Foreign Affairs to all Ministries Of. N° 1112 of 15th October 2020, requesting prompt, continuous and expedited information relating to grievances from foreign investments that could have the potential to develop in an investment dispute.

investment dispute, or to reduce the potential risk that the respective entity's response may have in the State's position if a dispute arises; and
- are conscious of the commitments undertaken by Chile in international agreements, in order to point out possible inconsistencies between those commitments and national legislation.

Additionally, short training sessions on the same issues should be held for relevant committees of the Congress.

To this end, the Defense Program has built its capacity to advise other State entities regarding the compatibility of their practices or internal regulations with the State's international commitments on foreign investment.

Through the prevention of disputes mandate given to the Vice-Ministry of International Economic Affairs by Law 21.080, as well as the coordination function in international dispute settlement provided in Decree 125, the Defense Program has implemented a mechanism to avoid potential claims by building capacity within the public sector.

In this context, the Program has advised the Ministry of Public Works and its entities as well as the Superintendent of Casinos, on the elements that should be taken into consideration when interacting with foreign investors. To this end, the Defense Program presented specific topics of international law, such as the obligations of the State in international investment agreements, the rules of attribution, and the broad concept of the State in international law.

The Defense Program also provided recommendations regarding the content of public statements, the importance of maintaining a record of all communications exchanged with foreign investors, the relevance of keeping the constructive nature of work meetings when dealing with grievances related to foreign investment, as well as certain clarifications related to the substantiation of administrative proceedings. In this sense, the Program highlighted that all decisions need to be based on technical and rational criteria, avoiding arbitrariness.

5.3.3 Pacific Alliance Instance of Cooperation and Discussion on Prevention and Defense in Investor-State Arbitration

In 2019, the entities responsible for the defense of the State in investment arbitration of the Pacific Alliance members[65] agreed to create a platform of discussion and exchange of experiences in managing ISDS disputes.

[65] The Pacific Alliance is a regional integration initiative formed by Chile, Colombia, Mexico, and Peru through a Framework Agreement that entered into force in July 2015. This Agreement aims to provide the necessary legal institutions to serve as a platform for economic and trade integration. The population of its four member states amounts to 230 million inhabitants. Together, the Pacific Alliance exported US$ 627 billion in 2019, and in 2018, it was host to 38% of Latin America's Foreign Direct Investment. *See* Vice-Ministry of International Economic Affairs data, available at: https://www.subrei.gob.cl/organismos-multilaterales/alianza-del-pacifico [last visit: 13th of June 2021].

One of the central ideas behind this project is to share best practices and create an institutional collaboration framework to advance the defensive interests of the region while strengthening the capacities of the internal defense teams of Chile, Colombia, Mexico and Peru.

Additionally, the creation of this permanent forum has allowed member States to jointly discuss the reform options in multilateral forums (such as ICSID and UNCITRAL) seeking to reach joint positions,[66] and consequently, to increase the degree of influence of the region in international negotiations, positioning the Pacific Alliance as a regional integration coalition before global forums.

Finally, this instance seeks to be instrumental for the exchange of experiences to jointly design future strategies for the prevention of investment disputes, as well as to identify and encourage the use of other dispute resolution methods that are less onerous for the investor-State relationship, such as mediation or conciliation.

Up until the time of this writing, the group has met on two occasions.[67] The Program has been working together with the investment arbitration defense agencies from Colombia, Mexico and Peru, exploring different avenues to explain to government officials the extension and relevance of the State's international obligations encompassed in investment agreements.

5.4 *Current Threats and Amicable Consultations*

5.4.1 Request for Amicable Consultation Presented by *Ohio National Financial Services Inc.* in Connection with the Enactment of Law 21.330[68] That Allows Annuity Withdrawals from Insurance Companies

On May 11, 2021, the United States-based insurance company *Ohio National Financial Services Inc.* ("Ohio National") and *ON Global Holdings LLC* notified the Minister of Foreign Affairs of their intention to request amicable consultations

---

[66] *See,* for instance, joint commentaries presented by Chile, Colombia, Costa Rica, Mexico and Peru on the ICSID amendment process; and the comments jointly presented by the Pacific Alliance Members at the 38th session of UNCITRAL Working Group III.

[67] September 2020 and April 2021.

[68] Law 21.330 of 28th April 2021, amends the Constitution to establish and regulate an exceptional mechanism for the withdrawal of pension funds and the advance payment of life annuities under certain conditions.

alleging the violation of the Chile-United States Free Trade Agreement (the "Treaty") and the breach of the General Agreement on Trade in Services. In their notification, they invited the State to initiate friendly consultations under Article 10.14 of the Agreement.

The dispute relates to the enactment of Law 21.330 that amended the Constitution to allow the withdrawal of ten percent of pension funds operated by insurance companies as annuities (*rentas vitalicias*). In this regard, *Ohio National* considers that through the enactment of Law 21.330, the State would have contravened certain provisions of the Agreement applicable to financial services, including the protection against expropriations that do not comply with the requirements of the Treaty (Art. 10.19). In addition, through the application of the most-favored-nation clause, *Ohio National* seeks the application of certain provisions of the investment chapter that are excluded from claims related to financial services, such as the minimum standard of fair and equitable treatment and full protection and security. Petitioners also noted that their long-term investments could be affected by the need for short-term liquidity, in order to meet the requested pension withdrawals.

5.4.2 Notice of Dispute Filed by ADP-Vinci, Primary Shareholders of *Sociedad Concesionaria Nuevo Pudahuel*, in Connection with Revenue Decreases as a Consequence of the COVID-19 Pandemic

On January 18, 2021, the major shareholders of *Sociedad Concesionaria Nuevo Pudahuel S.A.*, *ADP International SA* ("**ADP**"), and *VINCI Airports SAS* ("**Vinci**"), both French companies, notified the President of Chile of the existence of a dispute under the Agreement between the Government of the Republic of Chile and the Government of the Republic of France on the Reciprocal Promotion and Protection of Investments ("**Chile-France BIT**" or "**the Treaty**"). In their notice, ADP-Vinci requested the initiation of the negotiations' timeframe established in the Chile-France BIT ("**Notice of Dispute**"). In their Notice of Dispute, the companies referred to their consent to submit the claim to ICSID arbitration if the dispute is not amicably solved within the six months established in the Treaty.

In March 2021, the Interministerial Committee determined to participate in the consultation process requested by ADP and Vinci, establishing (a) that the consultations would be covered by a confidentiality agreement, and (b) that a technical table would conduct the consultations on behalf of the State. As stated in Sect. 5.2, this table would directly report to the Committee and the relevant authorities. On May 12, 2021, after a confidentiality agreement was established, the first formal meeting of the consultation process was held followed by a subsequent meeting that took place the June 10, 2021.

5.4.3 Potential International Arbitration Derived from the Process of Granting and Renewing Operating Permits for Gambling Casinos

Several economic groups operating in the gambling industry have expressed the possibility of resorting to ICSID arbitration as, in their opinion, the current process to grant and renew permits violates their rights. The casino operators' interpretation considers that by applying the 2005 version of Law 19.995 to the bidding process, instead of the current version of 2015, their right to legal certainty would be endangered. The main points differentiating these sets of rules lie in the application of a preferential adjudication right to casino operators requesting the renewal of a current operating permit. Additionally, the 2015 regulation includes certain modifications to the economic offer as a factor in the evaluation of the bidding process.

The Association of Casino Operators has launched a media campaign indicating that the State would "change the rules of the game" in relation to their concessions and has been categorical in affirming that if the results of their claims before local courts are not satisfactory, its members will initiate proceedings against the State before ICSID.

In February 2021, after learning of the ruling that rejected an appeal against the judgment on a *habeas corpus* filed by one of the Casino operators, the rest of the national operators withdrew subsequent appeals that were presented to stop the current bidding process. Additionally, on May 10, 2021, the respective Court of Appeals resolved to reject the claims of illegality filed by other operators against the bidding process. The court ordered the claimants to pay the costs of the proceedings after considering that the 2015 law was clear regarding the applicable procedure for the renewal of permits.

6 Conclusions and Path Forward

In the past twenty years Chile has witnessed major improvements in its international investment regime. Most importantly, the State has taken decisive steps in safeguarding its regulatory power while providing guarantees to foreign investors, thus advancing towards a necessary balance between both interests.

To achieve such balance, the State has built capacity among its public servants and has worked towards the modernization of its institutionality. The creation of the Program for the Defense of the State in International Investment Arbitration has been a key component to ensure sound coordination in responding to potential investment claims. Having a permanent defense team capable to assess the risks associated to the State's interactions with foreign investments has been a major improvement in Chile's readiness for potential disputes. Further efforts are being deployed to enhance the current legal regime and by the end of 2021 a new set of rules superseding Decree Law 125 is expected to be enacted improving the State's involvement in the prevention and management of investment disputes.

The elaboration of internal guidelines on dispute prevention, and the efforts that the Program for the Defense of the State has undertaken to increase awareness of Chile's international obligations among public officials, have translated into a robust mechanism to respond to potential claims.

Identifying grievances from an early stage has been a critical component of successful prevention, helping to solve potential disputes before they compromise the State's international responsibility. Preventing disputes has significant budgetary impacts, and may save costly and timely litigation against the State if satisfactory agreements are reached before a dispute arises. Such actions may have longstanding benefits for the international reputation of the country.

Furthermore, maintaining internal capacity to appropriately respond to investment claims, while elaborating the State's defense strategy, enhances Chile's capabilities while maintaining an adequate control of the economic and political considerations that are often central aspects of ISDS.

The State's right to regulate to achieve its legitimate public policy objectives is one of the cornerstones of a dynamic society that requires constant accommodations to meet the evolving needs of its population. It is therefore crucial to maintain a sound coordination among state organs to ensure that the necessary reforms are undertaken in a rational, non-arbitrary and non-discriminatory manner.

After Chile's social upheaval, an historic agreement between political parties was reached in November 2019. In October 2020, an overwhelming majority of Chile's population voted in favor of rewriting the Chilean Constitution.[69] In May 2021, the drafters of the Constitution were elected, showing a marked preference for citizens that were not affiliated with any political party.[70] The Constitutional Convention has remarkable characteristics to ensure representativity, such as a gender parity among its members[71] and reserved seats for indigenous people.[72]

The role that international treaties will play to draw the limits of the new text is established in the rules of the convention.[73] These set out that "*the text of the new Constitution submitted to plebiscite must respect the status of Republic of the State of Chile, its democratic regime, the final and enforced judicial judgments, and international treaties ratified by Chile which are in force*".

---

[69] Despite various reforms during the last decades, the 1980 Constitution was originally enacted during the military regime of General Augusto Pinochet that governed under a dictatorship from 1973 to 1990.

[70] *See Servicio Electoral de Chile* available at https://pv.servelelecciones.cl/ *Elecciones de Convencionales Constituyentes*. The results indicate that there will be no political party with the necessary majority to veto the decisions of the Convention [last visit: 12th of June 2021].

[71] *See* Law 21.216 of 24th of March 2020, amends the Constitution aiming to allow a balance in the representation of women and men in the Constitutional Convention.

[72] *See* Law 21.298 of 23rd December 2020, amends the Constitution to reserve seats for representatives of indigenous peoples in the Constitutional Convention and to safeguard and promote the participation of persons with disabilities in the election of Constitutional Convention members.

[73] Art. 135 para. 4 of the Constitution introduced by Law 21.200 of December 24th, 2019.

The Program for the Defense of the State in International Investment Arbitration, or any institution that succeeds it, may be called upon to transmit to the constitutional convention the scope of the State's international obligations *vis-a-vis* foreign investors. Such input may be pivotal to achieve an harmonious legal body that represents the views of the different stakeholders that conform Chile's society, while respecting the State's international commitments. It remains to be seen whether all these stakeholders will be able to agree on a text that satisfies the populations' concerns.

Acknowledgment This chapter has been submitted for publication in June 2021.

Chilean Legislation, Administrative Acts, and Diplomatic Communications

Chile's General Comptroller Authority's opinion E106514N21 of 19th May 2021.

Communication from the Ministry of Foreign Affairs to all Ministries Of. N° 1112 of 15th October 2020.

Decision 43 of 28th April 2000, of the Ministry of National Assets.

Law 19.568 of 23rd July 1998, which provided restitution or indemnification for property confiscated and acquired by the state through certain legal or administrative acts.

Law 19.589 of 14th November 1998, providing for tariff rates reduction and introducing amendment to other tax and economic regulations.

Law 21.080 of 20th March 2018, modifies various legal bodies in order to modernize the Ministry of Foreign Affairs.

Law 21.216 of 24th March 2020 amends the Constitution aiming to allow a balance in the representation of women and men in the Constitutional Convention.

Law 21.298 of 23rd December 2020, amends the Constitution to reserve seats for representatives of indigenous peoples in the Constitutional Convention and to safeguard and promote the participation of persons with disabilities in the election of Constitutional Convention members.

Law 21.330 of 28th April 2021, amends the Constitution to establish and regulate an exceptional mechanism for the withdrawal of pension funds and the advance payment of life annuities under certain conditions.

Letter 004948 of 18th October 1993, from President Patricio Aylwin Azócar to President William J. Clinton. Available at: https://archivospublicos.uahurtado.cl/

Note Verbale N° 6862 from the Ministry of Foreign Affairs to the Embassy of the Kingdom of Morocco in Chile, December 30th, 2015.

Official Message N° 725 of May 30th, 2003, from the General Directorate of International Economic Affairs to all Embassies of Chile, missions, and general consulates.

Official Message N° 196 from Vice Ministry of International Economic Affairs to all Embassies, General Consulates, and Official missions before International

Organizations, requesting prompt information regarding potential concerns that could lead to investor-State disputes, 2 October 2019.
Official Message N° 871 of General Directorate of International Economic Affairs to the Chilean Embassy in South Africa, September 2nd, 2016.
Political Constitution of the Republic of Chile.

International Investment Law Cases

Carlos Rios and Francisco Javier Rios v. Republic of Chile (ICSID Case No. ARB/17/16).
Eiser Infrastructure Limited and Energía Solar Luxembourg S.à r.l. v. Kingdom of Spain (ICSID Case No. ARB/13/36).
Interconexión Eléctrica S.A. E.S.P. v. Republic of Chile (ICSID Case No. ARB/21/27).
MTD Equity Sdn. Bhd. and MTD Chile S.A. v. Republic of Chile (ICSID Case No. ARB/01/7).
President Allende Foundation, Victor Pey Casado, Coral Pey Grebe v. Republic of Chile (PCA Case No. 2017-30).
Sociedad Anónima Eduardo Vieira v. Republic of Chile (ICSID Case No. ARB/04/7).
Victor Pey Casado and President Allende Foundation v. Republic of Chile (ICSID Case No. ARB/98/2).

UNCITRAL Investor-State Dispute Settlement Reform

A/CN.9/917 (2017), Possible future work in the field of dispute settlement: Reforms of investor-State dispute settlement (ISDS), 20th April 2017.
A/CN.9/935 (2018), Report of Working Group III (Investor-State Dispute Settlement Reform) on the work of its thirty-fifth session, 14th May 2018.
A/CN.9/WG.III/WP.142 (2017), Possible reform of investor-State dispute settlement (ISDS), 18th September 2017.
A/CN.9/WG.III/WP.167 (2019), Background information on a code of conduct, 31st of July 2019.
A/CN.9/WG.III/WP.173 (2019), Possible reform of investor-State dispute settlement (ISDS), Submission from the Government of Colombia, 14th June 2019.
A/CN.9/WG.III/WP.182 (2019), Possible reform of investor-State dispute settlement (ISDS) Submission from the Governments of Chile, Israel, Japan, Mexico and Peru.

International Agreements

Agreement of Economic Complementation N° 16 between the Republic of Chile and the Argentinian Republic, which entered into force in 1991.

Agreement of Economic Complementation N° 22 between the Republic of Chile and the Republic of Bolivia, which entered into force in 1993.

Agreement of Economic Complementation N° 38 between the Republic of Chile and the Republic of Peru, which entered into force in 1998.

Free Trade Agreement between the Government of Canada and the Government of the Republic of Chile, which entered into force in 1997.

Commercial Agreements ratified by Chile and year of entry into force: Bolivia (April 1993), Venezuela (July 1993), Mercosur (October 1996), Canada (July 1997), Mexico (July 1999), Central America (February 2002), European Union (February 2003), South Korea (April 2004), European Free Trade Association (December 2004), Unites States of America (January 2004), P4 (Brunei Darussalam, Chile, New Zealand, Singapore) (November 2006), China (October 2006), India (August 2007), Japan (September 2007), Cuba (June 2008), Panama (March 2008), Peru (March 2009), Australia (March 2009), Colombia (May 2009), Ecuador (January 2010), Turkey (March 2011), Malaysia (April 2012), Vietnam (January 2014), Hong Kong (November 2014), Thailand (November 2015), Pacific Alliance (Chile, Colombia, Peru and Mexico) (May 2016), Uruguay (December 2018), Indonesia (August 2019), Argentina (May 2019), and United Kingdom (January 2021).

Bilateral Investment Treaties ratified by Chile and year of entry into force: Spain (March 1994), France (July 1994), Norway (September 1994), Argentina (January 1995), Italy (February 1995), Venezuela (May 1995), China (August 1995), Malaysia (August 1995), Denmark (November 1995), Sweden (December 1995), Ecuador (February 1995), Finland (May 1996), Croatia (June 1996), Czech Republic (October 1996), United Kingdom (April 1997), Romania (July 1997), Philippines (August 1997), Ukraine (August 1997), Paraguay (December 1997), Portugal (February 1998), Uruguay (April 1999), Germany (May 1999), Bolivia (July 1999), BLEU (Belgium-Luxembourg Economic Union) (August 1999), South Korea (September 1999), Australia (November 1999), El Salvador (November 1999), Panama (December 1999), Poland (January 2000), Costa Rica (June 2000), Cuba (September 2000), Austria (October 2000), Nicaragua (January 2001), Peru (August 2001), Guatemala (December 2001), Honduras (January 2002), Dominican Republic (May 2002), Greece (October 2002).

Free Trade Agreements ratified by Chile and year of entry into force: Canada (July 1997), Mexico (July 1999), United States of America (January 2004), South Korea (April 2004), Japan (September 2007), Peru (March 2009), Australia (March 2009), Colombia (May 2009), China (April 2014), Pacific Alliance (May 2016), Argentina (May 2019).

ICSID Convention, which entered into force on October 14th 1966.

ICSID Rules and Regulations Amendment Process

Chile Comments to Code of Conduct, available at: https://www.subrei.gob.cl/docs/default-source/default-document-library/comments-on-draft-code-of-conduct%2D%2D-republic-of-chile.pdf?sfvrsn=bef1ffba_2, November 2020.
Comments on Working Paper # 3 (2019), available at: https://icsid.worldbank.org/sites/default/files/amendments/WP_3_Comment_Compendium.pdf [last visit: 13th of June 2021].
Compendium of Comments for Working Paper # 4 (2020), Updated as of September 17, 2020, available at: https://icsid.worldbank.org/sites/default/files/amendments/public-input/FOR%20WEBSITE%20PUBLIC%20WP%20%23%204%20Comment%20Compilation%20as%20of%2009.17.2020_DD_0.pdf [last visit: 13th of June 2021].
Rule Amendment Project (2019) – Member State & Public Comments on Working Paper # 2 of March 15, 2019, available at: https://icsid.worldbank.org/sites/default/files/amendments/State_Public_Comments_WP2.pdf [last visit: 13th of June, 2021].
Webinars of 18 November 2020 – The draft code of conduct for adjudicators in ISDS; 3–4 March 2021 – The draft Code of Conduct.

References

Others

Foreign Trade Information System, Dictionary of Trade Terms at http://www.sice.oas.org/dictionary/in_e.asp [last visit: 13th of June 2021]
Investment Arbitration Reporter (2020) ICSID releases fourth (and potentially last) working paper, with changes regarding disclosure of ownership and control, costs allocation, and transparency, March 20th 2020, available at: https://www.iareporter.com/articles/icsid-releases-fourth-and-potentially-last-working-paper-with-changes-regarding-disclosure-of-ownership-and-control-costs-allocation-and-transparency/ [last visit: 13th of June, 2021]
Investment Arbitration Reporter (2021) UNCITRAL working papers on appeal mechanism and selection and appointment of ISDS adjudicators reveal rift between parties as to desirability of standing investor-state dispute settlement body, January 14th 2021. Available at https://www.iareporter.com/articles/uncitral-working-papers-on-appeal-mechanism-and-selection-and-appointment-of-isds-adjudicators-reveal-rift-between-parties-as-to-desirability-of-standing-investor-state-dispute-settlement-body/ [last visit 13th of June, 2021]
Investor–State Disputes: Prevention and Alternatives to Arbitration. UNCTAD Series on International Investment Policies for Development, 2010. Available at: https://unctad.org/system/files/official-document/diaeia200911_en.pdf
Kaufman-Kohler G, Potesta M (2016) Can the Mauritius Convention serve as a model for the reform of investor-State arbitration in connection with the introduction of a permanent investment tribunal or an appeal mechanism? Analysis and roadmap, June, 2016

OECD (2020) Overview: enabling civil society through effective development co-operation. In: Development Assistance Committee Members and Civil Society. OECD Publishing, Paris. https://doi.org/10.1787/f2aef4ad-en

Servicio Electoral de Chile available at https://pv.servelelecciones.cl/ *Elecciones de Convencionales Constituyentes*

Subsecretaría de Relaciones Económicas Internacionales (2019) Impacto de los Tratados de Libre Comercio - Hacia una Política Comercial Inclusiva

Valderrama C (2018) Perú – Buenas Prácticas de Cómo Enfrentar Demandas Internacionales Iniciadas por Inversionistas Privados. ICSID Rev 33(1):103–124

Pablo Nilo Donoso is a lawyer from the Universidad de Chile with a Master of Laws in International Law (LL.M) from the University of Heidelberg. At the time of this writing (June 2021) he served as legal adviser at the Investment Arbitration Unit of the Vice-Ministry of International Economic Affairs of Chile. In this capacity, he worked coordinating Chile's defense strategy in investor-State dispute settlement proceedings. Previously, from 2015 to 2018, he was an investment and services negotiator at the Division of Investment, Services and Air Transport of the Vice-Ministry of International Economic Affairs, where he was responsible for negotiating investment agreements and investment chapters in free trade agreements. He has also been appointed as a representative of Chile to several multilateral and regional forums, such as WTO, APEC, UNASUR and UNCITRAL. He was a senior graduate teaching assistant of Public International Law at the Universidad Diego Portales in Santiago. He is the author of "Responsibility in the Antarctic Treaty System", which was awarded by the Chilean International Law Society as the best thesis in International Law submitted between 2010 and 2012 within Chilean universities.

International Investment Law and Its Scope in Argentina

Christian G. Sommer

1 The Legal Regulation of Foreign Investments in Argentina

Foreign investment has played an inportant role in Argentina's economic development process practically since the biginning of the modern state. A decisive factor in the promotion of Foreign Direct Investments (FDI) since the 1990s has been the adaptation of local regulatory systems to accommodate these new forms of international investment. This motivated, among other actions, the modification of public order norms for the incorporation of foreign subjects in the participation (among other matters) in the administration of public services or the elimination of legal restrictions that prevented the submission of States to foreign or international jurisdictions.

At different times, the intervention of foreign capital in the country has been, in part, a dynamic element of growth since it allowed the incorporation of technologies of the time that made possible a better development of the country's economy. Its foundation can be found in the ideology of promoting the settlement of foreigners in our country, which is constitutionally embodied in both the Preamble and Article 20 of the National Constitution of the State.[1]

Before the First World War, infrastructure and public services were the main recipients of foreign investments, in areas such as railroads, meatpacking plants,

[1] Article 20.- *Foreigners enjoy in the territory of the Nation all the civil rights of citizens; they may exercise their industry, commerce, and profession; own real estate, buy and dispose of it; navigate the rivers and coasts; freely exercise their worship; testament and marry according to the laws. They are not obliged to admit citizenship, nor to pay extraordinary forced contributions. They obtain nationalization by residing two continuous years in the Nation; but the authority can shorten this term in favor of the one who requests it, alleging and proving services to the Republic.*

C. G. Sommer (✉)
National University of Córdoba and Catholic University of Córdoba, Córdoba, Argentina

N. Monebhurrun et al. (eds.), *International Investment Law and Arbitration from a Latin American Perspective*, International Law and the Global South,
https://doi.org/10.1007/978-3-031-49382-9_4

trade and finance, although it is clear that the effect that many of these investments had on the country due to the lack of regulation and control by the national State[2] cannot be overlooked.

Foreign investment has played an important role in Argentina's economic development process practically since the beginning of the modern state. Since the end of the nineteenth century, foreign capital has played a key role in the development of the transportation infrastructure and services essential for the consolidation and growth of the agro-export model. Later, during the period of import substitution industrialization, there was a first stage (mainly that of the first two Perón governments) of retraction of foreign capital. However, at the end of the 1950s, with the arrival of President Arturo Frondizi, who liberalized the conditions for foreign investment, foreign investment gained new momentum, concentrating mainly on the industry, particularly in the automotive and chemical-petrochemical sectors.

It was around 1948, with national decree 3347/48, that a mechanism was established which gave rise to the National Commission for the Establishment of Industries, formalizing the requirements for the entry of foreign investments, which depended on the control of the Central Bank of the Argentine Republic (BCRA). But the policy of nationalization of public utilities that had arisen since the previous year caused that, contrary to what was expected, the investments existing at that time were reduced to less than half. Years later, in 1953, the law 14.222 was enacted, which established conditions for the incorporation of foreign capital into the country, equal treatment concerning national capital, and the possibility of repatriating the invested capital up to 8%, but after 10 years of having invested. This rule was later repealed with the coming to power of the so-called "Revolución Libertadora" of 1955, which liberalized the foreign exchange market, allowing the transfer of foreign currency to foreign companies without State control.

Years later, law 14.780 was enacted, which although it required special authorization for an investor to settle in the country, was less restrictive in terms of the transfer of foreign currency than the previous law of 1953. This law had a positive impact on the flow of investments, which made it possible for investments of close to 500 million dollars to enter the country in the first three years, mainly from the automotive and petrochemical sectors.[3]

In 1970, Law 18.587 was approved, which had a strong preponderance in assigning preferences to foreign investments made in association with national capitals. But by 1973, a new legislative modification was established, typical of the political conflicts of the past decades, through Law 20,557/73, allowing, among other measures, a limit on the transfer of remittances abroad of 12.5%, and not allowing the establishment of branches of foreign companies, among other points.

This last regulatory provision was modified with the implementation of Law 21.382 of 1976, in the context of the new economic regime of the de facto

---

[2] See Slame (1981); Cabanillas de Cuevas (1982); Ymaz Videla (1999). For a historical analysis see: Rapoport (2005).

[3] Slame (1981), p. 20.

government, which was later modified by Law 22.208 and its regulatory decree 103/81. This new law liberalized the incorporation of foreign investments in the country, establishing, among other measures, a waiting period of up to three years for the repatriation of capital invested in the country, and eliminating the transfer limits established by the previous law 20,557.

At the beginning of the last decade of the twentieth century, this national regulatory framework underwent a radical change with the enactment of National Laws 23,696, 23,697, and 23,928 (on the declaration of emergency of public utilities, modification of the capital market, and convertibility of the austral), as well as Law 24,156 of 1992, which established a new system of financial regulation and control of the national public sector.

As the new legal system for foreign investments, Law No. 21.382[4] and National Regulatory Decree No. 1.853/93[5] were approved, which favored a greater flow of capital, limiting the requirements for access to and control over investments.[6] This law defines foreign capital investment as (a) any contribution of foreign capital belonging to foreign investors applied to economic activities carried out in the country, and (b) the acquisition of shares in the capital of an existing local company by foreign investors (Art. 2. 1). The foreign investor is defined as any individual or legal entity domiciled outside the national territory that holds an investment of foreign capital, and local companies with foreign capital when they are investors in other local companies (Art. 2.2). Article 3 of Decree 1853/93 adds that "the concept of foreign investor includes Argentine individuals or legal entities domiciled outside the national territory". Regarding the transfer of profits abroad, the national regulation establishes that "foreign investors may transfer abroad the net and realized profits from their investments, as well as to repatriate their investment" (Art. 5). It also regulates the free choice of legal forms of business organization provided for in Argentine law (Art. 6); and access to domestic credit on equal terms with local companies of national capital (Art. 7).

This legislative incorporation maintained the equality of treatment between foreign and national investors. Although it should be clarified that years before, this process had already begun with the subscription by the country of the first Bilateral Investment Treaty (BIT) signed with the Republic of Italy in 1990.

Thus, during the 1990s, within the framework of a broad process of State reforms implemented by the government of President Carlos Menem, which included currency convertibility, commercial and financial openness, deregulation, and privatization of

---

[4]Online document. http://www.infoleg.gov.ar/infolegInternet/anexos/55000-59999/56254/texact.htm.

[5]Decree 1853/93. *Foreign investors who invest capital in the country, in any of the forms outlined in Article 3 for the promotion of economic activities, or for the expansion or improvement of existing ones, shall have the same rights and obligations that the Constitution and the laws grant to domestic investors, subject to the provisions of this law and those contemplated in special or promotional regimes.*

[6]Section 3 adds that *the concept of foreign investor includes Argentine individuals or legal entities domiciled outside the national territory.*

state enterprises, a new flow of foreign investment took place, which was strongly concentrated in the participation of public enterprises providing services or in natural resource extractive activities, mainly oil. The predominant form of foreign investment during this period was that of shareholding transfers, which was verified both in the privatization process and in the sale of private companies to foreign investors, which took place with greater intensity in the second half of the decade.

According to a report by Argentina's Ministry of Economy, the country received significant FDI flows during the 1990s, which showed an increasing trend from an average of 4 billion (1992–1995), to an average of 8 billion (1996–1998) until reaching a peak of 24 billion in 1999, an amount obtained as a consequence of the purchase of the national hydrocarbon company YPF. From that moment on, there was a profound change in the trend towards the first years of the 2000s, with flows of US$775 million. Shareholding transfers, the most important component of these flows in the last decade, dropped significantly, given the beginning of the recession, as a result of the economic crisis in the country. Contributions remained stable but were directed more towards sustaining the equity of the companies than towards financing new projects, while the other items (debt with related companies and reinvestment of profits) decreased to the point of becoming negative.[7]

According to experts, this new economic and financial order was resolved along three main lines: (a) equal treatment between foreign and local investors, in the sense that investors investing in the country for the promotion of economic activities have the same constitutional rights as nationals; (b) investors may make investments in the country without prior authorization from the State, and (c) investors may repatriate their profits at any time.[8] Some of these guarantees would be altered at the beginning of the 2000s, as a result of the economic and financial collapse of the country during the government of President Fernando De la Rúa.[9]

---

[7] MECON (2003). See to Stanley (2004).

[8] Bonchil (1994), p. 732.

[9] Although by the end of the 1990s there had been some cases of investor claims before the courts, it was after the modification of the exchange rate system and the enactment of the 2002 emergency laws that the number of investor arbitration claims increased exponentially, reaching almost half a hundred lawsuits for violation of investment agreements for economic estimates of close to US$ 75 billion. The economic crisis that occurred between 2001 and 2002 caused the collapse of the country's financial and economic system, forcing the State to issue a series of public order laws that modified the conditions agreed with investors up to that time, as a result of the agreements entered into at the beginning of the 1990s. As a result of the crisis, the Argentine State enacted Law 25,651, which declared the public emergency of the State until December 10, 2003, but which the National Congress has been extending until the present time. This law modified the scope of Law 23,923 of 1991 (known as the convertibility law), which established parity between the Argentine peso and the U.S. dollar, which led to the elimination of the tariff adjustment system held by the concessionaires of public utilities, most of which were in the hands of foreign investors. Such a tariff adjustment system was based on the United States Producer Price Index (US PPI), whereby tariffs were calculated in dollars and converted into pesos for the same amount and readjusted every 6 months. With the enacted emergency, the adjustment mechanisms were frozen and the national exchange rate system was specified. This change in the conditions under which investors had agreed to collect their profits, together with the amendments to other regulations on legal stabilization

As a consequence of a financial and economic crisis in 2001, the State enacted Law 25.651/02, which declared a State public emergency until December 10, 2003, which implied the cessation of payments to investors, the loss of the existing currency parity, and the limitation of transferring profits abroad. This rule implied the non-compliance with the BITs signed by the country and the consequent lawsuit before arbitration tribunals and foreign courts. Currently, part of this emergency law is still in force.

With the new government that emerged after a series of changes of Presidents in 2001, a process of normalization of the economy and relations with international creditors began. During that period until 2005 and, subsequently, during the commodity price boom of 2005–2011, the local policy encouraged domestic consumption relatively more than investment and the business climate did not generate signals for attracting new foreign investment.

Decree 1187/2010[10] eliminated the National Investment Development Agency, which operated within the Ministry of Industry (Section 3), and transferred the competencies of the former Agency to the Undersecretariat of Investment Development under the Secretariat of Trade and International Economic Relations of the Ministry of Foreign Affairs, International Trade and Worship (Section 5).

During the government of President Néstor Kirchner, foreign investment remained below the income of previous periods, due to the various financial problems that were being generated and the subsequent president of Cristina Fernández, would begin a process of de-escalation of foreign investment with various obstacles of benefits to investors and the impossibility of transferring funds abroad. During this period, the litigation with the investments that had sued before the ICSID, initiated a policy of paralyzing the agreement of new BITs, considering that the existing ones had been detrimental to the country.

Between 2012 and 2015, again the macroeconomic complications led to the imposition of controls that drove investors away. International companies already located in the country were subject to severe exchange controls. As a result, most of the modest FDI inflow was concentrated in the reinvestment of profits that could not be repatriated under the new controls.[11]

In 2016, the Argentine State has under the administration of President Mauricio Macri, sought to encourage foreign investment through Law 27.328 on national public-private participation contracts (PPP),[12] mainly aimed at the development of infrastructure works, which was not exempt from criticism for being a model that is no longer applied in many countries and that generates higher costs to the State.

---

clauses provided for in the BITs or the cancellation of public service concession contracts, led to the filing of claims before various arbitration tribunals (mainly before ICSID). As a result of the laws enacted, in 2003 the national government initiated a process of renegotiation of contracts with investors, mainly public service providers, through Decree 311/03, to which few companies agreed, renouncing, in turn, to file claims before foreign courts.

[10] Signed on 08/19/2010 and published in the Official Gazette on 08/27/2010, p. 1. Accessed at http://infoleg.mecon.gov.ar/infolegInternet/anexos/170000-174999/171086/norma.htm.

[11] Cristini and Bermúdez (2022), p. 24.

[12] Law 27.328. Public-Private Contract Law. November 16, 2016.

During this period of government, FDI flows resumed and new investment agreements were initiated (2018) but with a new change of government in 2019 and new economic crisis led to the resumption of restrictions on the movement of capital and imports that affected confidence again for investors to allocate their projects in the country.

On September 1, 2019, Argentina introduced a series of new restrictions on foreign currency transactions, reversing its four-year policy that had eliminated such controls. This move follows similar recent capital restrictions imposed by other states. Such regulations may give rise to investment treaty claims by foreign investors. In particular, depending on the circumstances, these measures may violate investors' rights to the free transfer of funds in and out of the host state; and fair and equitable treatment.

Since 2018 and until 2021, Argentina has again exhibited significant external financial fragility. At the same time, its business climate has moved away from the necessary conditions to attract new investments to improve its deteriorated productivity.[13]

Within the framework of the regional integration system, the country is also regulated by a series of norms. For out-of-zone investments, the States Parties to MERCOSUR approved the *Protocol of Buenos Aires on the Promotion and Protection of Investments from States not Parties to MERCOSUR*.[14] This was a model Bilateral Treaty that established maximum standards of treatment admitted and tolerated for extra-zone investors as of its entry into force, which did not occur. In turn, the integration zone has the *Protocol of Colonia for the Promotion and Reciprocal Protection of Investments in MERCOSUR*, which stipulates rules to promote investment among the Party States, guaranteeing the treatment of the nationals of such States, under standards applied in most BITs.[15] However, one of the particularities of these Protocols was the equal treatment of investors. Both provided for the possibility that the investor would receive treatment equal to that of a national of a State Party, but a *contrario sensu*, the investor was not guaranteed *better* treatment than a national. Because of the privileges usually sought by foreign investors, and not without mentioning that the treatment received by national investors by the MERCOSUR States is not usually very positive, it is understandable that such Protocols did not achieve their purpose. Furthermore, they allow the subjects contemplated in the Protocols to use ICSID, among others, as a reference arbitration mechanism.

Partly for this reason, in 2010, the Mercosur Common Market Council approved Decision CMC 30/10, which adopted the new "*Guidelines for the conclusion of a Mercosur Investment Agreement*",[16] leading to the termination of the Colonia and

[13] Cristini and Bermúdez (2022), p. 11.

[14] MERCOSUR/CMC/DEC N° 11/94. Approved on August 5, 1994.

[15] MERCOSUR/CMC/DEC/11/93. Signed on January 17, 1994 (not yet in force. Not ratified by any State Party of MERCOSUR). See on the subject: Chudnovsky and López (2000).

[16] MERCOSUR/CMC/DEC. N° 30/10. Signed on December 16, 2010.

Buenos Aires agreements, due to the lack of application of these agreements as investment promoters.

As recent advances in aspects related to investment rules, the Argentine State participated as a member of Mercosur, in the negotiation of an agreement between the European Union and MERCOSUR. On June 28, 2019, the blocks of the MERCOSUR and the European Union announced the end of the negotiation process to conclude a free trade agreement between both regional blocks. The agreement is currently under consideration for approval at the levels of the States Parties of the regional bodies. The Services chapter does not include any section with explicit reference to investment protection, nor does it include the investor-state dispute settlement (ISDS) mechanism. Investment regulation and protection will continue to be covered by the BITs signed by EU member countries bilaterally with Mercosur member countries. Except for Brazil, all Mercosur countries have a significant number of investment protection treaties with European countries, especially Argentina. Although there is no investment chapter, the document entitled "Agreement in Principle" issued by the EU explains that the agreement covers investment protection through the establishment of services with commercial presence. This is known as "mode 3" (or "establishment") of the WTO GATS classification of services.[17]

According to international reports, inward FDI flows to Argentina have been unstable in recent years. According to the World Investment Report 2020 published by UNCTAD, Argentina reduced its flows to USD 6.2 billion in 2019 (compared to USD 11.8 billion in 2018), which has been deepened by the economic crisis. Similarly, the stock of FDI fell in 2019, reaching USD 69.2 billion (a drop of USD 15 billion compared to 2010).[18] Although recent Argentine governments actively seek FDI, economic insecurity and recurrent crises hinder this task. At the same time the changes of governments in the hands of more populist parties, generate much uncertainty about investment expropriations and corruption practices. The general openness to foreign investment is below average. Even so, Argentina has obvious advantages: its natural resources are considerable (copper, gas, oil) and it has a skilled and competitive labor force. On the other hand, FDI restrictions continue to be applied in the agricultural sector, which is strategic for the country's food security. Also, recent measures (such as the restrictive mortgage law, increased regulations in the energy sector) have discouraged investors. However, Argentina has also adopted a preferential tax regime for the automotive sector to promote regional vehicle production chains among MERCOSUR countries. However, the business climate in Argentina remains rather poor. It should be recalled that most of the BITs with Argentina have not been modified in their original regulations of the 1990s and have been renewed automatically.

In the last decade, MERCOSUR countries have had increased investments with China. In February 2022, Argentina signed its adhesion to the Silk Belt and Road (BRI) program sponsored by the Asian country. This project was presented by the

---

[17] European Commission (2019); Sanahuja and Rodríguez (2019).

[18] UNCTAD. Word Investment Report. (2020).

Chinese authorities in 2013 and aimed to promote investment in land and sea transport infrastructure and digital communications infrastructure to link Eurasian markets. The initiative was later extended to 145 countries, including 20 Latin American countries. The projects are financed by China's state-owned development banks and private Chinese banks (10 entities in 2018), such as the Asian Infrastructure Investment Bank (which Argentina had already joined in 2017), and the implementation is mostly contracted with Chinese infrastructure companies.[19] Within the framework of the Economic and Investment Cooperation Agreement between Argentina and China (1992) and the need for investment in infrastructure, there are investment projects for constructing two hydroelectric dams in the south of the country and collaborating in the construction of a third nuclear power plant.

2 The Incorporation of BITs in Argentina

In the context of the so-called Washington Consensus, through the economic and financial reform carried out by President Menem's administration in the 1990s, there was a greater opening to foreign investment, whose legal framework was favored by the numerous signing of BITs with various investment exporting countries and others of various kinds.[20]

Around 1989, Argentina, following the parameters established by the 1962 OECD, elaborated its own model investment agreement, which was subsequently adopted in the various investment treaties. However, such treaties did not imply equivalent conditions of reciprocity (in practice) between the types of investments and their clauses agreed between the Argentine State and the third signatory States.

The first BIT signed by Argentina was with the Republic of Italy in 1990, followed by a dozen BITs, mainly with European and American countries.[21]

---

[19] Cristini and Bermúdez (2022), pp. 37–38.

[20] The first BIT signed by the Argentine Republic was with Italy (May 22, 1990), approved by Law 24,122.

[21] The Argentine Republic entered into bilateral treaties on the protection and promotion of foreign investments (BITS) with more than 50 countries. Among them, we can mention: People's Democratic Republic of Algeria: Date of signature: 04/10/2000; approving law: 25.538/02; Republic of India: Date of signature: 20/08/99; approving law: 25.540/2002; Republic of New Zealand: Date of signature: 08/27/99; enabling law: 25.539/2002; Thailand: Date of signature 02/18/2000; enabling law: 25.532/02; Philippines: Date of signature 09/20/99; enabling law: 25.481/01; Guatemala: Date of signature: 04/21/98; enabling law: 25.350/00; Republic of South Africa: Date of signature: 07/23/98; enabling legislation: 25.352/00; Nicaragua: Date of signature: 08/10/98; enabling legislation: 25.351/00; Russian Federation: Date of signature: 06/25/98; enabling legislation: 25.353/00; Costa Rica: Date of signature: 05/21/97; enabling legislation: 25.139/99; El Salvador: Date of signature: 09/05/96; enabling law: 25.023/98; Czech Republic: Date of signature: 27/09/96; enabling law: 24.983/98; Lithuania: Date of signature: 14/03/96; enabling law: 24.984/98; Panama: Date of signature: 10/05/96; enabling law: 24.971 /98: Mexico: Date of signature: 13/11/96; enabling law: 24.792/98; Morocco: Date of signature: 13/06/96; enabling law 24.890/97;

In turn, from the totality of BITs signed by Argentina, it is worth mentioning that there were evolutionary differences in terms of their scope and limits of action. Thus, the first BITs signed by the country with Italy, Germany, Austria, Canada, among others, state that, if an agreement is not reached with the Government, the investor must resort to the local courts of the State, to be able to exhaust the domestic remedies of the same, in the event of an eventual international claim, the terms were set at about 18 months. The purpose of this was to give the State receiving the investment the possibility of remedying its non-compliance through domestic mechanisms, thus avoiding the dispute reaching arbitration.

The BIT signed with France will modify these requirements, establishing the possibility of submitting the dispute to international courts without prior exhaustion of domestic remedies. Through this mechanism, the parties have a period of six months to reach an agreement on the dispute, in which case, if such a possibility is not achieved, the investor is allowed to choose the domestic or an international dispute settlement channel, including the jurisdiction of ICSID or an ad-hoc tribunal

---

Indonesia: Date of signature: 07/11/95; enabling law: 24.814/97; Cuba: Date of signature: 30/11/95; enabling law: 24.770/97; Vietnam: Date of signature: 03/06/96; enabling legislation: 24.778/97; Israel: Date of signature: 23/07/95; enabling legislation: 24.771/97; Australia: Date of signature: 23/08/95; enabling legislation: 24.728/96; Republic of Korea: Date of signature: 17/05/94; enabling legislation: 24.682/96; Ukraine: Date of signature: 09/08/95; enabling law: 24.681/96; Peru: Date of signature: 10/11/94; enabling law: 24.680/96; Malaysia: Date of signature: 06/09/94; enabling law: 24.613/96; Finland: Date of signature: 05/11/93; enabling law: 24.614/96; Portugal: Date of signature: 06/10/94; enabling law: 24.593/95; Croatia: Date of signature: 02/12/94; enabling law: 24.563/95; Jamaica: Date of signature: 08/02/94; enabling law: 24.549/95; Venezuela: Date of signature: 16/11/93; enabling law: 24.457/95: Ecuador: Date of signature: 02/18/94; enabling law: 24.459/95; Romania: Date of signature: 07/29/93; enabling law: 24.456/95; Bolivia: Date of signature: 03/17/94; enabling law: 24.458/95; Senegal: Date of signature: 04/06/93; enabling law: 24.396/94;. Bulgaria: Date of signature: 09/21/93; Adoptive law: 24.401/94; Armenia: Date of signature: 04/06/93; Adoptive law: 24.395/94; Tunisia: Date of signature: 06/17/92; Adoptive law: 24.394/94; Denmark: Date of signature: 11/06/92; Adoptive law: 24.397/94; Turkey: Date of signature: 08/05/92; Adoptive law: 24.340/94; Hungary: Date of signature: 05/02/93; Adoptive law: 24.335/94; People's Republic of China: Date of signature: 05/11/92; Adoptive law: 24.324/94; Republic of Austria: Date of signature: 07/08/92; enabling legislation: 24.238/94; Egypt: Date of signature: 11/05/92; enabling legislation: 24.248/93; Netherlands: Date of signature: 20/10/92; enabling legislation: 24.352/94: Great Britain and Northern Ireland: Date of signature: 1/12/90; enabling legislation: 24.184/92; Belgium and Luxembourg: Date of signature: 6/28/90; enabling legislation: 24.123/92; Canada: Date of signature: 11/05/91; enabling legislation: 24.125/92; USA: Date of signature: 11/05/91; enabling legislation: 24.125/92. USA: Date of signature: 11/14/91; enabling legislation: 24.124/92; Sweden: Date of signature: 11/22/91; enabling legislation: 24.117/92; Spain: Date of signature: 10/03/91; enabling legislation: 24.118/92; France: Date of signature: 07/03/91; enabling legislation: 24.100/92; Germany: Date of signature: 04/09/91; enabling legislation: 24.098/92; Switzerland: Date of signature: 04/12/91; approving law: 24.099/92; Poland: Date of signature: 07/31/91; approving law: 24.101/92; Chile: Date of signature: 08/02/91; approving law: 24.342/93; Italy: Date of signature: 05/22/90; approving law: 24.122/92. To this must be added the Buenos Aires Protocol for the Promotion and Protection of Investments from States not party to MERCOSUR: Date of signature: 04/08/1994, approving law 24.554 and the Convention on the Settlement of Investment Disputes between States and nationals of other States. Date of signature: 03/18/1965; approving law: 24.353/94. (B.O. 02/09/94).

for that purpose, generally under the rules of UNCITRAL/UNCITRAL. These types of options are often referred to a *fork in the road* clauses.[22]

Initially, the BITs signed in the 1990s were limited to establishing the general conditions under which the host States of the investment guarantee certain legal and economic conditions to the investors, known as investment clauses or standards.

These dozens of BITs were characterized by establishing in a very general and diffuse way what are the standards of protection to be and diffuse ways which are the standards of protection to which a State must adhere in the treatment of a foreign investor from another Party. Thus, the "fair and equitable treatment", "non-discrimination", the "umbrella" clause, or the "umbrella" umbrella, the "national treatment principle" or the "most-favored-nation clause", among others, were enshrined without determining exactly what their scope was. For example, the 1992 BIT between the Argentine Republic and the French Republic establishes that "Each of the Contracting Parties undertakes to grant, in its territory and in its maritime zone, fair and equitable treatment in accordance with the principles of international law, to investments made by investors of the other Party (. . .)", without determining exactly what this "fair and equitable treatment" implies. exactly what that "fair and equitable treatment" entails. These more generic definitions of investor protection standards later had their effects on the various arbitral tribunal proceedings in which the country was sued.

When new BITs were signed with some countries in 2016 (Qatar) and in 2018 (United Arab Emirates and Japan),[23] these "second or third generation" BITs clarified many of the more ambiguous terms of the BITs of the past decade and implemented new references to sustainable development and more detailed Most Favored Nation clauses, in the sense of invoking their scope to access the jurisdictional means of disputes of other BITs. In addition, the BITs mention that investors "shall endeavor to voluntarily incorporate corporate social responsibility guidelines". This means that these are not binding mandatory clauses, but it is up to the companies to follow the explicit guidelines, but it introduces new soft law conduct on corporate responsibility in business behavior and respect for the rights of the investment environment and inhabitants. In turn, these new agreements allude to the areas that will not be included or understood as "investment", linked to sovereign debts, public bonds, and exploitation of natural resources, which will be governed exclusively by national laws.

On the other hand, and having as experiences the BITs signed in the '90s, several countries in the region (Argentina, Brazil) together with other states (China, Russia), have been working in various international forums to advance the adoption of new types of agreements called "rules for investment facilitation", which were presented at meetings of the G-20 in Hamburg (2017) and Buenos Aires (2018).

The concept of investment facilitation is lax and indeterminate. On the one hand, it leaves out the typical investment protection issues found in bilateral investment

---

[22] See Kauffmann-Kohler and Postetà (2020), p. 39.

[23] https://investmentpolicy.unctad.org/international-investment-agreements/countries/8/argentina.

treaties (BITs), such as fair and equitable treatment, non-discriminatory treatment, and indirect expropriation clauses, all aimed at protecting investors, as well as the investor-state dispute settlement (ISDS) mechanism. On the other hand, this notion incorporates terms such as transparency, predictability, and stakeholder engagement to establish a new set of rules for foreign investment at the multilateral level.[24]

As a consequence of its modification of national norms in 2001 and 2002 that implied a substantial change in the conditions for investments, the Argentine state has been sued before ICSID and other investment arbitration mechanisms such as ad hoc tribunals under UNCITRAL rules in more than 60 cases over the last two decades.

In the context of these Argentine cases, it is possible to appreciate the scope of application of the main investment protection standards.

3 Standards and Rules Stipulated in the BITs with Argentina and Their Scope in Arbitration Awards

3.1 Fair and Equitable Treatment

This type of standard, although it has been developed by the doctrine and widely applied by arbitral jurisprudence, does not constitute in itself a standard that can be used in general terms, but rather, the conditions and circumstances that apply in each case must be analyzed to verify its use in the claim of breach of a contract or a BIT.[25] This implies that all investors must be guaranteed to be able to exercise their investments in the host State, free from any interference by State bodies or third parties that may involve discriminatory or abusive actions and which in turn imply a disadvantage compared to other public or private subjects.[26] The host State is thus

[24]Ghiotto and Guamán (2018), p. 4.

[25]Dolzer and Schreuer (2008), p. 119; Ymaz Videla (1999); Granato (2005); Tawil (2000), p. 1106; Barraguirre and Manzi (2010), pp. 145–188; Schreuer (2005), p. 356. The standard of fair and equitable treatment finds its first expression in the Havana Charter of 1948, when the first attempt was made to establish an international body for trade. It was subsequently raised in the drafts of the Abs-Schawcros Convention of 1960 and the Convention on the Protection of Property Abroad within the framework of the OECD of 1967. With the US BITs in the early 1970s, this clause began to be incorporated. Cf. UNCTAD (1999), pp. 10 et seq.

[26]It is also worth mentioning that although the investor must be guaranteed a non-discriminatory treatment for those reasons that the State may argue concerning particular situations, this principle cannot be subtracted from the social and economic reality to which a State may be subjected at a given time. It is worth remembering the "Doctrine of the Community of Fortune" formulated by the jurist Luis A. Podestá in 1922, in which he expressed that the foreigner acts under a personal resolution, freely adopted, when he, or his assets, are located in another State. In making that determination he knows what are the foreseeable advantages and disadvantages, and he enters to participate in the material and moral alternatives of the new environment in which he has decided to act. Like the other inhabitants of that environment, he must enjoy the benefits they enjoy and cannot

required to guarantee a minimum level of treatment towards the investor that cannot be violated and that makes it possible to achieve the agreed commitments, while at the same time, in the face of any difference or inconvenience in treatment between the investor and the State, the latter must act in a fair, reasoned and equitable manner.

Fair and equitable treatment shall in no case be less than that accorded by the rules and principles of international law. In other words, every investor must be able to receive treatment no less favorable than that received by another investor or a national, a standard also closely related to that of *national treatment*. However, when analyzing the conditions of treatment that are usually guaranteed to a foreign investor, in conjunction with the enforceability of other standards, the foreign investor often obtains more and better treatment than a national investor. Several BITs formulate in their clauses these standards necessary to guarantee a foreign investment. The BIT between Argentina and Australia stipulates it in its article 4, with Canada in its article II (4); with Italy in its article 2.2, with France in its article 3, among others.

This type of standard is the one mentioned in most of the awards against the Argentine Republic, whether in the *CMS,*[27] *Enron,*[28] *LG&E*[29] *Sempra*[30]*(*regarding

---

escape the evils they suffer. A tacit pact is thus established between the State and the foreigner, a relationship of coexistence, which creates a bond of reciprocal solidarity, a true "community of fortune". See Podestá Costa and Ruda (1979), p. 410.

[27] ICSID. *CMS Gas Transmission vs Argentine* (2001). CMS's claim (as a minority shareholder of the company Transportadora del Gas del Norte) was made due to the lack of adjustment of tariff adjustments in the provision of the gas transportation service that the Argentine government had suspended since 2000 and that the liquidation of the tariffs calculated in dollars had been devalued as a consequence of the emergency law and the pesification of the economy. The investor argued that this implied an expropriation and a violation of the fair and equitable treatment standard.

[28] ICSID. *Enron Corporation Ponderosa Assets LP vs Argentina* (2001). The claimant filed a claim for the lack of adjustment of tariffs for the U.S. PPI that had been guaranteed by the last decree in 2000 (No. 669) and that in the same year was no longer applied, and for the calculation of tariffs in dollars as a consequence of the pesification in 2001 onwards. The investor brought the case before ICSID against the State on the grounds of direct and indirect expropriation, as well as violation of the fair and equitable treatment standard and violation of the umbrella clause for breach of the contractual obligations assumed by the State through its special rules on the regulation of the gas market.

[29] ICSID. *LG&E Energy Corporation vs Argentine* (2002). The claim of the investor engaged in the transportation of gas was based on the modification of the indexation rules of the tariffs for the provision of services, which until the State emergency law of 2002 were calculated in dollars, and at the same time, it was claimed that since 1999 the tariffs were not adjusted every 6 months as agreed between the parties. The investor also argued that the umbrella clause had been breached due to the non-compliance with the obligations assumed by the State in the area of the gas transportation system in Argentina. For its part, the State rejected the investor's arguments, both because it considered that it did not meet the *ius standi requirements* to claim before ICSID and because of the exceptional circumstances that led to the enactment of the emergency laws.

[30] ICSID. *Sempra Energy International vs. Argentina.* (2002). In this case, at the beginning of the 1990s, the investor had acquired shares in the companies Sodigas Pampeana and Sodigas Sur which, in turn, held 90% and 86%, respectively, of the shares of two national companies: Camuzzi Gas Pampeana S.A. and Camuzzi Gas del Sur, which were granted licenses for gas distribution in

the modification by the State of the regulatory framework contrary to the terms of the agreed licenses); or in *Azurix,*[31] *Aguas del Aconquija (Vivendi),*[32] *Siemens,*[33] *Thales Spectrum*[34] (regarding the termination of long-term contracts) or *Continental Casualty*[35] (for the modification in the quotable values of bills of exchange), among others.

1996. With the economic crisis of 2000/2001, the companies were affected by a modification of the regulatory framework and tariffs in the gas market, as discussed in the CMS and Enron cases, among others, as well as for the pesification of service tariffs. The investor considered that such measures implied a violation of fair treatment and the umbrella clause of the Argentina-US BIT and brought the case before ICSID. Although the 2007 award was favorable to the investor, an ad-hoc Committee annulled the award in June 2010.

[31] ICSID. *Azurix Corporation vs. Argentine* (2001). The dispute arose from the cancellation of the concession contract for the provision of water and sewage services in the Province of Buenos Aires to the subsidiary Azurix Buenos Aires (ABA). The tribunal considered that the standard of fair and equitable treatment had been violated due to the existence of political conditions that distorted the adjustment of the tariff schedule, freezing it, and as a consequence of the precedents in other provinces (in Tucumán with the Aguas del Aconquija case).

[32] ICSID. *Compañía de Aguas del Aconquija SA and Vivendi SA v. Argentine* (2003). The investor's claim was related to the cancellation of the contract for the provision of water and sanitation services in the City of Tucumán by the Government of the Province, as a result of disagreements between the company and the State regarding the performance of the contract. While it was recognized that the investor should have exhausted domestic remedies for the claim for breach of contract, the case was subsequently accepted for jurisdiction in violation of the Argentina-France BIT for breach of the standard of fair treatment, among others. In 2019, the State agreed to pay US$220 million to the investors Agbar and Suez, together with international groups such as Vivendi, who entered the drinking water business in the cities of Santa Fe, Córdoba, and Buenos Aires.

[33] ICSID. *Siemens AG v. Argentine* (2002). The claim before ICSID arose from the cancellation of the contract that the Argentine State had signed with the national company SITS (a subsidiary of Siemens International), which consisted of providing the service of issuing new identity documents for the country's inhabitants as well as a new immigration control system. The government had terminated the contract in 2001 because the fees to be paid were disproportionate. ICSID accepted the claim for violation of fair and equitable treatment, expropriation, and breach of legal certainty, although after the award was rendered the company negotiated with the State not to continue with the claim.

[34] ICSID. *TSA Spectrum de Argentina SA vs. Argentina.* (2005). The case was brought to the ICSID arbitration body by the (apparent) French investor, due to the revocation by the national government in 2004 of the contract with the company for the provision of the service of radio-electric space control management in the country. The government alleged a breach of contract due to a lack of "operational synchronicity" and a collection that exceeded the rate of return. The investor filed a claim with ICSID for breach of fair and equitable treatment and for the expropriatory nature of the government's action. However, the tribunal rejected the jurisdiction of the Center because the claimant was not a foreign investor within the meaning of the Argentina-France BIT and the Washington Convention.

[35] ICSID. *Continental Casualty Company v. Argentina.* (2003). The investor filed a claim with ICSID in 2003 against the Argentine State alleging that with the modification of the economic emergency regulations and certain measures adopted by the Argentine Government to respond to the crisis, losses were caused to Continental in breach of Argentina's obligations under the Argentina-US BIT. 1996, the investor acquired 70% of the shares of the insurance company CNA Aseguradora de Riesgos del Trabajo, and by the year 2000 almost 100% of the shares.

The indetermination of this standard, in certain circumstances, causes legal uncertainty to the host State, so it becomes relevant that States can establish certain more objective parameters on which national legislation and public policy measures to be applied in certain circumstances can be based. The implementation of a mechanism that allows the State to determine high-quality standards in terms of investor treatment will imply, on the one hand, providing a more favorable environment for investment, but with its correlation of an effective mechanism for the control and resolution of disputes when they arise, to prevent situations of claims for breach of domestic contracts from escalating and implying the adoption of measures that a posteriori may be considered as a violation of the standard protected in the BIT.

3.2 The Most-Favored-Nation (MFN) Clause

This clause is widely used in BITs and regional investment promotion instruments (Article 1 of the Buenos Aires Protocol and Article 3 of the Cologne Protocol in the MERCOSUR sphere; Article 10 of the Energy Charter in the European sphere, among others) and has been used by investors, in some cases in an abusive manner. As such, the most favored nation standard has allowed what the doctrine has cataloged as the "multilateralization of treaties" in investment matters, as opposed to the protections to which an investor aspires.[36] This standard of treatment accorded to investors implies that in those cases where a BIT grants better treatment to an investor from a third State, but both have signed a BIT with the host State, the BIT more favorable to the investor may be applied.

It should be recalled that the International Law Commission of the UN General Assembly initially developed draft articles on the Most-Favored-Nation Clause.[37] Its article 4 defined it as "*... a provision of a treaty under which a State undertakes concerning another State the obligation to grant the treatment of the most favored*

Continental stated that CNA, like other insurance companies, maintained a portfolio of investment securities to obtain a return on its capital, which consisted mainly of "low-risk assets, such as cash deposits, treasury bills (LETE) and government bonds", and that, with some minor exceptions, investments were required to be made in Argentina. That with a series of regulations issued as from 2001 (Decree 1387/01-Voluntary bond exchange, Decree 1570/01 –"Corralito", Law 25.561 of Public Emergency of 2002; Decree 214/02 by which all obligations of sums of money), the investor saw its assets confiscated, which were in dollars, constituting acts of expropriation and treatment not under fair and equitable treatment, as well as violating the umbrella clause according to the BIT guidelines.

[36] Faya Rodríguez (2008), pp. 93–96; Fernández Masia (2007), pp. 16–20; Orrego Vicuña (1972), p. 17; Vesel (2007), pp. 154–192. In the field of international law, this clause represents a controversial standard at the time of its application. The ICJ has had the opportunity to refer to it in some rulings. See: *Anglo-Iranian Oil Company* Case (1952) and *Rights of U.S. Nationals in Morocco*. (1952), p. 191.

[37] ILC (1970), p. 204.

Nation in an agreed sphere of relations". In turn, Article 14 of the above-mentioned draft as adopted in 1978 established that "*...the treatment accorded by the granting State to the beneficiary State, or to persons or things in a particular relationship with that State, shall not be less favorable than the treatment accorded by the granting State to a third State, or to persons or things in the same relationship with that third State*".

Subsequently, this topic was taken up again in 2008.[38] Particularly the studies have been focused on establishing the existence or not of provisions in BITs on whether the MFN clause has effects on substantive and/or procedural (jurisdictional) provisions.

This principle needs to be stipulated under general conditions and not so much for particular investments, while in some cases access to these clauses applies to those BITs previously signed by the investor, while others only stipulate it in cases of BITs to be signed thereafter.[39]

Thus, for example, Article 3 of the Argentine-Italy BIT contains the MFN clause stating that:

> Article 3. National Treatment and Most-Favored-Nation Clause
>
> (1) Each Contracting Party shall, within its territory, accord to investments made by investors of the other Contracting Party, to profits and activities connected therewith and to all other matters governed by this Agreement, treatment no less favorable than that accorded to its investors or investors of third countries.

A point that has generated several controversies on the invocation of the MFN clause has been the use of the standard in seeking access to the jurisdiction of arbitral tribunals, to avoid the exhaustion of domestic remedies of the host State.

A paradigmatic case on this point has been *Maffezini v. Kingdom of Spain,* where the tribunal analyzed the MFN clause of the Argentine-Spain BIT about the provisions of the Chile-Spain BIT, which did not require the exhaustion of a certain

[38] At its sixtieth session, where the Commission decided to include the topic "Most-favored-nation clause" in its work program and to establish a Study Group on the issue at its sixty-first session. A Study Group, co-chaired by Mr. Donald M. McRae and Mr. A. Rohan Perera, was established at the sixty-first session (2009). The Study Group was re-established at the sixty-second session (2010) under the same co-chairmanship. At its 3119th meeting, on 8 August 2011, the Committee took note of the oral report presented by the co-chairmen of the Study Group. (*Official Records)* para. 354. In 2010 and 2011, the Study Group decided to seek to further identify the normative content of MFN clauses in the investment field and to undertake further analysis of the jurisprudence, including the role of arbitrators, factors explaining different approaches to interpreting MFN provisions, divergences, and actions taken by States in response to the jurisprudence. The Group focused its studies on the working paper on the "interpretation and application of MFN clauses in investment agreements" prepared by Donald McRae. The working paper built on an earlier study on "The MFN Clause and the *Maffezini* Case, prepared by Rohan Perera, and sought to identify the factors that tribunals had taken into account in reaching their decisions to gauge whether this shed any light on the divergences in the case law, intending to identify categories of factors that had been alleged in the various cases and assessing their relative importance in the interpretation and application of MFN clauses.

[39] Argentina - Italy BIT. (1990).

period before filing a claim. The Tribunal held that, in the absence of express provisions to the contrary, the investment dispute provisions of another treaty of the same nature can be extended to an investor from a third country because the purpose of the BIT is to protect foreign investors and their rights and because the investment dispute settlement provisions are intimately related to investment protection.[40]

However, as stated above, these clauses may give rise to the investor seeking to abuse the scope of the terms of the BITs. Therefore, the Tribunal also held that:

> (...). The distinction between the legitimate extension of rights and benefits through the application of the clause, on the one hand, and the harmful alternative of seeking to apply various treaties to alter the policy objectives underlying specific provisions, on the other, must be made clear" (...). To do otherwise would alter the finality of the agreed arrangements that many countries consider important as a matter of public policy (...).[41]

The reaction of the States that concluded investment agreements after the *Maffezini* case indicates a tendency to expressly state whether or not the MFN clause is applicable to dispute settlement procedures.

In line with the above, these debates on the scope of the application of MFN continue to manifest themselves in recent cases brought before ICSID. In the *Impregilo vs. Argentina* ***case***, two arbitrators upheld the jurisdiction of the Center, while Prof. Stern, with very good criteria, expressed her dissent. In this case, the majority of the Tribunal stated that:

> It is true, as noted, that the jurisprudence on the application of MFN clauses to dispute settlement rules is not consistent. However, in those cases where the MFN clause has referred to "all other matters" or to "any matter" regulated by the BIT, the conclusion has been almost unanimous in the sense of including dispute resolution rules. On this basis, the majority of the Tribunal concludes that Impregilo is entitled to rely, in this respect, on the dispute resolution rules contained in the Argentina-United States BIT and that the case cannot be dismissed for failure to comply with the requirements outlined in Articles 8(2) and 8(3) of the Argentina-Italy BIT.[42]

---

[40] ICSID. *Emilio Agustín Maffezini v. Kingdom of Spain,* (2000). The investor, an Argentine national, had a dispute with the Government of Spain arising out of an investment he had made in Spanish territory with a subdivision of the State. The investor, to request access to ICSID jurisdiction under the Argentina-Spain BIT, invoked the application of the most favored nation (MFN) clause, which obliged Spain to grant treatment no less favorable than to investors from third states, because the Spain-Chile BIT allowed direct access to ICSID (prior negotiations of 6 months), while the Argentina-Spain BIT required prior recourse to the local courts of the host State for a period of not less than 18 months. See also ICSID *Suez, Sociedad General de Aguas de Barcelona, S.A. and Vivendi Universal, S.A. v. Argentine Republic,* (2010) as well as ICSID *Suez, Sociedad General de Aguas de Barcelona S.A. and InterAguas Servicios Integrales del Agua S.A. v. Argentine Republic,* (2010).

[41] ICSID. *Emilio Agustín Maffezini v. Kingdom of Spain,* (2000) para. 63–64.

[42] ICSID. *Impregilo spA v. Argentine Republic.* (2011) para. 108. In 1996 the Italian investor, together with other national partners, formed the company AGBA, with which it won a bid for water and sewage services in the Province of Buenos Aires. In 1999 the investor reached an agreement with the provincial government for 30 years for the exclusive collection, processing, and distribution of drinking water and sewage. This authorized the collection of a tariff and its continuous

These "double routes" to which some investors have appealed to gain access to international arbitration, based on avoiding bringing cases before the local courts of the host States, is distorting the scope of these clauses, which refer to the treatment that a State must provide to an investor, for others, but without this, in turn, implying the de facto incorporation that such scope must also be applied to procedural issues regarding access to the dispute settlement areas that the various BITs stipulate. These positions that arbitrators end up applying through their rulings distort the scope that States commit to when they agree to BITs. It would be unreasonable that if two sovereign States decide to provide a dispute settlement mechanism between them, this would then imply that they would tacitly accept that the investor would choose any other "preference". In this sense, the disproportionate application of the MFN clause would be contrary to the good faith scope that should be given to the term "favorable treatment" under the 1969 Vienna Convention on the Law of Treaties.

For this reason, we agree with what Prof. Stern expressed in the dissenting opinion in the Impregilo case, when she stated that:

> (...) there are two different types of provisions in BITs that must be distinguished in this broad category of "all other matters", as I will discuss below. There are rights and there are substantive conditions for access to rights. In other words, some rules confer substantive and jurisdictional rights to foreign investors concerning their investments and some rules regulate the access of foreign investors to the substantive and jurisdictional rights granted by the base treaty. I consider that an MFN clause can only refer to the rights that an investor may enjoy, it cannot modify the fundamental conditions for the exercise of such rights, that is, the insurmountable conditions for accessing the rights granted under the BIT.[43]

These positions are not unanimous, as authors such as Van Harten leave open the possibility of a broader scope of the MFN clause.[44] Much depends on the wording of the particular MFN clause, he argues, as some BITs indicate whether an MFN clause applies in dispute settlement or not. In the absence of such an indication, there is no compelling reason to distinguish between substantive and dispute settlement rules and as a matter of treaty interpretation, it is difficult to understand why generally formulated MFN clauses referring to treatment should apply only to substantive issues, but not to the dispute settlement issue.

These positions can be glimpsed in some recent awards. In *Hochtief AG v. Argentine,* the tribunal analyzing its jurisdiction over a claim made by the German investor to ICSID, using the MFN clause in the context of the Argentina-Chile BIT, which excludes the possibility of waiting up to 18 months before bringing a case to

---

updating to cover service expenses. In 2001, given the difficulty in collecting the expected tariffs from users, the government was asked to modify the contractual conditions, which were rejected because this was part of the risks of an investment. With the 2001 economic crisis, the situation worsened and after several unsuccessful negotiations and reports of poor performance of the contract by the company, in 2006 the provincial government fined the company, and then the Governor ordered the cancellation of the contract and the transfer of the concession to a state-owned company (ABSA). In July 2007, the investor filed the case before ICSID.

[43] ICSID. *Impregilio*, Dissenting opinion of Prof. Brigitte Stern. Para. 47.

[44] Van Harten (2007).

the international instances provided for in the Germany-Argentine BIT, held as to whether the MFN clause included the jurisdictional aspects, that:

> The Tribunal considers that the phrase "the management, use, utilization, and development of an investment" includes the right to resort to dispute resolution mechanisms as an aspect within the management of the investment. Indeed, the ('procedural') right to enforce another ('substantive') right is a component within the compendium of rights and obligations that make up the legal concept of what constitutes property. (...) The Tribunal considers that the provisions of Article 10 which, whatever interpretation is adopted, provide investors with the possibility of recourse to arbitration, in addition to giving them the right to resort to domestic courts, constitute a form of protection enjoyed in the context of "the management, use, utilization and development of an investment".[45]

This reasoning was present when considering that the 18-month wait would not have modified the investor's access to ICSID in any way; it would only have delayed the time of presentation. In this sense, it expressed that:

> Second, avoiding the 18 months provided for in the Argentine-Germany BIT by resorting to the MFN clause would not affect the scope of the Tribunal's jurisdiction. It would not give rise to any case within the Tribunal's jurisdiction that Claimant, acting alone, could not subsequently bring before the Tribunal under Article 10 of the Argentine-Germany BIT. Nor would it deprive the Respondent of the right to invoke Article 10(2) of the BIT in any dispute, or to require that the matter be submitted to the domestic courts.[46]

To what is expressed by both positions, it is necessary to consider those positions that restrict the use of the MFN clause to cases referring to the enjoyment of better standards of protection of investment rights, rather than access to dispute settlement mechanisms. Disregarding what has been agreed by the States Parties in the BITs, in the sense of granting "reasonable periods" for national courts to hear investor claims, highlights the imbalance that is also generated by not questioning disputes arising from a breach (mainly regarding the contract between the State and the investor) in a jurisdictional sphere with greater knowledge of the scope and interpretation of local rules and their procedures, regarding the degree of enforceability (or not) on the fulfillment of the obligations of the parties.

A criticism should also be incorporated on the abuse by investors, as nationals of one of the States parties to the BIT, in seeking to achieve greater benefits than those that their States have granted them, turning in many cases, the search for jurisdictional bodies that accept them under the always questionable use of the so-called "treaties shopping". This *per saltum* that investors tend to seek, denotes a disregard for the role of local jurisdictions in dispute settlement matters since they are usually considered as a useless and dilatory resource for the investor's claims against the State. Although in some circumstances, it can be understood as such (the excessive application of administrative processes for an investor's claim or the payment of a judgment), in general nothing prevents local courts from upholding the investor's contractual claim, and in part, this would strengthen the investor's position in future

---

[45] ICSID. Hochtief AG v. Argentine Republic. (2011) para. 66 and 68.

[46] Ibid, para. 86.

litigation before an international tribunal if all the violated guarantees are not complied with. Exercising a "preventive action" for what the local courts would supposedly rule to pretend to omit the clauses of the BITs on the exhaustion of domestic remedies, constitutes an abusive malformation of investment arbitration.

3.3 The Umbrella Clause

The purpose of this type of clause is to include within the scope of the respective BIT the contractual obligations contracted by the State, thus being protected by it. The breach of the contract by the State receiving the investment would imply a breach of the BIT and could generate an eventual international liability.

Several BITs contain provisions according to which a breach by the host State of any of its obligations, whether of a contractual or BIT nature, is considered a breach of the treaty.[47] Thus, for example, in the event of an alleged breach of contract by the host State, the investor has the possibility of bringing two actions: one of a contractual nature and the other derived from the BIT. In addition, the protection of various provisions is sought, such as those guaranteeing the free transfer of dividends and repatriation of capital in freely convertible currency and the possibility of transferring employees of the foreign investor's nationality to the host State.

These distinctions on the scope of protection of umbrella clauses have given rise to a wide production of studies and arbitral decisions on the effects of the so-called "*treaty claims*" and "*contract claims*". However, it is clear that beyond the use that can be made of this clause, in case of doubt about its scope and limits, it always remains for the investor to make use of claims for possible violations of fair and equitable treatment to which he is entitled in any investment in a third State.

In several cases, arbitrators have not been systemic in agreeing on a common point on the scope of this type of clause, however, the most restrictive position on the scope of the clause has prevailed in the sense of differentiating between breaches of contracts and BITs since, in many cases, the responsible parties are not the same.

This has been reiterated in several rulings, among them in the *El Paso vs. Argentine* case, when the court stated that:

> (...) an umbrella clause cannot transform any contractual claim into a Saturday treaty claim, as this would necessarily imply that all the State's investment commitments, even minor ones, would be transformed into treaty claims. (...) it would indeed be strange if the acceptance of the BIT would entail the international responsibility of the State for the foreign investments embodied in the Treaty and make the State liable for breaches of any commitment under national or international law, "concerning investments".[48]

[47] The USA - Argentina BIT (Law 24.124), China - Argentina BIT (Law 24.325), among others.

[48] ICSID. *El Paso Energy International Co v Argentine,* (2006) para. 82. The investor is an energy company with U.S. nationality. It alleged before ICSID that, until 2003, it was the holder of indirect, non-controlling shareholdings in several Argentine entities: Compañías Asociadas Petroleras (CAPSA) and CAPEX SA (El Paso alleges that it held an indirect 45% interest in CAPSA,

This type of clause, although it can be understood in a broad sense or a more restrictive sense regarding the scope of application of the BIT, not any investor could wield such clauses when seeking to apply it by invoking the MFN clause, since the legal framework that regulates umbrella clauses is not expansive to a right to which the investor is not a party. The umbrella clauses, although designed for situations of possible political instability in countries receiving larger investments, have lost the objectives for which they were created, constituting at present a form of legal *corset* that often prevents States from updating their legislation under more equitable parameters and control over aspects of the economy and sustainable development.[49] The incorporation of greater principles of the adequacy of such rules, rather than infringing on the rights of the investor, would provide greater predictability to the agreements between the parties in the future life of the contract.

3.4 Stabilization Clauses

One of the objectives of these clauses is to limit the exercise of legislative competence by the State, by not allowing the State to unexpectedly modify the legislation on which the contract entered into by the investor is based. It is common to find in bilateral agreements provisions that keep the investor under the so-called "*alea legislative*", in some cases in a generic manner, and in others, with an enumeration of the frozen matters, such as labor, corporate or tax legislation, for the entire duration of the BIT, or a limited period. However, due to the constant changes that

---

which, in turn, held 60.36% of the shares of CAPEX); Central Costanera SA (Costanera), in which El Paso claims to have acquired an indirect 12.335% interest; and Gasoducto del Pacífico SA (Costanera), in which El Paso claims to have acquired an indirect 12.335% interest; and Gasoducto del Pacífico SA (Pacifico), where it claimed to have indirect participation of about 13.4% (in preferred shares) and 11.8% (in common shares), respectively. It also argued that in April 1997, El Paso acquired, through another subsidiary (KLT Power Inc.), an indirect non-controlling interest of 12.335% in Costanera. Costanera, a local company engaged in the generation and sale of electricity, with a total capacity of 2311 megawatt-hours (MWh), is the largest thermal generation company in Argentina. It owns approximately 10% of the country's total installed generation capacity, with a plant that has two state-of-the-art combined-cycle generators located in the city of Buenos Aires. In addition, in March 1998, it entered into an agreement with an Argentine branch of Bank of Boston for the lease of a gas processing plant located in the Agua de Cajón field in the Province of Neuquén. For its part, the State had rejected such a position, considering that the investor had not proved that it had such direct or indirect participation. The investor argued that in all these investments it had disbursed some US$ 300 million and that with the economic crisis of 2001 and the regulations issued by the government on tariff freezing and currency pesification, the investor's assets and shares were indirectly expropriated, and that this constituted a violation of fair and equitable treatment and arbitrary treatment by the State. Although the tribunal did not consider that expropriation had been caused to the investor, it condemned the State for the violation of fair and equitable treatment, not recognizing the existence of the state of necessity adduced by the State as an exoneration of liability.

[49] See Gutiérrez Haces (2015), pp. 23–59.

can occur in a State due to internal or external economic, political, technological, or social issues, in recent years modern BITs have made progress in the creation of "readjustment" clauses that seek to reduce the rigidity of the stabilization clauses. Thus, in long-term contracts, it is foreseen that the State may modify the contracts with the investor according to the aforementioned changes, without affecting the rights and investments made by the investor, through a mechanism of consultation and negotiation between the parties involved.

An example of this type of clause is the one established in the BIT signed with Panama which, in its third article, related to expropriations, nationalizations, or similar measures, establishes:

> Neither Contracting Party shall directly or indirectly take expropriation or nationalization measures, or any other similar measures, including modification or repeal of laws, having the same effect, against investments in its territory belonging to investors of the other Contracting Party, unless such measures are taken for reasons of public utility or social interest, as defined in the legislation of the host State, on a non-discriminatory basis and under due process of law.[50]

This type of clause has been widely used by investors when, for various reasons, they were unable to obtain favorable resolutions to their interests in disputes before local courts. In the light of the evolution in the economic and social life of a State, the attempt to maintain "stony" clauses without the possibility of progressive renegotiation according to the reality of the host State, constitutes an arbitrary mechanism that ends up damaging the relationship between the State and the investor, making compliance with the contracts more complex. As a frame of reference in the search for a greater "adaptation" of BITs to the new times, in 2004 the Argentine government exchanged interpretative reversal notes with the government of Panama, to establish more objective and specific guidelines on the implications of legislative modifications that cannot be understood as expropriation.

In this regard, the role played by the *Unit for the Renegotiation and Analysis of Public Service Contracts* (UNIREN), created under Decree 311/03, within the Ministry of Economy of the Nation, which carried out a series of contractual renegotiations with foreign investors that were harmed by the 2002 emergency regulations, should be borne in mind. In this settlement process, some investors withdrew their ICSID claims. It should be a model to be followed by other investors and especially by the States of which the investors are nationals, to understand that the negotiation and reinterpretation of clauses of BITs and contracts are positive facts that allow for greater stability in the investor and the confidence of the State.

[50]Panama-Argentine BIT. (Law 24.971).

3.5 *Expropriation*

Every State is entitled to expropriate property located on its territory, based on an act of sovereignty and law. However, such expropriations cannot be arbitrary. The expropriation to which foreigners may be subjected in this case can only be admitted when it serves a common interest or purpose of the State, without implying a discriminatory or targeted act against a particular investor, in the context of legality and due process, which must be coupled with due and fair compensation.[51] If these conditions are not met, a "confiscation" of the investor's property or rights is involved. An expropriation of the investment may result in the loss of the totality of the invested assets (direct) or restrictions that the State executes against the investor and that deprive him of normal development of the investment, limiting his legitimate rights of economic retribution for the investments made (indirect).

In Argentina, Art. 17 of the National Constitution states that "Property is inviolable, and no inhabitant of the Nation may be deprived of it, except by a judgment based on law. Expropriation for reasons of public utility must be qualified by law and previously compensated". For the Supreme Court of Argentina, the constitutional concept of property includes "Any right that has a value recognized as such by law, whether it originates in private law relations or arises from administrative acts (private or public subjective rights), provided that its holder has an action against anyone who attempts to interrupt its enjoyment, even if it is the State itself[52]".

The country has a law that regulates the expropriation of private property. Law 21499/75 establishes that the public utility that must serve as a legal basis for expropriation includes all cases in which the satisfaction of the common good, whether of a material or spiritual nature, is sought. (Art. 1). In this sense, it is a law that must declare the public utility of the good or goods and also requires that it must indicate who is designated as the "expropriating subject" (Art.2) Within a legal term the State must pay the price of the expropriation.

3.5.1 Direct Expropriation

All BITs stipulate clauses providing for the mechanisms and conditions under which the host State may proceed to nationalize or expropriate an investment since this is the origin and raison d'être of the treaties, which arose as a need to guarantee investors the intangibility of their investment. In the case of the BITs signed by the Argentine Republic, this can be seen, among others, in the agreements with France (Article 5.2); the United States (Article IV.1); Canada (Article 5). The

[51] See Dolzer (1986), p. 42; González de Cossio (2010), p. 21; Herdegen (1994), pp. 259–284; Jimenez de Arechaga (1978), pp. 179 et seq; Kriebaum (2007a), p. 70; Newcombe (2005), pp. 20:1; Páez (2006); Piran (1995); Reinisch (2007); Schwarzenberger (1969), p. 7; Stern (2009).

[52] CSJN. (1935) F145:307.

treaties, even when the syntax varies, refer to nationalization, expropriation, or measures of equivalent effect.

However, the scope of the BITs may be violated when the measures implemented by the States, through the expropriation of investments, dictate legislative measures in which the declaration of public utility is made in a considerably short time and/or arbitrary or disproportionate to market costs appraisals are made. In turn, the declaration of public utility, being subject to a future economic and financial appraisal, without the possibility of objection by the investor, usually obeys more to political criteria of the government in office than for purely public interest or strategic reasons of a State. Investment arbitrations have been presented to this extent, as in the case of *Repsol v. Argentine.*[53] The justification for the expropriation of Repsol's assets was based on corporate behavior that the government described as "predatory". In justifying the measure, the government accused Repsol of not making the necessary investments to ensure production (artificially reducing production), to benefit from the consequent rise in oil and gas prices, and to profit at the expense of Argentina's loss of energy sovereignty. Among the investors' arguments to claim the violation of the BIT between Argentina and Spain, it was stated that it was a "discriminatory expropriation" since the only nationalized shares were those of Repsol, the expropriation did not have an economic consideration and the appraisal had not yet been made at the time the Argentine Congress passed the expropriation law as established in the expropriation law 21,499. In this case, an agreement was reached between the State and the investors in 2014 to compensate the investor for the expropriation.

3.5.2 Indirect Expropriation

The situations in which indirect expropriations can be applied are of a higher degree of complexity, since the investor's assets or patrimony are not being physically deprived, but will be caused by the actions of the receiving State through the application of excessive tax measures, or the application of administrative or judicial measures that become arbitrary.[54] These measures equivalent to an expropriation

[53] ICSID. *Repsol, S.A. and Repsol Butano, S.A. v. Argentine Republic* (2012).

[54] Going back in time, these practices are not recent, so that the international tribunals on several occasions have had to analyze the scope of these measures. Thus, to mention a few, we can refer to the cases before the Permanent Court of International Justice, such as the *German Interests in Upper Silesia, Norwegian Claims,* or the *Chorzow Factory* case, *in which* it has been shown that a State may expropriate assets when it interferes with them, even if it manifests the absence of such intention. These cases, taken together, show that, even if a State does not intend to interfere with property rights, it may, by its acts, render them so useless that it will be understood to have expropriated them. Reference should also be made to the *Oscar Chinn* case of 1934, in which it was argued that a series of actions by the Belgian government in subsidizing transportation to the Congo for a company of which it was the majority shareholder had, by such state action, constituted an indirect expropriation of the British company which had hitherto carried on the business, reducing the value of the freight rates, thus making it unviable to continue the business. The

constitute an autonomous phenomenon to direct expropriation, however, they maintain the requirements demanded to the latter for its configuration. That is why several BITs refer to these possible situations.[55] In turn, for indirect expropriation to exist, the deprivation must be permanent, a transitory measure not being sufficient.[56]

In turn, for indirect expropriation to exist, the deprivation must be permanent, and a transitory measure is not sufficient. This was expressed in the *Metalclad* and *Tecmed cases*, among others.[57] In various cases against Argentina, positions have also been developed on the scope of this type of expropriation. In *CMS Gas Transmission Company vs. Argentine,* the tribunal held that:

---

court considered that the reduction in profits of the British company was due to the general economic situation and not to the measures adopted by the Belgian government, not accepting the arguments put forward by the United Kingdom that Belgium was responsible for Mr. Chinn's losses. ICJ Case *Oscar Chinn* (1934) para. 88h. In these situations, already in the ICJ sphere, it is enough to recall the famous *Barcelona Traction* case of 1970 where circumstances of administrative and judicial measures that would have led to indirect expropriation were analyzed, although in the present case the Court held that, according to international custom, the shareholders of a foreign investment company were not entitled to claim for damages suffered by indirect expropriation and only the company could do so. See ICJ Case. *Barcelona Traction Light and Power Company, Limited* (1970), p. 3.

[55] The BIT with Germany refers to measures that the State may apply against the investor and that (. . .) *in their effects are equivalent to expropriation or nationalization* (art. 4); *or in the case of the BIT with Italy, which expresses the limitations by which the investment "shall not be indirectly nationalized, expropriated or subjected to measures having equivalent effects* (art. 5).

[56] López Escarena (2014).

[57] ICSID. *Metalclad Corporation v. Mexico* (1997). This case involved a dispute arising out of an investment made by the claimant Metalclad (Metalclad Corporation, a Delaware corporation) in the State of San Luis Potosí. Metalclad was the 100% shareholder of the shares representing the capital stock of Ecosistemas Nacionales, S. A. de C. V. (Econsa). (Econsa), which it acquired from Confinamiento Técnico de Residuos Industriales, S. A. de C. V. (Coterin) (a company with a shareholding of 100%). (Coterin) (a Mexican corporation) to develop and operate the hazardous waste facility at Valle de la Pedrera, located in Guadalcazar, San Luis Potosí. Coterin obtained permits to build and operate a hazardous waste landfill in La Pedrera, Guadalcazar. The municipality ordered the suspension of activities in the absence of a construction permit, as the municipality argued that such authority was within *its* jurisdiction and outside of the federal permits obtained. Metalclad, because of this, argued its disagreement, since after processing all the corresponding permits, the authorities assured it that the only permits required were the federal ones. However, when this happened, the federal environmental authorities told Metalclad that all it had to do was request the permit; that it was just a formality and it would be granted almost immediately. Following the above advice, Metalclad resumed construction by requesting a permit from the municipality. Shortly thereafter, it obtained an additional (federal) permit from the National Institute of Ecology for this purpose. On December 5, 1995, more than a year after the permit was requested and construction was almost completed, the municipal permit was formally denied. This denial was motivated by the fact that Metalclad had begun construction before obtaining the municipal construction permit. The Arbitral Tribunal held that the conduct of the Mexican officials towards Metalclad was in violation of NAFTA. ICSID *Técnicas Medioambientales (Tecmed) vs. México* (2003) para 116.

> (...) it could be established that the enjoyment of the property had been effectively neutralized. The standard that many courts have applied in recent cases on indirect expropriation is consistent concerning substantial deprivation of the right to property.[58]

This type of expropriation has had different stages in the cases in which it has occurred, either through acts by the State where administrative or fiscal measures are established to limit the investor's activity or through economic regulations that make the use of the investor's assets unfeasible, depriving it of or restricting its profits. This last cause has also been called *regulatory expropriation, the* terminology used in North American law.[59] It should also be emphasized that the term indirect expropriation is comprehensive of situations known as *creeping expropriation*, in which the activities of the State cumulatively deprive the investor of the ownership of its assets or affect the right to receive from them.

In other cases, the Argentine state was sued by Spanish investors for breach of Article V of the BIT, in the *Aerolineas Argentinas* case for the progressive expropriation in 2008 of the private shareholders to whom the Argentine state had granted the management of two state-owned airlines.[60] In the award in this case the tribunal held that:

> The essence of expropriation is the taking or deprivation de facto or de jure of property rights. There is no doubt that the formal takeover of the Airlines through Law No. 26,466 dated December 17, 2008, was expropriation because it authorized the expropriation of indirectly held shares of the Airlines' investors and the exercise by the Government of the corporate rights granted by such shares.[61]
>
> (...) The Tribunal agrees that taking over the management of an investment constitutes an indirect expropriation, and that there is evidence that Argentina took control of the management at some point after the July 2008 Agreement and before the formal expropriation of Claimants' shares. In the Tribunal's view, this constituted an indirect expropriation.[62]

Recently, in 2019 the Spanish company *Orazul International Spain Holdings SL* has filed an arbitration claim against Argentina under the Argentine-Spain BIT, also arguing a violation of the treaty on grounds of indirect expropriation.[63]

---

[58] ICSID. *CMS Gas Transmission Company v. Argentine.* (2005) para 262.

[59] It had its first glimpses in 1922 when the Supreme Court of the United States established in the case *Pennsylvania Coal Co. vs Mahon* (1922) that, if a state regulation "goes too far", it may constitute an expropriation of private property that must be compensated. However, the validity of this position is relative, since later with the so-called *New Deal* legal process, the American courts practically abandoned these positions, leaving to the discretion of local legislatures the decision to compensate or not, although the Supreme Court in later cases alluded to these positions in cases such as *Nollan vs California Coastal Commission* (1987) and *Lucas vs South Carolina Coastal Council* (1992).

[60] ICSID, *Teinver S.A., Transportes de Cercanías S.A. and Autobuses Urbanos del Sur S.A. v. Argentine Republic.* (2009).

[61] Ibíd., para. 937.

[62] Ibid, para. 941.

[63] ICSID. *Orazul International Spain Holdings S.L. v. Argentine Republic* (2019).

Orazul Energy Argentina generates electricity and sells natural gas at a wholesale level, and manages the Planicie Banderita Hydroelectric Power Plant (Cerros Colorados) and the Alto Valle Thermoelectric Power Plant. Both plants are located in the province of Neuquén. The lawsuit is based on the fact that the Secretariat of Renewable Resources and Electricity Market of the Nation published a resolution that reduced the remuneration received by generators for operating thermal and hydroelectric power plants, which has had a significant impact on different plants and companies, including Orazul Energy.

4 Foreign Investment Treaties and Human Rights in the Context of Argentine Cases

Although every state must respect the international commitments it has assumed to encourage foreign investment in its territories, this State policy or the activities of investors can often lead to violations of the rights of its nationals, protected by human rights treaties. To this must be added the problem of the normative adequacy on the protection of human rights areas such as the implementation of environmental or social policies, access to basic resources such as water, gas, or electricity against the contractual commitments of the State not to alter the rules by which the investor agreed, as it is considered an alteration of the stabilization or expropriation clauses. However, the fact that foreign investment treaties do not establish specific rules on human rights does not imply that investors have no obligation to respect human rights, and these problems are often compounded by the lack of precise rules used in dispute settlement to accept possible human rights violations by investors.[64]

In Argentina, the lack of compatibility between the norms of investment treaties and human rights treaties (e.g. economic and social rights) could generate a "collision" of norms, because the norms of human rights treaties, which have a constitutional hierarchy, prevail over the content of the rest of the international treaties and, at the same time, as it is argued since the rules of interpretation do not apply to treaties with the same object, it is relevant to resolve these differences in a harmonious sense between the obligations of both treaties.[65]

Bolivia, the *Aguas Argentinas* case *(Suez-Aguas de Barcelona) vs. Argentina or Biwater vs. Tanzania*, as well as other environmental cases, such as the *Tecmed vs.* To this we can add more complex problems involving States and investors, such as the case of concessions for the exploitation of non-renewable natural resources in areas inhabited by indigenous communities, which in many cases had already obtained the formal recognition of their territories by the State. These have been the cases (among others) of *Mayagna (Sumo) Awas Tigni Community vs. Nicaragua;*

[64] See Kriebaum (2007b), p. 165; Francioni (2015), pp. 1739–1767; Dupuy and Viñuales (2015), pp. 1739–1767.

[65] Simma and Kill (2009), pp. 29–30.

Kichwa Indigenous People of Sarayaku vs. Ecuador, or *Sawhoyamaxa Indigenous Community vs. Paraguay*, before the Inter-American system for the protection of human rights.

More recently, the interactions between investment and human rights were also developed by arbitral tribunals in Argentine cases such as *Urbaser v. Argentina,* related to the provision of drinking water services.[66] As has been argued by specialists, human rights are objective rights that cannot be set aside by *peer-to-peer* agreements. The principle of party autonomy in BITs is limited by notions such as the public interest and the peremptory norms of international law.[67]

It is relevant to highlight the decision of the tribunal in the *Urbaser case* because it pointed out the importance of the norms of the Universal Declaration of Human Rights (art. 30) regarding the obligations of States not to allow the State itself, a group, or individuals in its jurisdiction to harm the rights established in the Declaration. That is, investors as part of their activity in the State are obliged not to generate actions that harm the rights of people, in this case, access to adequate water and sanitation services.[68]

These situations of complementarity and at the same time of collision between sub-systems of international law has motivated more than a decade ago that studies on the effects and responsibilities of investors in the respect of human rights began in the United Nations. In a first effort, in 2011, the so-called "Guiding Principles on Business and Human Rights," (A/HRC/17/31) were approved within the UN Human Rights Council. As a result of these general rules, several proposals have now been made within the Human Rights Council for a Working Group to draft an international treaty on the obligations of States, businesses and investors to promote, protect and remedy human rights violations arising from private activities (A/HRC/40/48/Add.1).

After the aforementioned case, in 2017 the Argentine State was sued by investors of the U.S. company *Metlife* for issues related to violations of the Argentina - USA BIT due to the decision of the Argentine State in 2008 to modify the social security system, retirement system, nationalizing the process of contributions.[69] In this case, several NGO's from Argentina and abroad have filed an *amicus curiae* before the Arbitral Tribunal in support of the Argentine State, considering that the efforts of the investing companies in the privatized regime were violating the human rights of the workers who could not have access to a dignified retirement in their retirement.[70]

[66]ICSID. *Urbaser S.A. and Consorcio de Aguas Bilbao Bizkaia, Bilbao Biskaia Ur Partzuergoa v. The Argentine Republic* (2007).

[67]Bohoslavsky (2010); Echaide (2017), pp. 81–114.

[68]ICSID. *Urbaser.* para 1195–99.

[69]ICSID. *MetLife, Inc., MetLife Servicios S.A. and MetLife Seguros de Retiro S.A. v. Argentine Republic.* (2017).

[70]CELS (2021).

In April 2019, Dutch investors[71] filed before the ICSID an arbitration claim for breach of the BIT between Argentina and the Netherlands stating the same situations of violations due to the modification of the social security system and the nationalization of the pension contributions process already discussed in the MetLife case.

5 Conclusion

BITs, as legal instruments within international economic law, have revolutionized the world of investments, making possible tools for the promotion, but above all, for the protection of investors in third States. At the same time, for the first time, an investor can have access, through these BITs or agreements between States, to jurisdictional bodies that allow it to raise its disputes *face to face* with the State receiving the investment, without the State of which it is a national having to intervene in its diplomatic protection. This implies a change of consideration in international law and in the role that individuals increasingly play as active subjects in the protection of their interests in the international sphere. According to the effects that certain standards in the BITs have generated in the breach of the agreements by the State, it becomes necessary to conciliate between the States Parties to the BITs, an evaluation of the current scope of the clauses of the treaties, either by renegotiating them or by establishing a more comprehensive reinterpretation of the BITs, allowing them to adapt to the new times. To this end, it would be useful to use the expiration dates of BITs, which tend to be approximately 10 years, to initiate these negotiations. The impact that the legal designs generated by BITs have had, in the face of the necessary modification of public policies or public order regulations, makes it necessary for the State to renegotiate BITs, while at the same time the possibility of excluding certain strategic sectors for the development and national security of the State should be studied with caution and responsibility, especially those that do not have a criterion of reciprocity towards Argentine investors in the counterpart State. The review and greater precision on the concept of investment in each treaty, the establishment of more flexible guidelines regarding the cases of State regulation in sensitive areas of its economy or social welfare (that may be excluded from being considered as indirect expropriations or that violate the regulatory stability clauses), are necessary subjects for a treaty renegotiation process.

Argentina has had the opportunity to appreciate the scope of BITs that did not have clear rules on the scope regulated in their clauses of investor protection guarantees, and the importance of updating those standards with the evolution of national regulations and state practices. A new and adapted investment regime is necessary to be able to encourage foreign investment, but above all that the different governments allow investors to visualize prospects of long-term legal certainty that

[71] ICSID. *Nationale-Nederlanden Holdinvest B.V. and others v. Argentine Republic* (2019).

do not unilaterally alter the conditions of investments and with its consequence of violations to BITs.

Norms

MERCOSUR/CMC/DEC/11/93. Signed on January 17, 1994.
MERCOSUR/CMC/DEC N° 11/94. Approved on August 5, 1994.
MERCOSUR/CMC/DEC. N° 30/10. Signed on December 16, 2010.

ICSID Awards

ICSID. Metalclad Corporation v. Mexico (1997). (n° ARB(AF) 97/1).
ICSID. Emilio Agustín Maffezini v. Kingdom of Spain, (2000). (n°. ARB/97/7).
ICSID. CMS Gas Transmission vs Argentine Republic (2001). (n° ARB/01/08).
ICSID. Enron Corporation Ponderosa Assets LP vs Argentine (2001). (n° ARB/01/3).
ICSID. Azurix Corporation vs. Argentine (2001). (n° ARB01/12).
ICSID. LG&E Energy Corporation vs Argentine (2002). (n° ARB/02/01).
ICSID. Sempra Energy International v. Argentine. (2002). (n° ARB/02/16).
ICSID. Siemens AG vs. Argentine (2002). (n° ARB/02/08).
ICSID. Compañía de Aguas del Aconquija SA and Vivendi SA v. Argentine (2003). (n° ARB/97/3).
ICSID. Continental Casualty Company vs. Argentine. (2003). (n° ARB/03/9).
ICSID Técnicas Medioambientales (Tecmed) vs. México (2003) (n° ARB/AF) /00/2).
ICSID. TSA Spectrum de Argentina SA vs. Argentine. (2005). (n° ARB/05/5).
ICSID. CMS Gas Transmission Company vs. Argentine Republic. (2005) para 262.
ICSID. El Paso Energy International Co vs Argentine Republic, (2006) (n° ARB/03/15).
ICSID. Urbaser S.A. and Consorcio de Aguas Bilbao Bizkaia, Bilbao Biskaia Ur Partzuergoa vs. The Argentine Republic (2007). (n°. ARB/07/26).
ICSID, Teinver S.A., Transportes de Cercanías S.A. and Autobuses Urbanos del Sur S.A. vs. Argentine Republic. (2009). (n°. ARB/09/1).
ICSID Suez, Sociedad General de Aguas de Barcelona, S.A. and Vivendi Universal, S.A. vs. Argentine Republic, (2010). (n°. ARB/03/19).
ICSID Suez, Sociedad General de Aguas de Barcelona S.A. and InterAguas Servicios Integrales del Agua S.A. vs. Argentine Republic, (2010). (n° ARB/03/17).
ICSID. Impregilo spA v. Argentine Republic. (2011). (n° ARB/07/17).
ICSID. Hochtief AG v. Argentine Republic. (2011) (n° ARB/07/31).

ICSID. Repsol, S.A. and Repsol Butano, S.A. v. Argentine Republic (2012). (n°. ARB/12/38).
ICSID. MetLife, Inc., MetLife Servicios S.A. and MetLife Seguros de Retiro S.A. v. Argentine Republic. (2017). (n°. ARB/17/17).
ICSID. Orazul International Spain Holdings S.L. v. Argentine Republic (2019). (n° ARB/19/25).
ICSID. Nationale-Nederlanden Holdinvest B.V. and others v. Argentine Republic (2019). (n° ARB/19/11).

List of All Arbitration Awards on Argentina

https://investmentpolicy.unctad.org/investment-dispute-settlement/country/8/argentina

ICPJ

ICJ Case Oscar Chinn (1934) United Kingdom vs. Belgium, ser A/B, No. 63. Par. 88h.

ICJ

Anglo-Iranian Oil Company Case (1952). United Kingdom vs. Iran, Sentence, July, 22, (Recueil, 1952, p. 2018.
Rights of U.S. Nationals in Morocco. (1952). France vs. United States of America. Sentence, August, 27 (Recueil, 1952, p. 191.
Barcelona Traction Light and Power Company, Limited (1970), Belgium vs. Kingdom of Spain), ICJ Report, 1970, p. 3.

CSJN

CSJN. (1935) F145:307. "Pedro Emilio Bourdieu v. Municipalidad de la Capital".

SCUSA

Pennsylvania Coal Co. vs Mahon (1922). 260 US 393.
Nollan vs California Coastal Commission (1987). 483 US 825.
Lucas vs South Carolina Coastal Council (1992). 505 US 1003.

References

Barraguirre, Manzi (2010) El sistema de solución de controversias en materia de inversiones. Anuario de la Asociación Argentina de Derecho Internacional, Córdoba, pp 145–188

Bohoslavsky (2010) Tratados de protección de las inversiones e implicaciones para la formulación de políticas públicas (especial referencia a los servicios de agua potable y saneamiento), 37 (Comisión Económica para América Latina y el Caribe, CEPAL, Santiago de Chile,

Bonchil (1994) El nuevo régimen de las inversiones extranjeras. Revista Jurídica La Ley 1994-A, p 732

Cabanillas de Cuevas (1982) Derecho de las Inversiones Extranjeras, 2nd edn. Heliasta SRL, Buenos Aires

CELS (2021) Amicus Curiae. 30 de marzo. https://www.cels.org.ar/web/wp-content/uploads/2021/03/Amicus-Curiae-Brief-ICSID-Case-No.-ARB1717_no-signatures.pdf

Chudnovsky, López (2000) El Boom de Inversión Extranjera Directa en el MERCOSUR en los años 1990: Características, determinantes e impactos. D.S, CENIT

Cristini, Bermúdez (2022) La inversión extranjera directa en Argentina: recuperando un factor imprescindible para crecer en un mundo de cambio. FIELD - Konrad Adenauer Stiftung. Buenos Aires

Dolzer (1986) Indirect expropriation of Alien Property. ICSID Rev 1:42

Dolzer, Schreuer (2008) Principles of international investment law. Oxford University Press, p 119

Dupuy, Viñuales (2015) Human rights and investment disciplines: integration in progress. In: Bungenberg, Griebel, Hobe, Reinisch (eds) . Hart Publishing, International investment law, pp 1739–1767

Echaide (2017) Demandas en el CIADI y el derecho humano al agua. ¿Tratados de inversión vs derechos humanos? International Law. Revista Colombiana de Derecho International. Bogotá (Colombia) N° 31: 81–114, julio - diciembre

European Commission (2019) New Mercosur - EU agreement. The Agreement in Principle. 1° de julio de 2019. https://trade.ec.europa.eu/doclib/docs/2019/june/tradoc_157964.pdf

Faya Rodríguez (2008) The most-favoured-nation clause in international investment agreements: a tool for treaty shopping? J Int Arbitr 25(1):88–102

Fernández Masia (2007) Atribución de competencia a través de la cláusula de la nación más favorecida: lecciones extraídas de la reciente práctica arbitral internacional en materia de inversiones extranjeras. REEI 13:16–20

Francioni (2015) Access to justice, denial of justice and international investment law. In: Dupuy, Petersmann, Francioni (eds) Human rights in international investment law and arbitration. Oxford University Press, pp 63–81

Ghiotto, Guamán (2018) ¿Facilitación o protección de inversiones extranjeras? Nuevos elementos del debate global. Ciclos XXV(51):4

González de Cossio (2010) Medidas equivalentes a expropiación en arbitrajes de inversión. In: Rodríguez Jiménez, Wöss (Coord). Arbitraje en Materia de Inversiones. Instituto de Investigaciones Jurídicas, Serie 155, UNAM, México, p 21

Granato (2005) Protección del inversor extranjero en los Tratados Bilaterales de Inversión, 2005, Disponible en www.eumed.net

Gutiérrez Haces (2015) Entre la observancia de los Acuerdos de Protección a la Inversión y el derecho a instrumentar políticas públicas de desarrollo en América Latina. In: Álvarez Zarate (edit) ¿Hacia dónde va América Latina respecto del derecho internacional de las inversiones? Universidad Externado de Colombia, Bogotá, pp 23–59

Herdegen (1994) Derecho de Expropiación internacional y derecho de inversiones. In: Derecho Económico Internacional. Edit. KAS – Dike. Medellín, pp 259–284

Jimenez de Arechaga (1978) State responsibility for the nationalization of foreign owned property. N Y Univ J Int Law Polit 11(2):179

Kauffmann-Kohler, Postetà (2020) Investor state dispute settlement and national courts. Current frameworks and reform options. European Yearbook of International Economic law – Special Issue. Springer, p 39

Kriebaum (2007a) Partial expropriation. J World Invest Trade 8(1):70 y ss

Kriebaum (2007b) Privatizing human rights. The interface between international investment protection and human rights. In: Reinissch, Kriebaum (eds) The law of international relations. Liber, Amicorum Hanspeter Neuhold. Eleven Publishing, Netherlands, pp 165 y ss

López Escarena (2014) Indirect expropriation in international law. Leuven Centre for Global Governance Studies, Edward Elger, USA-UK

MECON (2003) Informe sobre la inversión extranjera directa en Argentina (1992-2002) Buenos Aires 2003. http://www.mecon.gov.ar/cuentas/internacionales/documentos/inversion_extranjera_directa_arg1992-200.pdf

Newcombe (2005) The boundaries of regulatory expropriation under international law. ICSID Rev 20:1

Orrego Vicuña (1972) América Latina y la cláusula de la Nación Más Favorecida. Santiago de Chile, p 17

Páez (2006) La expropiación indirecta a frente al CIADI. Consideraciones para la auto regulación de los actos administrativos de los Estados. Revista Estudios Internacionales. Universidad de Chile. Abril, Santiago

Piran (1995) Indirect expropriation in the case law of the Iran-United States Claims Tribunal. Finnish Yearb Int Law 6:140–247

Podestá Costa, Ruda (1979) Derecho Internacional. Tomo 1, Tea, Buenos Aires, 1979, p 410

Rapoport (2005) Historia económica, política y social de la Argentina (1880-2003). Edit. Ariel, Buenos Aires

Reinisch (2007) Legality of Expropriations. 2007 Vienna Conference on Standards of Investment Protection. Vienna University

Sanahuja, Rodríguez (2019) Veinte años de negociación Mercosur-Unión Europea: Del Interregionalismo a la crisis de la globalización. Documento de Trabajo n° 13. Fundación Carolina, https://www.fundacioncarolina.es/wpcontent/uploads/2019/09/DT_FC_13.pdf

Schreuer (2005) Fair and equitable treatment in arbitral practice. J World Invest Trade 6(3), Geneva, p 356 y ss

Schwarzenberger (1969) Foreign investments and international law. Stevenson & Sons, London, p 7

Simma, Kill (2009) Harmonizing investment protection and human rights: first steps towards a methodology. In: Binder, Kriebaum, Reinisch (eds) International investment law for the 21st century: essays in honour of Christoph Schreuer. Oxford University Press 694, (n 3) pp 29–30

Slame (1981) Foreign Investments. Régimen legal y antecedentes jurídicos y económicos. Edit. Abeledo- Perrot. Buenos Aires

Stanley (2004) Acuerdos bilaterales de inversión y demandas ante Tribunales internacionales: la experiencia argentina reciente. CEPAL, Serie desarrollo productivo (158), Santiago de Chile

Stern (2009) What are the contours of indirect expropriation?. Perspectives 15- 01/09. LASIL-SLADI. http://www.lasil-sladi.org/articulos.html

Tawil (2000) Los Tratados de protección y promoción recíproca de inversiones. La Responsabilidad del Estado y el Arbitraje Internacional. revista Jurídica La Ley – D, 1106

UNCTAD (1999) Fair and Equitable Treatment. Vol III. UNCTAD/ITE/IIT/11. Series on Issues in International Investment Agreements. United Nations, pp 10 y ss
UNCTAD. Word Investment Report. (2020). Word Investment Report. Disponible en: https://unctad.org/system/files/official-document/wir2020_en.pdf
Van Harten (2007) Investment treaty arbitration and public law. Oxford University Press
Vesel (2007) Clearing a path through a tangled jurisprudence: most-favoured-nation in bilateral investment treaties. Yale J Int Law 32:154–192
Ymaz Videla (1999) Protección de inversiones extranjeras. Tratados Bilaterales. Sus efectos en las contrataciones administrativas. Edit. La Ley, Buenos Aires

Christian G. Sommer Lawyer and PhD in Law (National University of Córdoba). Chair of Public International Law (National University of Córdoba and Catholic University of Córdoba). Member of the Argentine Association of International Law (AADI), of the Latin American Society of International Law (SLADI), and Associate of the Hispanic Luso-American Institute of International Law (IHLADI).

Venezuelan Investment Arbitration Experience: From Unilateral Termination of Dutch Treaty, the Denunciation of ICSID Convention to Its Continued Participation as Respondent State in Investment Arbitration

Ivette Susana Esis Villarroel

1 Introduction

In the first decade of the twenty-first century, Bolivia, Ecuador, and Venezuela decided to denounce the Convention on the Settlement of Investment Disputes between States and Nationals of Other States (ICSID Convention) arguing reasons of national sovereignty and considering that the system created by the World Bank privileged the interests of foreign investors over those of the host States.[1] In the Venezuelan case—and unlike Ecuador—this decision was not accompanied by the denunciation or unilateral termination of bilateral treaties (it only occurred with the Dutch Treaty). The Venezuelan administration, faced with the imminent number of cases that would be filed against it, considered that the withdrawal of the multilateral treaty would be a good option. However, reality has shown that this was a circumstantial decision, which has not prevented several claims by foreign investors from being filed before the International Centre for Settlement of Investment Disputes—ICSID (Additional Facility Rules) or the Permanent Court of Arbitration (PCA) to date.

This paper proposes to analyze the Venezuelan position about International Investment Law. With this main objective, it briefly describes the political background in the decade of '90s, the most important changes of the legal system some years later, and the rise of arbitrations proceedings. Finally, the paper shows the actual problems of recognition and enforcement of investment arbitral awards against Venezuela and our reflections about this matter in the future.

[1] Durney (2013), p. 226; Hernández (2016), pp. 88–89.

I. S. Esis Villarroel (✉)
Finis Terrae University, Santiago, Chile
e-mail: iesis@uft.cl

N. Monebhurrun et al. (eds.), *International Investment Law and Arbitration from a Latin American Perspective*, International Law and the Global South,
https://doi.org/10.1007/978-3-031-49382-9_5

2 The Rollback of the Foreign Investment Legal Regime in Venezuela

During the last decade of the twentieth century, Venezuela entered into bilateral investment treaties with 28 countries and acceded in 1994 to ICSID Convention. In 1999, due to an "enabling law" granted by the Legislative Power to the Executive Power, the then President of the Republic enacted the Promotion and Protection of Investments Law—in Spanish Ley de Promoción y Protección de Inversiones, LPPI (Decree-Law No. 356 Official Gazette No. 5.390 Ext., dated 22 October 1999)—with the purpose to offer for local and foreign investors a stable legal framework for their investments and to favor national development.[2]

At the end of that same year, the new Constitution of the Republic was also enacted. In accordance with its articles 299, 301, and 302, both public and private initiatives must promote the national economy, in which individuals and legal entities may freely engage in the economic activity of their choice, except for the limitations contained in the national legal system. Foreign investment is subject to the same conditions as domestic investment and the former cannot be granted a more beneficial regime than the latter. Since then, a lot has happened with the passing of time and these constitutional precepts had not been complied with. In the next part, we will review of the evolution the Venezuelan national and international legal framework in this matter.

2.1 At the National Level: From the LPPI to the Recent Act on the Matter

The 1999 LPPI contained a number of articles whose content was quite similar to the wording of a traditional treaty or bilateral agreement for the promotion and protection of investments.[3] Indeed, this legal text provided in Chapter III a series of rules on the treatment of foreign investment in the country, guaranteeing the substantial obligations that Venezuela—as a host State—offered to foreign investors such as: fair and equitable treatment, national treatment, non-discrimination, most favored nation clause, expropriation under certain conditions, and free transfer of capital. It also included in Chapter IV an article about the resolution of Investor-States disputes through arbitration, provided that an investment treaty was in force between the States involved or that they were parties to the Washington Convention. This rule was subsequently studied by various arbitral tribunals.

On 18 November 2014, the Venezuelan Executive Power enacted a new Foreign Investment Act (in Spanish, Decreto Ley con Rango, Valor y Fuerza de Ley de

[2]Hernández-Bretón (2012), p. 291.

[3]Torrealba (2014), p. 1.

Inversiones Extranjeras)—LIE (Official Gazette No. 6.152 Ext.). This legislation derogated the entire chapter on the treatment of foreign investment in Venezuela established in the previous legislation. The elimination of the minimum guarantees offered by the Republic to investors constituted a serious setback to the security and legal certainty of local and foreign investment in the country.[4] The article referring to the resolution of investor-State conflicts was also abolished, obliging investors to resolve them before the Venezuelan ordinary jurisdiction. It was also included a solution according to which the Republic could participate and use other dispute resolution mechanisms under Latin American and Caribbean integration standards. In addition to this legislation, between 2006 and 2014 other regulations were enacted in economic sectors such as banking and finance, telecommunications, mining, insurance, and capital markets (among others) that modified the legal regime of foreign investment in such areas.[5]

If the enactment of the LIE was controversial, the Constitutional Act of Productive Foreign Investments—LCIEP of 2017 has been even more so (Official Gazette No. 41.310, dated 29 December 2017). This is due to the lack of legitimacy of the legislative body that promulgated it (National Constituent Assembly) due to the usurpation of functions that constitutionally and legally corresponds to the National Legislative Power of Venezuela (National Assembly).[6] The purpose of this legislation is to establish policies and processes that regulate the activity of investors and productive investments in goods and services. Although it provides that the treatment of investment is subject to the rules of predictability and legal certainty and conditions of equality between domestic and foreign investors, it does not incorporate other traditional guarantees such as non-expropriation, most favored nation clause, fair and equitable treatment or full protection and security. It maintains the dispute settlement rules of the LIE.

2.2 *At the International Level: From the Ratification of Investment Treaties to the Unilateral Termination of the Dutch Treaty and Subsequent Denunciation of the ICSID Convention*

During the last decade of the twentieth century, Venezuela not only adhered to the ICSID Convention, but also entered into and ratified several bilateral investment treaties (BITs) with countries such as the Kingdom of Spain, the Kingdom of the Netherlands, France, Chile, Argentina, Switzerland, Portugal, Barbados, Denmark, the United Kingdom, Ecuador, Lithuania, the Czech Republic, Peru, Germany,

[4] Esis (2015), p. 313.

[5] Abadi and García Soto (2020), pp. 1302–1303.

[6] Santana Pérez and Esis Villarroel (2020), p. 696.

Canada, Paraguay, Sweden, Cuba, Costa Rica, Uruguay, the Belgian Economic Union—Luxembourg, Indonesia, Iran, Russia, Belarus, and Vietnam. Of these treaties, two were left without effect: Ecuador's, due to the prevailing policy of that country to leave without effect all conventional instruments of this matter in order to adhere to a (failed) regional project of investor-state dispute settlement (i.e., UNASUR Centre for the Settlement of Investment Disputes);[7] and the Dutch treaty, due to Venezuela's unilateral termination of the agreement in 2008. In this year, the Venezuelan Government showed its position against the ICSID system and the decision of unilateral termination was an intent to stop the registration of new arbitral investment proceedings claiming the violation of the Dutch treaty.

During the 1990s, Venezuela went through a process of public policy and legislative reforms aimed to attract foreign investment in several areas, including oil and gas.[8] At that time important bids were held to explore and exploit important areas of the national territory where the existence of large deposits of petroleum was suspected. The Venezuelan State required capital and technology to undertake this task and, for this reason, once the public bidding process was over, it entered associative contracts (joint ventures) and formed partnerships with foreign operating companies.[9]

However, in the first two decades of the twenty-first century, several changes took place in the country, which led to a large extent, to greater State intervention in the institutional, political, and economic spheres. An exchange control system was imposed for several years; imports of goods and services were favored over domestic production; the currency was devalued on several occasions; a series of subsidies were created for the population which, far from helping it, contributed to its impoverishment; and several companies in different economic sectors were intervened.[10] The reform of the regulatory framework resulted in the expropriation (direct and indirect) and nationalization of foreign and local investments in the country and, in some cases, contributed to the unfeasibility of its operations continuity.

These changes gave rise to a series of litigation in various national and international arenas.[11] It is no coincidence that nowadays, according to statistics from the United Nations Conference on Trade and Development (UNCTAD), Venezuela ranks third on the list of most frequent respondent States (to the date of writing of this paper).[12] In view of this situation, an attempt was made to "unsuccessfully" stop the number of arbitrations against the Republic through various actions.

The first of these actions consisted of the unilateral termination, announced on 30 April 2008 and effective as of 01 November 2008, of the Treaty for the Promotion and Protection of Investments between Venezuela and the Kingdom of the

[7] Guerrero-Rocca (2018), p. 323. See also Titi and Fach Gómez (2016).

[8] Puerta Bautista (2005), pp. 15–33.

[9] Esis (2007).

[10] Hernández (2018), pp. 43–60.

[11] Bergolla (2016), p. 126.

[12] UNCTAD (2020), p. 2.

Netherlands (Official Gazette N° 35.269, dated 06 August 1993). Venezuela justified this decision by arguing that foreign investors were abusing the terms and conditions of the BIT.[13] The Venezuelan authorities did not denounce other treaties. Even though they did not explain the reason, we could argue that the Dutch treaty was the main jurisdictional base invoked by the investors to file several claims before the ICSID against the Republic between 2005 and 2008.[14] However, it should be noted that, according to Article 14(3) of the treaty, investments made within the framework of said BIT continue to be protected for a further 15 years (i.e., until 01 November 2023). And, for this reason, several investors have continued to invoke the treaty to sue the Republic at later dates.

The second action was a judicial request for interpretation of article 22 LPPI brought before the Venezuelan Supreme Court of Justice (Constitutional Chamber). The article states that investor-State disputes shall be submitted to international arbitration, in accordance with the provisions of the applicable investment promotion and protection agreement or the ICSID Convention, only if the treaty provides so. These conflicts may also be resolved by the mechanisms established by Venezuelan law.[15] The ambiguous wording of the Article gave rise to questions as to whether it contains an open offer to investment arbitration by Venezuela.[16]

The Venezuela Supreme Court of Justice (Constitutional Chamber), in its ruling No. 1541 dated 17 October 2008, recognized that the Venezuelan State may submit

[13] Hernández-Bretón (2010), p. 395.

[14] I&I Beheer B.V. v. Bolivarian Republic of Venezuela (ICSID Case No. ARB/05/4) discontinued; Mobil Cerro Negro Holding, Ltd., Mobil Cerro Negro, Ltd., Mobil Corporation and others v. Bolivarian Republic of Venezuela (ICSID Case No. ARB/07/27) decided in favour of investor; Eni Dación B.V. v. Bolivarian Republic of Venezuela (ICSID Case No. ARB/07/4) settled; ConocoPhillips Petrozuata B.V., ConocoPhillips Hamaca B.V. and ConocoPhillips Gulf of Paria B.V. v. Bolivarian Republic of Venezuela (ICSID Case No. ARB/07/30) decided in favour of investor; CEMEX Caracas Investments B.V. and CEMEX Caracas II Investments B.V. v. Bolivarian Republic of Venezuela (ICSID Case No. ARB/08/15) settled.

[15] Article 22 (in Spanish): "Las controversias que surjan entre un inversionista internacional, cuyo país de origen tenga vigente con Venezuela un tratado o acuerdo sobre promoción y protección de inversiones, o las controversias respecto de las cuales sean aplicables las disposiciones del Convenio Constitutivo del Organismo Multilateral de Garantía de Inversiones (OMGI - MIGA) o del Convenio sobre Arreglo de Diferencias Relativas a Inversiones entre Estados y Nacionales de Otros Estados (CIADI), serán sometidas al arbitraje internacional en los términos del respectivo tratado o acuerdo, si así éste lo establece, sin perjuicio de la posibilidad de hacer uso, cuando proceda, de las vías contenciosas contempladas en la legislación venezolana vigente". In English: "Disputes arising between an international investor, whose country of origin has in effect with Venezuela a treaty or agreement for the promotion and protection of investments, or disputes to which are applicable the provisions of the Multilateral Investment Guarantee Agency (MIGA), or the Convention on the Settlement of Investment Disputes between States and Nationals of Other States (ICSID), shall be submitted to international arbitration, according to the terms of the respective treaty or agreement, if it so provides, without prejudice to the possibility of making use, when appropriate, the contentious procedures mean provided for under the Venezuelan legislation in effect."

[16] Hernández-Bretón (2010), p. 402; Schreuer et al. (2009), p. 363; Santana Pérez and Esis Villarroel (2020), p. 704; Newcombe (2011).

to arbitration through an investment agreement or through a national legislation. However, regarding article 22 LPPI, it considered the non-existence of a unilateral open offer of State consent to investment arbitration, so the terms and conditions of each treaty must be considered. In arbitral practice, several arbitral tribunals reached the same conclusion, but not through this judicial interpretation, but through the analysis of the legislation itself in dialogue with the rules of International Law, as will be explained below.

The third action was the denunciation in 2012 of the ICSID Convention, arguing reasons of national sovereignty. Indeed, the Governmental Communiqué dated 24 January 2012 motivated its decision by an (alleged) incompatibility of international arbitration and the right to decide the social and economic affairs of the country.[17] This decision, oriented by the Calvo Doctrine,[18] paradoxically was based on Article 151 of the National Constitution, when in fact such provision allows the Republic to submit to international jurisdiction (judicial and arbitral) in contracts of public interest when its nature so recommends.[19]

Pursuant to Article 71 of the aforementioned Convention, the denunciation entered into force 6 months later, i.e. on 24 July 2012. Subsequently, two days later (on 26 July 2012), the National Assembly issued a Communiqué supporting the actions of the National Executive (Official Gazette No. 39.972), expressing that the ICSID had become an entity that only favored the interests of investors against the sovereignty and independence of the States.[20]

This decision generated many questions both in the academic sector and in the arbitration practice due to the jurisdictional and material effects it has produced.[21] However, we can affirm that the objective of avoiding future claims before the ICSID was not achieved, since the Republic continues to be a contracting party to various BITs, several of which have been the basis for the jurisdiction of various investment arbitral tribunals to date.

3 The Venezuelan Experience as a Respondent State in Investment Arbitrations

Several cases have been filed by investors from different economic sectors against the Republic before the ICSID and the PCA. Given the high number of claims filed mainly since 2011, we briefly analyze the main aspects discussed in these arbitrations.

---

[17] Hernández (2017).

[18] Hernández (2016).

[19] Esis Villarroel (2018), pp. 59–60.

[20] López Ortiz et al. (2016), pp. 1–38; Esis Villarroel (2018), pp. 58–60.

[21] Mezgravis and González (2012), pp. 1–25; Blas Vilizzio (2015), pp. 233–254; Tejera (2014), pp. 431–435; Peterson (2017).

3.1 *On Jurisdictional Phase: The Venezuelan Consent to Investment Arbitration and the Consequences of the ICSID Convention Denunciation*

As mentioned in the previous section of this paper, one of the main arguments presented by the Republic in several cases administered by the ICSID referred, in the jurisdictional venue, to the lack of consent of Venezuela to investment arbitration in accordance with the repealed Article 22 LPPI. In several arbitral proceedings, the argument was presented relying on ruling No. 1541 of the Constitutional Chamber of the Supreme Court of Justice, claiming that it should be considered as binding by the arbitral tribunals.

Thus, in *Mobil et al,*[22] *Cemex et al*[23] and *ConocoPhillips et al*[24] cases, the arbitral tribunals considered the non-existence of the unilateral State offer to investor-State arbitration administered by the ICSID, given the obscure and unclear nature of the wording of article 22 LPPI. They pointed out that the national judicial interpretation is not binding and, in accordance with the *Kompetenz-Kompetenz* principle, it is not possible for such a decision to control the arbitrators' decision. In *Cemex et al.* case, the arbitral tribunal explained that a unilateral state act consenting to accept the ICSID's jurisdiction, must be interpreted in accordance with the Washington Convention itself and in accordance with the principles of International Law relating to unilateral acts.[25] It should be noted that the arbitral tribunals considered the treaty with the Netherlands as the basis for their jurisdiction.

In *OPIC Karimun Corp.*[26] and *Brandes*[27] cases, the investors invoked the aforementioned article 22 as the basis for their jurisdiction. In both disputes, the arbitral tribunals were cautious in analyzing the rule and Venezuela's (unfriendly) track record in international arbitration, especially in public contracts matters. Faced with the ambiguous wording of the article 22 LPPI, the arbitral tribunals considered that it did not denote an open State offer to investment arbitration. In *Tidewater*

[22] Mobil Corporation Venezuela Holdings B.V., Mobil Cerro Negro Holding, Ltd., Mobil Venezolana de Petróleos Holding, Inc., Mobil Cerro Negro, Ltd. y Mobil Venezolana de Petróleos, Inc. v. Venezuela, ICSID, Case No. ARB/07/27, Decision on jurisdiction 10/06/2010, §97–111, §140–141.

[23] Cemex Caracas Investments B.V and Cemex Caracas II Investments, B.V. v. Venezuela, ICSID, Case No. ARB/08/15, Decision on jurisdiction 30/12/2010, § 79.

[24] ConocoPhillips Petrozuata B.V., ConocoPhillips Hamaca B.V. and ConocoPhillips Gulf of Paria B.V. v. Venezuela, ICSID, Case No. ARB/07/30, Decision on jurisdiction and merits 03/09/2013, § 261.

[25] Cemex Caracas Investments B.V and Cemex Caracas II Investments, B.V. v. Venezuela, supra, § 79.

[26] OPIC Karimun Corporation v. Venezuela, ICSID, Case No. ARB/10/14, Decision on jurisdiction 28/05/2013, § 165.

[27] Brandes Investment Partners, L.P. v. Venezuela, ICSID, Case No. ARB/08/03, Decision on jurisdiction 02/08/2011, § 86–91.

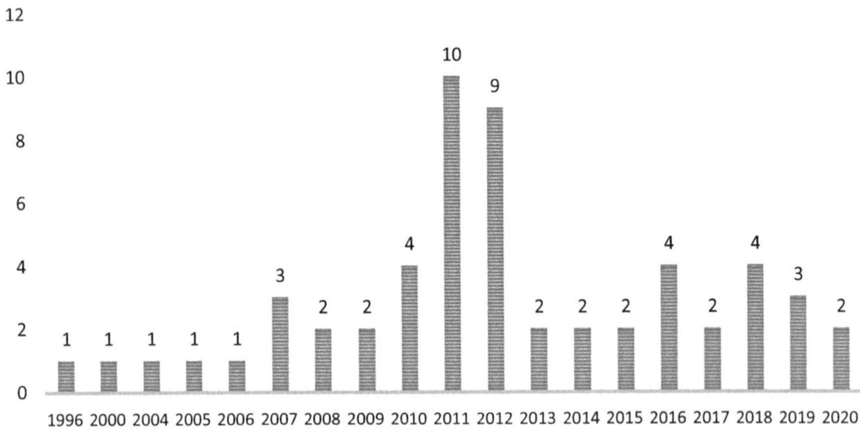

Fig. 1 Cases submitted against Venezuela per year. Source: Author's elaboration based on public information from investmentpolicyhub.unctad.org

et al,[28] the tribunal agreed with the other arbitral awards. However, it made some interesting observations: first, it considered the harmonious application of both the law of the respondent State and International Law and, second, it considered that the State offer contained in the article is limited and not clear enough to be interpreted as a general intention of the special legislation to protect local and foreign investment.

As can be seen in Fig. 1, although the first case was registered in 1996, between 2011 and 2012 more than ten lawsuits were filed before the ICSID against Venezuela. And, in January 2012, the Executive Branch formally submitted before the Secretariat the denounce of the ICSID Convention, which became effective on 24 July 2012. Several cases were registered before the end of the 6-month period provided for in Article 71 of the Convention. And, also, various claims have been filed after that date before the ICSID and the PCA.

The denunciation has raised many doctrinal and practical questions:[29] are foreign investments unprotected by Venezuela's withdrawal from ICSID Convention? Not in principle, especially those protected under the BITs in force. However, in the event of a dispute with the host State and the investor decides to sue: should it file its claim before ICSID, although under the rules of the Additional Facility, or should it initiate an *ad hoc* arbitration under the rules of the UNCITRAL Arbitration Rules? Since the denunciation of the Convention does not entail the derogation of BITs, they are still in force between Venezuela and other countries. For that reason, we consider that the answers to these questions depend on the *case-by-case* analysis of

[28] Tidewater Inc., Tidewater Investment SRL, Tidewater Caribe, CA, Twenty Grand Offshore, LLC, Point Marine, LLC, Twenty Grand Marine Service, LLC, Jackson Marine, LLC y Zapata Gulf Marine Operators, LLC v. Venezuela, ICSID, Case No. ARB/10/5, Decision on jurisdiction 08/02/2013, § 137–141.

[29] Mezgravis and González (2012), pp. 17–18: Guerrero-Rocca (2017), pp. 129–130.

the applicable BIT between the Republic and the investor's State of origin, in accordance with the precepts of the Vienna Convention on the Law of Treaties.

In practice, arbitral tribunals have been analyzing the coordination of dates between the day of filing of the request for arbitration by the investor before ICSID and the date of expiration of Venezuela's consent. That is: (i) before the notification of the denunciation (date prior to 24 January 2012); (ii) within 6 months between the notification and the denunciation entry into force (date between 24 January and 24 July 2012), and (iii) after the denunciation of the treaty becomes effective (24 July 2012 to the future).

In scenarios (i) and (ii), the arbitration proceedings have continued to be administered by ICSID, provided that the request of arbitration has been brought on those dates. This is evidenced in *Venoklin Holding*,[30] *Blue Bank*,[31] *Transban*[32] and *Rusoro Mining*[33] cases. However, it should be noted that the particularities of the applicable BIT may modify the rule explained above. In *Valores Mundiales*,[34] the Republic entered the BIT with Spain on 10 September 1997 and the Spanish investor informed Venezuela of the commencement of the dispute on 09 November 2011. The 6-month period of negotiations under the BIT expired on 9 May 2012. And the claimant filed the claim before ICSID on 10 May 2013, i.e. months after the denunciation of the ICSID Convention became effective. Since the BIT does not prohibit or temporarily limit the manifestation of the investor's consent, the arbitral tribunal considered that both parties perfected their consent to ICSID arbitration prior to the denunciation of the treaty. A different case scenario occurred in *Fabrica de Vidrios*,[35] where the arbitral tribunal declared that it did not have jurisdiction since, according to article 72 of the ICSID Convention, the investor had to sue (and consent to arbitration) prior to the notification of the denunciation of the treaty.

In scenario (iii), investors have chosen to sue Venezuela through the ICSID Additional Facility Rules or through the UNCITRAL Arbitration Rules, as has happened in *Serafín García Armas y Karina García Gruber*[36] y *US Venezuela*[37]

[30] Venoklin Holding B.V. v. Venezuela, ICSID, Case No. ARB/12/22, arbitral award 3 April 2015, § 67–79.

[31] Blue Bank International & Trust (Barbados) Ltd. V. Venezuela, ICSID, Case No. ARB/12/20, arbitral award 26 April 2017, § 120.

[32] Transban Investments Corp. v. Venezuela, ICSID, Case No. ARB/12/24, arbitral award 22 November 2017, §73–93.

[33] Rusoro Mining Limited v. Venezuela, ICSID, Case No. ARB(AF)/12/5, arbitral award 22 August 2016, § 260–273.

[34] Valores Mundiales SL y Consorcio Andino, SL v. Venezuela, ICSID, Case No. ARB/13/11, arbitral award 25 July 2017, S.L. §224.

[35] Fábrica de Vidrios Los Andes, C.A. & Owens Illinois de Venezuela, C.A., ICSID, Case No. ARB/12/21, arbitral award 13 November 2017, §282. Casas (2018).

[36] Serafin Garcia Armas and Karina Garcia Gruber v. Venezuela, PCA, Case No. 2013-3, Decision on jurisdiction 15 December 2014. See also for other interesting comments: Anzola (2016).

[37] Venezuela US, S.R.L. (Barbados) v. Venezuela, PCA Case No. 2013-34, interim award on jurisdiction 26 July 2016.

cases. In the first case, the issue of the dual nationality of the Spanish-Venezuelan claimants was widely discussed.[38] The arbitral tribunal confirmed its jurisdiction considering that the BIT does not limit a Spanish-Venezuelan investor from suing the host State, in this circumstance. And, in the second case, the Barbadian investor invoked the BIT Barbados - Venezuela (1993) to sue on 22 March 2016 the Republic, through an *ad hoc* arbitration administered by UNCITRAL Rules. Venezuela argued the non-existence of jurisdiction *ratione voluntatis*, arguing that there was not a valid and effective State consent to investment arbitration under the UNCITRAL Rules, while the investor claimed that the consent was valid since, due to Venezuela's denunciation to the ICSID Convention, it was not possible to sue by any other means. The arbitral tribunal pointed out that the wording of the article in its first paragraphs was designed for the prior event of Venezuela's adhesion to the treaty and confirmed the claimant's argument.

3.2 On Merits Phase: Fair and Equitable Treatment and Indirect Expropriation as Recurring Claims by Foreign Investors

The first investment arbitration case against Venezuela was registered in 1996 (*Fedax*).[39] In this dispute, the Dutch investor claimed a breach of Article 3 of the BIT (fair and equitable treatment) for the non-payment of promissory notes and penal interest from the dates of maturity on all notes. The arbitral tribunal ordered the Republic to honor its payment commitment. Then, in *Aucoven*[40]—filed in 2000—the arbitral tribunal considered that the Republic had failed to comply with the terms of the concession of an important highway that connects the capital of the country with the main port and airport of the country and ordered the payment of compensation to the investor.

As a result of the regulatory changes described in this paper, several investors have sued Venezuela for violation of investment treaties with Spain, Chile, The Netherlands, Barbados, and other countries. As can be seen in Fig. 2, the Republic has been successful in 25% of the cases (mainly in the jurisdictional analysis phase), while in 11% of the cases both parties have reached agreements that led to the termination of some arbitrations. Claimants have been successful in 32% of the cases related to unlawful expropriation and violation of fair and equitable treatment.

It is interesting to note that the arbitral tribunals have been careful in the analysis of the public interests that the Republic claims to take care (food security or national

---

[38] Anzola (2016).

[39] Fedax NV v. Venezuela, ICSID Case No. ARB/96/3, arbitral award 9 March 1998.

[40] Autopista Concesionada de Venezuela, C.A. v. Venezuela, ICSID Case No. ARB/00/5, award 23 September 2003.

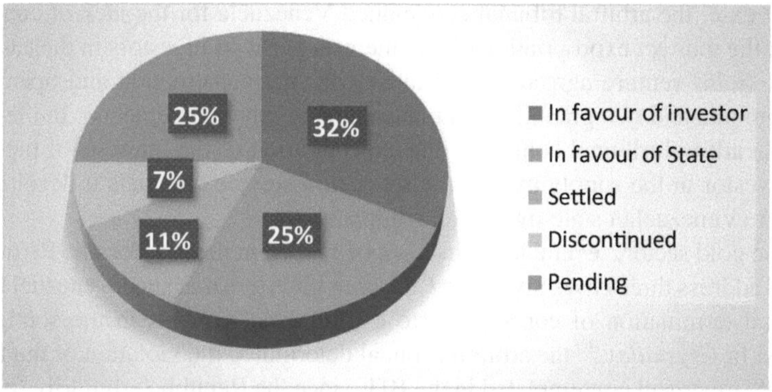

Fig. 2 Status of investment arbitrations against Venezuela. Source: Author's elaboration based on public information from UNCTAD (investmentpolicyhub.unctad.org)

sovereignty over natural resources, among others).[41] However, what has been objected to in many of the cases is the lack of due compensation in cases of expropriation, as well as the arbitrariness and lack of transparency of the decisions issued by the Venezuelan state bodies, which have affected the fair and equitable treatment, in accordance with the BITs.

In the hydrocarbons sector, due to the forced migration in 2007 of the association contracts and strategic associations to mixed enterprises where the Republic assumed 51% of their capital, several investors filed their claims before the ICSID. In *ConocoPhillips*,[42] the arbitral tribunal ordered Venezuela to pay a millionaire amount of money for not complying in good faith with its obligation to negotiate with the oil company, the compensation for the expropriation of its assets in the country. And in *Mobil*[43] case, the tribunal determined that the fair and equitable treatment contained in the Dutch Treaty had been violated, since the States' measures were contrary to the legitimate and reasonable expectations of the investors in accordance with the terms and conditions of the agreements previously signed by the parties. It also condemned Venezuela for the direct expropriation of claimants' assets.

In areas related to the petrochemical industry and activities related to the oil industry, *Koch Mineral*[44] and *Tidewater*[45] arbitrations are illustrative examples. In

---

[41] Hernández (2016); Guerrero-Rocca (2017), pp. 149–152.

[42] ConocoPhillips Petrozuata B.V., ConocoPhillips Hamaca B.V. and ConocoPhillips Gulf of Paria B.V. v. Venezuela, ICSID Case No. ARB/07/30, arbitral awards 03 September 2013 and 08 March 2019.

[43] Mobil Cerro Negro Holding, Ltd., Mobil Cerro Negro, Ltd., Mobil Corporation and others v. Venezuela, ICSID Case No. ARB/07/27, Award 9 October 2014, §273 and § 301.

[44] Koch Minerals Sárl and Koch Nitrogen International Sárl v. Venezuela, ICSID Case No. ARB/11/19, Award 30 October 2017, §7.17–7.54.

[45] Tidewater Investment SRL and Tidewater Caribe, C.A., ICSID Case No. ARB/10/5, Award 13 March 2015, § 103–121.

the first case, the arbitral tribunal condemned Venezuela for the lack of compensation for the indirect expropriation of the interests of Swiss investors in the east of the country (joint venture agreed with Pequiven for the construction and operation of two ammonia and two granular urea plants, among other agreements). In the second case, the arbitral tribunal confirmed the expropriation of the interests of the Barbadian investor in the supply marine transportation service contracts it developed for PDVSA (Venezuelan state-owned oil company).

In the gold sector, several lawsuits have been filed in the last decade. Particularly, we will address three cases involving Canadian investors that sued Venezuela for the unilateral termination of concessions to exploit gold deposits in the south of the country. In *Crystallex*,[46] the arbitral tribunal determined the violation of the fair and equitable treatment contemplated in the BIT, since the Republic arbitrarily frustrated the legitimate expectations of investor arising from the promise of the Ministry of the Environment of the future granting of a permit to exploit the deposits, its subsequent denial and the termination of the contract. It also declared the indirect expropriation of the contractual rights derived from the granted concession. In *Rusoro Mining*,[47] the arbitral tribunal considered that the Republic violated the BIT for not paying due compensation to the investor on occasion of the expropriation of its assets. And in *Gold Reserve*,[48] although the expropriation claim was declared unfounded, the arbitral tribunal determined the violation of fair and equitable treatment due to the disrespect of the investor's legitimate expectations to continue with the concession, due to the State's actions in withdrawing it.

The problems between foreign investors and Venezuela were evident in other areas of the economy. Thus, in the airport sector, *Flughafen*[49] case evidenced the unclear performance of the State authorities in the claim of the Chilean and Swiss investors for the expropriation of the administration contract of the international airport of Margarita Island. The arbitral tribunal condemned the Republic for violation of fair and equitable treatment (in particular, due process) and for expropriation, due to the deprivation of their rights derived from the concession contract. In the steel area, the cases of *Tenaris Talta I and II*[50] arose from the expropriation of the shareholding of Portuguese and Luxembourg companies engaged in this area,

[46] Crystallex International Corporation v. Venezuela, ICSID Case No. ARB(AF)/11/2, award 4 April 2016, §543–546, 705–706.

[47] Rusoro Mining Ltd. v. Venezuela, ICSID Case No. ARB(AF)/12/5, award 22 August 2016.

[48] Gold Reserve Inc. v. Venezuela, ICSID Case No. ARB(AF)/09/1, award 22 September 2014, §579–591.

[49] Flughafen Zürich A.G. and Gestion e Ingenieria IDC S.A. v. Venezuela, ICSID Case No. ARB/10/19, award 18 November 2014, §494–503, §595–597.

[50] Tenaris S.A. and Talta - Trading e Marketing Sociedade Unipessoal Lda v. Venezuela (I), ICSID Case No. ARB/11/26, award 29 January 2016; Tenaris S.A. and Talta - Trading e Marketing Sociedade Unipessoal Lda. v. Venezuela (II), ICSID Case No. ARB/12/23, award 12 December 2016.

without due compensation. Likewise, in *Saint-Gobain,*[51] the Republic was also condemned for the expropriation of the proppants plant, which was built and operated by a French investor.

In *OI European Group B.V.*,[52] Dutch investors claimed Venezuela for the expropriation of two industrial plants for production and distribution of glass containers and the violation of the guarantees of fair and equitable treatment, full protection and security, and equal treatment enshrined in the BIT. Venezuela argued that the measures adopted were aimed at guaranteeing the nation's food safety and that the company had developed certain practices contrary to free-market competition. The arbitral tribunal considered that the evidence presented by the defendant was not sufficient and upheld the claimants.

Finally, in *Serafín García Armas and Karina García Gruber*[53] case, related to the food sector, the arbitral tribunal considered that the state measures of seizure and temporary occupation executed against the defendants' assets, constituted an indirect expropriation. Likewise, in *Valores Mundiales*,[54] the plaintiffs—also engaged in the food industry with the production and commercialization of cornflour and wheat—sued Venezuela for indirect expropriation, violation of fair and equitable treatment, and limitations to the free transfer of capital. The arbitral tribunal dismissed the first claim but decided in favor of the investors with respect to the other two. In particular, the tribunal found that the investors had been placed in a situation of uncertainty due to the initiation of an expropriation process for almost a decade, without any progress in the negotiations between the parties. This process was later suspended, but the state measures prevented the companies from normal operation in the country.

4 The Venezuelan Experience as a Respondent in Claims for Recognition and Enforcement of Investment Arbitral Awards

As previously stated, only 32% of the cases filed before the ICSID and the PCA has been ruled in favor of the investors (to the date of writing of this paper). At present, adding the amounts ordered to be paid in each arbitral award, Venezuela must pay approximately USD 10,492,200,000, as shown in Table 1. This does not include the calculation of interest or future awards in pending cases (if any) and investor-State

---

[51] Saint-Gobain Performance Plastics Europe v. Venezuela, ICSID Case No. ARB/12/13, Decision on liability and principles of quantum 30 December 2016, §415–421.

[52] OI European Group B.V. v. Venezuela, ICSID Case No. ARB/11/25, award 10 March 2015.

[53] Serafín Garcia Armas and Karina Garcia Gruber v. Venezuela, PCA, Case No. 2013-3, award 26 April 2019.

[54] Valores Mundiales SL and Consorcio Andino, SL v. Venezuela, ICSID, Case No. ARB/13/11, arbitral award 25 July 2017, S.L. §582–588.

Table 1 Amount for compensation (claimed by investors vs. awarded by arbitral tribunals)

Case	Amount claimed by investors (US Million)	Amount awarded by arbitral tribunals (US Million)
Vestey Group	157.40	98.10
Conoco Phillips	30305	8366.10
Gold Reserve	1735	713
Tidewater	234	46.40
Flughafen	82.20	19.40
Tenaris (I)	299.30	87.30
Tenaris (II)	243.70	137.00
OIEG	929.50	372.40
Longreef	500	43
Koch Minerals	672.40	325.10
Crystallex	3160	1202
Saint-Gobain	115.10	29.60
Rusoro	2318.90	967.80
Garcia Armas	1155.50	214.00
Valores Mundiales	629.70	430.40

Source: Author's elaboration based on Public information from UNCTAD (investmentpolicyhub.unctad.org)

litigation that may eventually arise in the short and medium-term. However, as can also be seen, the amount ordered to be paid is considerably less than the amount claimed by the investors.

One of the main concerns of the winner investors is that Venezuela would voluntarily complies with the arbitral award effectively. Indeed, Article 53 of the ICSID Convention establishes that the arbitral award is binding for both parties, and according to Article 54 the States parties to the ICSID Convention are under the obligation to recognize them as if they were domestic court judgments. Likewise, according to Article II of the New York Convention on the Recognition and Enforcement of Arbitral Awards, the signatory States have the duty to recognize the binding effect of arbitration agreements and to give full recognition to arbitral awards issued by arbitral tribunals, provided that the case does not fall within any of the grounds for refusal set forth in the Convention itself, either *ex officio* or at the request of a party. Once the award has passed judicial control and been recognized, the enforcement procedure corresponds to the procedural law of the requested country.[55]

The challenge for investor-creditors lies in the recognition and subsequent enforcement of these arbitral awards. To date, several lawsuits on this matter are being processed in the United States Courts, as has occurred in *Gold Reserve,*

[55] Paluma et al. (2020), p. 564; Gaillard and Mitrev-Penusliski (2021), p. 5: Gerlich (2015), p. 48

Rusoro, and *Crystallex* cases, since that the Republic has a series of assets in that country. Thus, in *Gold Reserve*, Venezuela alleged that the arbitral award exceeded the terms of the arbitration agreement, the violation of due process and that such decision was contrary to the public policy of the United States. In 2015, The District Court for the District of Columbia dismissed such allegation and upheld the recognition of the award.[56] In *Crystallex*, the Court also dismissed the argument arguing that the award did not violate either public policy or U.S. notions of morality or justice.[57] In 2018, the same Court dismissed Venezuela's request to deny recognition of the arbitral award in *Rusoro case*, considering that the parties had consented to submit to investment arbitration.[58] Likewise, in 2019 the Court confirmed the recognition of the arbitral award in *OIEG* case.[59]

Once the recognition phase is over, investors face the last and no less complicated phase of enforcement of the arbitral award. The practice has shown that respondent States (debtors) bring in the courts the argument that their assets enjoy enforcement immunity.[60] In the Venezuelan scenario, the *Crystallex* case has been paradigmatic, and its outcome may open the door to other preceding litigations to enforce arbitral awards against the country. In this case, the Canadian claimant has succeeded in obtaining a court order to enforce the award against assets owned by the Venezuelan state-owned oil company—PDVSA—in the United States, under the *alter ego* doctrine.[61] Since Venezuela controls PDVSA, both form a single entity and, therefore, are responsible for the compliance of arbitral awards rendered against them. However, given the humanitarian and institutional crisis that Venezuela is suffering, the Treasury Department's Office of Foreign Assets Control (OFAC) has issued a number of resolutions that prevent the enforcement of awards and judicial decisions on Venezuelan assets in that country.[62] Therefore, the execution continues to be in the hands of the American justice system and the special authorization of OFAC.

[56]US District Court for the District of Columbia, Gold Reserve Inc. v. Bolivarian Republic of Venezuela, Order 20 November 2015. https://www.italaw.com/sites/default/files/case-documents/italaw10201.pdf.

[57]US District Court for the District of Columbia, Crystallex International Corporation v. Bolivarian Republic of Venezuela, Memorandum Opinion March 25 2017. https://www.italaw.com/sites/default/files/case-documents/italaw8579.pdf.

[58]US District Court for the District of Columbia, Rusoro Mining Limited v. Bolivarian Republic of Venezuela, Memorandum Opinion 01 March 2018. https://www.italaw.com/sites/default/files/case-documents/italaw9547.pdf.

[59]US District Court for the District of Columbia, OI European Group NV v. Bolivarian Republic of Venezuela, Memorandum Opinion 21 May 2019. https://www.italaw.com/sites/default/files/case-documents/italaw10546.pdf.

[60]See cases Anatolie Stati, Gabriel Stati, Ascom Group SA and Terra Raf Trans Traiding Ltd v. Kazajstán and Mr. Franz Sedelmayer v. Russia Federation, detailed in https://www.italaw.com. Also see: Volterra and Nistal (2018); Hernández-Bretón (2005).

[61]Santana Pérez and Esis Villarroel (2020), p. 665; Torrealba (2019), pp. 1450–1456.

[62]Executive Order No. 13884 of 05 August 2019, available at https://www.treasury.gov/resource-center/sanctions/Programs/Documents/13884.pdf. See also: Department of the treasury, OFAC,

This fact concerns not only the Republic, but also Venezuelan future generations. The amount of money ordered to be paid in arbitral awards corresponds to non-financial public debt which, only in 2017 reached the sum of US16 billion.[63] Logically, the payment obligation must be honored. But also, as a result of a series of governmental measures and legal reforms, Venezuela confronts a serious socio-economic and institutional situation. Indeed, according to World Bank, ECLAC, and other institutions data, Venezuela has lost a significant percentage of its Gross Domestic Product (−15.7% for 2018[64]) during the last few years. As a consequence of this crisis, according to UNHCR the number of Venezuelan migrants and refugees in the world amounts to 5.4 million.[65] This forces us to reflect on the future decisions to be made. In the matter addressed in this paper, we do not doubt that the debt with foreign investors (creditors) should be negotiated and restructured in favorable terms for both parties.

5 Closing Remarks

The decision to denounce the ICSID Convention did not exactly respond to the demands of a citizenry in the protection of public interests, but rather to political criteria that the former Administration had to avoid a significant number of claims against it. Logically, the change in the legal and economic framework seriously affected legal security and predictability, as well as the property rights of local and foreign investors. It is no coincidence that, as of 2006, the number of arbitration cases against the Republic began to increase. Since Venezuela—unlike Ecuador—did not denounce the BITs with other countries, except for the Dutch Treaty, the State's offer to arbitrate investments conflicts continues. Evidently, these arbitrations are being administered either by the ICSID Additional Facility or by the UNCITRAL Arbitration Rules.

Contrary to what might be thought, the Republic has won 25% of the cases. In the disputes it has lost, the tribunals have awarded the claimant investors considerably less amount of money than requested. In expropriation cases, in many of them, it was not challenging the sovereign power of the State to dictate measures that caused a deprivation of property rights. However, what has been objected to is the lack of due compensation, in accordance with the applicable BITs. And, in those cases in which was claimed the violation of fair and equitable treatment, the tribunals only upheld

31 CFR Part 591 Venezuela Sanctions Regulations of 22 November 2019, available at: https://home.treasury.gov/system/files/126/fr84_64415.pdf.

[63] See Prodavinci (2017) Venezuela: la deuda externa en cifras, at: https://especiales.prodavinci.com/deudaexterna/.

[64] See: https://datosmacro.expansion.com/pib/venezuela https://datos.bancomundial.org/indicador/NY.GDP.MKTP.KD.ZG?locations=VE https://repositorio.cepal.org/bitstream/handle/11362/46071/89/ES2020_Venezuela_en.pdf.

[65] See UNHCR (2021) Venezuelan situation at: https://www.unhcr.org/venezuela-emergency.html.

them when there was evidence of arbitrary and disproportionate action on the part of the respondent State.

The problem now is that the non-financial public debt, generated by the condemnatory arbitral awards, continues to increase and is a matter of concern. Its execution will depend, to a large extent, on the resilience of the winner investor; but also, on Venezuela's economic conditions. At present, given the institutional, political, economic, and social crisis in the country, it seems to foresee that the execution will not occur as soon as the investor wishes, and will require negotiations and a debt restructuring process, in convenient terms for both the Republic and its creditors.

References

Abadi A, García Soto C (2020) Inversión extranjera en Venezuela: diagnóstico y algunas ideas para discusión. In: Libro Homenaje al Profesor Eugenio Hernández-Bretón. Academia de Ciencias Políticas y Sociales, Editorial Jurídica Venezolana, Baker & McKenzie, Caracas, pp 1293–1318

Anzola JE (2016) Dual nationality in investment arbitration: the case of Venezuela. Transnatl Dispute Manag 2:1–43

Bergolla LA (2016) The Venezuela awards: tribunals should not rule out expropriation risk. Ariz J Int Comp Law 34(1):123–133

Blas Vilizzio M (2015) Solución de controversias en los tratados bilaterales de inversión: mapa de situación en América del Sur. Revista de la Secretaría del Tribunal Permanente de Revisión de Mercosur 3(5):233–254

Casas M (2018) When the bell doesn't save you: Favianca and jurisdiction after ICSID denunciation. Kluwer Arbitration Blog, January 5, 2018. http://arbitrationblog.kluwerarbitration.com/2018/01/05/bell-doesnt-save-favianca-jurisdiction-icsid-denunciation/

Durney M (2013) Legal effects and implications of the denunciation of the ICSID convention on unilateral consent contained in bilateral investment treaties: a perspective from Latin American cases. In: Max Planck yearbook of United Nations law, vol 17, pp 223–304

Esis I (2007) Régimen jurídico del contrato de *joint venture* internacional en Venezuela. In: Avances Legales en la Industria del Gas en Venezuela, Serie Publicaciones, Asociación Venezolana de Procesadores de Gas (AVPG), No. 3, Caracas

Esis I (2015) Comentarios sobre la nueva Ley de Inversiones Extranjeras de Venezuela. Revista Secretaría Tribunal Permanente de Revisión de Mercosur 5:295–315

Esis Villarroel I (2018) La expropiación en el sistema internacional de protección de inversiones. Tirant lo blanch, Valencia

Gaillard E, Mitrev-Penusliski I (2021) State compliance with investment awards. ICSID Rev - Foreign Invest Law J:1–55. https://doi.org/10.1093/icsidreview/siaa034

Gerlich O (2015) State immunity from execution in the collection of awards rendered in international investment arbitration: the Achilles' heel of the investor-State arbitration system. Am Rev Int Arbitr 26(1):47–99

Guerrero-Rocca G (2017) In case of fire, please denounce the ICSID Convention: the socio-legal risks of adopting a pro-State approach towards articles 71-72 dealing with sovereign repeat players. World Arbitr Mediat Rev 11(2):129–186

Guerrero-Rocca G (2018) The prodigal son comes home: Ecuador returns with investment arbitration. World Arbitr Mediat Rev 12(3):319–369

Hernández JI (2016) Balances y perspectivas del arbitraje internacional de inversiones. Revista Electrónica de Derecho Administrativo Venezolano 10:69–94

Hernández JI (2017) La experiencia de Venezuela en el arbitraje internacional de inversiones. Lex Latin, February 23, 2017. https://lexlatin.com/opinion/la-experiencia-venezuela-arbitraje-internacional-inversiones

Hernández JI (2018) La apertura petrolera o el primer intento por desmontar el pensamiento estatista petrolero en Venezuela. In: Brewer-Carias A (ed) Crónica de una destrucción (concesión, nacionalización, apertura, constitucionalización, desnacionalización, estatización, entrega y degradación de la industria petrolera). Editorial Jurídica Venezolana, Caracas, pp 43–60

Hernández-Bretón E (2005) Problemas contemporáneos del Derecho procesal civil venezolano. Sherwood, Caracas

Hernández-Bretón E (2010) El arbitraje y las normas constitucionales en Venezuela: lo bueno, lo malo y lo feo, Boletín de la Academia de Ciencias Políticas y Sociales, No. 149 (julio-diciembre), pp 391–407

Hernández-Bretón E (2012) La inversión extranjera de 2012, Anuario de Derecho Público, No. 6, Centro de Estudios de Derecho Público de la Universidad Monteávila, pp 279–311

López Ortiz A, Caicedo JJ, Ahern W (2016) Two solutions for one problem: Latin America's reactions to concerns over investor-state arbitration. Transnatl Dispute Manag 13(2):1–38

Mezgravis A, González C (2012) Denunciation of the ICSID Convention: two problems, one seen and one overlooked. Transnatl Dispute Manag 9(7):1–25

Newcombe A (2011) Arbitration under the Venezuelan Foreign Investment Law – The Mobil and Cemex Decisions, Kluwer Arbitration Blog, January 18, 2011. http://arbitrationblog.kluwerarbitration.com/2011/01/18/arbitration-under-the-venezuelan-foreign-investment-law-the-mobil-and-cemex-decisions/

Paluma T, Esis I, Briceño G (2020) El (largo) camino de reconocimiento y ejecución de laudos arbitrales de inversión. Revista de Direito Internacional 17(3):558–577. https://doi.org/10.5102/rdi.v17i3.6981

Peterson EL (2017) Analysis: what have we learned from the first wave of post-denunciation ICSID claims against Venezuela – and why do investors keep suing Venezuela there? IA Reporter November 30, 2017. https://www.iareporter.com/articles/analysis-what-have-we-learned-from-the-first-wave-of-post-denunciation-icsid-claims-against-venezuela-and-why-do-investors-keep-suing-venezuela-there/

Puerta Bautista L (2005) La inversión extranjera en Venezuela: De las casas comerciales a las compañías petroleras (1850 – 1975). Tiempo y Espacio XXXIII(63):15–33

Santana Pérez M, Esis Villarroel I (2020) Régimen jurídico internacional de las inversiones extranjeras en Venezuela. In: Esplugues C (ed) Tratado de Inversiones Extranjeras y Arbitraje de Inversiones en Iberoamérica. Tirant lo blanch, Valencia, pp 698–719

Schreuer C, Malintoppi L, Reinisch A, Sinclair A (2009) The ICSID Convention: a commentary, 2nd edn. Cambridge University Press, Cambridge

Tejera V (2014) Unraveling ICSID's denunciation: understanding the interaction between Articles 71 and 71 of the ICSID Convention. ISLA J Int Comp Law 20(3):423–438

Titi C, Fach Gómez K (2016) UNASUR Centre for the Settlement of Investment Disputes: Comments on the Draft Constitutive Agreement, Investment Treaty News, International Institute for Sustainable Development, 10 August 2016. https://www.iisd.org/itn/en/2016/08/10/unasur-centre-for-the-settlement-of-investment-disputes-comments-on-the-draft-constitutive-agreement-katia-fach-gomez-catharine-titi/

Torrealba JG (2014) Comentarios al Decreto con rango, valor y fuerza de Ley de Inversiones Extranjeras. Revista de Derecho Público 140:212–223

Torrealba JG (2019) La ejecución de laudos arbitrales que condenan al Estado sobre activos de empresas del Estado. A propósito de la teoría del alter ego en el caso Crystallex vs. Venezuela. In: Libro Homenaje al Profesor Eugenio Hernández-Bretón. Academia de Ciencias Políticas y Sociales, Editorial Jurídica Venezolana, Baker & McKenzie, Caracas, pp 1427–1458

UNCTAD (2020) Investor-State dispute settlement cases pass the 1,000 mark: cases and outcomes in 2019. IIA Issues Notes No. 2, July, pp 1–14

Volterra R, Nistal A (2018) Enforcing investment treaty awards, financierworldwide.com, 2018. https://www.financierworldwide.com/enforcing-investment-treaty-awards#.XsBkXWj0nIV

Ivette Susana Esis Villarroel PhD International Law (University of Valencia). Post-doctoral researcher (Federal University of Uberlândia, Brazil and University Centre od Brasília – PNPD Capes Fellowship). Venezuelan lawyer with managerial experience in private institutions as senior positions in the field of Banking Law and Arbitration Law; and, also, with academic experience as a researcher & university professor in the field of Private International Law. Lecturer in many academic congresses related to International Law and Arbitration. Author of academic articles and technical studies published in Brazil, Spain and Venezuela.

Philip Morris v. Uruguay Through the Lens of the ISDS Trilemma

Magdalena Bas Vilizzio

1 Starting Point: A Legitimacy Crisis

Investor-state dispute settlement (ISDS) is in the midst of a legitimacy crisis. The regime had been profoundly attacked for procedural and substantial issues, particularly the tensions with sovereign powers. Most common criticisms on procedural issues refer to inconsistencies in jurisprudence, unappealable awards, lack of transparency, or the bypass of local courts. Regarding sovereignty, especially regulatory sovereignty, the two main arguments against the ISDS focused on *ad hoc* tribunal powers and regulatory chill.

ISDS legitimacy crisis lays on both normative and sociological senses. In terms of Keohane, "normatively an institution is legitimate when its practices meet a set of standards that have been stated and defended," while sociological legitimacy depends on the acceptance that practice is "appropriate and worthy of being obeyed by relevant audiences."[1] Relevant audiences accept the set of principles of a legal system as worthy to be followed when both ideas coincide. Bolivia, Ecuador, and Venezuela withdrawal from the Centre for Settlement of Investment Disputes (ICSID) Convention or the Brazilian new international investment agreement (IIA) model without ISDS provisions are examples of legitimacy crisis rooted in the Global South.

[1] Koehane (2006), p. 57.

M. B. Vilizzio (✉)
University of the Republic, Montevideo, Uruguay

University of Monterrey, Monterrey, Mexico

N. Monebhurrun et al. (eds.), *International Investment Law and Arbitration from a Latin American Perspective*, International Law and the Global South,
https://doi.org/10.1007/978-3-031-49382-9_6

But Global North has also experienced this phenomenon. In Achmea judgment,[2] the Court of Justice of the European Union concluded that Netherlands – Slovakia Bilateral Investment Treaty (BIT) ISDS mechanism was incompatible with European Union (EU) Law. Consequently, in 2020, 23 members signed the Agreement for the termination of Bilateral Investment Treaties between the Member States of the EU. With nuances, the tendency that originated in the Global South became global.

The legitimacy crisis is fed back by the fragmentation of International Law in different self-contained regimes, as a result of the diversification and expansion of issues that could be under international regulation as well as the prerogative of the States to be part of international agreements.[3] Self-contained regimes are regulation spheres that have their own rules, values, principles and even sources,[4] which are not necessarily shared with the General International Law or other self-contained regimes.

Even though the International Law Commission has deeply examined the International Law fragmentation, the final report[5] presents criteria and guidelines for interpretation of International Law relations with self-contained regimes, rather than resolving the risks of self-contained regimes collision. Investor-State disputes that are related to human rights portray the risks of said fragmentation of International Law: (1) public health *vis-à-vis* foreign investment protection as in Philip Morris v. Uruguay case;[6] (2) ambient air quality standards (environmental protection) as in Renco v. Peru;[7] (3) human right to water, as in Aguas del Tunari v. Bolivia,[8] among others.

In light of the above, the legitimacy crisis reveals that we should rethink the assumption that ISDS global governance, foreign investors' *locus standi,* and regulatory sovereignty (the three vertexes of a triangle) can be attained at the same time. Namely, ISDS regime confronts a trilemma in which only two of the vertexes can be pursued simultaneously. This chapter aims to examine the trilemma and focus on Philip Morris v. Uruguay case as an example of how ISDS global governance and foreign investors' *locus standi* challenges regulatory sovereignty.

---

[2]Case C-284/16, Judgment of the Court (Grand Chamber) of 6 March 2018, Slowakische Republik v Achmea BV, available at https://eur-lex.europa.eu/legal-content/EN/TXT/PDF/?uri=CELEX:62016CJ0579.

[3]Nasser (2015).

[4]Lima (2014), p. 220.

[5]Koskenniemi (2006), p. 11.

[6]ICSID case number ARB/10/7, award, decisions and other documents available at https://www.italaw.com/cases/460.

[7]ICSID case number UNCT/13/1, decisions and other documents available at https://www.italaw.com/cases/57. Even though the dispute is finished, and the tribunal ruled in favour of the State, the investor filed a new claim under the same agreement (United States – Peru BIT) but in a different jurisdiction. Renco II: PCA case number 2019-46, decisions and other documents available at https://www.italaw.com/cases/6179.

[8]ICSID case number ARB/02/3, decisions and other documents available at https://www.italaw.com/cases/57.

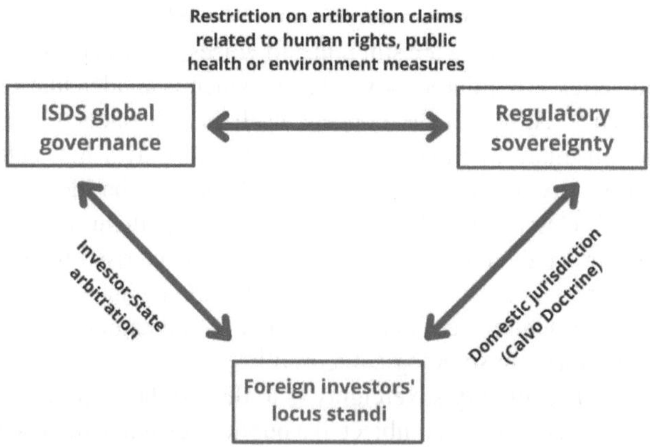

Fig. 1 The ISDS trilemma. Source: author's elaboration

2 The ISDS Trilemma

ISDS suffers from a trilemma: it is impossible to achieve regulatory sovereignty, foreign investors' *locus standi,* and ISDS global governance (see Fig. 1). If States decided to deeper regulatory sovereignty, they must choose between maintaining *locus standi* to foreign investors—mostly transnational corporations—or being part of the regime's global governance—a set of rules and institutions created to protect foreign investments. If States focused on foreign investors' *locus standi*, they have to choose between ISDS global governance and their sovereignty powers. Finally, if said election focuses on regulatory sovereignty, the State cannot deepen at the same time ISDS global governance and foreign investors' *locus standi* in international arbitration.

Global ISDS governance is rooted in a network of more than 3200 IIA (bilateral investment treaties, investment chapters in free trade agreements, plurilateral agreements such as Energy Chart Treaty, among others). Despite the absence of a specific international organisation that governs the ISDS regime, some bodies fulfil different roles such as, *ad hoc* tribunals' administration (e.g., ICSID, Permanent Court of Arbitration, or International Chamber of Commerce International Court of Arbitration), or investment attraction for developing countries[9] and regime reform (United Nations Conference for Trade and Development).

According to Koskenniemi, International Law should not be considered exclusively as a mechanism to govern things: States and foreign investors' relationship. Even though "it is also – and perhaps above all – about constructing a public space

[9] At this point, it is pertinent to mark that development is an objective in developing countries BITs and it has a legal function. Development has never been defined in International Investment Law; although investment tribunals usually consider it as criteria for identifying an investment contribution to the host State (Monebhurrun 2017).

within which also groups whose interests are not well-represented in governance bodies receive a voice,"[10] there are still unheard voices, such as local communities.[11]

The second vertex is regulatory sovereignty, which is an idea that I introduced in previous research.[12] Although the concept itself is still under construction, it is defined bearing in mind the three elements proposed by Krasner: authority, legitimacy and control.[13] As regulatory sovereignty challenges the idea of being limited by its exercise, it is characterised by authority as it is the path through which the State enforces its power. Regulatory sovereignty is also characterised by legitimacy, as it focuses on the defence of a basic set of norms (legitimacy in normative terms) and the support of relevant audiences that accept them as indicators of the behaviours to be followed (legitimacy in sociological terms).[14]

The objective of regulatory sovereignty is to defend the national policy space—the set of measures taken in areas subject to a public decision, which heart is the right to regulate.[15] Since the concept has not become fixed yet, its content is still not well-delimited. The list of regulatory areas included is flexible: environment protection, public health—including tobacco control measures, human security measures, right to water, among others. At a higher level of abstraction, the list should contain all human rights measures. The role of the States is considered essential by negotiating treaties that protect those areas of regulation.

Finally, the third vertex in said trilemma is foreign investors' *locus standi*. The foreign investor is entitled to a *locus standi in judicio* (procedural capacity) and the *jus standi* (direct access to international courts). Therefore, in this regime, the institute of diplomatic protection does not apply. According to diplomatic protection, it is the State of the nationality of the affected physical or legal person, which presents the claim as its own.[16]

The refusal to select only two vertexes is the basis of the trilemma, and it is the reason why the legitimacy crisis is still unresolvable. As Fig. 1 illustrates, in a trilemma, only one side of the triangle is chosen and said selection derives in

---

[10] Koskenniemi (2004), p. 253.

[11] They received investment's direct impacts, but, paradoxically, apart from *amicus curiae* presentations, they have no rights or remedies (Perrone 2019).

[12] For initial analysis see: Bas Vilizzio (2020a), pp. 284–288.

[13] Krasner (1999).

[14] Keohane (2006).

[15] According to Titi (2014, p. 18), the right to regulate "denotes the legal right exceptionally permitting the host state to regulate in derogation of international commitments it has undertaken by means of an investment agreement without incurring a duty to compensate." The right to regulate is precisely what establishes a brake on international agreements so the State does not constrain its own sovereignty. Investment tribunals recognised right to regulate in Parkerings Companient AS v. Lithuania (ICSID case ARB/05/8) and Philip Morris v. Uruguay (ICSID case ARB/10/7). On the opposite side, in ADC v. Hungry (ICSID case ARB/03/16) the tribunal used a restricted approach, arguing that "when a State enters into a bilateral investment treaty (. . .), it becomes bound by it and the investment protection obligations it undertook therein must be honoured rather than be ignored by a later argument of the State's right to regulate" (paragraph 423).

[16] Torroja Mateu (2012).

(1) investor-State arbitration mechanisms as we know them until today; (2) domestic jurisdiction instead of international arbitration—a sort of Calvo doctrine revisited; and (3) restriction on arbitration claims related to human rights, public health, or environmental measures.

The first side of the trilemma is current investor-State international arbitration that lays in a set of IIA that gives foreign investors *locus standi* and *jus standi*. The system has five main rules: (1) controversies are settled by *ad hoc* tribunals; (2) there is no obligation to exhaust local remedies; (3) existence of a cooling-off period before international arbitration; (4) awards are unappealable; (5) there are nor general exceptions for arbitration, not even for measures related to human rights, public health of the environment.

Because of the following reasons, this side of the trilemma mainly relegates regulatory sovereignty: *ad hoc* tribunal powers and regulatory chill. On the one hand, IIA—not Constitutional provisions—usually establish *ad hoc* tribunals that work as external bodies that control the legality of State activity or inactivity.[17] On the other hand, a regulatory chill may also arrive as a result of claims or threat of claims, and it leads States to refrain from regulating, in other words, to stop legislative discussions, to postpone the adoption or the entry into force of new domestic rules, or to delay the approval or ratification of treaties.[18]

Two examples may be illustrative: Pac Rim v. El Salvador[19] and Philip Morris Asia v. Australia.[20] In the first one, the big-scale metal mining prohibition was approved by Congress five months after the International ICSID award rejected the claims. The second dispute shows how regulatory chill could affect third States. In 2012, New Zealand decided to interrupt the legislative discussion on the tobacco plain packaging act as a result of the Philip Morris Asia lawsuit against Australia. In 2018, three years after the award dismissing the claims, New Zealand's plain packaging act entered into force.[21]

The second side of the trilemma joins foreign investors' *locus standi* and regulatory sovereignty but relegates ISDS global governance. The decision paths the way to the reinforcement of domestic jurisdiction to settle disputes between foreign investors and host States. Brazilian experience is a good example of this practice as it was the Latin American traditional outsider of the ISDS regime.[22] In 2001, the

[17] Hernández González (2017), p. 182; Van Hurten and Loughlin (2006), p. 149; Postiga (2013), p. 182.

[18] De Zayas (2015).

[19] ICSID case number ARB/09/12. Award, resolutions and other documents available at https://www.italaw.com/cases/783.

[20] Permanent Court of Arbitration case number 2012-12. Award, resolutions and other documents available at https://www.italaw.com/cases/851.

[21] The regulatory chill could affect national or international regulations created to protect areas of public interest, such as environment, public health, access to water, created to protect human being as a vulnerable subject, in terms of Fineman (2010, 2019).

[22] A typology built for previous research divides States' positions into members, outsiders, dissidents and confronters. For further analysis see: Bas Vilizzio (2019b), p. 4.

Executive Power decided to withdraw from Congress six bilateral investment treaties which were being under discussion. The new investment agreement model—Agreement on Cooperation and Facilitation of Investments (ACFI)[23]—maintains Brazilian tradition: it does not include ISDS provisions, innovates in corporate social responsibility, and provides bilateral institutions[24] to coordinate and facilitate investors-State and interstate dialogues.[25]

Other original pieces in the global cartography of IIA are United Kingdom-Australia Free Trade Agreement (Agreement in principle, 2021) and the Indian BIT Model (2016), but they present differences from the Brazilian ACFIs. The investment chapter in the first one maintains investment protections but does not include ISDS provisions or provide bilateral institutions. On the contrary, traditional ISDS provisions are included in the Indian BIT Model (2016), but to access international arbitration, foreign investors must follow a complex path which makes access difficult or almost impossible. The 2016 Indian BIT Model is still part of ISDS global governance, but its intricate engineering strengthens domestic jurisdiction, resulting in a direct impact on the protection of sovereign measures.[26]

Finally, the third side of the trilemma does not destroy ISDS global governance, it enhances it by preserving regulatory sovereignty and forgetting about the unrestricted foreign investors' international *locus standi* model. The claim for preserving regulatory sovereignty, in other words, broadening national policy space, has different interpretations in Global North and Global South. While in the first it is usually part of the debates for "correcting negative externalities, illustrated by health, safety and environmental exceptions," it is part of constitutional provisions for the South States.[27] For instance: Bolivia, Ecuador, and Venezuela in Latin America or South Africa after the post-apartheid constitution.

This side of the triangle has some antecedents in International Investment Law regarding the exception of tobacco control measures in the Comprehensive and Progressive Agreement for Trans-Pacific Partnership (2015) and the Agreement to Amend the Singapore-Australia Free Trade Agreement (2017). With a wider exception on any measure regarding tobacco or related products can be mentioned the Singapore – Kazakhstan BIT (2018).

It could also be seen as an extension of the proposal of a moratorium on pending ISDS disputes, as well as a restriction on future claims related to health, social and economic measures taken to tackle the spread of covid-19 made by academia[28] and

---

[23]Since 2015, Brazil signed ACFIs with Angola, Chile, Colombia, United Arab Emirates, Ethiopia, Malawi, Morocco, Mexico, Mozambique, Peru, Surinam, Guyana, Ecuador and India, as well as the Cooperation and Investment Facilitation Protocol within Mercosur.

[24]These institutions are not part of ISDS global governance, since ACFI does not include ISDS provisions.

[25]For further analysis see: Monebhurrun (2016).

[26]For further analysis see: Bas Vilizzio (2019a) and Nedumpara (2018).

[27]Morosini and Ratton Sanchez Badin (2018), p. 33.

[28]Columbia Center for Sustainable Investment (2020); Gallagher and Kozul-Wright (2020).

more than 600 civil society entities.[29] Even though both proposals can be considered temporary or intermediate, since they do not solve the core problem, they are still pertinent[30] during this syndemic.[31] Temporal measures could be the kick-off for the third side of the trilemma, thinking of a generalised restriction on arbitration claims related to measures that protect the human right to water, fight climate change, or safeguard public health before the next pandemic/syndemic.

Taking the trilemma in mind, we could paraphrase Rodrik and ask: has ISDS gone too far?[32] In other words, what was the experience in the ISDS regimen regarding specific disputes? For regulatory sovereignty, one of the vertexes, the answer is yes, and the Uruguayan case is paradigmatic. Philip Morris v. Uruguay is a fine example to illustrate the trilemma side effects.

3 Philip Morris v. Uruguay and Regulatory Sovereignty

Uruguay has a late entry into the ISDS regime. It was part of the "No of Tokyo" and in the 90s joined the regional tendency to sign BITs and accessed ICSID Convention.[33] Uruguay has 31 BITs in force (71% signed during the 90s under Washington Consensus [34]) and the Intra-Mercosur Cooperation and Facilitation Investment Protocol (Brazilian alternative model without ISDS). The BITs follow the traditional model in the Investment Law cartography with most favoured nation treatment, national treatment, transparency, minimum standard, compensation for expropriation, State-State and investor-State dispute settlement, etc. Regarding ISDS, 97% of BITs in force in Uruguay refer to ICSID mechanism.

The first known investor-State dispute was the Philip Morris case in 2010,[35] a phenomenon that goes hand in hand with the idea that fulfilment of International

---

[29] ACAFREMIN et al. (2020).

[30] A generalised moratorium during covid-19 would prevent eventual rejection to requests of suspension on a case-by-case basis, as in Orlandini v. Bolivia (Permanent Court of Arbitration case number 2018-39, Procedural Order No. 7) and Glencore v. Bolivia (Permanent Court of Arbitration case number 2016-39, Procedural Order No. 11).

[31] The term "syndemic" was coined by Singer to introduce multidimensional analysis to epidemics.

[32] Rodrik (1997).

[33] In the typology built for previous research, Uruguay is a member of the ISDS regime. For further analysis see: Bas Vilizzio (2019b), p. 4.

[34] Only the Uruguay-Czech Republic BIT was modified and the investment chapter in the Uruguay-Mexico FTA complemented the previous BIT.

[35] Philip Morris is the first known dispute against Uruguay, the first dispute took place in 1998 with Stéphane Benhamou's lawsuit. The indirect shareholder in Banco Pan de Azúcar claimed 103.80 million dollars after Central Bank intervened in the management of the Uruguayan private bank. The *ad hoc* tribunal (Permanent Court of Arbitration) ruled in favour of the State on December 19, 2002.

Table 1 Uruguay in ISDS regime[a]

Year	Case	Sector	Situation	IIA invoked
2019	LARAH v. Uruguay (ICSID Case No. ARB/19/16)	Transportation and storage	Pending	Panama - Uruguay BIT (1998)
2017	Agarwal and Mehta v. Uruguay (PCA Case No. 2018-04)	Mining and quarrying	Decided in favour of State (2020)	United Kingdom - Uruguay BIT (1991)
2016	Italba v. Uruguay (ICSID Case No. ARB/16/9)	Information and communication	Decided in favour of State (2019)	The United States of America - Uruguay BIT (2005)
2010	Philip Morris v. Uruguay (ICSID Case No. ARB/10/7)	Manufacturing	Decided in favour of State (2016)	Switzerland - Uruguay BIT (1988)
1998	Benhamou v. Uruguay (PCA)	Financial and insurance activities	Decided in favour of State (2002)	France - Uruguay BIT (1993)

Source: author's elaboration based on UNCTAD Investment Policy Hub data
[a] The table does not include the cases that do not invoke IIAs, for instance, Conecta v. Uruguay case that was based on a contract between the corporation and the State

Law is a common characteristic of small countries.[36] Moreover, until today, all the disputes involving Uruguay were decided in favour of the State (see Table 1).

Without a doubt, the most famous dispute is the Philip Morris case, a leading case for tobacco control global regulation. The lawsuit was the response to a set of measures taken by Uruguay to protect public health, especially tobacco control. The cornerstone of the tobacco control policy is Decree number 268, dated September 5, 2005, which provides that all closed premises for public use and all work areas must be 100% smoke-free (article 2). Consequently, on March 1, 2006, Uruguay became the first smoke-free State in the American continent and the seventh in the world.[37]

Other regulations complemented the tobacco control policy, such as Law number 18,256, which established the prohibition of smoking in closed public or private places and it limited advertising at points of sale and prohibits the advertising, promotion and sponsorship of tobacco products—including sporting events. The Ministry of Public Health Ordinance number 514 (August 18, 2008) reinforced these provisions that prohibit manufacturers selling more than one variant of cigarette per brand family to avoid misleading descriptions, such as "light," "low," or "mild" (the "single presentation requirement").

Subsequently, the sanction of Decree number 287 (June 15, 2009) and Ordinance number 466 (September 1, 2009) complemented the regulatory map by increasing graphic health warnings on cigarette packages' front and back (the "80/80 regulation") to illustrate tobacco harmful effects. Both measures were taken in compliance

[36] Bizzozero (2000), p. 24.
[37] Vázquez (2009).

with the World Health Organisation (WHO) Framework Convention on Tobacco Control. The agreement is characterised by its high number of parties[38] and because it is the only international instrument that regulates the prevention and control of the consumption of a good whose commercialisation is legal.

President Vázquez (2005–2010; 2015–2020), also an oncologist, internationally stood up against the enforcement of the tobacco control policy. He spoke before the United Nations General Assembly on September 23, 2009, about this. He addressed the necessity to implement measures to improve the well-being of the population since smoking causes five million deaths per year around the world, a figure bigger than that related to alcoholism, traffic accidents, AIDS, illegal drugs, homicides and suicides all together. Thus, the Uruguayan tobacco control policy constituted a partial but auspicious advance in the fight against a phenomenon that could be considered an epidemic.[39]

A few weeks after the end of Vázquez's first presidency, on March 26, 2010, ICSID registered the request submitted by Philip Morris Brand Sàrl (Switzerland), Philip Morris Products SA (Switzerland) and Abal Hermanos SA (Uruguay). In Vázquez words, the lawsuit was a mechanism to intimidate countries that are implementing public policies related to tobacco control or those preparing to do so.[40] The comparison with the fight between David and Goliath was inevitable, due to the power of the tobacco corporation, which in 2020 registered a net income of 77,927 million dollars,[41] compared to a South American State of 3.4 million inhabitants and a GDP of 56,046 million dollars in the same year.[42]

The claimants argued that Uruguay breached Uruguay-Switzerland BIT, particularly protection and treatment of investments, expropriation and compensation, and observance of commitments provisions. Since the single presentation requirement and the 80/80 regulation restricted their right to display the trademarks in a proper form, they considered the measures as an indirect expropriation of seven trademarks without due compensation. Therefore, they claimed compensation of 22,267 million dollars.

During the arbitration, the tribunal accepted an *amicus curiae* submitted by the World Health Organization and the Pan American Health Organization, in accordance with ICSID Convention rule 37 (2). The tribunal's decision was motivated by the public interest in the controversy and the knowledge and experience of qualified institutions. The acceptance of the participation of the two organizations as amicus curiae provided a professional analysis of the challenged measures considering the international commitments assumed by Uruguay to protect public health.

On July 8, 2016, the tribunal—Gary Born, James Crawford, and Piero Bernardini (president)—issued the award. Assuming that the trademarks were under the

---

[38] 180 at the date of the award, 182 at May 3, 2021.

[39] Vázquez (2009).

[40] Vázquez (2010), p. 243.

[41] Statista (2021).

[42] World Bank (2021).

protection of the Uruguayan Trademark Law (Law No. 17.011) the tribunal concluded that "the Challenged Measures were a valid exercise by Uruguay of its police powers for the protection of public health" (paragraph 307). Thus, Philip Morris' investment was not indirectly expropriated. The recognition of police powers is the key element of the award, and it will probably have consequences to avoid future lawsuits from the tobacco industry. However, since there are no precedents in tobacco control measures, the question arises about possible arbitrations challenging other actions also taken in a valid exercise of national policy space, for instance, front-of-pack food and beverage labelling.[43]

Additionally, the tribunal dismissed the violation of fair and equitable treatment since the investors could not have legitimate expectations that such measures are not applied, given the growing global concern about the effects of smoking. For the same reasons, since the actions cannot be considered unjustified or arbitrary, the claimants did not lose the use, enjoyment, and extension of their investment (paragraphs 444–446).

In third place, the rejection of non-observance of the commitments regarding the use of trademarks. The tribunal argued that in Trademark Law, "if investors want stabilization they have to contract for it" as "a trademark is not a promise by the host State to perform an obligation" (paragraph 481). In this respect, the international trend towards greater tobacco control is noteworthy. At the date of the award other States already had measures similar to the 80/80 regulation, increasing graphic health warnings above the minimum established in the WHO Framework Convention on Tobacco Control (50%), namely: Namibia (55%), Ecuador (60%), Canada (75%), Sri Lanka (80%).[44] Other countries had led the way towards the implementation of plain packaging, such as Australia (2012), the United Kingdom (2016), France (2016), Ireland (2017), Norway (2017), New Zealand (2018), Canada (2019), Belgium (2019), Thailand (2019),[45] Turkey (2019), Saudi Arabia (2019), Hungary (2019), Slovenia (2020), Israel (2020), Singapore (2020), Netherlands (2020), Uruguay (2020).

All in all, the tribunal dismissed Philip Morris' claims and concluded that the investors were responsible for the costs incurred by the parties and the fees, expenses and charges (1.5 million dollars), as well as reimbursing Uruguay 7 million of the

[43] The WTO document "Tackling NCDs: 'best buys' and other recommended interventions for the prevention and control of noncommunicable diseases" (2017) proposes cost-effective and feasible "best buy" policies, including health warning labelling, limiting portion and package size, among others. These measures are similar to those challenged by Philip Morris. According to Brewin, it is maybe a matter of time before food and beverage corporations move to international courts. Brewin (2018).

[44] According to the Canadian Cancer Society International Tobacco Packaging Report (2018), the top 10 countries ranked by graphic health warning size (average of the front and back) are: East Timor (92.5%), Nepal (90%), Vanuatu (90%), New Zealand (87.5%), Hong Kong (85%), India (85%), Thailand (85%), Australia (82.5%), Sri Lanka (80%) and Uruguay (80%).

[45] Thailand is the first low-to-middle income country in the world to adopt plain packaging for cigarettes.

10 million dollars for the costs incurred during the process. Putting the ISDS trilemma to work, even though the Philip Morris case was decided in favour of the State, the object of the controversy (public health measures) and the six years of litigation show that regulatory sovereignty was challenged. The system prioritised ISDS global governance and foreign investors' *locus standi*, sweeping away regulatory sovereignty.

Moreover, the next step for Uruguay was plain packaging in accordance with WHO Framework Convention on Tobacco Control articles 11 and 13. However, *amparo* actions filed by national corporations led towards changes in domestic regulations and delayed the application of the new requirements until January 2020—implementation of Law number 19.723. The shift in power from States to markets as far as Strange[46] highlights the growing weight of non-state actors *vis-à-vis* the States. In effect, Uruguayan decision-making capacity was limited, and an invisible brake operated on its regulatory sovereignty, not only in terms of investment tribunals' powers but also regulatory chill.

4 Concluding Remarks

The ISDS regime is going through a legitimacy crisis. Procedural issues, as well as impacts on regulatory sovereignty, are profoundly questioned. In the beginning, detractors spoke of the Global South as a traditional place of resistance to hegemonic regimes. But recent discomfort and confrontation come from both the Global South and the Global North. The fragmentation of International Law fuels this crisis, which derives in investment tribunals hearing cases related to human rights, public health or environmental protection measures. In addition, the COVID-19 syndemic strengthens this phenomenon, since most IIAs were signed at a time when the priority was not the protection of global public goods such as public health or the environment.[47]

Today the ISDS regime faces a trilemma: ISDS global governance, foreign investors' *locus standi* and regulatory sovereignty cannot be attained at the same time, and the selection of two of the vertexes has consequences: (1) investor-State arbitration, (2) domestic jurisdiction—return to Calvo doctrine, or (3) restriction on arbitration claims related to human rights, public health or environment measures. Philip Morris v. Uruguay is a paradigmatic example of the advancement of investor-State arbitration and foreign investors' *locus standi* over regulatory sovereignty, even though the award was in favour of the State. The challenged measures, the six years of arbitration, and the regulatory chill regarding plain packaging confirms the previous statement.

[46] Strange (1996). For further analysis of Strange's ideas from ISDS, see: Bas Vilizzio (2020b).
[47] UNCTAD (2020), p. 12.

At this point, the question is whether it is possible to solve the trilemma. Any attempt to solve it should start by accepting that States must select only two vertexes of the triangle. The second step is to define which ones, in other words, to decide which global public goods are going to be prioritised, and if regulatory sovereignty is going to play a dominant role or not.

References

ACAFREMIN et al (2020) Open letter to governments on ISDS and COVID-19. http://s2bnetwork.org/wp-content/uploads/2020/06/OpenLetterOnISDSAndCOVID_June2020.pdf

Bas Vilizzio M (2019a) ¿Hacia una nueva era en los Acuerdos de Inversiones? Soberanía y reforzamiento de la jurisdicción doméstica en el nuevo modelo de TBI de la India. Revista Iberoamericana de Derecho Internacional y de la Integración 11

Bas Vilizzio M (2019b) Acuerdo Mercosur – Unión Europea: Sombras y ausencia de la solución de controversias inversor – Estado. Fundación Carolina, Documento de Trabajo 21/2019. https://www.fundacioncarolina.es/wp-content/uploads/2019/11/DT_FC_21.pdf

Bas Vilizzio M (2020a) Estado-empresas transnacionales: cambios en el régimen de solución de controversias inversor-Estado y redefinición de la soberanía a la luz de la protección de los derechos humanos. Relaciones Internacionales 29(59):271–294. Instituto de Relaciones Internacionales, Universidad Nacional de La Plata, La Plata. https://doi.org/10.24215/23142766e116

Bas Vilizzio M (2020b) Releyendo a Susan Strange en clave de solución de controversias inversor-Estado. Revista Tribuna Internacional 9(18):1–17. https://doi.org/10.5354/0719-482X.2020.58871

Bizzozero L (2000) Socios pequeños en procesos de integración. El caso de los países del Benelux en la integración europea. In: Mateo F (ed) Los países pequeños. Su rol en los procesos de integración. Documento de divulgación 8. BID-INTAL. Buenos Aires

Brewin S (2018) Food for thought: weighing up health and investment in the age of the new pandemic. International Institute for Sustainable Development, May 14, 2018. https://iisd.org/blog/food-thought-weighing-health-and-investment-age-new-pandemic

Canadian Cancer Society (2018) Cigarettes packaging health warnings: international status report. Sixth Edition, September 2018. https://www.tobaccofreekids.org/assets/global/pdfs/en/WL_status_report_en.pdf

Columbia Center for Sustainable Investment (2020) Call for ISDS moratorium during COVID-19 crisis and response. http://ccsi.columbia.edu/2020/05/05/isds-moratorium-during-covid-19/

De Zayas A (2015) Report of the Independent Expert on the promotion of a democratic and equitable international order. A/70/285. United Nations, New York. https://www.un.org/en/ga/search/view_doc.asp?symbol=A/70/285

Fineman MA (2010) The vulnerable subject and the responsive state. Emory Law J 60(2):251–275. https://scholarlycommons.law.emory.edu/elj/vol60/iss2/1

Fineman MA (2019) Vulnerability and social justice. Valaparaiso Univ Law Rev 53(2):341–369. https://scholar.valpo.edu/vulr/vol53/iss2/2

Gallagher K, Kozul-Wright R (2020) Breaking out of the double squeeze: the need for fiscal and policy space during the COVID-19 crises. Global Policy Journal, June 26 2020. https://www.globalpolicyjournal.com/blog/26/06/2020/breaking-out-double-squeeze-need-fiscal-and-policy-space-during-covid-19-crises

Hernández González J (2017) Regulación económica y arbitraje internacional de inversiones. In: RED: Revista Electrónica de Direito (1). Facultad de Derecho de la Universidad de Porto, Porto. https://dialnet.unirioja.es/servlet/articulo?codigo=6421947&orden=0&info=link

Keohane R (2006) The contingent legitimacy of multilateralism. In: Newman E et al (eds) Multilateralism under challenge: power, international order, and structural change. UNU Press, p 57

Koskenniemi M (2004) Global governance and public international law. Kritische Justiz 37(3): 241–254. https://www.nomos-elibrary.de/10.5771/0023-4834-2004-3-241/global-governance-and-public-international-law-jahrgang-37-2004-heft-3

Koskenniemi M (2006) Fragmentation of international law: difficulties arising from the diversification and expansion of international law. A/CN.4/L.682. United Nations, New York. http://legal.un.org/ilc/documentation/english/a_cn4_l682.pdf

Krasner S (1999) Sovereignty: organised hypocrisy. Princeton University Press, Chichester

Lima G (2014) Conceitos de relações internacionais e teoria do direito diante dos efeitos pluralistas da globalização: governança global, regimes jurídicos, direito reflexivo, pluralismo jurídico, corregulação e autorregulação. Braz J Int Law 11(1):215–228. UniCEUB, Brasilia. https://www.publicacoesacademicas.uniceub.br/rdi/article/view/2069

Monebhurrun N (2016) Novelty in international investment law: the Brazilian Agreement on cooperation and facilitation of investments as a different international investment agreement model. J Int Dispute Settlement idv028. https://doi.org/10.1093/jnlids/idv028

Monebhurrun N (2017) The (mis)use of development in international investment law: understanding the jurist's limits to work with development issues. Law Dev Rev 10(2). https://doi.org/10.1515/ldr-2017-0021

Morosini F, Ratton Sanchez Badin M (2018) Reconceptualizing international investment law from the global south an introduction. In: Morosini F, Ratton Sanchez Badin M (eds) Reconceptualizing international investment law from the global south. Cambridge University Press, Cambridge

Nasser S (2015) Direito Global em pedaços: fragmentação, regimes e pluralismo. Braz J Int Law 12(2):98–126. UniCEUB, Brasilia. https://www.publicacoes.uniceub.br/rdi/article/view/3707

Nedumpara J (2018) India's trade and investment agreements. Striking a balance between investor protection rights and development concerns. In: Morosini F, Ratton Sanchez Badin M (eds) Reconceptualizing international investment law from the global south. Cambridge University Press, Cambridge

Perrone N (2019) The 'invisible' local communities: foreign investor obligations, inclusiveness, and the international investment regime. AJIL Unbound 113:16–21. https://doi.org/10.1017/aju.2018.92

Postiga A (2013) A emergência do direito administrativo global como ferramenta de regulação transnacional do investimento estrangeiro direto. Braz J Int Law 10(1):171–193. UniCEUB, Brasilia. https://www.publicacoesacademicas.uniceub.br/rdi/article/view/2369

Rodrik D (1997) Has globalization gone too far? Institute for International Economics, Washington, DC

Statista (2021) Net revenue of Philip Morris International worldwide 2010-2020. Published by Jan Conway, April 15, 2021. https://www.statista.com/statistics/500455/net-revenue-of-philip-morris-worldwide/

Strange S (1996) The retreat of the state: the diffusion of power in the world economy. Cambridge University Press, Cambridge

Titi A (2014) The right to regulate in international investment law. Nomos, Munich

Torroja Mateu H (2012) Protección diplomática. In: Sánchez V (Dir) Derecho Internacional Público, 315–330. Huygens Editorial, Barcelona

UNCTAD (2020) Investment policy responses to the COVID-19 pandemic. Special Issue No. 4. https://unctad.org/system/files/official-document/diaepcbinf2020d3_en.pdf

Van Hurten G, Loughlin M (2006) Investment treaty arbitration as a species of global administrative law. Eur J Int Law 17(1):121–150. https://doi.org/10.1093/ejil/chi159

Vázquez T (2009) Discurso ante la 64° Asamblea General de la Organización de Naciones Unidas. http://uruguayescribe.com/2009/09/23/discurso-del-presidente-dr-tabare-vazquez-en-la-onu-el-23-setiembre-2009/

Vázquez T (2010) Políticas públicas contra el tabaquismo. In: Revista Uruguaya de Cardiología 25(3):241–244. Sociedad Uruguaya de Cardiología, Montevideo. http://www.suc.org.uy/revista/v25n3/pdf/rcv25n3_7_3.pdf
World Bank (2021) PIB (US$ a precios actuales) – Uruguay. https://datos.bancomundial.org/indicator/NY.GDP.MKTP.CD?locations=UY

Magdalena Bas Vilizzio Professor at the University of the Republic (Uruguay) and the University of Monterrey, Mexico, Member of the National Researchers System (Uruguay). She holds a PhD in International Relations from the National University of La Plata, Argentina. Her current research focuses on investor-State dispute settlement, Mercosur, multilateralism, International Economic Law, and didactics of International Relations.

Part II
Trends in Dispute Governance and Settlement

Dispute Prevention Methods in the Brazilian Agreements on Cooperation and Facilitation of Investments (CFIAs)

Nitish Monebhurrun and Leonardo Vieira Arruda Achtschin

1 Introduction

Brazil is viscerally opposed to investor-State international arbitration.[1] Its first generation of bilateral investment agreements signed in the 90s were never ratified by the local Congress, namely because of the specific transnational arbitration provision.[2] It therefore comes as no surprise that the Brazilian Agreements on Cooperation and Facilitation of Investments (CFIA), a new bilateral investment agreement model signed with 14 States[3] since 2015, contain no provision on investor-State arbitration. Still in 2015, an aperture took shape with the adoption of Statute no.13.129[4] which amended the local Brazilian arbitration law,[5] enabling arbitration procedures against the public administration.[6] This was however

The authors would like to thank the representatives of the Brazilian Ministry of Foreign Affairs and of the Executive Secretariat of the Foreign Trade Board who kindly agreed to answer their interview queries.

[1]Vidigal and Stevens (2018), p. 486; Kalicki and Medeiros (2008), pp. 432 *et seq.*

[2]ICSID (1968), p. 306 (reprinted in 2009). See also: Morosini et al. (2020), p. 304.

[3]The agreements were namely signed with: Angola, Mozambique, Malawi, Morocco, Ethiopia, Colombia, Chile, Mexico, Suriname, Guyana, Ecuador, India, Sao Tome and Principe and the United Arab Emirates. The CFIA signed with Chile no longer exists and its content was transferred to the Free Trade Agreement signed between Brazil and Chile in 2018. It entered into force in 2022. The CFIAs signed with Angola, Mexico and the United Arab Emirates have been ratified.

[4]Statute no.13.129 (Brazil) (26/05/2015).

[5]Statute no.9.307 (Brazil) (23/06/1996).

[6]Wald and de Borja (2016), pp. 21–52; Carmona (2016), pp. 7–21.

N. Monebhurrun (✉) · L. V. A. Achtschin
University Center of Brasilia, Brasilia, Brazil
e-mail: nitish.monebhurrun@ceub.edu.br; leovarruda@sempreceub.com

N. Monebhurrun et al. (eds.), *International Investment Law and Arbitration from a Latin American Perspective*, International Law and the Global South,
https://doi.org/10.1007/978-3-031-49382-9_7

restricted to domestic private-public arbitration and did not foreshadow any trend at the international level as evidenced by the CFIAs signed between 2015 and 2023. This Brazilian traditional resistance echoes the more recent outcry against investor-State arbitration,[7] namely in cases like *Philip Morris*,[8] *Vattenfall*[9] or *Achmea*[10] and more generally regarding the recurrent questioning of the States' right to regulate before arbitral tribunals.[11] The insertion of an Investment Tribunal System in the recent investment agreements signed by the European Union—which includes an Appeals mechanism—acknowledges this backlash. A similar resistance has already been flagged by Australia. [12] The United Nations Commission on International Trade Law (UNCITRAL) has joined the movement in entrusting its Working Group III to address the issue of dispute settlement reform in international investment law.[13] The concerns discussed by the Working Group III were divided in three groups ("consistency, coherence, predictability and correctness of arbitral decisions by ISDS tribunals; arbitrators/decision makers; and costs and duration"[14]) which commentators have categorised as "(1) excessive legal costs; (2) duration of proceedings; (3) legal consistency; (4) decisional correctness; (5) arbitral diversity; and (6) arbitral independence and impartiality".[15] These concerns are real and must conspicuously be addressed although it seems that they have been raised because many capital exporting countries are now facing more arbitration procedures wherein their right to regulate is being questioned by foreign investors.

If States which, until recently, did not consider investment arbitration as *problematic* are now longing for reform,[16] it would be fair to say that Brazil's position has always been coherent in this regard. Its known skepticism[17] has in fact remained untouched. Arbitration is provided for in its CFIAs but is restricted to disputes between the investor's host and home State.[18] The noteworthy aspect of the

[7] Nolan (2015), pp. 429–445; Weghmann and Hall (2021), pp. 1–17.

[8] Philip Morris v. Uruguay. ICSID ARB. 10/7 (08/07/2016). For a case comment, see: Zarra (2017), pp. 96–120; Voon and Mitchell (2012), pp. 137–172.

[9] Vattenfall AB and others v. Germany. ICSID Case no. ARB/12/12. See also: Damjanovic and Quirico (2019), pp. 102 *et seq.*

[10] Slowakische Republik v. Achmea BV. CJEU. Case C-284/16 (06/03/2018). Para. 60.

[11] See generally: Titi (2014), 376 p. See also the contribution of Magdalena Bas in this book.

[12] Kurtz (2012), pp. 65–86.

[13] UNCITRAL (2017) Report of the United Nations Commission on International Trade Law Fiftieth Session. A/72/17: para. 264. See also: Langford et al. (2020), p. 167.

[14] UNCITRAL (2018) Possible Reform of Investor-State Dispute Settlement. A/CN.9/WG.III/WP.149. para. 8.

[15] Langford et al. (2020), p. 171.

[16] Monebhurrun (2015), pp. 12–14.

[17] Monebhurrun (2019), p. 71.

[18] CFIA Brazil/India (2020), art. 19; CFIA Brazil/Morocco (2019), art. 20; CFIA Brazil/Colombia (2015), art. 23; CFIA Brazil/Chile (2015), art. 25; CFIA Brazil/Ethiopia (2018), art. 24; CFIA Brazil/Suriname (2018), art. 25; CFIA Brazil/Guyana (2018), art. 25; CFIA Brazil/United Arab Emirates (2019), 25; CFIA Brazil/Ecuador (2019), art. 25; CFIA Brazil/Mexico (2015), art. 19;

CFIAs dispute settlement mechanism is the dispute prevention governance due to be activated upstream. If public information is not yet available on this mechanism, the latter is already on call given that three CFIAs have been ratified.[19] It is only a matter of time for it to start being used constantly and consistently by the parties. This dispute avoidance mechanism will operate by the means of two main bodies instituted by the CFIAs: The Joint Committee ('Comitê Conjunto', in Portuguese) and the Ombudsperson ('Ponto Focal', in Portuguese).

The main concerned actors, States, and investors, as well as other stakeholders must anticipate the operations of these bodies. Brazil, which is new to this world of International Investment Law, must also prepare its administration, its institutions, and civil servants to deal with foreign investors via the Joint Committee and the Ombudsperson to avoid unnecessary future controversies. The prevention mechanism is namely designed to mitigate dispute and should conspicuously not be the cause of future misunderstanding between the parties. For this reason, the dispute avoidance machinery must be duly oiled before being tested. This can be done by anticipating some technical contingencies related to both the Joint Committee and the Ombudsperson.

It is in this vein that this article critically presents and discusses the CFIAs' dispute prevention governance with the aim of highlighting its potential—namely for other States who are interested in understanding the Brazilian model—, while alerting on its grey areas. The CFIA bears some originality in professionalizing the dispute prevention mechanism through the operations of the aforementioned bodies. Brazil's intention and objective to consolidate the dispute prevention framework was confirmed during the interviews which the authors conducted with both the Ombudsperson (Executive Secretariat of the Foreign Trade Board—CAMEX) and the Brazilian Ministry of Foreign Affairs under whose aegis the Joint Committees will operate. The main argument addressed to uphold the observed professionalization of dispute prevention will be twofold: the CFIAs' dispute prevention mechanism has put together a multi-layered dialogue method for dispute avoidance (Sect. 2) with a specific procedural organization which bestows a quasi-jurisdictional function on the Joint Committee (Sect. 3).

2 A Multi-layered Dialogue Method for Dispute Prevention

The prevention of disputes hints at the '**cooperation**' element of the **Cooperation** and Facilitation of Investments Agreements. Cooperation is based on dialogue and the latter acts as the cornerstone of the CFIAs dispute prevention mechanism. This dialogue operates in layers, the main layers and the secondary ones. In the main

---

CFIA Brazil/Mozambique (2015), art. 15 (6); CFIA Brazil/Angola (2015), art. 15 (6); CFIA Brazil/Malawi (2015) art. 13 (6).

[19]The CFIA with Angola, Mexico and the United Arab Emirates.

layers, a dispute prevention governance is provided for through a dialogical articulation between the CFIAs Joint Committees and Ombudspersons (Sect. 2.1). In the secondary layers, the main dispute prevention governance body integrates other stakeholders to the dialogue (Sect. 2.2).

2.1 The Main Layers: The Dispute Prevention Governance Organized Through a Dialogical Articulation Between the CFIAs Joint Committees and Ombudspersons

All CFIAs institute a Joint Committee and an Ombudsperson.[20] This practice is not new. South Korea, for instance, holds an Office of the Foreign Investment Ombudsperson (OFIO), which is part of the so-called Home Doctor System.[21] In their bilateral investment agreement signed in 2016, Morocco and Nigeria also instituted a Joint Committee for—amongst others—the friendly settlement of disputes.[22] The essence of such institutions is to knit transparent and friendly relations with foreign investors with the objective of minimizing disputes and misunderstandings. This is in line with UNCTAD's guideline to diversify dispute management processes.[23] An expected consequence is the non-systematic association of international investment law to arbitration and to an underlying (supposed) permanent tension between States and foreign investors. These institutions are therefore also helpful to raise public awareness and understanding of international investment protection law. The CFIAs' Joint Committee and Ombudsperson have been created with a series of missions amongst which dispute management is central. Their future practice is being eagerly and impatiently awaited in Brazil. They have been respectively described elsewhere as the dialogue coordinator for the first and as the dialogue facilitator for the second.[24] If the Joint Committee has been bestowed with a quasi-jurisdictional function, as this shall be addressed in Sect. 3, it has also been granted a policy function in the governance of dispute prevention (Sect. 2.1.1) and under this title it is expected to complement the administrative function conferred to the Ombudsperson (Sect. 2.1.2).

---

[20] CFIA Brazil/India (2020), art. 13, art. 14; CFIA Brazil/Morocco (2019), art. 14, art. 15; CFIA Brazil/Colombia (2015), art. 16, art. 17; CFIA Brazil/Chile (2015), art. 18, art. 19; CFIA Brazil/Ethiopia (2018), art. 17, art. 18; CFIA Brazil/Suriname (2018), art. 18, art. 19; CFIA Brazil/Guyana (2018), art. 18, art. 19; CFIA Brazil/United Arab Emirates (2019), art. 18, art. 19; CFIA Brazil/Ecuador (2019), art. 18, art. 19; CFIA Brazil/Mexico (2015), art. 14, art. 15; CFIA Brazil/Mozambique (2015), art. 4, art. 5; CFIA Brazil/Angola (2015), art. 4, art. 5; CFIA Brazil/Malawi (2015) art. 3, art. 4. The CFIA with Angola and Mexico.

[21] Nicolas et al. (2013), p. 24 [available at: https://doi.org/10.1787/5k4376zqcpf1-en].

[22] BIT Morocco/Nigeria (03/12/2016), art. 4.

[23] UNCTAD (2010) Investor–State Disputes: Prevention and Alternatives to Arbitration. UNCTAD Series on International Investment Policies for Development, 28–30.

[24] Monebhurrun (2017), pp. 84 *et seq.*

2.1.1 The Joint Committee's Policy Function in Dispute Prevention

The Joint Committees will be composed of representants of the States parties to a CFIA and shall operate with a rotating presidency.[25] Their main functions rest in a political and diplomatic nest aimed at monitoring the agreements application while discussing investment policies to stimulate investment flows.[26] On other grounds, the Committees also offer political and diplomatic support in terms of dispute management. The CFIA between Brazil and India states, for example, that one of the responsibilities of the instituted Joint Committee is to "discuss issues and seek to resolve disputes concerning investments of investors of a Party in an amicable manner[27]".

Owing to a functional duplication logic, the Joint Committees' participation in the dispute management system is, it is argued, twofold. As mentioned, they have been expressly granted a quasi-jurisdictional function, with a specific procedure and deadlines, in matters of dispute prevention.[28] At the upstream, it can be inferred that they also have an implicit competence to prevent disputes on political and diplomatic grounds. It is not a trivial choice if, in Brazil, the Joint Committees act under the aegis of the Ministry of Foreign Affairs. This competence is policy oriented. The main idea in the background of this argument is that all policy measures adopted to improve transparency in the investor-State operations are likely to better calibrate the investors' expectations and thus reduce the risk of disputes. For such purposes, the Joint Committees have the power to issue recommendations to the Ombudsperson[29] which must relate to the Joint Committees' statutory competences. As dispute prevention is not only a pedestal of the CFIAs' architecture but also an ingredient of their general philosophy, the subject matter will undoubtedly be the object of at least one recommendation—considering that the Ombudsperson is the other pole of the dispute prevention governance mechanism. And in general, any recommendation aiming at governing the investor-State relationship, through greater access to information for instance, will have a positive impact on dispute reduction. Therefore, more proactivity in facilitating the investors' local integration and in

[25]CFIA Brazil/India (2020), art. 13; CFIA Brazil/Morocco (2019), art. 14; CFIA Brazil/Colombia (2015), art. 16; CFIA Brazil/Chile (2015), art. 18; CFIA Brazil/Ethiopia (2018), art. 17; CFIA Brazil/Suriname (2018), art. 18; CFIA Brazil/Guyana (2018), art. 18; CFIA Brazil/United Arab Emirates (2019), art. 18; CFIA Brazil/Ecuador (2019), art. 18; CFIA Brazil/Mexico (2015), art. 14; CFIA Brazil/Mozambique (2015), art. 4; CFIA Brazil/Angola (2015), art. 4; CFIA Brazil/Malawi (2015) art. 3.

[26]CFIA Brazil/India (2020), art. 13; CFIA Brazil/Morocco (2019), art. 14; CFIA Brazil/Colombia (2015), art. 16; CFIA Brazil/Chile (2015), art. 18; CFIA Brazil/Ethiopia (2018), art. 17; CFIA Brazil/Suriname (2018), art. 18; CFIA Brazil/Guyana (2018), art. 18; CFIA Brazil/United Arab Emirates (2019), art. 18; CFIA Brazil/Ecuador (2019), art. 18; CFIA Brazil/Mexico (2015), art. 14; CFIA Brazil/Mozambique (2015), art. 4; CFIA Brazil/Angola (2015), art. 4; CFIA Brazil/Malawi (2015) art. 3.

[27]CFIA Brazil/India (2020), art. 13.4(e).

[28]This will be further discussed in Sect. 3.

[29]For instance: CFIA Brazil/India (2020), art. 14.4 (a).

ensuring their adaptation to the local business mores does have an indirect influence in narrowing the margin of potential disputes.

In a similar vein, noteworthy is the possibility given to the Committees to establish *ad hoc* working groups to assist them in their work.[30] Working Groups are established with the aim of gathering expertise on specific topics and complex questions. Composed of specialists, they can be of a variable duration and are meant to shed light on a curtailed problematic issue or to monitor an ongoing debate or negotiation. Working groups are a common feature of the practical work of international organizations.[31] For instance (and to remain within the area of international economic law), the UNCITRAL's Working Group III was instituted and given a "broad mandate to work on the possible reform of investor-State dispute settlement".[32] UNCITRAL's working group II focused on arbitration and conciliation, working group I examined the issue of micro, small and medium-sized enterprises.[33] Similarly, the possibility offered to the Joint Committees to confer given missions to working groups are meant to enshrine the Committees' political attributions in a technical background. The working groups will support the committees' tasks and findings through its technical inputs. When established, these working groups and their insight on the investor-State relationship will help the dispute prevention agenda in at least two ways. Firstly, they may be mandated to produce an advisory opinion on dispute prevention as such. Secondly, and as mentioned, their technical advice on consolidating the investor-State relations will be used by the State as an input with the prospective and indirect result of abating tensions with the foreign investors. The instituted working groups will have the possibility of inviting the investors to participate in their work.[34] Maintaining the investors close to the State is a tactic of the CFIAs' dispute prevention mechanism which finds an echo in the administrative function of the Ombudsperson therein.

2.1.2 The Ombudsperson's Administrative Function in Dispute Prevention

In mainstream arbitration procedures, investors have sometimes sued developing States alleging unfair and unequitable treatment because of a lack of coherence, consistency, predictability, or transparency of the States' administration.[35] Even

[30] CFIA Brazil/India (2020), art. 13.4.

[31] Beate (2000), pp. 296 *et seq.*

[32] UNCITRAL (2021) Report of the United Nations Commission on International Trade Law Fifty Fourth Session. A/72/17: 2.

[33] UNCITRAL's working groups can be found at: https://uncitral.un.org/en/working_groups.

[34] CFIA Brazil/India (2020), art. 13.5.

[35] See for example: Metalclad Corporation v. The United Mexican States (30/08/2000), ICSID Case No. ARB (AF)/97/1; Waste Management Inc. v. United Mexican States, (30/04/2004) ICSID Case No. ARB (AF)/00/3; MTD Equity Sdn. Bhd. and MTD Chile S.A. v. Republic of Chile, ICSID Case No. ARB/01/7, (25/05/2004);CMS Gas Transmission Company v. Argentina, Final Award, (25/05/

though the CFIAs do not, as such, make provision for fair and equitable treatment,[36] all CFIAs uphold the need for transparency in the investor-State relationship,[37] be it in their preamble or in their very provisions. The Ombudsperson, as provided for by the CFIAs, is the potential conveyor of transparency. It has been instituted to bring flesh to the concept thereby fulfilling the equation as per which more transparency is equivalent to reducing the risk of disputes. In Brazil, the Ombudsperson has its seat at the Executive Secretariat of the Foreign Trade Board (CAMEX). The CFIAs' Ombudsperson is an articulator. Acting as a hyphen between one and the other, it is supposed to bring together the foreign investor and the State for day-to-day issues. Should the foreign investor have any doubts or any lack of knowledge and/or information regarding the legal and administrative aspects/status of its operations, enquiries can be submitted to the Ombudsperson, the latter having an obligation to inform back the investor[38]—obviously, on the understanding that the information given be precise, relevant and useful.[39] Brazil being a Federation with a complex administrative structure, foreign investors are not necessarily always acquainted to the distribution of competences between the Federal and the local levels—for example, in matters of issuance of permits, of environmental impact assessments or, more simply, in those of the applicable laws and regulations. With the objective of injecting more transparency, the Ombudsperson has been designed to lessen bureaucracy in that it is on-call to provide prompt and ready-made information to investors, on demand. It is the investors' local point of reference and can even register and treat its complaints.[40] Due to its knowledge of the local reality and due to its proximity with all the State's institutions, the Ombudsperson is expected to mobilize its forces on a timely basis to meet the investors' demands. In so doing, the CFIAs count on the Ombudsperson's proactivity in the exercise of its functions so as to dispel to a maximum the possibility of a dispute with the host State by stabilizing the investment atmosphere. Because of the nature of its attributions, it can also be inferred that the Ombudsperson has the competence to intervene and act on

2005) ICSID Case No. ARB/01/08; Occidental Exploration and Production Company (OEPC) v. Ecuador, (01/07/2004) UNCITRAL Rules, Final Award; Walter Bau v. Thailand, (01/09/2009) UNCITRAL, Award; Mohammad Ammar Al-Bahloul v. The Republic of Tajikistan (02/09/2009) SCC Case No. V (064/2008); Glencore International A.G. and C.I. Prodeco S.A. v. Republic of Colombia (27/08/2019), ICSDI ARB/16/6, Award. Kontinental Conseil Ingénierie v. Gabonese Republic (23/12/2016) PCA Case No. 2015-25.

[36] It is important to note that the CFIAs make no provision for fair and equitable treatment as such, even though studies do inform that the legal guarantee, security and treatment offered by the Brazilian legal system do not fall short of the international standard. See: Achtschin (2021).

[37] For instance: CFIA Brazil/India (2020), art. 8.

[38] CFIA Brazil/India (2020), art. 14.4 (b).

[39] CFIA Brazil/India (2020), art. 14.4 (e).

[40] CFIA Brazil/India (2020), art. 14.4 (c); CFIA Brazil-Angola, art. 5.4 (ii); CFIA Brazil-Mozambique, art. 5.4 (ii); CFIA Brazil-Mexico, art. 15.4 (b); CFIA Brazil-Malawi, art. 4.4 (ii); CFIA Brazil-Chile, art. 19.4 (c); ACDI Brazil-Ethiopia, art. 18.3 (c); CFIA Brazil-Colombia, art. 17.4 (b); CFIA Brazil-Guyana, art. 19.4 (c); CFIA Brazil-Suriname, art. 19.4(c).

its own—by informing the Joint Committee if needed[41]—should there be a degradation of the investor-State relationship or of the investment environment.[42] By addressing these matters, it would indirectly contribute to prevent future disputes.[43]

In reason of its key function as a facilitator as described by the CFIAs, foreign investors will vest high level of confidence in the Ombudsperson. Apart from being the investors' web of information, the Ombudsperson is the depositary of their trust which it cannot frustrate. It was designed to reduce bureaucracy: therefore, it cannot itself work as per cumbersome procedures and processes. It should act as a timely *question and answer panel* for investors: hence, it cannot work with recurrent delays. As it must bring meat to the bone of transparency, it cannot operate obscurely or provide unclear, imprecise or incoherent information to the investors. This point of concern is here mostly brought up as an alert especially in the Brazilian context where the Ombudsperson will be operated from the Foreign Trade Board (CAMEX), which is itself a governmental body with manifold competences and functions.[44] In other words, the CAMEX is not integrally dedicated to ombudsmanship. For this reason, the CFIAs state that the signatory parties must ensure that the Ombudsperson be granted the "means and resources" to efficiently conduct its activities[45]—being implied that the investors would expect it to be always readily available. If the Ombudsperson is an unquestionable asset of the CFIAs, the signatory States must however see to their efficient operability as any deficiency would imply a potential violation of the agreements in that an inefficient Ombudsperson would account for a low standard of treatment.

Like the Joint Committees, the Ombudsperson is programmed to engage in dispute prevention in two ways: prevention by more transparency while stabilizing the investor-State relationship; prevention *per se* in case of a potential incipient dispute. To this first layer of dispute prevention through the articulation between these two main dispute prevention bodies, the CFIAs aggregate a secondary layer by enabling the participation of stakeholders.

2.2 The Secondary Layers: The Dialogical Connection Between the Dispute Prevention Governance Body and Stakeholders

Another original characteristic of the CFIAs which relates to dispute prevention is the possibility of stakeholders' participation. The stakeholders are divided into two

[41] CFIA Brazil/India (2020), art. 14.4 (f).

[42] Monebhurrun (2020), pp. 227–242.

[43] CFIA Brazil/India (2020), art. 14.4 (d).

[44] For example, currently, another department of the Foreign Trade Board (CAMEX) also hosts the OECD National Contact Point in Brazil.

[45] CFIA Brazil/India (2020), art. 14.7.

categories: the investor and the civil society. The investor is here uncommonly put on the bench of stakeholders because the CFIAs give preference to State-State relationships as compared to the majority of existing investment agreements. This said, investors are expected to have an active participation in the dispute prevention procedure (Sect. 2.2.1) and, quite interestingly, other stakeholders, like representants of the civil society, may also be invited to participate (Sect. 2.2.2).

2.2.1 The Expected Participation of the Investor

Both the Joint Committee and the Ombudsperson can work directly with the investors in matters of dispute prevention. When it comes to dispute prevention by the Joint Committee, some CFIAs are clear at making room for investors' participation[46] whilst others state that participation is not automatic but on invitation.[47] In both cases, the investors' participation is, needless to say, more than expected given that they will be at the very center of an incipient conflict and their insight and contribution can only help in preventing its worsening. Even if the CFIAs are mostly based on inter-State relations, establishing a partnership with the investors—the main concerned stakeholders—is a sound policy for an efficient dispute management, considering *en passant* that the business world is sensible to the cost[48] and time parameters of dispute prevention and apply the latter for in-house problems or for external cases.[49] The CFIAs are novel in many respects and the dedication to dispute prevention and conflict management is surely part of the novelty.[50] However, partnering with the concerned investors is a must so as not to condemn the novelty to a mere paper proposal. Partnering, as argued in doctrine, "is a proactive dispute prevention tool that seeks to resolve conflicts at the earliest stages while other dispute resolution mechanisms, together with litigation, are reactive dispute management modalities that operates within and already presumes the existence of formal disputes and complaints[51]". If the partnering logic is quite explicit in the CFIAs, its implementation rests upon a culture of investor-State partnership in matters of dispute prevention. This culture will need to be fomented by the signatory States and especial care must be attributed to this aspect of the CFIAs by Brazil, which is a newcomer to the field of international investment law, and which must

[46] CFIA Brazil/Ecuador (2019), art. 24 (3) (c) (i); CFIA Brazil/Mexico (2015), art. 18 (3) (c) (i); CFIA Brazil/Mozambique (2015), art. 15 (3) (iii) (a); CFIA Brazil/Angola (2015), art. 15 (3) (iii) (a); CFIA Brazil/Malawi (2015) art. 13 (3) (c) (i).

[47] CFIA Brazil/India (2020), art. 18 (3) (b); CFIA Brazil/Morocco (2019), art. 19 (3) (a); CFIA Brazil/Colombia (2015), art. 22 (3) (c) (i); CFIA Brazil/Chile (2015), art. 24 (3) (c) (i); CFIA Brazil/Ethiopia (2018), art. 23 (3) (b); CFIA Brazil/Suriname (2018), art. 24 (3) (b); CFIA Brazil/Guyana (2018), art. 24 (3) (b); CFIA Brazil/United Arab Emirates (2019), art. 24 (3) (b).

[48] Lipsky and Seeber (1998), p. 142.

[49] Masucci and Suresh (2017), pp. 664–665; Lipsky et al. (2020), pp. 431–455.

[50] Monebhurrun (2017), pp. 83 *et seq.*

[51] Purisima (2019), pp. 38–39. See also: El-Hakim (1997), p. 350.

still build experience therein. Relatedly, this non-adversarial culture creation will be better achieved with the investors' active contribution: de-escalating and cooling off a conflict requires the understanding and the good will of all concerned parties; mobilizing such conditions obviously depends on their permanent participation. Besides, considering that investor-State arbitration is not provided for by the CFIAs, it would be only fair to (at least) always enable investors' participation in the dispute prevention process so as not to confine them to the role of mere spectators. The CFIAs are sometimes criticized for not being as protective as the other existing international investment agreements. For example, they make no provision for the fair and equitable treatment, for the full protection and security, for indirect expropriation, let alone for investor-State arbitration. As such, the CFIAs' protective appeal might easily dwindle for investors. Therefore, making room for their participation in the dispute management might add some balance or some compensation and enhance the CFIAs attractiveness—in bringing together investors and States for non-litigation purposes. This, it is claimed, is the CFIAs' main force together with an unusual opening they offer to civil society participation in matters of dispute prevention.

2.2.2 The Possible Formal Participation of Civil Society

From its inception, international investment law has focused on investors' protection,[52] providing the latter a series of well-known privileges on a red carpet.[53] The participation of other stakeholders in the international investment law system remains rare and exceptional—taking, for instance, the form of amicus curiae in the strict ambit of arbitration.[54] Yet, it is also known that the activities of foreign investors sometimes potentially produce negative externalities for the local population or for the local communities.[55] Many of these investors are protected by an array of investment agreements and UNCTAD itself underpinned that international investment agreements "bite".[56] In the microcosmos of international investment law, investors appear to be untouchable, with their own legal protection regime and dispute settlement mechanism. Coalitions from the civil society[57] have resultantly launched grassroot actions and petitions to block negotiations of economic agreements like the EU-Mercosur Trade Agreement[58] or the Transatlantic Trade and

---

[52] Ho (2021), p. 14; Miles (2013), p. 48.

[53] Alvik (2020), p. 290.

[54] Ascensio (2001), pp. 897–930; Grisel and Vinuales (2007), pp. 380–432.

[55] Miles (2013), pp. 133 *et seq.*; Perrone and Cotula (2021), pp. 78–80; Monebhurrun and De Andrade (2021), p. 263.

[56] UNCTAD (2018). UNCTAD Reform Package for the International Investment Regime. UNCTAD Publication: 17–18.

[57] On social movements, see: Miles (2013), pp. 100 *et seq.*

[58] This initiative was taken by the Stopeumercosur coalition (see: https://stopeumercosur.org/).

Investment Partnership.[59] The Brazilian CFIAs have taken a step towards non-investors stakeholders by granting them a say in the CFIA operations and, namely, in the dispute prevention procedure. The agreements state that parallelly to the investors, other stakeholders may be consulted by the Joint Committee on questions related to its attributed works and competence, including matters of dispute prevention.[60] As an illustration of this possibility, the Brazil-India CFIA purports that "[w]henever relevant to the consideration of the measure in question, the Joint Committee may invite other interested stakeholders to appear before the Joint Committee and present their views on such measure".[61] The Brazil-Angola CFIA's Joint Committee's internal regulation,[62] which is the first one to have been adopted, confirms that one of the competences of the Committee is to seek and welcome stakeholders' participation.

However, if they can be consulted in matters of dispute prevention, the exact substantial nature of the stakeholders' participation is not clearly described in the CFIAs which do not detail the content of the stakeholders' prospective contribution to the Joint Committees' work. This could theoretically be unraveled by the Committees' internal regulation but if the latter mirrors the one adopted for the Brazil-Angola's Joint Committee's operations the regulations will surely be of generic character. Still, the scope of the stakeholders' participation can be construed from the very CFIAs. The latter indistinctly contains a provision on corporate social responsibility (CSR).[63] The novelty rests in that these provisions contain detailed CSR standards which are addressed directly to the investors.[64] Under the CSR provisions, investors have a duty of diligence in matters of corporate social responsibility which

[59] This initiative was launched by the Collectifstoptafta (see: https://www.collectifstoptafta.org/). See also: Monebhurrun (2015), pp. 12–14. Generally: Sornarajah (2017), pp. 84–85.

[60] CFIA Brazil/India (2020), art. 13 (4) (d), art. 18.4; CFIA Brazil/Morocco (2019), art. 14 (4) (d), art. 19.4; CFIA Brazil/Colombia (2015), art. 16 (4) (d) (i), art. 22 (3) (c) (ii); CFIA Brazil/Chile (2015), art. 18 (4) (d), art. 24 (3) (c) (ii); CFIA Brazil/Ethiopia (2018), art. 17 (4) (d), art. 24 (4); CFIA Brazil/Suriname (2018), art. 18 (4) (d), art. 24 (4); CFIA Brazil/Guyana (2018), art. 24 (4), art. 18 (4) (d); CFIA Brazil/United Arab Emirates (2019), art. 18 (4) (d), art. 24 (4); CFIA Brazil/Ecuador (2019), art. 18 (4) (d) (i), art. 24 (3) (c) (ii); CFIA Brazil/Mexico (2015), art. 14 (4) (d), art. 18 (3) (c) (ii); CFIA Brazil/Mozambique (2015), art. 15 (3) (b), art. 4 (4) (iv); CFIA Brazil/Angola (2015), art. 4 (4) (iv), art. 15 (3) (iii) (a); CFIA Brazil/Malawi (2015) art. 3 (4) (d), art. 13 (3) (c) (ii).

[61] CFIA Brazil/India (2020), art. 18.4.

[62] The authors had access to the internal regulation of the Brazil-Angola Joint Committee by the means of the Brazilian Statute on Access to Information (Statute no. 12.527 of 2011) which created an online platform on the website of all Ministries and of the Public Administration in general enabling citizens to have an active access to information. The Public Administration has a legal obligation to answer to the citizens' request for information.

[63] CFIA Brazil/India (2020), art. 12; CFIA Brazil/Morocco (2019), art. 13; CFIA Brazil/Colombia (2015), art. 13; CFIA Brazil/Chile (2015), art. 15; CFIA Brazil/Ethiopia (2018), art. 14; CFIA Brazil/Suriname (2018), art. 15; CFIA Brazil/Guyana (2018), art. 15; CFIA Brazil/United Arab Emirates (2019), art. 15; CFIA Brazil/Ecuador (2019), art. 14; CFIA Brazil/Mexico (2015), art. 13; CFIA Brazil/Mozambique (2015), art. 10 and Annex II; CFIA Brazil/Angola (2015), art. 10 and Annex II; CFIA Brazil/Malawi (2015) art. 9.

[64] Monebhurrun and De Andrade (2021), pp. 275–276; Monebhurrun (2017), pp. 95–99.

range from environmental and human rights protection to workers' protection and anti-corruption measures.[65] They have, under this token, a duty to endeavor their best efforts—reminiscent of an obligation of means—to keep up with the detailed and precise CSR standards set by the agreements. This said, despite their originality, the CFIAs' CSR provisions face important limits in that they are (surprisingly) not arbitrable. For instance, pursuant to article 25 (3) of the Brazil-United Arab Emirates CFIA:

> The following may not be subject to arbitration: Article 13 - Security Exceptions; Article 14 - Compliance with Domestic Legislation; **Article 15 - Corporate Social Responsibility**;[66] Paragraph 1 of Article 16 - Investment Measures and Combating Corruption and Illegality; and Paragraph 2 of Article 17 - Provisions on Investment and Environment, Labor Affairs and Health.

We here argue that the CSR provisions are not meant to be a dead letter: if they are not arbitrable, nothing indicates that they cannot be invoked during the dispute prevention procedure. The Brazil-Morocco CFIA expressly mentions that the Joint Committee must supervise the agreement's implementation, including CSR-related questions.[67] Concerning the other CFIAs, it can be claimed that the Joint Committees have an implicit competence to monitor the observance of the CSR standards by

---

[65] The CFIAs' provisions on corporate social responsibility are very detailed ones. Here is, for example, the content of article 12 of the Brazil-India CFIA (2020):

"12.1 Investors and their investments shall strive to achieve the highest possible level of contribution to the sustainable development of the Host State and the local community, through the adoption of a high degree of socially responsible practices, based on the voluntary principles and standards set out in this Article and internal policies, such as statements of principle that have been endorsed or are supported by the Parties. 12.2 The investors and their investments shall endeavour to comply with the following voluntary principles and standards for a responsible business conduct and consistent with the laws adopted by the Host State: a) contribute to the economic, social and environmental progress, aiming at achieving sustainable development; b) respect the internationally recognized human rights of those involved in the companies' activities; c) encourage local capacity building through close cooperation with the local community; d) encourage the creation of human capital, especially by creating employment opportunities and offering professional training to workers; e) refrain from seeking or accepting exemptions that are not established in the legal or regulatory framework relating to human rights, environment, health, security, work, tax system, financial incentives, or other issues; f) support and advocate for good corporate governance principles, and develop and apply good corporate governance practices, including anti-corruption measures; g) develop and implement effective self-regulatory practices and management systems that foster a relationship of mutual trust between the companies and the societies in which their operations are conducted; h) promote the knowledge of and the adherence, by workers, to the corporate policy, through appropriate dissemination of this policy, including professional training programs; i) refrain from discriminatory or disciplinary action against employees who submit grave reports to the board or, whenever appropriate, to the competent public authorities, about practices that violate the law or corporate policy; j) encourage, whenever possible, business associates, including service providers and outsources, to apply the principles of business conduct consistent with the principles provided for in this Article; and k) refrain from any undue interference in local political activities.

[66] Highlighted by the authors.

[67] CFIA Brazil/Morocco (2019), art. 14 (4) (a).

the investors. If CSR-related conundrums cannot be, as such, the object of an arbitration, the CFIAs do put the investors' corporate behavior under the spotlight from which they can be observed by the Joint Committees and in so doing, the latter can be assisted by stakeholders, especially by the civil society. We argue that the CSR provisions do have a legal purpose and can be accordingly matched with the expected stakeholders' participation in assisting the Joint Committees, acting therein as a watchdog of the investors' corporate social responsibility. In a dispute prevention procedure, whereby the host States' acts and omissions are under scrutiny for having potentially infringed a foreign investor's rights, the investor's behavior can parallelly be put in the balance. The stakeholders' (local communities, indigenous people, NGOs, consumers, academia, for instance) participation can here be useful in helping the Joint Committees to assess how clean are the investor's hands, that is, to what extent its corporate behavior is/was respectful of the CSR standards set in the CFIA. In this sense, the CFIA's corporate social responsibility provision also provide useful parameters to assess the investors' social license to operate[68] Stakeholders' participation is here relevant and important because an investor's corporate misconduct might not always be brought to the debate by the State parties for strategic or for political reasons.[69] Concerns on investors' accountability are often voiced by the civil society given that it is often the one to be affected in the flesh by corporate misconduct, namely when it comes to local communities.[70] Therefore, in a dispute prevention environment, the Joint Committee can—with the stakeholders' collaboration in matters of fact-finding or field research for example—call the investor to order and remind it of its corresponding CSR duties which are paired with its protected rights. This could be an indirect means to enforce or, at least, to give an *effet utile* to the CSR provision whilst construing the stakeholders' function as a CSR guardian in the dispute prevention procedure.

It is through this manifold participation that the CFIAs establish a multilayered dispute prevention governance. The latter's implementation also depends on a specific procedural dispute prevention method which gives a quasi-jurisdictional function to the Joint Committees. This will be addressed in the next section.

---

[68] Monebhurrun (2023).

[69] Ho (2021), p. 28.

[70] Ho (2021), p. 28. Generally: Perrone and Cotula (2021), pp. 71 *et seq.*

3 A Procedural Dispute Prevention Method Giving a Quasi-Jurisdictional Function to the CFIAs' Joint Committees

Under the CFIAs, bringing a potential controversy before the Joint Committee is a compulsory procedural step of dispute prevention before having recourse to State-State arbitration.[71] Consulting the Joint Committees is not symbolical in nature. If they are not tantamount to arbitral tribunals with an authority of *res judicata*, the legal procedure before the Committee confirms that dispute prevention is taken seriously and indicates that the Joint Committees are expected to have a quasi-jurisdictional function. The argument to support this thesis is two-pronged. It is first based on the formality of the dispute prevention submission procedure by the parties (Sect. 3.1) and secondly grounded in the formalism of the dispute prevention evaluation procedure by the Joint Committees (Sect. 3.2).

3.1 The Formality of the Dispute Prevention Submission Procedure by the Parties

A measure adopted by the host State which is not in conformity with the CFIA can be the starting point of a dispute prevention procedure due to be activated by the investor's home State. The investor is, of course, expected to notify its home State of the inconformity measure and will surely be in the background of the dispute prevention mechanism in a manner remindful of the dispute settlement method of the World Trade Organization.[72] Such notification is, however, informal and implicit, in that it is not provided for by the CFIAs. Formally, the official activation of the dispute prevention mechanism belongs to the States. For example, pursuant to article 18.1 of the Brazil/India CFIA "[i]f a Party considers that a specific measure adopted by the other Party constitutes a breach of this Treaty, it may invoke this Article to initiate a dispute prevention procedure within the Joint Committee".[73] "Party", in the CFIAs context, refers to State parties. Still, initiating a dispute prevention procedure pertains to the home State's discretionary powers—just as it would be in matters of diplomatic protection.[74] This could be a limitation of the CFIAs and their esteemed dispute prevention governance.[75] Political circumstances,

[71] See for example: CFIA Brazil/Colombia (2015), art. 22(2); CFIA Brazil/Chile (2015), art. 24(1); CFIA Brazil/Suriname (2018), art. 15; CFIA Brazil/Ecuador (2019), art. 24(2); CFIA Brazil/Mozambique (2015), art. 15(2); CFIA Brazil/Angola (2015), art. 15(2); CFIA Brazil/Malawi (2015) art. 13(3). See also: Badin and Morosini (2017), p. 233.

[72] Ascensio (2020), pp. 123–124.

[73] CFIA Brazil/India (2020), art. 18.1.

[74] De Nanteuil (2017), p. 17; Lim et al. (2018), p. 5.

[75] Monebhurrun (2019), p. 76.

sensitive conundrums or other strategic reasons might deter the home State's will to activate the dispute prevention mechanism. The political relationship between the concerned investor and its home State will also be a shadow criterion in determining the State's motivation to act. For instance, it is not clear if Brazil, as a home State, would be ready to intervene in cases concerning small or medium Brazilian investors abroad or if it would readily accept to trigger the procedure several times a year before the same Joint Committee on behalf of different Brazilian investors. These are some dim spots of the dispute prevention mechanism. Granting to investors the right to bring a case directly before the Committees would have undoubtedly been less bureaucratic and maybe less discriminatory given that any investor would have had the legal possibility to do so, regardless of its size, of its business sector or of its political connections.

Having said that, once the investor's home State is convinced that there are sufficient grounds to commence a dispute prevention procedure, it can have recourse to the Joint Committee before which it will however act in its own name, with the objective of settling any nascent controversy. The formality rests in that the procedure before the Joint Committee is the first steppingstone of the dispute governance system. It is a prior compulsory procedure which, once started, must be fully completed before eventually referring the case to an arbitral tribunal in a State-State arbitration. An arbitral tribunal constituted under the auspices of an CFIA will deny jurisdiction absent a prior dispute prevention report of the Joint Committee. The trust and mission conferred upon the Joint Committee to find a friendly solution elevates the Committees to a quasi-jurisdictional entity, which is more so confirmed by the procedural formalism to be fulfilled before and by it.

3.2 *The Formalism of the Dispute Prevention Evaluation Procedure by the Joint Committee*

Submitting a case before the Joint Committee follows some formal rules and steps. The home State must accordingly formalize its demand by a written statement, thereby highlighting the inconformity measure as well as the points of law and facts relevant to the case. Curiously (or confusingly), some CFIAs state that the written statement must be sent to the Joint Committee[76] whilst others inform that it must be notified to the host State[77] or even to the Ombudsperson.[78] If a clear pattern

[76]For example: CFIA Brazil/Angola (2015), art. 15.3; CFIA Brazil/Mozambique (2015), art. 15.3; CFIA Brazil/Colombia (2015), art. 22.3; CFIA Brazil/Malawi (2015) art. 13.3. See also: Badin and Morosini (2017), p. 233.

[77]For example: CFIA Brazil/India (2020), art. 18.2; CFIA Brazil/Morocco (2019), art. 19 (2) (a); CFIA Brazil/Suriname (2018), art. 24 (2) (a); CFIA Brazil/Guyana (2018), art. 24 (2) (a); CFIA Brazil/United Arab Emirates (2019), art. 24.2.

[78]ACFI Brazil/Morocco (2019), art. 19.2.

has yet to established therein by practice, it is logically expected that the request be addressed to the Joint Committee and to the host State or to the latter via the Joint Committee. In any case, the Joint Committee must, for a fact, be informed because it is the body having the competence to act formally in the dispute prevention procedure. Once notified, the Joint Committee must set a meeting within an established deadline which ranges from 60[79] to 90[80] days depending upon the CFIA. As from the first meeting, the Joint Committees have 60 days, extendable if need be (120 days in the Brazil/India CFIA), to evaluate the case and adopt a report.[81] In so doing, the Committees are expected to match the facts of the case with the applicable law in order to reach a solution and thereby prevent the exacerbation of a nascent dispute. It is expected that the home and the host State also present their oral submissions before the Joint Committees by the means of their representatives. As mentioned in Sect. 2, the concerned investor[82] as well as other stakeholders[83] may be granted the possibility to participate in the round(s) before the Joint Committees. Their position will as such be duly considered; their arguments will be heard as per the partnering principle[84] consecrated in the CFIAs as a tool enabling to solve the problem and avoid arbitration *in fine*. This part of the procedure can be determining considering that the investors and the other stakeholders will have an opportunity to influence the content of the final report. The Joint Committees have been accorded the competence to empower a constructive and friendly dialogue between the concerned parties and actors; nevertheless, on a formal note, the procedure inherent to their work is tantamount to a hearing. After the audiences and after examining the details of the case, the Joint Committees must adopt a report which contains the: (i) identification of the submitting State; (ii) a description of the

---

[79] All the CFIAs, with the exception of the Brazil/India one, provide for a 60 days meeting deadline.

[80] CFIA Brazil/India (2020), art. 18.2 (a).

[81] For instance: CFIA Brazil/Mozambique (2015), art. 15.3 (ii); CFIA Brazil/Angola (2015), art. 15.3 (ii); CFIA Brazil/Malawi (2015) art. 13.3 (b); CFIA Brazil/United Arab Emirates (2019), art. 24.2 (b); CFIA Brazil/Guyana (2018), art. 24 (2) (b); CFIA Brazil/Morocco (2019), art. 19 (2) (b); CFIA Brazil/Suriname (2018), art. 24 (2) (b); CFIA Brazil/India (2020), art. 18.2 (b).

[82] CFIA Brazil/Ecuador (2019), art. 24 (3) (c) (i); CFIA Brazil/Mexico (2015), art. 18 (3) (c) (i); CFIA Brazil/Mozambique (2015), art. 15 (3) (iii) (a); CFIA Brazil/Angola (2015), art. 15 (3) (iii) (a); CFIA Brazil/Malawi (2015) art. 13 (3) (c) (i); CFIA Brazil/India (2020), art. 18 (3) (b); CFIA Brazil/Morocco (2019), art. 19 (3) (a); CFIA Brazil/Colombia (2015), art. 22 (3) (c) (i); CFIA Brazil/Chile (2015), art. 24 (3) (c) (i); CFIA Brazil/Ethiopia (2018), art. 23 (3) (b); CFIA Brazil/Suriname (2018), art. 24 (3) (b); CFIA Brazil/Guyana (2018), art. 24 (3) (b); CFIA Brazil/United Arab Emirates (2019), art. 24 (3) (b).

[83] CFIA Brazil/India (2020), art. 13 (4) (d), art. 18.4; CFIA Brazil/Morocco (2019), art. 14 (4) (d), art. 19.4; CFIA Brazil/Colombia (2015), art. 16 (4) (d) (i), art. 22 (3) (c) (ii); CFIA Brazil/Chile (2015), art. 18 (4) (d), art. 24 (3) (c) (ii); CFIA Brazil/Ethiopia (2018), art. 17 (4) (d), art. 24 (4); CFIA Brazil/Suriname (2018), art. 18 (4) (d), art. 24 (4); CFIA Brazil/Guyana (2018), art. 24 (4), art. 18 (4) (d); CFIA Brazil/United Arab Emirates (2019), art. 18 (4) (d), art. 24 (4); CFIA Brazil/Ecuador (2019), art. 18 (4) (d) (i), art. 24 (3) (c) (ii); CFIA Brazil/Mexico (2015), art. 14 (4) (d), art. 18 (3) (c) (ii); CFIA Brazil/Mozambique (2015), art. 15 (3) (b), art. 4 (4) (iv); CFIA Brazil/Angola (2015), art. 4 (4) (iv), art. 15 (3) (iii) (a); CFIA Brazil/Malawi (2015) art. 3 (4) (d), art. 13 (3) (c) (ii).

[84] El-Hakim (1997), p. 350.

contested measure and the provisions of the CFIA which have been allegedly violated; (iii) their findings.[85] These findings are supposed to express a mutually agreed solution. A few CFIAs mention that the report must state the identification of the concerned party and investor, the contested measure and the parties' position thereto related[86] but are silent on the exigency of the Committees' specific findings, the latter being certainly the expected result of the dispute prevention procedure. Some CFIAs indicate a specific deadline for the report to be presented, ranging from 15[87] to 30[88] days after one of the parties has decided to end the consultation procedure; others do not make provision for specific deadlines.[89] If confidentiality is the rule regarding the Committees' meetings and documentation, the adopted report will however be rendered public as per the forms and procedures of the parties' domestic law.[90] Transparency—in terms of the publication of the Committees' reports—is, in this context, a must in that it is a tool of dispute prevention but also an indicator of the Joint Committees' legitimacy as a technically competent body. Transparency is a hallmark of efficient governance[91] and marks the independence of an adjudicatory or a non-adjudicatory body.[92] The Joint Committees' reports constitute a major asset which the State parties, future investors and other stakeholders can use to understand how given legal questions were tackled by the Committees and how dispute prevention was effectively achieved. The reports' publicness is furthermore important if ever a question of public interest is embedded in the dispute.[93] If the submitted legal questions encroach upon issues of environmental law, human rights, health care, cultural heritage, or indigenous and tribal rights, the outcome will evidently be of general interest. This reasoning also applies in matters of corruption or whenever a corporate social misconduct is in debate. Such transparency is also likely to facilitate the social acceptability of the dispute prevention mechanism provided for by the CFIAs—especially in Brazil where reins a skepticism regarding international investment law in general. In the longer run, the collection of these reports will be able to express the Joint Committees' best practices as the CFIAs main dispute prevention body, thereby acting as a repository of the dispute avoidance "jurisprudence". It is also worth noting that if the dispute is not settled within the deadlines established by the CFIAs or if one of the State parties

[85] For example: CFIA Brazil/India (2020), art. 18.2 (c); CFIA Brazil/United Arab Emirates (2019), art. 24.2 (c); CFIA Brazil/Guyana (2018), art. 24 (2) (c); CFIA Brazil/Suriname (2018), art. 24 (2) (c); CFIA Brazil/Morocco (2019), art. 19 (2) (c); CFIA Brazil/Ethiopia (2018), art. 23 (2) (c).

[86] For example: the CFIA signed with Mexico, Angola, Mozambique, Chile or Malawi.

[87] See: CFIA with Ecuador and Colombia.

[88] See: CFIA with Chile.

[89] See: CFIA with Mozambique, Angola, Mexico, Guyana, Ethiopia, Morocco, Suriname, United Arab Emirates and India.

[90] CFIA Brazil/India (2020), art. 18.5; CFIA Brazil/United Arab Emirates (2019), art. 24.5; CFIA Brazil/Mozambique (2015), art. 15(5); CFIA Brazil/Angola (2015), art. 15(5).

[91] Schewe (2016), pp. 396–398; Calamita (2014), p. 650.

[92] Schewe (2016), p. 399.

[93] Calamita (2014), p. 651.

does not participate in the procedure, an arbitration procedure may be initiated by the other party.[94] On this last point, it is however unclear whether the concerned investor will have to make a formal request to its home State to start an arbitration or if the initiative belongs solely to the State. The concern is here of procedural importance: the need of a request by the investor might be construed as a diplomatic protection case[95]—or presented/defended as such by the host State—whereby the investor will have to exhaust all local remedies before any eventual State-State arbitration.[96] But overall, the characteristics examined in this topic are those which collectively boil down to equating the Joint Committees to quasi-jurisdictional bodies.

4 Closing Remarks

The Brazilian CFIAs are theoretically fit to inaugurate a differentiated era of international investment dispute settlement method which could act as a model in line with the objective of dispute avoidance and of harmonizing the relationship between States, investors and other stakeholders. The dispute settlement mechanism, once put to test, will enable to assess the soundness of Brazil's strategic choice in prioritizing prevention or in allowing the intervention of third parties in the procedure. Cases in international investment law are known to be highly technical and the technicity also applies at the dispute prevention level. Even if it is rooted in international law, international investment law has its own language and techniques which must be duly mastered not only for the purposes of dispute settlement but also for the general relations to be established with foreign investors. Brazil is starting to learn the language of international investment law and must prepare its bodies (especially the Joint Committee and the Ombudsperson) and their civil servants to understand the underlying techniques of this law field. An anticipation of and a prior *investment* in this preparatory work would, for this reason, be duly recommendable. These could firstly take the form of legal training through seminars and workshops. They could secondly be achieved by the establishment of a situation room whereby dispute prevention could be simulated and where policies and strategies could be

[94] See for instance: CFIA Brazil/India (2020), art. 18.2 (d); CFIA Brazil/Ecuador (2019), art. 24 (3) (f); CFIA Brazil/Morocco (2019), art. 19 (2) (d); CFIA Brazil/United Arab Emirates (2019), art. 24 (2) (d).

[95] The Mavrommatis Palestine Concessions, PCIJ, Series A, no.2, Judgement (30/08/1924), p. 12: "It is an elementary principle of international law that a State is entitled to protect its subjects, when injured by acts contrary to international law committed by another State, from whom they have been unable to obtain satisfaction through the ordinary channels. By taking up the case of one of its subjects and by resorting to diplomatic action or international judicial proceedings on his behalf, a State is in reality asserting its own rights its right to ensure, in the person of its subjects, respect for the rules of international law".

[96] Monebhurrun (2019), p. 76. See also: Case concerning Avena and other Mexican nationals (Mexico v. United States of America), I.C.J., Judgement (31/03/2004), para. 40.

discussed by experts to anticipate future cases through the elaboration of inputs and guidelines on dispute prevention in international investment cases.

References

Achtschin LVA (2021) A Aplicabilidade da Cláusula do Tratamento Justo e Equitativo ao Brasil. Lumen Juris, Rio de Janeiro

Alvik I (2020) The justification of privilege in international investment law: preferential treatment of foreign investors as a problem of legitimacy. Eur J Int Law 31:290

Ascensio H (2001) L'amicus curiae devant les juridictions internationales. Revue générale de Droit international public 4:897–930

Ascensio H (2020) Droit international économique. PUF, Paris, pp 123–124

Badin MR, Morosini F (2017) Navigating between resistance and conformity with the international investment regime. In: Badin MR, Morosini F (eds) Reconceptualizing international investment law from the global south. Cambridge University Press, Cambridge

Beate R (2000) Thematic Rapporteurs and Working Groups of the United Nations Commission on Human Rights. Max Planck Yearb United Nations Law 4:296 e ss

Calamita NJ (2014) Dispute settlement transparency in Europe's evolving investment treaty policy. J World Invest Trade 15

Carmona CA (2016) Arbitragem e Administração Pública – Primeiras reflexões sobre a arbitragem envolvendo a administração pública. Revista brasileira de arbitragem 51:7–21

Centro Internacional para a Arbitragem de Disputas sobre Investimentos (CIADI) (1968) History of the ICSID Convention. Document concerning the Origin and the Formulation of the Convention on the Settlement of Investment Disputes between States and Nationals of Other States. ICSID Publication, Washington, ICSID. Vol. II. Part 1. 1968: p 306

Comissão das Nações Unidas para o Direito Comercial Internacional (UNCITRAL) (2017) Report of the United Nations Commission on International Trade Law Fiftieth Session. A/72/17: para. 264

Comissão das Nações Unidas para o Direito Comercial Internacional (UNCITRAL) (2018) Possible Reform of Investor-State Dispute Settlement. A/CN.9/WG.III/WP.149. para. 8

Comissão das Nações Unidas para o Direito Comercial Internacional (UNCITRAL) (2021) Report of the United Nations Commission on International Trade Law Fifty-Fourth Session. A/72/17: 2

Conferência das Nações Unidas sobre Comércio e Desenvolvimento (UNCTAD) (2010) Investor–State Disputes: Prevention and Alternatives to Arbitration. UNCTAD Series on International Investment Policies for Development, 28–30

Conferência das Nações Unidas sobre Comércio e Desenvolvimento (UNCTAD) (2018) UNCTAD Reform Package for the International Investment Regime. UNCTAD Publication: 17–18

Damjanovic I, Quirico O (2019) Intra-E investment Dispute Settlement under the Energy Charter Treaty in Light of Achmea and Vattenfall: matter of priority. Columbia J Eur Law 26:102 e ss

De Nanteuil A (2017) Droit international de l'investissement. Pédone, Paris

El-Hakim J (1997) Les modes alternatifs de règlement des conflits dans le droit des contrats. Revue internationale de Droit comparé 49:350

Grisel F, Vinuales JE (2007) L'amicus curiae dans l'arbitrage d'investissement. ICSID Rev - Foreign Invest Law J 22:380–432

Ho J (2021) International law's opportunities for investor accountability. In: Ho J, Sattorova M (eds) Investors' international law. Hart, Oxford

Kalicki J, Medeiros S (2008) Investment arbitration in Brazil. Revisiting Brazil's traditional reluctance towards ICSID, BITs and Investor-State Arbitration. Arbitr Int 4:432 e ss

Kurtz J (2012) Australia's rejection of investor–state arbitration: causation, omission and implication. ICSID Rev - Foreign Invest Law J 27:65–86

Langford M, Potestà M, Kaufman-Kohler G, Behn D (2020) Special Issue: UNCITRAL and investment arbitration reform: matching concerns and solutions: an introduction. J World Invest Trade 21:167
Lim CL, Ho J, Paparinskis M (2018) International investment law and arbitration. Cambridge University Press, Cambridge
Lipsky DB, Seeber RL (1998) In search of control: the corporate embrace of ADR. Univ Pa J Labor Emp Law 1:142
Lipsky DB, Avgar AC, Lamare JR (2020) Organizational conflict resolution and strategic choice: evidence from a survey of fortune 1000 firms. Ind Labor Relat Rev 73:431–455
Masucci D, Suresh S (2017) Transforming business through proactive dispute management. Cardozo J Conflict Resol 18:664–665
Miles K (2013) The origins of international investment law: empire, environment and the safeguarding of capital. Cambridge University Press, Cambridge
Monebhurrun N (2015) E eles descobriram a arbitragem investidor-Estado. Braz J Int Law 12:12–14
Monebhurrun N (2017) Novelty in international investment law: the Brazilian Agreement on cooperation and facilitation of investments as a different international investment agreement model. J Int Dispute Settlement 8:84 e ss
Monebhurrun N (2019) What would change in Brazil's practice with the adoption of an investor-state dispute settlement mechanism in its investment agreements? Nomos 39:76
Monebhurrun N (2020) O mecanismo de resolução de disputas nos novos Acordos de Cooperação e de Facilitação dos Investimentos do Brasil. In: Mota CE (ed) Tratado de inversiones extranjeras y arbitraje de inversiones en Iberoamérica. Tirant Lo Blanch, Valencia, pp 227–242
Monebhurrun N (2023) Incorporating the social license to operate into international investment law: taking stock from the Brazilian experience. J World Invest Trade 24 (forthcoming)
Monebhurrun N, De Andrade PP (2021) Mapping investors' environmental commitments and obligations. In: Ho J, Sattorova M (eds) Investors' international law. Hart, Oxford
Morosini FC, Gabriel VDR, Costa A (2020) Solução de controvérsias em Acordos de Investimento: as experiências do CPTPP, CETA e dos ACFIs. Braz J Int Law 17:304
Nicolas F, Thomsen S, Bang M-H (2013) Lessons from investment policy reform in Korea. OECD Working Papers on International Investment 2:24. Disponível em: https://doi.org/10.1787/5k4376zqcpf1-en. Acesso em: 24 set. 2021
Nolan M (2015) Challenges to the credibility of the investor-state arbitration system. Am Univ Bus Law Rev 5:429–445
Perrone NM, Cotula L (2021) Investors' international law and its asymmetries: the case of local communities. In: Ho J, Sattorova M (eds) Investors' international law. Hart, Oxford, pp 78–80
Purisima KJE (2019) Participatory dispute prevention: managing risks and partnering for Marawi's big rise. Ateneo Law J 64:38–39
Schewe C (2016) Clearing up transparency in the dispute settlement of international trade agreements, vol 59. German Yearb Int Law
Sornarajah M (2017) The international law on foreign investment. Cambridge University Press, Cambridge
Titi A (2014) The right to regulate in international investment law. Hart, Baden-Baden
Vidigal G, Stevens B (2018) Brazil's new model of dispute settlement for investment: return to the past or alternative for the future? J World Invest Trade 19:486
Voon T, Mitchell AD (2012) Implications of international investment law for plain tobacco packaging: lessons from the Hong Kong–Australia BIT. In: Voon T et al (eds) Public health and plain packaging of cigarettes legal issues. Edward Elgar Publishing, Cheltenham

Wald A, De Borja AG (2016) The New Brazilian Arbitration Law. Univ Miami Inter-Am Law Rev 47:21–52

Weghmann V, Hall D (2021) The unsustainable political economy of investor-state dispute settlement mechanisms. Int Rev Adm Sci:1–17

Zarra G (2017) Right to regulate, margin of appreciation and proportionality: current status in investment arbitration in light of Philip Morris v. Uruguay. Braz J Int Law 14:96–120

Nitish Monebhurrun is a Tenured Law Professor at the Law Faculty (Master, Doctoral and Undergraduate Programmes) of the University Centre of Brasília, Brazi. He is also a visiting Professor at the Universidad de la Sabana, Bogota, Colombia, where he teaches International Investment law and Arbitration. He is the Director of the Business, Human Rights and Public Policy Clinic of the University Centre of Brasília. He is a consultant in international law and an arbitrator [CAMESC/ALAM]. Nitish is an associate researcher at the Department of Latin American Studies of the University of Brasilia and a researcher at the Observatory of International Migrations, Brazil. He holds a PhD – International Law (Sorbonne Law School) and has written extensively in matters of international investment law. He is a member of the Pool of Experts of the United Nations Regular Process for Global Reporting and Assessment of the State of the Marine Environment, including Socioeconomic Aspects. He is the Chief-Editor of the Brazilian Journal of International Law.

Leonardo Vieira Arruda Achtschin PhD Candidate (University Center of Brasília), PhD Research Fellow (Max Planck Institute, Luxembourg). Civil Servant and Trade Specialist at the Brazilian Competition Authority.

The Brazilian Branches in the Arbitration Bench: Challenges and Possibilities in Face of the "Precatório" System and Consensuality

João Paulo Santos Borba and Gustavo Ferreira Ribeiro

1 Introduction

Brazil's rejection of investor-state dispute settlement (ISDS) provisions is well known in the literature.[1] Against the mainstream, in which developing countries celebrated investor protection agreements containing the clause, Brazil remained resistant to ISDS provisions throughout its history. Even after the 2000s, when the country experienced a broader internationalization of Brazilian companies in foreign markets, the Brazilian government´s aversion to ISDS clauses remained still.

Since an ISDS alternative seems unplausible as a legal option to foreign investors in Brazil, what are the possibilities left to companies in case of disputes against an illicit act of any entity of the Brazilian branches?

One may think on the grounds of state-to-state disputes found in the Cooperation and Investment Facilitation Agreements (ACFI, in the Portuguese acronym). However, these agreements have not been put under test so far, and whether they will come out as an alternative will depend on the practice.[2]

The investor may consider, as well, domestic institutions instead of the ISDS regime. Resorting to the Judiciary can be the first option, but the response can take a considerable time. Courts are filled up with proceedings and the Public Administration, in the quality of defendant, counts with multiple prerogatives regarding, for instance, extra time to act in legal proceedings.

[1] Campello and Lemos (2015), pp. 1055–1086. Reis and Ribeiro (2019), pp. 56–60.

[2] Vidigal and Stevens (2018), pp. 475–512. For an overview of the Brazilian ACFI, *see* Monebhurrun (2017).

J. P. S. Borba · G. F. Ribeiro (✉)
University Center of Brasilia, Brasilia, Brazil
e-mail: joao.borba@sempreceub.com; gustavo.ribeiro@ceub.edu.br

N. Monebhurrun et al. (eds.), *International Investment Law and Arbitration from a Latin American Perspective*, International Law and the Global South,
https://doi.org/10.1007/978-3-031-49382-9_8

Another possibility came after the enactment of Law No. 13.129 (2015), which amended Law No. 9,307 (1996), the Brazilian Arbitration Law (LBA). The amended law expressly established the possibility for the Public Administration to use arbitration to settle conflicts related to property rights available, pacifying the admissibility of arbitration by or with public law entities.[3]

While exploring the inclusion of the Public Administration as a part of arbitration proceedings in Brazil, this chapter exposes difficulties that arise from the enforcement of obligations to pay against Public Administration.

On one hand, the system of public debt payments, known as *precatórios*, represents a formidable challenge to arbitration principles, as it will be demonstrated. On the other hand, by revisiting contemporary administrative law doctrine, this chapter presents an alternative. In line with the perspective of consensualism and dialogic action, it suggests that the Public Administration can carry out transaction or spontaneous performance of the awarding arbitration decision, provided that legal standards or rules are available.

2 The Public Administration as a Party in Arbitration Proceedings and the *Precatório* System

As pointed out, the LBA is relatively new. Even newer is the possibility of the inclusion of the public entities as a party in arbitration.

Curiously, arbitration itself, as an ADR method, has been long provided as an option in Brazil, but it lost traction along the evolution of Brazil´s legal institutions.

Just as a context, the Constitution of 1824 provided that civil legal disagreements could be decided by arbitrators. The arbitration process was even raised to mandatory in commercial matters, in the interstice between 1850 and 1866. With the institutionalization of the Brazilian Republic (1889) and the progressive strengthening of the Judiciary Power, a shift of dispute settlement mechanisms to the hands of the State began. The Civil Code of 1916 and the Code of Civil Procedure 1939 shaped, at an infra-constitutional level, this new model. Arbitration was recognized,

[3]LAB (1996): Art. 1: “Persons capable of contracting may avail themselves of arbitration to settle disputes relating to available property rights. § 1 *The direct and indirect public administration may use arbitration to settle disputes relating to available property rights*. (Included by Law No. 13.129 of 2015) § 2 The competent authority or body of the direct public administration for the execution of an arbitration agreement is the same for the execution of agreements or transactions. (Included by Law No. 13.129 of 2015)(emphasis added). LAB (1996), Art. 2: “The arbitration may be of law or equity, at the discretion of the parties (. . .) § 3o *Arbitration involving the public administration will always be under the rule of law and will respect the principle of publicity*” (emphasis added). *See* also Rocha (2016), pp. 103–126. Before the LAB amendment, there were already discussions about the possibility of using arbitration by the Public Administration. See Grinover (2003), pp. 382–385, demonstrating the doubt that existed at the time about the (im)possibility of using arbitration by the Public Administration, though the author concluded that there was no doubt about the admissibility of arbitration involving the Public Administration, directly and indirectly.

for example, as a method of conflict resolution, but it was subjugated to the State's will once decisions needed double recognition. The Constitution of 1946 reinforced the approach by stating that the Judiciary Power would not be deprived from analyzing any claims regarding the violation of individual rights.[4] Decades have passed and neither the "Buzaid's Civil Code reform", nor the following Constitutions, such as the Federal Constitution of 1988, changed the situation.[5] On the contrary, there seems to have been a combination, in a self-reinforcing dynamic, of the strengthening of the State as the only instance to settle disputes and the lack of familiarity and credibility of arbitration, and ADR methods, in general.

While arbitration expanded in Latin America as an ADR method, especially in commercial disputes, Brazil was falling behind. Notwithstanding the enactment of the LAB (1996), doubts remained about the constitutionality of the arbitration bill. It was only in 2001, during a recognition proceeding of a foreign arbitral award at the Brazilian Federal Supreme Court (STF), which held this competence for recognition by that time, that the constitutionality of arbitration was finally settled down.[6] Moreover, it should not come as a surprise that the prospects of arbitration with public entities would involve some level of controversies along the way.[7]

Today, at least, one can say that the much of this debate had been overcome. The constitutionality of arbitration and the possibility of public entities as parts in arbitration are clear. In this sense, the number of arbitrations having the Public Administration as a party has been increasing. One research informs that approximately 17% (48) of the total number of new arbitration cases (277), initiated in seven out of eight of the main arbitration chambers in Brazil, had the Public Administration as a party. This share represents a growth of 7 p.p. as compared to 2018. The increased participation derives, most likely, from claims for damages by breach of contract, economic and financial balance of contracts related to concessions and public-private partnership contracts.[8]

However, the enforcement of awards still represents a challenge. The LAB is silent about the procedure to be adopted for the fulfillment of the obligation to pay as a result of an arbitration award issued against a legal entity governed by public law.

---

[4] *See* Samtleben (1996), pp. 35–39.

[5] We refer to the very miscomprehended article 5, item XXXV of the 1988 Federal Constitution: "the law will not exclude from the Judiciary Power's assessment an injury or threat to a right". For a long time, the Judiciary interpreted the provision as a "monopoly" to settle disputes.

[6] STF Decision Ag. Reg. na Sentença Estrangeira 5.206-7 Reino da Espanha (2001).

[7] Indeed, the Brazilian Superior Court of Justice (STJ) had the chance to resolve many cases addressing arbitration with the so-called indirect public administration (semipublic corporations, known as "Sociedades de Economia Mista" in Brazil). STJ Decision REsp No. 606.345-RS (2003); STJ Decision REsp No. 612.439-RS (2003); STJ Decision MS 11.308/DF (2008).

[8] *See* Lemes (2020), pp. 4; 7. The report does not disclose whether those cases involved foreign investors and the Public Administration. It only details (section 12) some figures about the participation of "foreign parts" in arbitration of international contracts. Also *see* Cunha (2020), revisiting the idea of "justice of multiple doors", which involves mediation, conciliation, and arbitration in Brazil; Aragão (2017), pp. 19–58.

The new Brazilian Code of Civil Procedure (NCPC), Law No. 13,105 (2015), in its turn, simply establishes that the arbitration award is a judicial enforceable title. And, most importantly, article 100 of the Brazilian Constitution establishes that payments due by the National Treasury, by virtue of a judicial decision, will be made exclusively through the so-called system of "*precatórios*".[9]

The system involves the issuance of a court-ordered for cash payment and, most likely, a long wait in a public line of scheduled debts. Although the constitutional provision refers to "judicial decision", the prevailing understanding is that the article 100 applies to the fulfillment of the obligation to pay established in an arbitration award.[10] In other words, the enforcement of an arbitration award in the face of the National Treasury would necessarily follow the *precatório* system.

In practical terms, the system of *precatório* allows the execution against the National Treasury by including in its budget the amount necessary to pay the debt established in a court decision, so that the amount due is paid in compliance with the order of presentation of the respective requests.[11] The procedure established in the Federal Constitution is a result of the determination that, in the Brazilian legal system, public assets are, in general, unseizable and inalienable. This is the reason that the National Treasury, once faced with a money demand to pay, is not submitted to ordinary execution rules such as the adoption of expropriation measures for the satisfaction of credit.

Once article 100 has been introduced, the next section explores the lack of effectiveness of the *precatório* scheme and its consequences.

3 The Adoption of the Precatório System and the Possibility of Compromising Arbitration Principles

Before the advent of the Federal Constitution in 1988, the *precatório* system was already in place and already considered ineffective. In 1986, a study highlighted that, once prompted to reimburse, state and municipal administrations frequently alleged that there were no funds available to pay without the sacrifice, for example, of public payroll. The *precatório* methodology should be rethought, advised the study, to preserve the effectiveness of enforcement against public entities and to respect the balance and harmony among the Powers.[12]

---

[9]Article 100 Brazilian Constitution, *caput*: "Payments due by the Federal, State, District and Municipal National Treasury, by virtue of a judicial decision, will be made exclusively in the chronological order of the presentation of the court orders ["precatórios"] and to the account of the respective credits, and the designation of cases or persons in the budget appropriations and additional credits opened for this purpose is prohibited".

[10]See Fichtner et al. (2019), Megna (2019), pp. 288–289; Timm and Richter (2016), pp. 255–276.

[11]Dantas (2005), pp. 81–100.

[12]Greco Filho (1986), p. 48.

Later, administrative law experts continued to emphasize that the demoralization of the coercive execution against the National Treasury was notorious. The crisis to honor commitments arising from court convictions resulted from the gradual growth of debts at the federal, state and municipal levels.[13] The Federal Constitution of 1988 defined a complicated *precatório* system and unveiled a litigious expedient of installments that made the enforcement against the National Treasury, with few exceptions, practically inextinguishable. As a former judge pointed out, the administrative insolvency would not be resolved by transferring it to the Judiciary and the *precatório* system resembled the Myth of Sisyphus: a repetitive, useless, and endless job.[14]

In terms of figures, in 2010, the Federal Justice Council (CJF) informed that the public sector owned R$ 60 billion in court orders. The president of the National Council of Justice (CNJ) at that time stated that irresponsibility has been a hallmark in the public sector, as there have already been three *moratoria* – in 1988 the public sector gained eight years for payment; in 2000 it gained another 10 years; and in 2009 another 15 years - and none of the deadlines were met.[15]

A 2020 study prepared by the CNJ updated the estimates of total debt of the Union, states and municipalities to R$ 97.3 billion.[16] Moreover, the relationship between the total budget of the Union and the allocation of resources for the payment of *precatórios* showed that, from 2016 to 2020, there was an annual allocation of less than 1.20% of the budget for this type of payment, as can be seen by comparing CJF reports and the transparency dashboard of the General Controller of the Union (CGU).[17]

Aside from the financial impossibility of paying debts accumulated by public entities, it is worth noticing other intricacies of article 100. Paragraphs 19 and 20 of

---

[13] Dallari (2005), pp. 177–192.

[14] Beneti (2005), pp. 369–378. Specifically regarding the comparison between the Myth of Sisyphus and the *precatório* system, the author states that: "(...) in the current court-ordered system, in which so much work is required from the parties, lawyers, judges and civil servants, one can see the representation of Sisyphus, condemned by Hades to the task of carrying a heavy stone to the top of the mountain, and then seeing it slide down to the valley, from where he was again forced to transport it to the top, in the useless labor of eternal torment."

[15] Conselho da Justiça Federal (2010), https://www.cjf.jus.br/cjf/outras-noticias/2010/setembro/setor-publico-deve-r-60-bilhoes-em-precatorios **It should also be mentioned that the moratoria on the payment of debts arising from court orders, informally called "calote" in Portuguese, were approved several times by the constituent power through the edition of constitutional amendments that inserted provisions in the Transitory Constitutional Provisions Acts (ADCT). However, at least one of this amendment was considered unconstitutional. STF Decision ADI n. 4.357/DF (2009) and STF Decision ADI n. 4.425/DF (2009).**

[16] Conselho Nacional de Justiça (2020), https://www.cnj.jus.br/tribunais-tem-ate-30-de-agosto-para-enviar-ao-cnj-dados-sobre-precatorios.

[17] Conselho Nacional de Justiça CNJ (2020). https://www.cjf.jus.br/cjf/corregedoria-da-justica-federal/corregedoria-geral-da-justica-federal/estatisticas-da-justica-federal-1/precatorios-e-rpvs. *See* also Controladoria-Geral da União CGU- (2021) http://www.portaltransparencia.gov.br/orcamento?ano=2020.

the concerned provision, for instance, opens the door for debt installments and rescheduling, regardless of the creditor's consent, if the public entity's net revenue is compromised by the payment.

In this context, it seems that the enforcement of an arbitration decision containing an obligation to pay through the *precatório* system may compromise the expected speediness in the effective resolution of conflicts.

As an example, in one case, the National Agency of Petroleum, Natural Gas and Biofuels (ANP) was ordered to pay a certain amount in an arbitral award. Approximately 5 (five) years elapsed between the filing of the enforcement action, embodied in the arbitration decision, and the payment of the debt through a court order. Thus, it appears that the fulfillment of the obligation to pay, established in the arbitration decision, could have been carried out more quickly, with no need for a period exceeding half a decade for the enforcement of the decision, which it could, for example, have occurred after the issuance of the arbitration award.[18]

Thus, it is imperative to rethink the mandatory application of the *precatório* system to comply with the obligation to pay established by an arbitration award. The practical effect of the system in Brazil is that the mechanism offsets the speed and informality of the arbitration procedure, which are relevant characteristics to justify the choice of arbitration as a method of conflict resolution.

But could the *precatórios* limitations be surmounted? For an adequate response to this question, the definition of a theoretical framework encompassing "consensualism" in the Public Administration will be presented.

4 The Application of Consensualism by the Public Administration

The option for adopting arbitration to resolve conflicts involving the Public Administration demonstrates the convergence towards one of the trends in contemporary administrative law. That is the search for consensus in the conduct of administrative management.

The quest is not trivial. One of the consequences of the characterization of a State governed by the rule of law is found in the principle of legality that informs the activities of Public Administration.[19] The understanding of this principle must encompass the observance of the formal law, voted by the Legislative, and also of

[18] The enforcement proceeding occurred at the 16th Federal Court of the Judiciary Section of Rio de Janeiro. At the end of 2014, the ANP was responsible for the payment of roughly R$ 5,4 million. *See* also JF 16 Seção Judiciária do Rio de Janeiro Lawsuit n° 0019013-98.2009.4.02.5101/RJ (*ANP v. Newfield Brasil LTDA)*.

[19] Federal Constitution (1988), article 37: "The direct and indirect Public Administration of any of the Powers of the Union, States, Federal District and Municipalities shall comply with the principles of *legality*, impersonality, morality, publicity and efficiency, as well as the following: (...)(emphasis added)".

the precepts arising from a Democratic State of Law, which is the way of being of the Brazilian State, as stated in art. 1st, caput, of the Constitution; and, still, it must include the observance of the other fundamentals and principles of constitutional base.[20]

As an author puts it, the use of consensualism and dialogue as means of Public Administration actions is undeniably an alternative, representing a beneficial renewal for politics and the legal system. It would contribute to improving governability (efficiency), providing more mechanisms against abuses (legality), ensuring the attention of all interests (justice), providing the wisest and prudent decision (legitimacy), avoiding moral deviations (lawfulness), developing the responsibility of the people (civism) and making state commands more acceptable and easily obeyed (order).[21]

The application of consensualism in Public Administration has resulted in the reduction of unilateral and unreasonable state measures to certain areas involving administrative action. Consequently, the so-called "consensual administration" flourishes, as well as the change in the axis of administrative law, which is now guided by the logic of authority leaned towards the logic of consensus. Therefore, administrative acts and administrative contracts are seen as legal instruments adopted by the Public Administration to carry out its duties, which are governed by the same similar logic, directed to the search for consensus.[22]

The performance of the Public Administration as a business can also be seen in the growing use of negotiating instruments signed between the Public Administration as a means of achieving the collective interest, such as the signing of administrative contracts for the concession of public service. This shift helps to demonstrate the overcoming of old practices that privilege the view of authority and the unilateral imposition of decisions by the public power. The application of consensus by the Public Administration has a singular relevance. It stimulates the creation of private solutions applied by the Public Administration, enriching its ways and forms of serving the public interest.[23] Consensualism, put in the perspective of conflict resolution, characterizes the dialogic Public Administration.[24]

Surely, arbitration is not a consensual means of solving disputes, since it represents a hetero composition, not a self-composition, mechanism. Consensus in arbitration is externalized in its establishment, as the consent of the parties involved, including the Public Administration itself, is essential for the conflict to be resolved in the "arbitration bench" and not by the Judiciary.

In this sense, the invocation of the arbitration agreement to settle conflicts related to administrative contracts exemplifies the dialogic action in administrative

[20] Medauar (2018).

[21] Moreira Neto (2003), pp. 129–156.

[22] Oliveira (2005), pp. 241–271.

[23] Moreira Neto (2003), pp. 129–156.

[24] Cunha (2020), pp. 140–162.

management, since in these adjustments the parties voluntarily adjust which conflict related to the signed contract will be submitted to arbitration.

Thus, the voluntary option of the use of arbitration by state entities, as an alternative method of resolving conflicts, is in line with the trend of contemporary administrative law that there should be a search for consensus and dialogue as a method of action of the Public Administration.

5 The Possibility of Voluntary Compliance with the Arbitration Decision

Arbitral courts do not have coercive powers, which is why the execution of its decision, if there is resistance to voluntary compliance, will depend on the apparatus of the State.[25]

Thus, an arbitral decision containing a money demand, if not voluntarily complied with, may trigger a judicial process of execution. The LAB considers the arbitration award binding, to the extent that it has the same effects of an award rendered by the bodies of the Judiciary Power.[26] The NCPC, likewise, categorizes the arbitration award as an enforceable title.[27]

But what if the defendant, the Public Administration, in this case, wants to spontaneously comply with the arbitration award, avoiding the filing of a lawsuit for the execution of an enforceable title?

First, that position would be in line with the voluntariness principle embedded in the arbitration agreement. Parties agreed to grant powers to the arbitration court to resolve any conflict of interest and to comply with what would be determined in the

---

[25] About this aspect, *see* Scavone Júnior (2019).

[26] LAB, Art. 31: "The arbitral award produces, between the parties and their successors, the same effects as the award rendered by the bodies of the Judiciary Power and, if condemning, constitutes an enforceable title".

[27] CPC, Art. 515, item VII: "These are judicial executive titles, which will be enforced in accordance with the articles provided for in this Title: (. . .) VII - the arbitration award." For further commentaries, *see* Carmona (2009), pp. xxx. To the extent that the arbitration proceeding may need court action in specific steps, makes the Brazilian nuances not different from the international harmonization efforts. *See* UNCITRAL (1985). UNCITRAL Model Law on International Commercial Arbitration. Article 6 https://uncitral.un.org/sites/uncitral.un.org/files/media-documents/uncitral/en/19-09955_e_ebook.pdf. The United Nations Commission for International Trade Law (UNCITRAL), which influenced and influences the domestic legislation of several countries, including Brazil, has a similar parameter on the legal discipline of arbitration. As the United Nations body responsible for the modernization and harmonization of rules concerning international trade, the UNCITRAL drafted, through a committee formed by 58 countries and 18 international organizations, the Model Law on Arbitration. Its final text was approved by the General Assembly of the United Nations on December 11, 1985, through resolution 40/72, and the success of the legislation was remarkable, as countries that handle most of the international trade have adopted laws based on the Convention. Diz and Ribeiro (2013), pp. 219–230.

arbitration award. Second, procedural loyalty would be met, since the defendant has the duty to comply with the determination in the award, without putting up undue obstacles to the satisfaction of the debt.[28]

However, spontaneous compliance with the arbitration award could collide with the mandatory observance of the *precatório* system established in the Federal Constitution, as exposed before.[29]

One alternative to consider is the situation in which a public interest exists. The National Treasury can pay the obligation voluntarily, when, for example, an advantage in carrying out a transaction in a dispute is tangible, such as a debt abatement or some gain identified by a cost benefit analysis.[30] In addition, legally speaking, there is no express prohibition regarding the implementation of a transaction by the Public Administration whereas the safeguarding of the public interest or its best satisfaction occurs precisely by the agreement. It is also noteworthy that coercive enforcement through the *precatório* system does not prevent the adoption of consensual solutions. There is no sense in hampering the Public Administration from seeking, among the possible solutions, the one that best meets the public interest.[31]

Indeed, enforcement of Judiciary awards bears the same option. No rule exists to prevent the Public Administration from entering into an agreement with the private party, with the purpose of resolving a pending matter that is the object of a lawsuit. If the judicial proceeding is in the execution phase, it is possible for the Public Administration to resolve the dispute by consensual means, without the issuance of a court order. The existence of ongoing judicial proceeding, even at the level of final enforcement, does not prevent a transaction.[32]

These arguments are in line with the perspective that Public Administration should act in a dialogical manner and be guided by the search for consensus in administrative management, without unnecessary delays. As the administrative literature points out, the adoption of the *precatório* system, as a rule, does not prevent public entities, guided by dialogic action and consensuality, from creating, under legal boundaries, "private solutions" so that there is effectiveness in fulfilling the obligation to pay determined in the arbitration award. In this context, freedom of choice meets the Public Law regime.[33]

[28] Nery Júnior and Nery (2015).

[29] Cunha (2017), p. 341.

[30] Bacellar (2016), p. 151, lists many advantages for the Public Administration with the use of arbitration, among them, the prevalence of the autonomy of the will of the parties, security, expertise, effectiveness and speed.

[31] Dallari (2005), pp. 177–192.

[32] Sundfeld and Câmara (2010), pp. 43–58.

[33] Moreira Neto (2003), pp. 129–156. As the author posits, "[t]hrough consensus, the Government goes beyond encouraging the practice of private conduct in the public interest, starting to encourage the creation of private solutions in the public interest, contributing to enrich its modes and forms of service." See also Oliveira (2005), pp. 241–271, "This is one of the main consequences of the intensification of relations and closer ties between the State, companies and civil society organizations in the contemporary world. The path of negotiation - and not the path of imposition - for the

Finally, the implementation of alternatives to the *precatório* system is a corollary of a consensus based and voluntary framework. It would be contradictory to choose arbitration as a method of conflict resolution, adopted due to the existing advantages for its use, and, at the same time, not improving the legal background or mitigating the historical difficulties involved in the judicial enforcement against the National Treasury.

Yet, one thing to consider should be the adoption of standards or rules by which the Public Administration would base its decision to spontaneously comply. The spontaneity relates to the arbitration award decision, not to an arbitrary choice.

6 Conclusion

This chapter made three initial assumptions: ISDS dispute mechanisms are not available in Brazil; State-to-State arbitration, as provided by ACFI has not been tested; and judicial proceedings in Brazil are overwhelmed and can take considerable time. From these starting points, this chapter explored the perspective for investors of domestic arbitration against public entities as provided by the LAB, after the 2015 amendment, i.e. the possibility of having the "Brazilian branches" in the arbitration "bench".

Though from the legal standpoint, public entities can be challenged under the LAB, the mandatory application of the *precatório* system for compliance with the arbitration decision may impact procedural informality. It also hampers, above all, speediness.

The *precatório* system indeed represents an obstacle not only to the enforcement of arbitration but to court awards, as well; not only to investors but also to any sort of companies or citizens litigating against the Brazilian Public Administration. However, once arbitration proceedings are confronted with the *precatório* mechanism, the clash of principles becomes obvious.

This chapter then invoked the doctrine that conceives contemporary administrative law as guided by consensus and dialogic action. This trend can involve the adoption of ADR methods, as one can already verify from the increased use of arbitration by the Brazilian Public Administration. It also can include the use of an effective mechanism to implement what the award decision had determined, such as the payment of cash amounts. Therefore, while arbitration is generally seen as an efficient ADR to settle disputes, the overall functioning of the *precatório* mechanism requires the improvement of this old-fashioned system or the possibility of spontaneous payments.

In the last case, the paradigm change would require the creation of standards, parameters, or rules to inform how the Public Administration should act.

---

composition of any disagreements between the parties, presupposes the recognition (although relativized by the legal-administrative regime) of the autonomy of the parties involved".

References

Aragão A (2017) A Arbitragem no Direito Administrativo. Revista da AGU 16(3):19–58

Bacellar R (2016) Mediação e Arbitragem, 2nd edn. Saraiva, São Paulo

Beneti S (2005) Os precatórios e o Mito de Sísifo. Revista Ibero-Americana de Direito Público 5(18):369–378

Campello D, Lemos L (2015) The non-ratification of bilateral investment treaties in Brazil: a story of conflict in a land of cooperation. Rev Int Polit Econ 22(5):1055–1086. https://doi.org/10.1080/09692290.2014.987154

Carmona C (2009) Arbitragem e processo: um comentário à Lei n° 9.307/96. 3nd edn. Atlas, São Paulo

Conselho da Justiça Federal – CJF (2010). https://www.cjf.jus.br/cjf/outras-noticias/2010/setembro/setor-publico-deve-r-60-bilhoes-em-precatorios. Accessed 5 July 2021

Conselho Nacional de Justiça – CNJ (2020). https://www.cjf.jus.br/cjf/corregedoria-da-justica-federal/corregedoria-geral-da-justica-federal/estatisticas-da-justica-federal-1/precatorios-e-rpvs. Accessed 5 July 2021

Conselho Nacional de Justiça – CNJ. https://www.cnj.jus.br/tribunais-tem-ate-30-de-agosto-para-enviar-ao-cnj-dados-sobre-precatorios/. Accessed 5 July 2021

Controladoria-Geral da União – CGU (2021). http://www.portaltransparencia.gov.br/orcamento. Accessed 5 July 2021

Cunha L (2017) A Fazenda Pública em juízo, 14nd edn. Forense, Rio de Janeiro

Cunha L (2020) Justiça multiportas: mediação, conciliação e arbitragem no Brasil. Revista ANNEP de Direito Processual 1(1):140–162. https://doi.org/10.34280/annep/2020.v1i1.33

Dallari A (2005) Acordo para recebimento de crédito perante a Fazenda Pública. Revista de Direito Administrativo 239:177–192. https://doi.org/10.12660/rda.v239.2005.43866

Dantas F (2005) O sistema dos precatórios e a efetividade do processo. Revista do Processo 30(127):81–100

Diz J, Ribeiro C (2013) Impacto e influência dos tratados e convenções internacionais sobre a lei brasileira de arbitragem. Revista de Direito Internacional 10(1):219–230

Fichtner J, Mannheimer S, Monteiro A (2019) Teoria geral da arbitragem. Forense, Rio de Janeiro

Greco Filho V (1986) Da execução contra a Fazenda Pública. Saraiva, São Paulo

Grinover A (2003) Arbitragem e Prestação de Serviços Públicos. R. Dir. Adm. 233:377–385 http://bibliotecadigital.fgv.br/ojs/index.php/rda/article/viewFile/45459/45041. Accessed 5 July 2021

Lemes S (2020) Arbitragem em Números e Valores. Oito Câmaras. 2 anos. Período de 2018 (jan./dez.) a 2019 (jan./dez.) http://selmalemes.adv.br/artigos/Analise-Pesquisa-ArbitragensNseValores-2020.pdf. Acessed 5 July 2021

Medauar O (2018) Direito Administrativo moderno. 21 nd edn. Belo Horizonte, Fórum

Megna B (2019) Arbitragem e Administração Pública: fundamentos teóricos e soluções práticas. Belo Horizonte, Fórum

Monebhurrun N (2017) Novelty in international investment law: the Brazilian agreement on cooperation and facilitation of investments as a different international investment agreement model. J Int Disp Settlement 8(79-100):2017

Moreira Neto D (2003) Novos institutos consensuais da ação administrativa. Revista de Direito Administrativo 231:129–156

Nery Júnior N, Nery R (2015) Comentários ao Código de Processo Civil. Revista dos Tribunais, São Paulo

Oliveira G (2005) A arbitragem e as parcerias público-privadas. R. Dir. Adm 241:241–271. https://doi.org/10.12660/rda.v241.2005.43372

Rocha C (2016) Arbitragem e Administração Pública: nova disciplina normativa após a Lei 13.129/2015. Revista de Arbitragem e Mediação 49(13):103–126

Samtleben J (1996). Histórico da Arbitragem no Brasil. In: Casella, P (ed.) Arbitragem: a nova lei brasileira (9.307/96) e a praxe internacional. LTr, São Paulo, pp. 29-86.

Scavone Júnior L (2019) Arbitragem - Mediação, Conciliação e Negociação, 9nd edn. Forense, Rio de Janeiro
Sundfeld C, Câmara J (2010) Acordos na execução contra a Fazenda Pública. Revista Brasileira de Direito Público – RBDP 8(30):43–58
Timm T, Richter M (2016) Os contratos administrativos e a arbitragem: aspectos jurídicos e econômicos. Revista de Arbitragem e Mediação 50(13):255–276
UNCITRAL (1985) UNCITRAL Model Law on International Commercial Arbitration https://uncitral.un.org/es/texts/arbitration/modellaw/commercial_arbitration. Accessed 5 July 2021
Vidigal G, Stevens B (2018) Brazil's new model of dispute settlement for investment: return to the past or alternative for the future? J World Investment Trade 19(3):475–512. https://doi.org/10.1163/22119000-12340100

João Paulo Santos Borba holds a master's in law (CEUB). Postgraduate in Public Law (University of Brasilia). Lawyer at the Federal Attorney General Office (AGU).

Gustavo Ferreira Ribeiro holds a S.J.D. from Maurer School of Law - 2009 (Fulbright/CAPES grantee). He also holds a Master's in Law (UFSC, 2004), Bachelor's in Law (UFMG, 2002), and a Bachelor's Degree of Computer Science (UFMG, 1996). Mr. Ribeiro currently teaches International Economic Law, Law and Technology and Methodology at the University Centre of Brasília (CEUB). Mr. Ribeiro is, since 2018, part of the staff and the Head of The Market Access Division of the Intelligence Department at ApexBrasil.

Part III
Trends in Connecting Investment Law to Human Rights

The 2017 BIT Model of Colombia: A Human Rights Assessment from Investment Disputes Against the State

Carolina Olarte-Bácares, Enrique Prieto-Rios, and Juan P. Pontón-Serra

1 Introduction

The International Investment Law (IIL) system, understood as the principles, norms and institutions that are in place for the protection of foreign investors in host countries has been the subject of criticisms from different stakeholders. One of the main criticisms has been linked with the relationship between states obligations to respect, protect and promote human rights, on the one hand, and to respect international obligations towards foreign investors, on the other hand. Sources of conflict between and IIL and human rights mainly emerge from, first, the possibility that foreign investors protected by international investment agreements (IIAs) challenge the host state's laws, regulations and policies aimed at protecting human rights in its territory, and second, the adoption of foreign investment attraction policies characterized by a relaxation by states of the respect of human rights.[1] This was recognized back in 2009 by the Special Representative of the Secretary-General on the issue of human rights and transnational corporations and other business enterprises who observed on investment and trade agreements that "recent experience suggests that some treaty guarantees and contract provisions may unduly constrain the host

[1] Abdullah Al Faruque (2010), pp. 552–553.

C. Olarte-Bácares (✉)
Pontificia Universidad Javeriana, Bogotá, Colombia
e-mail: c.olarte@javeriana.edu.co

E. Prieto-Rios
Faculty of Law, Universidad del Rosario, Bogota, Colombia
e-mail: enrique.prieto@urosario.edu.co

J. P. Pontón-Serra
Universidad del Rosario, Bogota, Colombia
e-mail: juan.ponton@urosario.edu.co

N. Monebhurrun et al. (eds.), *International Investment Law and Arbitration from a Latin American Perspective*, International Law and the Global South,
https://doi.org/10.1007/978-3-031-49382-9_9

Government's ability to achieve its legitimate policy objectives, including its international human rights obligations".[2] In this regard, in 2011, the United Nations Guiding Principles on Business and Human Rights, unanimously endorsed by the Human Rights Council includes principle 9 which requires States to "*maintain adequate domestic policy space to meet their human rights obligations when pursuing business-related policy objectives with other States or business enterprises, for instance through investment treaties or contracts*".[3] This principle arises from the potential conflict between State's obligations under trade and foreign investment agreements and their duty to respect, protect and fulfil human rights through domestic measures.

Similarly, the United Nations Committee on Economic, Social and Cultural Rights noted in its General Comment 21 encouraged states "to insert, in future treaties, a provision explicitly referring to their human rights obligations" and to encourage that investor-state dispute settlement (ISDS) mechanisms "take human rights into account in the interpretation of investment treaties or of investment chapters in trade agreements".[4]

Within this context, bilateral investment treaties (BIT) models, which at first were adopted by developed countries to set in motion negotiations with developing countries,[5] have been one of the main instruments used by developing states to rebalance IIL obligations, through the clarification of the scope of substantive provisions or the limitation of the power of interpretation granted to arbitral tribunals. In the current context of IIL criticism and reform of the ISDS mechanism, BIT Models have served as an instrument for states to mirror its stance on the IIL and on politically sensitive issues. Accordingly, this chapter will focus on how Colombia adopted in 2017 a new version of BIT Model, which, in addition to continuing trends of delimitation of the scope and content of substantive and ISDS provisions, contains several references to human rights. Specifically, this chapter assesses the 2017 Colombian BIT model using as a comparative element ISDS cases with human rights features.

The chapter is divided in four sections, the first section deals with Colombia's relationship with IIL since the 1990s, when the state started to regularly sign IIAs, including BITs and treaties with investment provisions, mostly free trade agreements (FTAs). A presentation of previous BIT models adopted in 2003, 2006, 2009 and

[2]Human Rights Council. Eleventh session, 'Business and Human Rights: Towards Operationalizing the "Protect, Respect and Remedy" Framework. Report of the Special Representative of the Secretary-General on the Issue of Human Rights and Transnational Corporations and Other Business Enterprises' (United Nations, 22 April 2009), para. 30.

[3]Human Rights Council. Seventeenth session., 'Guiding Principles on Business and Human Rights. Implementing the United Nations "Protect, Respect and Remedy" Framework' (New York: United Nations General Assembly, 21 May 2011) principle 9.

[4]Committee on Economic, Social and Cultural Rights, 'General Comment No. 24 (2017) on State Obligations under the International Covenant on Economic, Social and Cultural Rights in the Context of Business Activities' (United Nations, 10 August 2017), para. 13.

[5]Vandevelde (2011), pp. 307–316.

2011, as well as the Colombia state's introduction to the investor-State dispute settlement (ISDS) in 2015, will be included. With this background, the third section will present the main provisions of the 2017 BIT Model, with particular focus on human rights related and human rights relevant provisions. The fourth section will discuss current ISDS cases against Colombia that involve significant human rights features, particularly by identifying the main source of tension between protection of human rights and enforcement of the applicable IIA.

2 Building the Path Towards the 2017 BIT Model

Colombia began to regularly sign IIAs in the 1990s, following the enactment of the 1991 Colombian Constitution, which was embedded in the context of economic liberalization and global integration policies.[6] As stated by the commission of the National Constituent Assembly in charge of economic, social and ecological matters, economic integration fell within a broader integration process that was the expression of a "transcendental trend of contemporary international law".[7] In this form, the Colombian Constitutions contains several clauses that deal with economic liberalization, the protection of economic freedoms, the protection of property and private initiative,[8] among other relevant clauses of what is usually referred as the "economic constitution".[9] For instance, articles 226 and 227 of the Constitution instructed the promotion of the internationalization of international relations and economic integration through the signature of international treaties.

As direct consequence of the liberalization agenda, that started in the 1990s and came along with neoliberal ideology, Colombia began adopting domestic policies to be an active participant of the global market and to attract foreign direct investment (FDI) as part of the national economic policy. FDI was (and still is) seen as a driver for economic growth and development. In this context, the first IIA signed by Colombia after the 1991 Constitution came into force was, the BIT signed with United Kingdom in 1994. This BIT contained 11 pages and standard provisions on fair and equitable treatment (FET), most favoured nation (MFN) and national

[6] See generally: Velásquez Ruiz (2020).

[7] Comisión Quinta, Asamblea Nacional Constituyente, 'Internacionalización de Las Relaciones Económicas e Integración Supranacional' (Colección digital: Asamblea Nacional Constituyente, 15 April 1991), 1, https://babel.banrepcultural.org/digital/collection/p17054coll28/id/322/rec/69.

[8] Guinard Hernandez (2017), p. 96.

[9] The concept of 'Economic Constitution', which has its origins in German constitutionalism, has been defined by the Constitutional Court as 'the constitutional norms that direct the economic life of society and establish the essential legal framework for the structuring and functioning of the material productive activity' (Corte Constitucional de Colombia, Sentencia C-265 de 1994 (M.P. Alejandro Martínez Caballero) [2 June 1994]); and that encompasses matters related to private property, freedom of enterprise, public expenditure, state budget and goods and services (Corte Constitucional de Colombia, Sentencia T-505 de 1992 (M.P. Eduardo Cifuentes Muñoz) [28 August 1992]).

treatment, and protection against expropriation without compensation, as well as referral to ICSID arbitration in case of investor-state disputes. The BIT signed with United Kingdom was followed by three almost identical BIT, with Peru, Cuba, and Spain. The Colombian Constitutional Court when making the automatic constitutional revision of the mentioned treaties deemed that they were partially constitutional. The Court ruled that the BITs expropriation provisions, were contrary to paragraph four of article 58 of the Constitution that allowed for expropriation without compensation for reasons of equity. The declarations of unconstitutionality of the expropriation provisions of the first four BITs signed by the state, which prevented their ratification, led to a reform of the Colombian Constitution in 1999. Article 58 was amended to remove its paragraph four, establishing that expropriation was always followed by compensation without any exception. Thus, the Colombian Constitution was amended to follow the same legal logic as the one followed by IIAs.

After the constitutional amendment, the commitment to the integration of the Colombian economy to the international market and the protection and attraction foreign investment persisted in the following decades. Some of the policies have been the elimination of barriers to international trade and foreign investment and the persistent signing of BITs and FTAs among others.[10] In the last two decades, Colombia has ratified 19 IIAs, out of which 8 are BITs (Spain, Switzerland, Perú, China, India, United Kingdom, Japan, and France) and 11 FTAs with investment provisions (México, Chile, Northern Triangle of Central America, EFTA, Canada, United States, European Union, North Korea, Costa Rica, Pacific Alliance, and Israel).

With the purpose of establishing a standardized basis for the negotiation of IIAs, the Colombian government adopted in 2003 its first BIT Model. This was an eight-page document with the usual substantive provisions drafted in a short and broad manner that did not specify neither their content nor the guiding criteria for its determination. This BIT model was ambiguous making the state vulnerable to investment claim in case of any dispute.[11] The 2003 BIT Model served as the basis of the Colombia – Spain BIT, the Colombia – Switzerland BIT and the Colombia – United States FTA, all signed in 2006. It is worth mentioning that out of all the arbitration cases against Colombia registered by the ICSID, at the time of writing this chapter, 11 are based on one of these three IIAs. The 2003 BIT Model was revised in 2006 to incorporate new discussions and trends within the IIL system.[12] However, the 2006 BIT model did not incorporate any specific provision aimed at protection Colombian state's interests.[13]

In 2009, a new BIT Model, later revised in 2011, was adopted by the Colombian government. This time the model included more precise definitions on the scope of

[10] Matamoros and Victoria (2019).

[11] García Matamoros, 105.

[12] UNCTAD (2006), p. 22.

[13] García Matamoros, 'La Relación Entre Las Políticas de Inversión Extranjera En Colombia y Los Acuerdos Internacionales de Inversión', 106.

investment and investor, on the FET standard—which was confined to the customary minimum standard of treatment–, on the protection against expropriation and on the settlement of disputes between the state and investors. In this 2011 model, non-discriminatory measures based on public purpose or social interest, aimed at the protection of public health, security and environment, were explicitly excluded from the definition of indirect expropriation. While no direct reference was made to human rights, the 2011 Model included a provision stating that the BIT was not be construed as an obstacle to the adoption or enforcement of measures aimed at guaranteeing that investments were made in conformity with environmental and labour legislation. A provision on general exceptions was also included. These provisions had been included in previous IIAs signed by Colombia, mainly with the aim of protecting international security, public order, and financial services. The 2011 Model further includes as legitimate objectives of the general exceptions provision the protection of the environment and of human, animal and vegetal life and health.[14]

Contrary to most of its regional peers, such as Argentina, Mexico and Venezuela, Colombia was a stranger to ISDS in the years that followed the signature of the first IIA. As such, the perceived benefits of signing IIAs were put forward while its drawbacks were rarely acknowledged. Only in 2010, with the adoption of Document 3684 of the National Council for Economic and Social Policy, the possibility that a foreign investor brought an international claim against the state under IIAs was recognized. In this document, the Council diagnosed that "the country is not prepared to prevent and solve timely and effectively the possible disputes that arise from IIAs" as a result of "the lack of understanding by officials at all levels of the reach of IIAs".[15] Consequently, the Council established a course of action aimed at adjusting the institutional capacity of the state to prevent and face ISDS claims.

The first ever international investment arbitration claim against Colombia was filed by the investors Cosigo Resources and Tobie Mining in 2015.[16] Since then, Colombia has faced a significant number of international investment arbitrations. So far, the claims against Colombia have arisen from the sectors of oil, gas & mining,[17]

---

[14]The Republic of Colombia, 'Bilateral Agreement of the Promotion and Protection of Investments of Colombia and _____. Colombian Model 2011' (n.d.), https://investmentpolicy.unctad.org/international-investment-agreements/countries/45/colombia.

[15]Consejo Nacional de Política Economica y Social, 'Fortalecimiento de La Estrategia Del Estado Para La Prevención y Atención de Controversias Internacionales de Inversión. Documento CONPES 3684', 19 October 2010, 13.

[16]Cosigo Resources, Ltd., Cosigo Resources Sucursal Colombia, Tobie Mining and Energy, Inc. v. Republic of Colombia, No. UNCITRAL (n.d.).

[17]Glencore International A.G. and C.I. Prodeco S.A. v. the Republic of Colombia, No. ICSID Case No. ARB/16/6 (n.d.); Eco Oro Minerals Corp. v. the Republic of Colombia, No. ICSID Case No. ARB/16/41 (n.d.); Red Eagle Exploration Limited v. the Republic of Colombia, No. ICSID Case No. ARB/18/12 (n.d.); Galway Gold Inc. v. the Republic of Colombia, No. ICSID Case No. ARB/18/13 (n.d.); Gran Colombia Gold Corp. v. the Republic of Colombia, No. ICSID Case No. ARB/18/23 (n.d.); Amec Foster Wheeler USA Corporation, Process Consultants, Inc., and

finance,[18] energy,[19] telecommunications,[20] and construction.[21] Most of the claims have involved issues of public interest, generally involving decisions by high courts or control agencies. Out of all the cases, only five have been solved on the merits, with a balance mostly favourable to the state. However, none of the cases that deal at their core with issues of human rights, which will be analyzed further on, have been solved.

The first wave of claims against Colombia, as well as new developments of IIL, prompted the government to adopt two important decisions. On the one hand, the Higher Council for Foreign Trade decided to halt the subscription and ratification of new IIAs, while at the same time honoring the existing IIAs.[22] On the other hand, the Ministry of Commerce, Industry and Tourism, in charge of the negotiation of IIAs, decided in 2015 to launch a public consultation for the adoption of a new version of BIT Model. The new BIT Model was drafted with insights from academics, practitioners, and organizations like the United Nations Conference on Trade and Development (UNCTAD) and the International Institute for Sustainable Development (IISD).[23] Moreover, the new BIT Model was nurtured both by previous experiences of Latin American states in investor-state arbitrations and by Colombia's own first-hand experience as respondent in investor-state arbitration claims.[24]

Joint Venture Foster Wheeler USA Corporation and Process Consultants, Inc. v. the Republic of Colombia, No. ICSID Case No. ARB/19/34 (n.d.); South32 SA Investments Limited v. the Republic of Colombia, No. ICSID Case No. ARB/20/9 (n.d.); Glencore International A.G. v. Republic of Colombia, No. ICSID Case No. ARB/21/30 (n.d.); Glencore International A. G., C. I. Prodeco S.A., and Sociedad Portuaria Puerto Nuevo S.A. v. Republic of Colombia, No. ICSID Case No. ARB/19/22 (n.d.); Anglo American plc v. the Republic of Colombia, No. ICSID Case No. ARB/21/31 (n.d.).

[18] Astrida Benita Carrizosa v. the Republic of Colombia, No. ICSID Case No. ARB/18/5 (n.d.); Alberto Carrizosa Gelzis, Felipe Carrizosa Gelzis and Enrique Carrizosa Gelzis v. the Republic of Colombia, No. PCA Case No. 2018-56 (2021); AFC Investment Solutions S.L. v. the Republic of Colombia, No. ICSID Case No. ARB/20/16 (n.d.).

[19] Naturgy Energy Group, S.A. and Naturgy Electricidad Colombia, S.L. (formerly Gas Natural SDG, S.A. and Gas Natural Fenosa Electricidad Colombia, S.L.) v the Republic of Colombia, No. ICSID Case No. UNCT/18/1 (n.d.).

[20] América Móvil S.A.B. de C.V. v. the Republic of Colombia, No. ICSID Case No. ARB(AF)/16/5 (n.d.); Telefónica, S.A. v. Republic of Colombia, No. ICSID Case No. ARB/18/3 (n.d.); Neustar, Inc. v. the Republic of Colombia, No. ICSID Case No. ARB/20/7 (n.d.).

[21] Angel Samuel Seda and others v. the Republic of Colombia, No. ICSID Case No. ARB/19/6 (n. d.).

[22] Consejo Superior de Comercio Exterior, 'Sesión 100. Política de Aprovechamiento de Los Acuerdos Comerciales', 9 October 2018.

[23] García Matamoros, 'La Relación Entre Las Políticas de Inversión Extranjera En Colombia y Los Acuerdos Internacionales de Inversión', 109.

[24] García Matamoros, 111; Duggal et al. (2019), p. 227.

3 The 2017 BIT Model

The 2017 BIT Model maintains a commitment to the global integration and foreign investment attraction policies that have been prevalent since 1991 while trying to balance any negative impact of IIL in the state's right to regulate, including any "chilling effect" on the adoption of public interest measures.[25] The 2017 BIT Model serves two main functions, as noted by two state officials behind its elaboration. On the one hand, it provides a predictable road map for the negotiation, re-negotiation, or adoption of joint interpretative declarations of IIAs. On the other hand, it establishes an interpretative guideline for the assessment of the understanding by the Colombian state of its commitments on IIL.[26] The former aspect is highly relevant given that, while the state has not signed new IIAs since 2014, it is currently renegotiating some of the earliest IIA in force, notably those signed with Spain in 2005 and with Switzerland in 2006. Moreover, the state adopted in 2020 joint interpretative declarations with France and Israel to clarify and limit the scope of some of its provisions.[27] While focus will be made on the provisions relating to human rights (3.2), it is worth mentioning other important additions of the 2017 BIT Model (3.1).[28]

On general jurisdictional aspects, the Model restricts the definition of investor and investments. In the case of "investment", the standard four elements of definition are included: commitment of capital, expectation of gain or profit, duration, and assumption of risk. However, in the case of duration, what is assessed is the investor's intention to maintain a long-term presence in the territory of the host state. This aims to bring flexibility to the definition, allowing for a focus on each investor business model instead of on fixed periods of time.[29] Furthermore, the model includes a closed list of assets that can be considered as investment, instead of an open-ended list. The Model also provides more careful drafting of concepts such as "effective control" and "substantial business activities". In the case of the former, it is established that any investor must exercise effective control over an investment,

[25] García Matamoros, 'La Relación Entre Las Políticas de Inversión Extranjera En Colombia y Los Acuerdos Internacionales de Inversión', 111.

[26] Nicolás Palau van Hissenhoven and Samuel Trujillo Murcia, 'El nuevo AII Modelo de Colombia: una herramienta necesaria para re-balancear el sistema arbitral de inversiones', *Debate Global* (blog), 1 September 2017, https://debateglobal.wordpress.com/2017/09/01/el-nuevo-aii-modelo-de-colombia-una-herramienta-necesaria-para-re-balancear-el-sistema-arbitral-de-inversiones/.

[27] Carolina Olarte-Bácares, Enrique Prieto-Ríos, and Juan P. Pontón-Serra, 'Are Interpretative Declarations Appropriate Instruments to Avoid Uncertainty? The Cases of the Colombia–France BIT and the Colombia–Israel FTA', IISD, *Investment Treaty News* (blog), 19 December 2020, https://www.iisd.org/itn/en/2020/12/19/are-interpretative-declarations-appropriate-instruments-to-avoid-uncertainty-the-cases-of-the-colombia-france-bit-and-the-colombia-israel-fta-carolina-olarte-bacares-enrique-prieto-rios-juan-ponton-se/.

[28] A thorough account on the most relevant provisions of the 2017 BIT Model can be found at: Duggal et al., 'Colombia's 2017 Model IIA'.

[29] Duggal et al., 228.

which can only be determined by a closed list of criteria. In the case of the latter, the concept is included to define an enterprise from a contracting party and is defined by detailed criteria that must be considered to determine its existence.[30]

On the substantive provisions, the 2017 BIT Model continues the global trend to carefully define and circumscribe the scope of the standards of treatment to limit the room for interpretation of arbitral tribunals. The national and MFN treatment provisions of the Model stem from the recognition that the interpretation of the concept of "treatment" in IIL has become blurred and has departed from the states' original intention.[31] As such, only treatment for the purposes of protecting the covered investor and investments against any impact on the competitive relationship with other investors or investments are included, that is, treatment related to "expansion of productive capacity, management and direction, operation, sale, and other forms of disposal of investments in the host state territory".[32] Definitions, substantive standards of treatment, procedural obligations, and dispute settlement mechanisms are explicitly excluded from the national and MFN treatment provisions. In the case of FET, there is a closed list of conducts that amount to a breach of the standard; and no references to "legitimate expectations" are included. Previous practice of assimilating the FET to the customary minimum standard of treatment, which has been deprived of any practical effects by arbitral tribunals, is avoided. Regarding the expropriation clause, the Model does not include the payment of compensation as a requirement of the lawfulness of an indirect expropriation. Moreover, the determination of compensation is made dependent on "an equitable balance between the public interest and the interest of the affected Covered Investor",[33] among others.

On the settlement of disputes, the BIT Model contains a detailed regulation of ISDS. Its provisions evidence the state's intent to prevent first and foremost investor-state disputes. As such, the Model provides precise time limits on the submission of both the notice of dispute to the respondent state and, if the disputing parties have not reached an agreement, the intention to submit a request for arbitration through a notice of intent. An entire article deals with consultations, which are to be carried out in a six-month period and, in the case of Colombia, are to be governed by domestic law. The Model also limits the possibility for the investor to raise claims in the arbitration that were not identified in the notice of dispute. It also conditions the submission of a claim by the investor to the communication of the matter of controversy to the foreign investment ombudsman of the host respondent state, if such a figure has been established by the latter. This for the ombudsman to attempt to

[30]The Republic of Colombia, 'Bilateral Investment Treaty between the Republic of Colombia and _____. Colombian Model 2017' (2017) SECTION [AA]-SCOPE AND DEFINITIONS.

[31]Nicolás Palau van Hissenhoven and Samuel Trujillo Murcia, 'Descripción general del AII Modelo', *Debate Global* (blog), 1 September 2017, https://debateglobal.wordpress.com/2017/09/01/descripcion-general-del-aii-modelo/.

[32]The Republic of Colombia, Bilateral investment treaty between the Republic of Colombia and _____. Colombian Model 2017 Article [##]-National Treatment, Article [##]-Most-Favoured Nation Treatment.

[33]The Republic of Colombia Article [##]-Compensation arising from an Expropriation.

solve the investor's situation. Moreover, the Model provides an article that lists a set of omissions by the claimant investor that amount to a tacit withdrawal of the dispute. This aims to penalize the procedural inactivity of investors following the submission claim, a practice that has been common in cases against Colombia.[34]

Regarding human rights, the 2017 BIT Model contains several references aimed at reinforcing the states' right to regulate. Its preamble reaffirms "the right of each Contracting Party to regulate the investments made in its Territory to protect legitimate public welfare objectives such as human rights, health, public order and safety, labour rights and environment".[35] The reference to the right to regulate in the preamble can inform the interpretation of the object and purpose of the BIT by arbitral tribunals,[36] particularly in application of article 31(2) of the Vienna Convention on the Law of Treaties that includes the preamble as part of the context to be considered in the interpretation of treaties.

The right to regulate is then again mentioned in the Model as an operative clause in Section [CC] entitled "Right to regulate and investment related obligations". Its wording is similar to the one included in the preamble, this time incorporating those "legitimate public policy objectives such as those enshrined in their Constitutions or in international agreements that promote and protect human rights (...)".[37] The scope of this clause is further broadened by Annex 6, which provides that any measures adopted, maintained or modified in order to implement the Peace Agreements between the Colombian government and any armed group will not be considered in breach of the BIT unless they are discriminatory and arbitrary. Not only this provision incorporates obligations of other international law regimes, particularly of international human rights law, but it also aims at defending interests of great importance for the Colombian state, such as the protection of the Constitution and the implementation of the 2012 Peace Agreement signed between the government and the FARC guerrilla group, instead of the usual one-size-fits-all interests that are included in IIAs. While the indication of "any" armed group allows to encompass future peace agreements involving other armed groups in addition to the FARC guerrilla, a specific mention of the 2012 Peace Agreements would have been adequate, considering how it has been alerted that its implementation could result in investment claims against the state.[38]

Section [CC] of the 2017 BIT Model contains other relevant additions regarding human rights. A provision on general exceptions, that exempt from the breach of the treaty the adoption, maintaining and enforcement of measures deemed necessary by

---

[34] The Republic of Colombia SECTION [DD]-INVESTOR-STATE DISPUTE SETTLEMENT.

[35] The Republic of Colombia Preamble.

[36] Coleman et al. (2020), p. 304.

[37] The Republic of Colombia, Bilateral investment treaty between the Republic of Colombia and _____. Colombian Model 2017 Article [##]-Chapeau on Investment and Regulatory Measures.

[38] For an analysis of the challenges that IIL poses to the Colombian Peace Agreement, see: Prieto-Rios et al. (2016), pp. 223–247; Urueña and Prieto-Rios (2017), pp. 159–182; Velásquez Ruiz (2016).

the host state to protect human rights, among others legitimate objectives, is included.[39] As previously mentioned, general exceptions clauses in IIAs signed by Colombia have not been uncommon, first with reference only to national security, public security, or public order,[40] then also to human, animal or plant life and health, environment, and non-living exhaustible natural resources.[41] However, two highly relevant additions of the Model in relation to both IIAs signed by Colombia and other states,[42] are the explicit reference to the protection of human rights and the self-judging nature of exceptions. This latter aspect has been subject of much debate surrounding general exceptions and their interpretation by arbitral tribunals. Doubts have been raised regarding general exceptions that leave open to determination whether a measure corresponds to a listed public policy objective or not and, more specifically, whether this can result in an even further hinderance of the regulatory powers of states.[43] The general exception clause is followed by a "non-lowering of standards" provision that includes the recognition that the promotion of investment by Contracting Parties is not made by "detracting from or diminishing environmental, human rights or labour standards". The provision adds that no modification or derogation of laws and regulations that imply the detraction from these standards can result from a measure to promote foreign investment.[44]

In addition to the reaffirmation of the right to regulate in both the preamble and operative provisions, the BIT Model includes an article on social responsibility, entitled "Investor's Social Responsibility". Paragraph one establishes the obligation of Contracting Parties to endeavor to ensure that investors "incorporate and practice the Organization for Economic Development (OECD) Guidelines for Multinational Enterprises on a voluntary basis".[45] Paragraph two goes beyond and imposes an obligation to Claimant investors to "respect the prohibitions established in international instruments, to which any Contracting Party is or becomes a party, pertaining to human rights and the environment". Furthermore, paragraph two conditions the submission of an ISDS claim to the acceptance by Claimant investors of "the

---

[39] The Republic of Colombia, Bilateral investment treaty between the Republic of Colombia and _____. Colombian Model 2017 Article [##]-General Exceptions.

[40] 'Bilateral Agreement for the Promotion and Protection of Investments between the Government of the United Kingdom of Great Britain and Northern Ireland and the Republic of Colombia' (2010) Article IV.

[41] 'Agreement between the Government of the Republic of Colombia and the Government of the Republic of Turkey Concerning the Reciprocal Promotion and Protection of Investments' (2014) Article 6.

[42] Jesse Coleman et al. (2020), p. 306.

[43] Alschner and Hui (2018); Martini (2018), p. 2877.

[44] The Republic of Colombia, Bilateral investment treaty between the Republic of Colombia and _____. Colombian Model 2017 Article [##]-Non-detraction from environmental, human rights and labour standards.

[45] The Republic of Colombia Article [##]-Investors' Social Responsibility.

aforementioned prohibitions as mandatory throughout the making of its investment and its operation".[46]

Also included in Section [CC] but with broader effects besides the preservation of the right to regulate is the Denial of Benefits clause, which lists a set of situations that allow a Contracting Party to deny to an investor the benefits of the treaty. The clause includes usual grounds of IIAs for the denial of benefits, such as the absence of substantial business activities in the territory of the home contracting party and the lack of effective control of the investment by a home contracting party enterprise. However, the BIT Model expands on these grounds by including the commission of "serious human rights violations", "serious environmental damage" and grave violations of labour laws, as well as the sponsorship of "persons or organisations sentenced because of serious human rights violations or violations against International Humanitarian Law" or the sponsorship of "internationally-listed terrorist organisations", that have been proven by "an international court of judicial or administrative authority of any State with which the Contracting Parties have diplomatic relations".[47] This latter inclusion is another significant evidence of a willingness by the government to incorporate aspects relevant to the Colombian context of internal armed conflict and transitional justice.

Two provisions that do not refer specifically to human rights but that may have significant impacts on their protection are both included in the ISDS section: one relates to counterclaims and the other to *amicus curiae* intervention. On the one hand, the BIT Model provides that the respondent state may submit a claim against the claimant investor before the decision of the tribunal on the merits and on the terms of the ISDS scope of application established by the treaty.[48] Indeed, the latter extends the application of ISDS to claims raised by the respondent state either in relation to the subject matter of the dispute or to any of the grounds included in the denial of benefits clause.[49] Moreover, the Model provides that the consent to arbitration by the investor must explicitly recognize the possibility that states submit claims against it. [50] Under these provisions, the respondent state in a dispute may submit a claim against the investor if for instance a judicial authority in Colombia has proven that it has committed serious human rights violations. On the other hand, the BIT Model allows for the intervention by *amicus curiae* under the invitation of the arbitral tribunal and upon the identification "of the author, and any person who provides financial or any other assistance for the preparation of such submission". This drafting differs from the one that governs interventions by Non-Disputing

[46]'Agreement between the Government of the Republic of Colombia and the Government of the French Republic for the Promotion and Protection of Investments' (2014) Article 11.

[47]The Republic of Colombia, Bilateral investment treaty between the Republic of Colombia and _____. Colombian Model 2017 Article [##]-Denial of Benefits.

[48]The Republic of Colombia Article [##]-Disputes and Claims raised by the Respondent State.

[49]The Republic of Colombia Article [##]-Scope of Application of Investor-State Dispute Settlement.

[50]The Republic of Colombia Article [##]-Submission of a claim before a Court of Law or Arbitral Tribunal.

Party, which must be accepted by the arbitral tribunal and is not dependent on any invitation by it. [51]

The provisions of the 2017 BIT Model have disparately found their way into the agreed text of newly concluded investment treaties to which Colombia is party. Provisions requiring an intention to maintain a long-term presence for an operation to qualify as "investment" can be found in the 2023 Venezuela-Colombia BIT. Exclusions from the scope of MFN of the provisions on definitions, denial of benefits and ISDS can be found in the 2021 Spain BIT. Omission of "legitimate expectations" as part of the FET standard can be observed in the United Arab Emirates 2017 BIT, while the FET standard is omitted altogether in the 2023 Venezuela BIT. Provisions on the State's right to regulate and on social responsibility standards are included in the 2021 Spain BIT. While it may be difficult to link the inclusion of these provisions exclusively to the 2017 BIT Model, and not to a global trend in the modernization of investment treaties, some examples evince more clearly such a link. For instance, the 2021 Spain BIT contains a provision on denial of benefits for grounds different than absence of business activities, as well as a provision on amicus curiae intervention, that are drafted identically to the corresponding provisions of the BIT Model.

4 Assessing the 2017 BIT Model from a Human Rights Perspective

From a quick reading of the 2017 BIT Model adopted by Colombia it is possible to easily evidence the purpose of the government to implement human rights aspects and to preventively avoid any tension with obligations towards foreign investors. However, these additions most be analyzed with caution, by analyzing potential impacts on disputes and adequate incorporations of international human rights law that allow for a real correspondence between IIL and human rights.[52] While it is difficult to assess the impact that provisions from the 2017 BIT Model may have in upcoming ISDS cases involving Colombia, if effectively incorporated in future IIAs, it is nonetheless possible to assess them considering existing disputes.

As it was stated in previous sections, Colombia was a newcomer to the ISDS system, becoming respondent in an international investment arbitration only in 2015, almost two decades after the signature of the first IIA. As registered by the UNCTAD, Colombia was the most respondent state in 2018[53] and among the four most respondent states in 2019.[54] At the time of writing this chapter, 20 ISDS cases against Colombia have been registered. Out of these, only on six cases a decision on

---

[51] The Republic of Colombia Article [##]-Intervention by Amicus Curiae and Non-Disputing Party.

[52] Jesse Coleman et al. (2020), p. 309.

[53] UNCTAD (2019), p. 103.

[54] UNCTAD (2020), p. 111.

the merits has been issued by the respective tribunal, with two being decided in favour of the investor[55] and five in favour of Colombia.[56] The following paragraphs introduce cases which have strong human rights features, that is, cases in which the tension between the protection of human rights and the enforcement of IIAs is evident.

The first ISDS case against Colombia was registered in 2005 under both the Colombia – United States FTA and the Colombia—Canada FTA by the companies Cosigo Resources (Canada), Cosigo Resources Sucursal Colombia (Colombia) and Tobie Mining Energy Inc. (United States). These mining companies challenged a 2009 resolution that ordered the creation of the Yaigojé Apaporis national park in the Taraira region, which led to the suspension of all mining activities in the territory of the park. The resolution was passed almost simultaneously as the signing of a mining gold concession contract between the Colombian national mining agency and Andrés Rendle, the legal representative of Cosigo Resources. The conclusion of the contract had been authorized following the informed consent and prior consultation of indigenous communities of the region, some of which were opposed to mining. The consultations resulted in the granting to an indigenous association of 20% of the concession right. However, after inconsistencies were found in the prior consultation procedure, the national mining agency requested the annulment of the contract to an administrative judge, which effectively annulled it in 2015. The companies filed an arbitration claim against Colombia arguing that the prohibition to conduct mining activities that resulted from the creation of the national park resulted in an indirect expropriation of its investments. Moreover, the investors argued that the procedure for the creation of the park was based on fraudulent acts and had not fulfilled the requirements of prior consultation of indigenous communities in the region. The companies further argued that the approval for the conclusion of the contract was unduly delayed as a deliberate attempt by the government to set it back until the creation of the park was in place.[57]

---

[55] Glencore International A.G. and C.I. Prodeco S.A. v. Republic of Colombia, Award, No. ICSID Case No. ARB/16/6 (27 August 2019), Eco Oro Minerals Corp. v. Republic of Colombia, Decision on Jurisdiction, Liability and directions on quantum, ICSID Case No. ARB/16/41 (9 September 2021).

[56] América Móvil S.A.B. de C.V. v. the Republic of Colombia, Award, No. ICSID Case No. ARB (AF)/16/5 (7 May 2021); Astrida Benita Carrizosa v. the Republic of Colombia, Award, No. ICSID Case No. ARB/18/5 (19 April 2021); Alberto Carrizosa Gelzis, Felipe Carrizosa Gelzis and Enrique Carrizosa Gelzis v. the Republic of Colombia; Naturgy Energy Group, S.A. and Naturgy Electricidad Colombia, S.L. (formerly Gas Natural SDG, S.A. and Gas Natural Fenosa Electricidad Colombia, S.L.) v the Republic of Colombia, Award, No. ICSID Case No. UNCT/18/1 (12 March 2021); AFC Investment Solutions S.L. v the Republic of Colombia, ISCID Case No. ARB/20/16, Award on Respondent's Rule 41(5) Preliminary Exception (24 February 2020).

[57] Maria Alejandra Latorre Bastidas and Daniela Zambrano Cerro, 'Caso Cosigo Resources, Ltd., Cosigo Resources Sucursal Colombia, Tobie Mining Energy Inc. vs La República de Colombia' (Trabajo para optar por el título de abogada, Santiago de Cali, Pontificia Universidad Javierana Cali, Facultad de Humanidades y Ciencias Sociales, Departamento de Ciencia Jurídica y Política, Programa de Derecho, 2016); Luke Eric Peterson and Zoe Williams, 'Two New Treaty-Based

No procedural activity has been registered by the claimants since the submission of the notice of arbitration in 2016. Thus, it is fair to affirm that no decision on the merits will be issued by the tribunal, which has not been constituted. However, elements of analysis can be drawn from the notice of intent and the notice of arbitration, as well as from the state's response to the latter. In its response, Colombia put in context the construction of the Yaigojé Apaporis national park by referencing that since the 1950s a series of regulations have been adopted to "protect areas of particular ecological importance for the country, which due to their biological and cultural diversity, warrant special protection by the state, by excluding in them industrial, mining and oil activities".[58] It further specified how the protection of environment diversity and the conservation of those areas was explicitly included as a state duty in the 1991 Constitution and stems from international treaties as the Convention on Biological Diversity (CBD). Finally, the state provided a description of the national park, which "hosts 18 different ecosystems, 1.638 flora species, more than 1.115 fauna species and around 1.616 inhabitants from the 19 indigenous communities that inhabit the 'Yaigojé Indigenous Reservation". Moreover, the state specified how the construction of the natural park was a result of a procedure started from the request of traditional indigenous authorities of the Reservation to the state's environmental agency.[59] On jurisdictional issues, the state formally notified the companies of the denial of benefits under the Colombia – United States FTA on the ground of lack of substantial activities in the United States territory. On substantive issues, the state specified that even before the creation of the natural park, the area requested for concession was encompassed in both the Amazon Forest Reserve and the Yaigojé Indigenous Reservation, which precluded Andrés Rendle to conduct any exploitation and exploration activities without demonstration that the latter coexisted with the objectives of the forest area.[60]

In the cases of Eco Oro Minerals, Galway Gold and Red Eagle, Canadian-based companies, the protection of the environment is at stake. The Colombian state's actions regarding the regulation of mining activities in the Santurbán *paramo* is at the core of these disputes. In 2010, Law 1382, which prohibited mining *in paramo*

Disputes Center on Friction between Colombian Mining and National Parks – and Highlight Differing Transparency Rules in Canadian and U.S. FTAs', IAREPORTER, *Investment Arbitration Reporter* (blog), 9 March 2016, https://www.iareporter.com/articles/analysis-two-new-treaty-based-disputes-center-on-friction-between-colombian-mining-and-national-parks-and-highlight-differing-transparency-rules-in-canadian-and-u-s-ftas/; Damien Charlotin and Zoe Williams, 'Latin American Round-up: Updates on the Dominican Republic, Peru and Colombia', IAREPORTER, *Investment Arbitration Reporter* (blog), 22 November 2017, https://www.iareporter.com/articles/latin-american-round-up-updates-on-the-dominican-republic-peru-and-colombia/.

[58] República de Colombia, Cosigo Resources, Ltd., Cosigo Resources Sucursal Colombia, Tobie Mining and Energy, Inc. c. la República de Colombia, Respuesta de la República de Colombia a la Solicitud de Arbitraje de las Demandantes (19 March 2016).

[59] República de Colombia, at 4–5.

[60] República de Colombia, Cosigo Resources, Ltd., Cosigo Resources Sucursal Colombia, Tobie Mining and Energy, Inc. c. la República de Colombia, Respuesta de la República de Colombia a la Solicitud de Arbitraje de las Demandantes.

ecosystems, was passed. This prohibition was again included in Law 1450 of 2011, which instructed the environmental agency to *demarcate paramos* ecosystems. Law 1753 of 2015 further established a transitional regime that allowed mining titles granted over before 2010 over areas that overlapped *with paramos* to continue until their expiration, without possibility for any extension. The *Santurbán paramo* was demarked in 2014. In 2016, the Constitutional Court declared the unconstitutionality of the transitional regime provided in Law 1753 and ordered the immediate suspension of all mining activities in the Santurbán *paramo*.

The first of these claims was submitted by Eco Oro Minerals, a Canadian-based company, in December 2016. The company had held a mining title for the exploration and exploitation of gold in the Angostura region in Santander since 2007. In 2011, the state's environmental agency issued a resolution that revoked a license in favour of the company on the ground that it would generate an irreversible damage to the Santurbán *páramo*. Following the demarcation of the Santurbán *páramo* in 2014, it was found that around 50% of the area in which the company held its mining title overlapped with the protected area. Despite this, the Colombian government exempted the company's project from the suspension of its activities in application of Law 1753. However, this decision was annulled by the Constitutional Court in its 2016 decision. In its claim, Eco Oro argued that the different state actions and omissions regarding the Santurbán *páramo* resulted in legal uncertainty that affected its investment, making it unviable. Specifically, Eco Oro stated that Colombia breached the minimum standard of treatment, which included the FET and full protection and security standards "by taking unfair and inequitable measures (...) by acting in an arbitrary, inconsistent, non-transparent and disproportionate manner and by frustrating Eco Oro's legitimate expectations".[61] Eco Oro also argued that Colombia's actions and omissions resulted in an indirect expropriation of its investments that was not accompanied by payment of prompt, adequate and effective compensation.[62]

The Eco Oro case was followed by two new claims, both submitted in April 2018 by Red Eagle Exploration Limited and Galway Gold Inc. In the case of Galway Gold, the company had held a mining concession since 2009, when it acquired from another company its contracting rights. In the case of Red Eagle, the company's protected investments, three mining concession contracts and a license for exploitation held by one of its branches in Colombia, were all affected by the prohibition to conduct mining activities in the Santurbán *páramo*. Both companies argued in their arbitration requests that their investments were first affected and then devastated because of fluctuations and uncertainties surrounding decisions related to the regulation of the Santurbán *páramo*, which in turn resulted in a breach of the customary

[61] Eco Oro Minerals Corp., Eco Oro Minerals Corp. v. the Republic of Colombia, Request for Arbitration (8 December 2016).

[62] Eco Oro Minerals Corp., at 30–32.

minimum standard of treatment, including of the obligation to provide a FET, and in measures amounting to an indirect expropriation.[63]

One particular issue that evidences the human rights relevance of these cases is the request to intervene as non-contending parties made by the following six non-governmental organisations (NGO) to the Eco Oro Minerals tribunal: Comité para la Defensa del Agua y el Páramo de Santurbán, the Centre for International Environmental Law (CIEL), Asociación Interamericana para la Defensa del Ambiente (AIDA), MiningWatch Canada, Institue for Policy Studies (IPS) – Global Economy Projecto and Centre for Research on Multinational Corporations (SOMO). This request was based on article 37(2) of the ICSID Arbitration Rules and on article 841 and Annex 831 of the Colombia – Canada FTA, which sets as one of the requirements for *amicus curiae* submissions the identification by the petitioner of a significant interest in the arbitration and the specification of the nature of this interest, as well as accounting for the reasons why its intervention should be accepted by the tribunal. Both the request and the decision of the tribunal are significant for any human right analysis of these cases.

These NGOs argued that it had significant interest in the arbitration, inasmuch as "[t]here is a strong civil society movement within and outside of Colombia concerned with the effects of the commercial activities of Eco Oro Minerals Corp. in relation to the Eco Oro gold mine".[64] They further informed that their intervention would focus "on international law regarding human rights and particularly the right to live in a healthy environment".[65] The Colombian state confirmed that the NGO had a significant interest in the proceedings as its outcome "may have a direct or indirect impact on the rights or principles [they represent and defend]".[66] In its decision, the tribunal denied the request based on a lack of relevance to the scope of the dispute. Accordingly, it stated "the Tribunal does not consider that the Petitioners have sought to show how generalised issues of human rights, and particularly the right to live in a healthy environment, may be said to relate to the scope of the specificities of this dispute".[67] Furthermore, the tribunal asserted that neither the NGO, through their knowledge of the Santurbán *páramo* and social and environmental issues, could assist the tribunal, nor that they had a significant interest in the case.

---

[63] Red Eagle Exploration Limited, Red Eagle Exploration Limited v. Republic of Colombia, Request for Arbitration (21 March 2018); Galway Gold Inc., Galway Gold Inc. v. Republic of Colombia, Request for Arbitration (21 March 2018).

[64] Eco Oro Minerals Corp. v. the Republic of Colombia, Procedural Order No. 6. Decision on Non-Disputing Parties' Application, No. ICSID Case No. ARB/16/41 (18 February 2019).

[65] Eco Oro Minerals Corp. v. the Republic of Colombia, Procedural Order No. 6. Decision on Non-Disputing Parties' Application paragraph 18.

[66] Eco Oro Minerals Corp. v. the Republic of Colombia, Procedural Order No. 6. Decision on Non-Disputing Parties' Application paragraph 22.

[67] Eco Oro Minerals Corp. v. the Republic of Colombia, Procedural Order No. 6. Decision on Non-Disputing Parties' Application paragraph 28.

The four cases introduced evidence tensions and conflicts between IIL and human rights in Colombia. The specific case of *Cosigo Resources and others v. Colombia* exemplifies how IIL may come into conflict with the state's human rights objectives of protection of the environment and of flora and fauna, as well as of protection of indigenous peoples' rights and the respect of their traditions and cultures through participation and consultations in decisions that may be harmful for them. This case has been characterized as one in which there were concurring interests over one territory and in which the adoption by the state of a perfectly harmonizing decision between interests of foreign investors and interests of indigenous communities was not possible.[68] Such direct conflict between indigenous peoples and foreign investors rights has been a commonplace in ISDS cases involving Latin American states, with clashes relating "inter alia, to ancestral lands, traditional heritage and knowledge, access to water and prior consultation"[69] From a human rights perspective, the approach of investment arbitral tribunals to indigenous issues has been problematic. As a general issue, indigenous peoples' rights and interests are generally analyzed by tribunals exclusively through the lens of the disputing parties. In the high-profile case *Chevron v. Ecuador*, where such clashes were at the core of the dispute, the requests of the NGOs Fundación Pachamama and IISD to participate in the procedure on the basis that "the arbitration raised a number of issues of vital concern to specific indigenous communities and peoples in Ecuador"[70] were rejected by the arbitral tribunal.

At its turn, the Santurbán *páramo* saga, composed of the cases Eco Oro Minerals, Galway Gold and Red Eeagle, also exemplifies a tension between IIL and objectives of environment protection, which in the case of *páramos* are connected to the access to water of local populations. As stated by a local activist: "not only does the *páramo*'s rich biodiversity make it a precious ecosystem – its distinctive hydrological cycle provides water for a growing population of some two million people in the province".[71] However, these cases not only highlight a tension between human rights of access to water and healthy environment, but they also raise important issues of participation of those individuals and communities whose rights may be at stake in the decision. Local activists in Santander feel that they have a stake in these disputes. Public mobilisations and legal interventions were key in the decisions of the Constitutional Court that led to the prohibition of mining in *páramo* territories.

---

[68] Robledo Silva and Rivas-Ramírez (2019), p. 68.

[69] Prieto-Ríos and Rivas-Ramírez (2020), p. 86.

[70] Fundación Pachamama and The International Institute for Sustainable Development (IISD), 'Chevron Corporation and Texaco Petroleum Company v. the Republic of Ecuador, Petition for Participation as Non-Disputing Parties', 22 October 2010, para. 3.1.

[71] Lorenzo Cotula, 'Investment Disputes from below: Whose Rights Matter? Mining Environment and Livelihoods in Colombia', International Institute for Environment and Development, 23 July 2020, https://www.iied.org/investment-disputes-below-whose-rights-matter.

Advocators for the protection of the Santurbán *paramo* feel that they are protagonists in these cases.[72]

Other issues involving human rights that do not necessarily stem from these four previous cases can also be mentioned. Some scholars have warned how the implementation of the land restitution programme established in 2011, which aims to protect the right to reparation and the right to restitution of internally displaced persons and of victims of the internal armed conflict, can be hampered by interests of foreign companies protected by IIAs.[73] In 2017, the administrative unit in charge of representing victims before judges in land restitution cases explicitly mentioned IIAs and the risks that the state responsibility was compromised as a reason not to request a legal remedy favourable to the victims that might have been to harmful for foreign companies with economic interests in the land requested for restitution.[74] These warnings can be framed in a broader call for greater attention of the tensions that the implementation of the 2012 Peace Agreements between the Colombian government and the FARC guerrilla group.[75]

Other sources of tension might be exemplified by the 2021 investment arbitration claim of the company Anglo American plc., partially owner of the mining company Cerrejón, submitted during the writing of this article. While details of the claim are not public, the claim could challenge either a decision by a local court to block the expansion of a coal mine for environmental reasons and-or the blockades of access to the mine by workers and indigenous people opposed to the project. It is worth noting, on the one hand, that labour disputes between Cerrejón and its workers have been prominent over working conditions and, on the other hand, that a 2019 decision by the Constitutional Court ordered the company to protect the life and health of indigenous communities whose rights to a healthy environment, including the protection of water sources and of flora and fauna, were being vulnerated by its mining activities.[76]

---

[72] Lorenzo Cotula, 'Investment Disputes from below: Whos Rights Matter? Mining Environment and Livelihoods in Colombia', International Institute for Environment and Development, 23 July 2020, https://www.iied.org/investment-disputes-below-whose-rights-matter.

[73] Van Ho (2016), pp. 60–85; Tamayo-Álvarez (2018), p. 114.

[74] Ethnic Affairs Directorate, 'Cocolatu Concept' (Bogotá, 27 September 2017).

[75] Prieto-Rios, Gomez-Suarez, and Perrone, 'Foreign Investors and the Colombian Peace Process'; Urueña and Prieto-Rios, 'Derecho de La Inversión Extranjera y Acuerdos de Paz: Tensiones y Soluciones'.

[76] Lisa Bohmer, 'COLOMBIA IS FACING SECOND ICSID CLAIM OVER COAL MINING DISPUTE', IAREPORTER, *Investment Arbitration Reporter* (blog), 2 June 2021, https://www.iareporter.com/articles/colombia-is-facing-second-icsid-claim-over-coal-mining-dispute/; Jack Ballantyne, 'Colombia Faces Second ICSID Claim over Mine Expansion Project', GAR, *Global Arbitration Review* (blog), 3 June 2021, https://globalarbitrationreview.com/colombia-faces-second-icsid-claim-over-mine-expansion-project?utm_source=social-media&utm_medium=linkedIn; 'Anglo American Presenta Arbitraje De Inversión Contra Colombia', *Ciar Global* (blog), 3 June 2021, https://ciarglobal.com/anglo-american-presenta-arbitraje-de-inversion-contra-colombia/.

With these sources of tension set out, it is worth establishing how does the 2017 BIT Model may affect the outcome of future claims arising out of similar facts or if it may prevent them altogether. Regarding cases involving environmental issues, the BIT Model contains several provisions that may protect the state from compromising its international responsibility. As it was stated in previous sections, the inclusion of a provision of reaffirmation of the states right to regulate investments to protect legitimate public welfare objectives such as the environment may inform the interpretation of the arbitral tribunal, who may accord a greater deferential attitude towards state action. However, this remains in the realm of discretion of arbitral tribunals and its real impact in future disputes is uncertain. Something similar can be said of the reaffirmation of the right to regulate included in the operative section of the Model as part of Section [CC], as well as of the non-lowering of standards provision. In any case, the real impact of these provisions may be found in the interpretation of the treaty made by state officials in charge of adopting decisions that could result in an engagement of the state responsibility.

Of greater relevance is the explicit exclusion from the qualification of indirect expropriation of measures adopted in a non-discriminatory manner to protect public objectives, including the environment. Considering that the Santurbán saga involves cases founded for the most part on indirect expropriation claims that challenge measures adopted to protect the environment, this provision is of great importance as it would, at least in theory, exclude the state responsibility for their adoption, if they are not discriminatory. At the same time, an almost identical provision exists in the applicable Colombia – Canada FTA, and that did not prevent the submission of three indirect expropriation-based claims, nor they necessarily guarantee a favorable outcome to the state in the tribunal's decisions. A similar case can be made for the "general exceptions" clause, which states that the treaty shall not prevent the adoption of measures aimed at protecting the environment, provided that they do not amount to an arbitrary or discriminatory treatment against the investor. Nonetheless the Eco Oro Minerals award, in which the majority of the investment arbitral found that the State had breached the FET standard despite the environmental exception found in the FTA.[77] This decision has attracted general criticism, including by the dissenting arbitrator, and has raised concerns about the general usefulness of general exception-type clauses in investment treaties.[78]

If compared to the environment protection, a noticeable omission of the BIT Model is the lack of provisions that aim at preserving the right to adopt measures adopted to protect the rights of indigenous people, which are not mentioned once in the whole document. While it could be argued that the rights of indigenous people are encompassed in provisions relating to human rights or that relate to "other public policy objectives", the lack of a specific provision on indigenous rights is surprising.

[77] Eco Oro Minerals Corp. v. Republic of Colombia, Decision on Jurisdiction, Liability and directions on quantum, ICSID Case No. ARB/16/41 (9 September 2021).

[78] Robert Garden, Eco Oro v Colombia: The Brave New World of Environmental Exceptions, ICSID Review, 2022, https://doi.org/10.1093/icsidreview/siac020.

This is even more so considering that at the time of the adoption of the 2017 BIT Model clashes between indigenous rights and foreign investors' interests had been prominent in Colombia, not only in the realm of IIL, but also of domestic constitutional law and international law of human rights. Moreover, previous IIAs signed by Colombia with other states have included specific derogations regarding non-conforming measures aimed at protecting indigenous people and minority groups or traditional expressions.[79] Such an inclusion is significant given that private adjudicators from developed countries may not necessarily recognize indigenous peoples' rights as human rights as much as they might do so in regard to the environment, health or labour.

This also leads to another problematic issue of the BIT Model, which is its framing of *amicus curiae* intervention. As previously noted, the Model states that the tribunal "may invite, prior consultation with the Disputing Parties, submissions from *amicus curiae* that are not a disputing party".[80] The allowance of *amicus curiae* intervention is not necessarily innovative given that the ICSID Arbitration Rules were amended in 2006 specifically to open the possibility that tribunals accept non-disputing parties' submissions.[81] Similarly, the UNCITRAL Rules on Transparency that are being incorporated in an increasing number of IIAs, including the Colombia – France BIT, explicitly enable third party interventions.[82] The Model fails to properly address two contemporary problems surrounding *amicus curiae* intervention in ISDS. First, the discretional faculties that pervade the arbitral tribunals' final decision on the acceptance of these submissions, and second, the general lack of real engagement by arbitral tribunals with *amicus curiae* arguments on their decisions, with the *Philip Morris v. Uruguay* case being a notable exception.

The most significant contribution of the 2017 BIT Model from a human rights perspective does not necessarily relates to the state defense in ISDS cases. The denial of benefits clause and its connection with counterclaims is probably the most important aspect in the prevention of disputes. Any investor involved in "serious human rights violations" or in sponsoring "persons or organisations sentenced because of serious human rights violations or violations against International Humanitarian Law" or "internationally-listed terrorist organisations", may feel deterred to act as claimant in an ISDS case if it contemplates the possibility that

[79] For instance, the Colombia-Japan 2011 BIT states that 'Colombia reserves the right to adopt or maintain any measure according rights or preferences to socially or economically disadvantaged minorities and ethnic groups, including with respect to the communal lands held by ethnic groups in accordance with Art. 63 of the Constitución Política de Colombia.' 'Agreement between Japan and the Republic of Colombia for the Liberalization, Promotion and Protection of Investment' (2011) Article 6, Annex II.

[80] The Republic of Colombia, Bilateral investment treaty between the Republic of Colombia and _____. Colombian Model 2017 Article [##]-Intervention by Amicus Curiae and Non-Disputing Party.

[81] International Center for Settlement of Investment Disputes, 'ICSID Convention Arbitration Rules' (2006) art. 37.2.

[82] UNCITRAL (2014) art. 4.1.

the state denies it the protection of the treaty and, most importantly, that the state submits a counterclaim for these facts.[83]

The BIT Model does not limit the evidence of commission of "serious human rights violations" and of sponsoring "persons or organisations sentenced because of serious human rights violations or violations against International Humanitarian Law" or "internationally-listed terrorist organisations" to that of courts and authorities of only one of the Contracting Parties. This is to be saluted, as it evidences an engagement with the condemnation of human rights violations by businesses worldwide, and not only in Colombia. Such provision, if replicated in a significant number of IIAs around the globe, could obstruct the access to ISDS of investors involved in human rights violations altogether. However, when referring to the commission of "serious environmental damage", the ground for the denial of benefits is limited to the damage caused in the territory of the host state. Questions arise as how this could harmonize with the first ground of human rights violations and how the commission of serious environmental damage in the territory of a non-contracting party could not be considered as one.

The obligation provided in the BIT Model that imposes to Claimant investors the acceptance of "the prohibitions established in international instruments, to which any Contracting Party is or becomes a party, pertaining to human rights and the environment (. . .) as mandatory" in the making and operation its investment to submit an ISDS claim may also serve as a deterrent to the access of the ISDS mechanism, as well as an instrument for the promotion of more socially responsible investments.

5 Conclusion

Despite non-negligible shortcomings in the protection of indigenous rights and in the inclusiveness in arbitration procedures of individuals and communities that may have human rights stakes in the outcome of the dispute, the 2017 BIT Model adopted by the Colombian government is a noteworthy advancement for discussions surrounding relations between investment protection and human rights, both in the Colombian and in the global context. Further research will have to study whether other provisions such as denial of benefits for human rights violations will be incorporated in future IIAs signed by Colombia or by other states, as well as their

[83] *Urbaser v. Argentina* is a case that shows the importance of such a provision. In this case, Argentina submitted a counterclaim against the investor alleging that the latter had acquire the obligation to guarantee the human right of access of water, which was breached as a result of the deficiencies in the service it provided. The tribunal accepted its jurisdiction over the claim in the application of a broad jurisdictional clause, recognizing the existence of a human right to water, as well as the fact that human rights obligations can be imposed on foreign investors. (Urbaser S.A. and Consorcio de Aguas Bilbao Bizkaia, Bilbao Biskaia Ur Partzuergoa v. The Argentine Republic, Award, No. ICSID Case No. ARB/07/26 [8 December 2016]).

impact in future ISDS cases. For more common provisions like reaffirmations of the right to regulate and general exceptions, a consistent approach by arbitral tribunals that enables an adequate analysis on its impacts on human rights protection is yet to be found. Nevertheless, the Model's most substantial advancements may not be found within the context of ongoing ISDS cases, but on their prevention and on the promotion of human rights respect by foreign investors in their operations. Moreover, for the Model to be successful, the Colombian government must adopt strong standing in the renegotiation of previous IIAs and in the negotiation of new IIAs to follow the main features included in the 2017 Model. Further revisions will have to include sensitive issues omitted by the Model, including the protection of indigenous peoples.

References

AFC Investment Solutions S.L. v. the Republic of Colombia, No. ICSID Case No. ARB/20/16 (n.d.)

Agreement between Japan and the Republic of Colombia for the Liberalization, Promotion and Protection of Investment (2011)

Agreement between the Government of the Republic of Colombia and the Government of the French Republic for the promotion and protection of investments (2014)

Agreement between the Government of the Republic of Colombia and the Government of the Republic of Turkey concerning the Reciprocal Promotion and Protection of Investments (2014)

Al Faruque A (2010) Mapping the relationship between investment protection and human rights. J World Investment Trade 11(4):539–560. https://doi.org/10.1163/221190010X00248

Alberto Carrizosa Gelzis, Felipe Carrizosa Gelzis and Enrique Carrizosa Gelzis v. the Republic of Colombia, No. PCA Case No. 2018-56 (2021)

Alschner W, Hui K (2018) Missing in Action: General Public Policy Exceptions in Investment Treaties. SSRN Scholarly Paper. Rochester, NY: Social Science Research Network, 22 August 2018. https://doi.org/10.2139/ssrn.3237053

Amec Foster Wheeler USA Corporation, Process Consultants, Inc., and Joint Venture Foster Wheeler USA Corporation and Process Consultants, Inc. v. the Republic of Colombia, No. ICSID Case No. ARB/19/34 (n.d.)

América Móvil S.A.B. de C.V. v. the Republic of Colombia, Award, No. ICSID Case No. ARB (AF)/16/5 (7 May 2021)

América Móvil S.A.B. de C.V. v. the Republic of Colombia, No. ICSID Case No. ARB(AF)/16/5 (n.d.)

Angel Samuel Seda and others v. the Republic of Colombia, No. ICSID Case No. ARB/19/6 (n.d.)

Anglo American plc v. the Republic of Colombia, No. ICSID Case No. ARB/21/31 (n.d.)

Astrida Benita Carrizosa v. the Republic of Colombia, Award, No. ICSID Case No. ARB/18/5 (19 April 2021)

Astrida Benita Carrizosa v. the Republic of Colombia, No. ICSID Case No. ARB/18/5 (n.d.)

Ballantyne J (2021) Colombia Faces Second ICSID Claim over Mine Expansion Project. GAR. *Global Arbitration Review* (blog), 3 June 2021. https://globalarbitrationreview.com/colombia-faces-second-icsid-claim-over-mine-expansion-project?utm_source=social-media&utm_medium=linkedIn

Bilateral agreement for the Promotion and Protection of Investments between the Government of the United Kingdom of Great Britain and Northern Ireland and the Republic of Colombia (2010)

Bohmer L (2021) Colombia Is Facing Second Icsid Claim Over Coal Mining Dispute. IAREPORTER. Investment Arbitration Reporter (blog), 2 June 2021. https://www.iareporter.com/articles/colombia-is-facing-second-icsid-claim-over-coal-mining-dispute/

Charlotin D, Williams Z (2017) Latin American Round-up: Updates on the Dominican Republic, Peru and Colombia. IAREPORTER. Investment Arbitration Reporter (blog), 22 November 2017. https://www.iareporter.com/articles/latin-american-round-up-updates-on-the-dominican-republic-peru-and-colombia/

Ciar Global (2021) Anglo American Presenta Arbitraje De Inversión Contra Colombia. 3 June 2021. https://ciarglobal.com/anglo-american-presenta-arbitraje-de-inversion-contra-colombia/

Coleman J, Cordes KY, Johnson L (2020) Human rights law and the investment treaty regime. In: Deva S, Birchall D (eds) Research handbook on human rights and business. Edward Elgar Publishing Limited, pp 290–314

Comisión Quinta, Asamblea Nacional Constituyente. 'Internacionalización de Las Relaciones Económicas e Integración Supranacional'. Colección digital: Asamblea Nacional Constituyente, 15 April 1991. https://babel.banrepcultural.org/digital/collection/p17054coll28/id/322/rec/69

Committee on Economic, Social and Cultural Rights. 'General Comment No. 24 (2017) on State Obligations under the International Covenant on Economic, Social and Cultural Rights in the Context of Business Activities'. United Nations, 10 August 2017

Consejo Nacional de Política Economica y Social. 'Fortalecimiento de La Estrategia Del Estado Para La Prevención y Atención de Controversias Internacionales de Inversión. Documento CONPES 3684', 19 October 2010

Consejo Superior de Comercio Exterior. 'Sesión 100. Política de Aprovechamiento de Los Acuerdos Comerciales', 9 October 2018

Corte Constitucional de Colombia. Sentencia T-505 de 1992 (M.P. Eduardo Cifuentes Muñoz) (28 August 1992)

Corte Constitucional de Colombia. Sentencia C-265 de 1994 (M.P. Alejandro Martínez Caballero) (2 June 1994)

Cosigo Resources, Ltd., Cosigo Resources Sucursal Colombia, Tobie Mining and Energy, Inc. v. Republic of Colombia, No. UNCITRAL (n.d.)

Cotula L (2020) Investment disputes from below: whose rights matter? Mining environment and livelihoods in Colombia. International Institute for Environment and Development, 23 July 2020. https://www.iied.org/investment-disputes-below-whose-rights-matter

Duggal KAN, Garciá Clavijo DF, Trujillo S, Rincón MC (2019) Colombia's 2017 Model IIA: Something Old, Something New, Something Borrowed. ICSID Rev 34(1):224–240. https://doi.org/10.1093/icsidreview/siz004

Eco Oro Minerals Corp. Eco Oro Minerals Corp. v. the Republic of Colombia, Request for Arbitration (8 December 2016)

Eco Oro Minerals Corp. v. the Republic of Colombia, No. ICSID Case No. ARB/16/41 (n.d.)

Eco Oro Minerals Corp. v. the Republic of Colombia, Procedural Order No. 6. Decision on Non-Disputing Parties' Application, No. ICSID Case No. ARB/16/41 (18 February 2019)

Ethnic Affairs Directorate (2017) Cocolatu Concept. Bogotá, 27 September 2017

Fundación Pachamama and The International Institute for Sustainable Development (IISD). 'Chevron Corporation and Texaco Petroleum Company v. the Republic of Ecuador, Petition for Participation as Non-Disputing Parties', 22 October 2010

Galway Gold Inc. Galway Gold Inc. v. Republic of Colombia, Request for Arbitration (21 March 2018)

Galway Gold Inc. v. the Republic of Colombia, No. ICSID Case No. ARB/18/13 (n.d.)

Garden, Robert Eco Oro v Colombia: The Brave New World of Environmental Exceptions, ICSID Review, 2022, https://doi.org/10.1093/icsidreview/siac020

Glencore International A.G. and C.I. Prodeco S.A. v. Republic of Colombia, Award, No. ICSID Case No. ARB/16/6 (27 August 2019)

Glencore International A.G. and C.I. Prodeco S.A. v. the Republic of Colombia, No. ICSID Case No. ARB/16/6 (n.d.)

Glencore International A.G., C. I. Prodeco S.A., and Sociedad Portuaria Puerto Nuevo S.A. v. Republic of Colombia, No. ICSID Case No. ARB/19/22 (n.d.)
Glencore International A.G. v. Republic of Colombia, No. ICSID Case No. ARB/21/30 (n.d.).
Gran Colombia Gold Corp. v. the Republic of Colombia, No. ICSID Case No. ARB/18/23 (n.d.)
Hernandez G, Mauricio D (2017) Discussing the Tension between States' Right to Regulate and Foreign Investment Protection in Recent Colombian Cases. Con-Texto: Revista de Derecho y Economia 47:89–120
Human Rights Council (2009) Eleventh session. 'Business and Human Rights: Towards Operationalizing the "Protect, Respect and Remedy" Framework. Report of the Special Representative of the Secretary-General on the Issue of Human Rights and Transnational Corporations and Other Business Enterprises'. United Nations, 22 April 2009
Human Rights Council (2011) Seventeenth session. 'Guiding Principles on Business and Human Rights. Implementing the United Nations "Protect, Respect and Remedy" Framework'. New York: United Nations General Assembly, 21 May 2011
International Center for Settlement of Investment Disputes. ICSID Convention Arbitration Rules (2006)
Latorre B, Alejandra M, Cerro DZ (2016) Caso Cosigo Resources, Ltd., Cosigo Resources Sucursal Colombia, Tobie Mining Energy Inc. vs La República de Colombia'. Trabajo para optar por el título de abogada, Pontificia Universidad Javierana Cali, Facultad de Humanidades y Ciencias Sociales, Departamento de Ciencia Jurídica y Política, Programa de Derecho, 2016
Martini C (2018) Avoiding the planned obsolescence of modern international investment agreements: can general exception mechanisms be improved, and how? Boston College Law Rev 59(8):2877
Matamoros G, Victoria L (2019) La Relación Entre Las Políticas de Inversión Extranjera En Colombia y Los Acuerdos Internacionales de Inversión. Anuario Colombiano de Derecho Internacional
Naturgy Energy Group, S.A. and Naturgy Electricidad Colombia, S.L. (formerly Gas Natural SDG, S.A. and Gas Natural Fenosa Electricidad Colombia, S.L.) v the Republic of Colombia, Award, No. ICSID Case No. UNCT/18/1 (12 March 2021)
Naturgy Energy Group, S.A. and Naturgy Electricidad Colombia, S.L. (formerly Gas Natural SDG, S.A. and Gas Natural Fenosa Electricidad Colombia, S.L.) v the Republic of Colombia, No. ICSID Case No. UNCT/18/1 (n.d.)
Neustar, Inc. v. the Republic of Colombia, No. ICSID Case No. ARB/20/7 (n.d.)
Olarte-Bácares C, Prieto-Ríos E, Pontón-Serra JP (2020) Are interpretative declarations appropriate instruments to avoid uncertainty? The cases of the Colombia–France BIT and the Colombia–Israel FTA. IISD. Investment Treaty News (blog), 19 December 2020. https://www.iisd.org/itn/en/2020/12/19/are-interpretative-declarations-appropriate-instruments-to-avoid-uncertainty-the-cases-of-the-colombia-france-bit-and-the-colombia-israel-fta-carolina-olarte-bacares-enrique-prieto-rios-juan-ponton-se/
Palau van Hissenhoven N, Murcia ST (2017) Descripción general del AII Modelo. Debate Global (blog), 1 September 2017. https://debateglobal.wordpress.com/2017/09/01/descripcion-general-del-aii-modelo/
Palau van Hissenhoven N, Murcia ST (2017) El nuevo AII Modelo de Colombia: una herramienta necesaria para re-balancear el sistema arbitral de inversiones. Debate Global (blog), 1 September 2017. https://debateglobal.wordpress.com/2017/09/01/el-nuevo-aii-modelo-de-colombia-una-herramienta-necesaria-para-re-balancear-el-sistema-arbitral-de-inversiones/
Peterson LE, Williams Z (2016) Two New Treaty-Based Disputes Center on Friction between Colombian Mining and National Parks – and Highlight Differing Transparency Rules in Canadian and U.S. FTAs. IAREPORTER. Investment Arbitration Reporter (blog), 9 March 2016. https://www.iareporter.com/articles/analysis-two-new-treaty-based-disputes-center-on-friction-between-colombian-mining-and-national-parks-and-highlight-differing-transparency-rules-in-canadian-and-u-s-ftas/

Prieto-Ríos E, Rivas-Ramírez D (2020) Neocolonialism and the tension between international investment law and indigenous peoples: the Latin American Experience. In: Borrows J, Schwartz R (eds) Indigenous peoples and international trade building equitable and inclusive international trade and investment agreements. Cambridge University Press

Prieto-Rios E, Gomez-Suarez A, Perrone NM (2016) Foreign investors and the Colombian peace process. Int Commun Law Rev 18(3–4):223–247

Red Eagle Exploration Limited. Red Eagle Exploration Limited v. Republic of Colombia, Request for Arbitration (21 March 2018)

Red Eagle Exploration Limited v. the Republic of Colombia, No. ICSID Case No. ARB/18/12 (n.d.)

República de Colombia. Cosigo Resources, Ltd., Cosigo Resources Sucursal Colombia, Tobie Mining and Energy, Inc. c. la República de Colombia, Respuesta de la República de Colombia a la Solicitud de Arbitraje de las Demandantes (19 March 2016)

Robledo Silva P, Rivas-Ramírez D (2019) Cuando La Leyenda de El Dorado Se Hace Realidad: Análisis Sobre Las Tensiones Entre Los Intereses Económicos y Los Derechos de Los Pueblos Indígenas. In: Martínez JJT (ed) Derechos Humanos y La Actividad Empresarial En Colombia: Implicaciones Para El Estado Social de Derecho. Universidad Externado de Colombia, Bogotá

South32 SA Investments Limited v. the Republic of Colombia, No. ICSID Case No. ARB/20/9 (n.d.)

Tamayo-Álvarez R (2018) Colombia's land restitution programme and international investment law: normative tensions and possible convergences concerning investor diligence. Manchester J Int Econ Law 15(1):114

Telefónica, S.A. v. Republic of Colombia, No. ICSID Case No. ARB/18/3 (n.d.)

The Republic of Colombia. Bilateral investment treaty between the Republic of Colombia and _____. Colombian Model 2017 (2017)

The Republic of Colombia. Bilateral agreement of the promotion and protection of investments of Colombia and _____. Colombian Model 2011 (n.d.). https://investmentpolicy.unctad.org/international-investment-agreements/countries/45/colombia

UNCITRAL (2014) UNCITRAL Rules on Transparency in Treaty-based Investor-State Arbitration

UNCTAD (2006) Investment Policy Review: Colombia. United Nations, Geneva

UNCTAD (2019) World Investment Report 2019. United Nations Publications. United Nations, New York

UNCTAD (2020) World Investment Report 2020. United Nations Publications, New York

Urbaser SA and Consorcio de Aguas Bilbao Bizkaia, Bilbao Biskaia Ur Partzuergoa v. The Argentine Republic, Award, No. ICSID Case No. ARB/07/26 (8 December 2016)

Urueña R, Prieto-Rios E (2017) Derecho de La Inversión Extranjera y Acuerdos de Paz: Tensiones y Soluciones. In: Céspedes-Báez LM, Prieto-Rios E (eds) Utopía u Oportunidad Fallida. Análisis Crítico Del Acuerdo de Paz. Editorial Universidad del Rosario, Bogotá, pp 159–182

Van Ho TL (2016) Is it already too late for Colombia's land restitution process?: The impact of international investment law on transitional justice initiatives. Int Human Rights Law Rev 5(1): 60–85. https://doi.org/10.1163/22131035-00501003

Vandevelde KJ (2011) Model bilateral investment treaties: the way forward. Southwestern J Int Law 18(1):307–316

Velásquez Ruiz MA (2016) The Colliding Vernacullars of Foreign Investment Protection and Transitional Justice in Colombia: A Challenge for the Law in a Global Context. Graduate Program in Law York University – Osgoode Hall Law School

Velásquez Ruiz MA (2020) Genealogy of the Protection of Foreign Investment through International Investment Agreements in Colombia. In: Cera SI (ed) Implementación Normativa Del Tratado de Libre Comercio Entre Colombia y Estados Unidos ¿Potestad o Imposición? Tirant lo Blanch, Bogotá DC

Carolina Olarte-Bácares Associate Professor, Pontificia Universidad Javeriana. Ambassador of Colombia to the Kingdom of The Netherlands. Agent of Colombia before the International Court of Justice, Member of the Permanent Court of Arbitration. Former Dean Law School, Pontificia Universidad Javeriana, Bogota, Colombia. Ph.D. in International Law University Paris 1 Panthéon-Sorbonne, Master of research in international law, Robert Schuman University, Strasbourg. Lawyer, Pontificia Universidad Javeriana, Law School, Bogota. Independent Consultant in international law, investment arbitration, human rights, and business and human rights, and external consultant for diplomatic representations in Colombia on matters related to diplomatic privileges and immunities. Founding member of the Colombian Academy of International Law (ACCOLDI), Board Member of the Global Business and Human Rights Scholars Association, and the Latin American Business and Human Rights Academy. Co-Chair of the International Law Association (ILA) Committee on Business and Human Rights.

Enrique Prieto-Rios is an Associate Professor, at the Faculty of Law-Universidad del Rosario. Enrique holds a Phd in Law from Birkbeck – University of London, a MA in International Law from University College of London UCK and an LLB from Universidad del Rosario (Bogotá Colombia). Enrique's research focuses on International Economic Law, the Teaching and Learning of International Law, International Human Rights Law and Business and Human Rights. Enrique is Commissioner at the Advisory Commission on Peace and Human Rights that was created by the 2016 Peace Accord. Enrique has been a visiting research fellow at the Max Planck Institute of Comparative and International Law, Osgoode School of Law – University of York, the School of Law – University of Warwick, a visiting lecturer at the School of Law- Universidad de los Andes, and a sessional lecturer at the School of Law – Birkbeck University of London. Enrique has been clerk at the Colombian Constitutional Court, the Director of the British and Colombian Lawyers Association –BRICOL, intern at the International Bar Association –IBA- and a consultant for law firms in Bogotá and in London.

Juan P. Pontón-Serra Junior Researcher at the Faculty of Law at Universidad del Rosario. He holds a postgraduate degree in international law from the Paris 1 Panthéon-Sorbonne University.

Peru and International Investment Agreements: Legal and Institutional Challenges Under a Business and Human Rights Perspective

Salvador Herencia-Carrasco

1 Introduction

For a country that was only featured in international news when natural tragedies, human rights violations or political scandals happened, the beginning of the twenty-first century showed a significantly different Peru to the world. News of economic development and social progress indicated that the country could be (finally) moving in the right direction.

Following years of economic crisis, poverty and terrorism, particularly between the 1970s and 1990s, the 1993 Constitution[1] established a model that fostered the inclusion of the country into the global economy by opening its national markets to foreign trade and investment while prioritizing the subscription of international investment agreements (hereinafter, "IIA").[2] This model of development focused on the exploration of natural resources[3] and export of agro-industrial products.[4] This was a significant shift from the 1979 Constitution, where the state had a prominent role in the control of the economy, the market and the means of production.

The economic chapter of the 1993 Constitution and the laws and policies adopted to implement this model seemed to have a positive effect, as Peru became one of the

[1] See: Political Constitution of Peru, adopted on 29 December 1993 (entry into force: 31 December 1993).

[2] See: UN Working Group on Business and Human Rights (27 July 2021) Human rights-compatible international investment agreements, A/76/238.

[3] Banco (2021).

[4] See: Agüero et al. (2020).

S. Herencia-Carrasco (✉)
University of Ottawa, Ottawa, ON, Canada
e-mail: shere045@uottawa.ca

N. Monebhurrun et al. (eds.), *International Investment Law and Arbitration from a Latin American Perspective*, International Law and the Global South,
https://doi.org/10.1007/978-3-031-49382-9_10

leading economies in Latin America,[5] portraying the country as a success story for the region.[6] However, behind these positive developments, Peru remained a country with great institutional fragility and growing social inequality.[7] Corruption, the concentration of economic progress in urban areas and the lack of social reforms prevented this progress from reaching all sectors of society.[8]

For many years, any questioning of this model was rejected by political and business elites,[9] as social and economic indicators suggested the model was working.[10] But the political crisis of recent years, triggered by the Odebrecht *Lava Jato* scandal, corruption and kickbacks received by senior government officials and members of Congress[11] as well as the coronavirus pandemic, proved that this model, without social reforms to include historically vulnerable groups, was fragile.[12]

The coronavirus pandemic has caused a severe economic crisis in the country. According to the *Instituto Nacional de Estadística e Informática* (Statistics Peru), by the end of 2020, approximately 30.1% of the population was living under poverty, an increase of 9.9% in comparison to 2019. In the case of people living in extreme poverty, the percentage went from 2.9% to 5.1% of the population during that same period.[13]

This fragility may be best represented in the precarious working conditions of the population. The informality of the economy, which never fell below 72% of the workforce,[14] was estimated to be at 78.1% during the second quarter of 2021.[15] This meant that the vast majority of the economically active population did not have access to social benefits, insurance or any other social safety nets. This fragility helps

[5] See: Comisión Económica para América Latina (CEPAL) (2020) La Inversión Extranjera Directa en América Latina y el Caribe 2020. CEPAL, Santiago.

[6] See: Castilla (2015).

[7] Contreras et al. (2015).

[8] See: Programa de las Naciones Unidas para el Desarrollo (PNUD) (2019).

[9] See: Durand (2021).

[10] See: Crabtree and Durand (2017).

[11] See: Lagunes and Svejnar (2020).

[12] See: Aldana et al. (2020).

[13] See: Instituto Nacional de Estadística e Informática (INEI) (2021) Informe Técnico Evolución de la Pobreza Monetaria 2009-2020. INEI, Lima. https://www.inei.gob.pe/cifras-de-pobreza/.

[14] See: Instituto Nacional de Estadística e Informática (INEI) (2020) Producción y Empleo Informal en el Perú, Cuenta Satélite de la Economía Informal 2007-2019. INEI, Lima, p. 101. https://www.inei.gob.pe/media/MenuRecursivo/publicaciones_digitales/Est/Lib1764/.

[15] See: Instituto Nacional de Estadística e Informática (INEI) (2021b) Perú: Comportamiento de los indicadores de mercado laboral a nivel nacional, Informe Técnico N° 03 Empleo Nacional. Trimestre: Abril-Mayo-Junio 2021. INEI, Lima, p. 19. https://www.inei.gob.pe/media/MenuRecursivo/boletines/03-informe-tecnico-empleo-nacional-abr-may-jun-2021.pdf.

understand the sharp increase of people living in poverty just 9 months after a global pandemic was declared by the World Health Organization in March 2021.[16]

In the 2021 Presidential election, left-wing candidate Pedro Castillo Terrones was elected President. He assumed office on 28 July 2021 for a period of five years, after defeating right-wing candidate Keiko Fujimori Higuchi in a close run-off election.[17] His party, Perú Libre, has announced its intention to renegotiate contracts[18] with transnational corporations (hereinafter, "TNC") and to convene a Constitutional Assembly to draft a new Constitution.[19] Among their political priorities, the ruling party will attempt to reinstate the role of the state as the leading actor in the country's economic activity, following the model set in the 1979 Constitution.

In December 2022, Congress voted Castillo out-of-office, following his announcement to shut down Congress, to arrest senior state officials and to rule by decree in a national emergency government for six-months, until elections could be held. [20] Castillo was arrested and ousted as President, sparking a series of protests in the country.[21] A group of protesters are advocating for a Constitutional Assembly[22] that would, among other things, redraft the economic section of the Constitution, including the section related to IIAs. At the time of drafting this chapter, the crisis is ongoing and 61 people have died and uncertainty reigns as to what will happen to the country, socially, politically and economically.

As it will be seen in this chapter, IIAs have played a significant role in the country's economy and TNCs have led investments in strategic sectors like mining, oil, gas and forestry. The drive to sign these IIAs, particularly with Global North countries, led state officials to accept clauses that could undermine its ability to protect public goods such as the environment or human rights.

---

[16] World Health Organization (11 March 2020), WHO Director-General's opening remarks at the media briefing on COVID-19 - 11 March 2020. https://www.who.int/director-general/speeches/detail/who-director-general-s-opening-remarks-at-the-media-briefing-on-covid-19%2D%2D-11-march-2020.

[17] Organismo Nacional de Procesos Electorales (ONPE) (2021), Presentación de Resultados: Elecciones Generales y Parlamento Andino 2021. https://resultadoshistorico.onpe.gob.pe/EG2021/EleccionesPresidenciales/RePres/T.

[18] Perú Libre (2020), Perú Libre: Ideario y Programa, pp. 11-16. http://perulibre.pe/wp-content/uploads/2020/03/ideario-peru-libre.pdf.

[19] Perú Libre (2020), Perú Libre: Ideario y Programa, p. 12. http://perulibre.pe/wp-content/uploads/2020/03/ideario-peru-libre.pdf.

[20] The Guardian (8 December 2022), Peru president removed from office and charged with 'rebellion' after alleged coup attempt. https://www.theguardian.com/world/2022/dec/07/peru-president-detained-pedro-castillo-coup.

[21] New York Times (7 December 2022), Peru's President Tried to Dissolve Congress. By Day's End, He Was Arrested. https://www.nytimes.com/2022/12/07/world/americas/peru-pedro-castillo-coup.html.

[22] Americas Quarterly (2 February 2023), Is This Peru's "Constitutional Moment"? https://www.americasquarterly.org/article/is-this-perus-constitutional-moment/.

How IIAs may affect a country's capacity to regulate corporate behaviour and respect for human rights is nothing new.[23] For example, the UNCTAD has recognized that IIAs may constrain the ability of states (particularly in the Global South) to regulate and protect public goods as it prioritizes rights and not obligations of TNCs in host countries.[24] UNCITRAL has emphasized the need for transparency in arbitrations between investors and states.[25] In June 2021, the UN Working Group on Business and Human Rights, building on the UN Guiding Principles on Business and Human Rights,[26] has stated the need for states to achieve policy coherence between investment and human rights.[27]

These problems are faced by different developing nations and Peru follows a similar trend as other Latin American countries included in this book. Peru has IIAs with the United States, the European Union, Canada and China and most of Latin American countries, among others states and international organizations. All of these agreements are already in force. However, an on-going process to become a member of the Organisation for Economic Co-operation and Development (hereinafter, "OCDE"), which has a strong IIA component, could be an opportunity to foster economic development without compromising on the state's duty to protect human rights, labour rights or environment.

The purpose of this book is to study the impact that international economic law has had in Latin America. Peru can serve as a cautionary tale to the region as to what happens when IIAs are adopted without taking the necessary measures to assure its duty to protect public goods without the fear of retaliation by TNCs, particularly before the International Centre for the Settlement of Investment Disputes (ICSID)[28]. But this is also a chance for countries and international organizations that advocate for sustainable development and the protection of human rights to include specific sections on these IIAs, allowing developing nations to regulate public goods without the fear of diplomatic pressures, penalties or being taken to arbitration tribunals.[29]

Following this introduction, Sect. 2 will analyze how IIAs have been included in national legislation and policies, including some decisions from the Constitutional Court on the matter. This section will conclude with a reference to the 2009 Bagua socio-environmental conflict, where it can be seen how the adoption of IIAs are done without taking into account its impact on the human rights of vulnerable groups.

---

[23] See: Dupuy et al. (2009).

[24] United Nations Conference on Trade and Development (UNCTAD) (2012) World Investment Report 2012: Towards a New Generation of Investment Policies. UNCTAD, New York.

[25] See: UNCITRAL Working Group III: Investor-State Settlement Reform, https://uncitral.un.org/en/working_groups/3/investor-state.

[26] Human Rights Council (6 July 2011), *Human rights and transnational corporations and other business enterprises*, A/HRC/RES/17/4. [UN Guiding Principles].

[27] See: UN Working Group on Business and Human Rights (27 July 2021) Human rights-compatible international investment agreements, A/76/238.

[28] See: Saco (2016), pp. 654–670.

[29] See: Steininger (2021), pp. 406–427.

Section 3 will focus on the social and environmental conflicts around extractive industries in Peru. This industry is led by TNCs and it highlights many of the criticisms posed by academia and UN bodies:[30] TNCs are perceived as receiving many benefits and no responsibilities to assure policy coherence between states duty to foster development while respecting environmental, human rights and labour standards.

The fourth and final section of the chapter will analyze the potential of the National Action Plan on Business & Human Rights (BHR), adopted in June 2021, as a tool for the private sector to contribute to the development of society, and will end with some conclusions and challenges. This National Plan could be an opportunity for the Organization for Economic Co-Operation and Development (hereinafter, "OECD") to push for state and TNCs to implement responsible business conducts and achieve policy coherence.

2 Peru's Legal Framework for International Investment Agreements: Many Protections, Not Enough Responsibilities

The economic chapter of the 1993 Political Constitution establishes the foundation for a social market economy.[31] However, it also limits the state to a subsidiary role in the management of the economy.[32] The Constitution includes several articles that foster foreign direct investment, including the equal treatment of national and foreign businesses,[33] guarantees, albeit not absolute, against expropriations[34] and it grants the state the possibility to shield contracts executing strategic projects by giving it the same status as a law (*contratos-ley*).[35]

Peru, like many Latin American countries, has subscribed IIAs as a means to provide legal security, fiscal and financial stability to TNCs.[36] According to the United Nations Conference on Trade and Development database, between 1991 and 2019, Peru has signed 33 bilateral investment treaties and other 31 international instruments with investment provisions, like free trade agreements (hereinafter, "FTA") and other economic integration conventions.[37] Most of these IIAs have been with Global North countries, China, South Korea and Latin America.

[30] See: Radi (2018).

[31] Political Constitution of Peru, *supra* note 1, Art. 58.

[32] Political Constitution of Peru, *supra* note 1, Art. 60.

[33] Political Constitution of Peru, *supra* note 1, Art. 63.

[34] Political Constitution of Peru, *supra* note 1, Art. 70.

[35] Political Constitution of Peru, *supra* note 1, Art. 62.

[36] Calvert (2018), pp. 46–65.

[37] See: UNCTAD's Investment Policy Hub for Peru. https://investmentpolicy.unctad.org/international-investment-agreements/countries/165/peru.

Under the Constitution, the state has created a wide array of laws and institutions to promote foreign direct investment in the country,[38] which include Ministries, specialized agencies and a foreign policy aimed at attracting foreign investment. Peruvian authorities have adopted legal and policy reforms to promote and protect such investments,[39] without putting into due consideration the possible impact to labour issues, the environment or human rights. This narrow vision on the role and benefits of IIAs can be seen throughout the public service, including the judiciary.

For example, the Constitutional Court has heard a limited number of cases about IIAs, without addressing issues around policy coherence or the duty of the state to assure that these agreements do not generate an adverse impact to human rights or the environment. For example, a lawsuit against the free trade agreement with the United States was dismissed by the Court because the case was filed before the entry into force of such a treaty.[40] In the case of an IIA with Chile,[41] a lawsuit filed by members of Congress focused on issues related to national sovereignty and tariffs. But the most relevant aspect of this judgment was that the Constitutional Court acknowledged the importance of international arbitration to settle disputes between investors and States, without analyzing what this may imply for access to justice, particularly of vulnerable populations like Indigenous Peoples.[42]

Although the ruling does not mention it explicitly, it gives an understanding that being subject to the jurisdiction of the International Centre for the Settlement of Investment Disputes (hereinafter, "ICSID") and to honour the decisions of the arbitration panels means that the Peru is a rule of law country. Finally, in the ruling that analyzed the free trade agreement with China, the Constitutional Court did not take into account the possible implications that this treaty could have in limiting the capacity of local governments to regulate matters under their competence.[43]

In the context on how human rights were seen as a problem to foster investments, I can only exemplify it with a personal experience. In 2013, I was part of the Ministry of Justice and Human Rights, helping to draft the second National Human Rights Plan of the country. These national policies are adopted by a Supreme Decree (*Decreto Supremo*), which means that all members of the Cabinet must approve it as a means to show the political commitment of the Executive branch.

In the drafting of the National Human Rights Plan, following the recent adoption of the UNGP in July 2011, the drafting team included an activity titled "to carry a diagnostic on the impact of business activities on human rights of vulnerable groups". The purpose was only to commission a study that could start assessing the impact of business activities to human rights. No policy or legal reforms were

[38] Metaxas and Kechagia (2016), pp. 160–173.

[39] Stanley (2020).

[40] Tribunal Constitucional del Perú, Resolución No. 00036-2007-PI/T (20 November 2007).

[41] Tribunal Constitucional del Perú, Sentencia No. 00002-2009-PI/TC (5 February 2010).

[42] Tribunal Constitucional del Perú, Sentencia No. 00002-2009-PI/TC (5 February 2010), paras. 27–41.

[43] Tribunal Constitucional del Perú, Sentencia No. 00021-2010-AI/TC (20 March 2012).

included as this was, at the time, a fairly new field. Approximately 30 minutes after the draft was sent for consultation to other members of the Cabinet, the Minister of Justice and Human Rights received the instruction to remove that activity from the draft plan, as it was going to "scare investments away" and "outrage TNCs". The plan was adopted in 2014 without any reference to issues around business and human rights.

In all fairness, the following Human Rights plans in Peru have included these BHR section and the country now has a National Action Plan on the matter. A lot has changed in the past 8 years but the reluctance to add a human rights or environmental component in the regulation of business activities continues.

2.1 Bagua: Indigenous Protests and Free Trade Agreement

In 2009, the government of then President Alan García was about to ratify the FTA with the United States, which was seen as a great achievement and recognition of the country's economic and political stability. In this context, the U.S. government had requested a series of legal reforms prior to ratifying this agreement. Part of these legal reforms included measures that could undermine environmental protections and territorial rights of Indigenous Peoples. It should be noted that Peru was, at the time of the events, a party to ILO Convention 169 on the Rights of Indigenous and Tribal Peoples [44] and had voted in favour of the 2007 UN Declaration on the Rights of Indigenous Peoples,[45] in addition to its obligations under the American Convention on Human Rights and the case-law established by the Inter-American Court of Human Rights regarding Indigenous Peoples.

In the face of protests against reforms regarding forestry concessions on Indigenous land, the government stated that if these reforms were not adopted, the FTA would not be approved. This generated widespread polarization within the public opinion and Indigenous Peoples protested against these measures, particularly against Decree 1090 and Decree 1064. The focus of the protests was centered in the town of Bagua, in the Peruvian Amazon. The confrontation between the public forces and the Indigenous Peoples caused the death of 33 people, including 21 members of the Police.

The confrontation ended with a truce, facilitated by the Catholic Church and the Office of the Ombudsperson. Days later, Congress struck down Decree 1090 and Decree 1064, which were the ones most objected by Indigenous organizations.[46] The

[44] *Convention No. 169, Convention concerning Indigenous and Tribal Peoples in Independent Countries*, June 27, 1989, 28 ILM 1382 (entered into force 5 September 1991).

[45] *Declaration on the Rights of Indigenous Peoples*, 13 September 2007, G.A. Res. 61/295, U.N. Doc. A/RES/47/1 (2007).

[46] Ibid, paras. 19–20.

FTA was adopted and has been in force for the past 12 years. To this date, no senior political authority that participated in this conflict has been convicted.

For the purpose of this chapter, this case is illustrative because it was a lost opportunity for governmental authorities to negotiate a FTA, respecting its international human rights obligations. The claim of Indigenous Peoples that the implementing decrees affected their territory and therefore, should have been consulted was not heard by government officials. Instead, a member of the Cabinet warned Congress that if those decrees were struck down, the FTA was not going to be approved.[47]

In addition, this showed the lack of vision from the private sector (including TNCs) to position themselves in favor of measures that would benefit all sectors of society. It was not true that the adoption or reform of a specific law conditioned the approval of a treaty that took years to negotiate. But the government's position at that time was supported by the business community, both domestic and foreign.

Although the Bagua conflict took place almost twelve years ago,[48] It shows the problems that developing nations like Peru face in the negotiation and approval of IIAs. Social and political elites accept these agreements without understanding (or caring) how these IIAs may impact vulnerable groups.[49] Anybody that poses questions to the social benefits of IIA is seen as an enemy. Indigenous Peoples concerns are ignored, despite that many of these IIAs tend to foster access of transnational corporations to mining, oil, gas and forestry projects located in Indigenous land.

One of the focuses of the next section will show how the increase in foreign investment in extractive projects has also led to an increase in socio-environmental conflicts. But perhaps of all the socio-environmental conflicts that the country has faced over the years, the Bagua conflict[50] exemplifies the consequences of IIAs that do not take into consideration the views of all stakeholders.[51]

[47] Radio Programas del Perú (9 June 2009), Ministra Aráoz advierte que derogar DL 1090 haría peligrar TLC con EEUU. https://rpp.pe/economia/economia/ministra-araoz-advierte-que-derogar-dl-1090-haria-peligrar-tlc-con-eeuu-noticia-186949.

[48] Zambrano et al. (2017).

[49] See: Li (2015).

[50] See: Defensoría del Pueblo del Perú (2010).

[51] See: Report of the Special Rapporteur on the situation of human rights and fundamental freedoms of indigenous people, James Anaya (18 August 2019), Observations on the situation of the indigenous peoples of the Amazon region and the events of 5 June and the following days in Bagua and Utcubamba provinces, Peru. A/HRC/12/34/Add.8.

Fig. 1 Source: Banco Central de Reserva del Perú

3 Impact of IIAs: A Growing Gap Between the Economy and Public Goods

IIAs have played a significant impact in the Peruvian economy. Major TNCs, particularly those operating in the mining, oil, gas and agro-industrial sectors, participate in different projects throughout the country. According to the *Banco Central de Reserva del Perú*, the country's Central Reserve Bank, foreign direct investment has significantly increased in the past forty years, reaching its peak in 2012 with almost USD $12,000 million in investment.[52] The two sharp declines seen in the graph below were caused by external factors such as the end of the commodity boom and the coronavirus pandemic in 2020 (Fig. 1).

This increase in foreign direct investment also reflects in the growth of the country's GDP. On average, the country's economy grew approximately 4.9% per year between 2007 and 2019. [53] Poverty was reduced from 33.5% to 20.2% while extreme poverty went from 9.5% to 2.9% of the population, between 2001 and 2019.[54] As stated in the introduction, this growth was fragile and highly dependent on external factors such as the end of the commodity boom and the coronavirus pandemic.

[52] Banco Central de Reserva del Perú, https://estadisticas.bcrp.gob.pe/estadisticas/series/consultas/grafico.

[53] See: Instituto Nacional de Estadística e Informática (INEI) (2021) Panorama de la Economía Peruana 1950-2020. INEI, Lima, 2021, https://www.inei.gob.pe/media/MenuRecursivo/publicaciones_digitales/Est/Lib1799/libro.pdf.

[54] Instituto Nacional de Estadística e Informática (INEI) (2021a) Informe Técnico Evolución de la Pobreza Monetaria 2009-2020, *supra* note 13.

Cuadro N.° 16:
PERÚ: CONFLICTOS SOCIOAMBIENTALES, SEGÚN ACTIVIDAD, ENERO 2023
(Número de casos)

Actividad	Conteo	%
TOTAL	**141**	**100.0%**
Minería	94	66.7%
Hidrocarburos	28	19.9%
Residuos y saneamiento	8	5.7%
Otros	7	5.0%
Agroindustrial	2	1.4%
Energía	1	0.7%
Forestales	1	0.7%

Fuente: Defensoría del Pueblo - SIMCO

Fig. 2 Net foreign direct investment in Peru 1980–2020 (in USD)

3.1 Social-Environmental Conflicts and Legal Measures to Undermine Human Rights

Throughout the country, the increase of economic activities in the mining and gas sectors, where licenses and permits are usually given with little or no participation of the population in the area of influence of the project, particularly Indigenous Peoples, has sometimes led to violent confrontation.

Since 2008, the Office of the Ombudsperson (*Defensoría del Pueblo*) has produced a monthly report on the state of social conflicts in the country. In its January 2023 report,[55] the Ombudsman reported 198 social conflicts in the country, of which 141 were of a socio-environmental nature. As it can be seen from the table below, of all the socio-environmental conflicts, 94 are caused by mining activities, 28 from hydrocarbons activities, and 1 from energy projects (Fig. 2):[56]

In some cases, violent clashes between the community that opposes the project and police forces result in violations of the right to life, security of the person and property. According to a report of the Peruvian Ombudsman regarding to violence that has risen from socio-environmental conflicts, 2312 people have been injured and 195 have lost their lives between January 2006 and September 2011.[57]

TNCs are not the sole responsible for all socio-environmental conflicts in the country. It is the state's primal responsibility to prevent and address human rights and environmental concerns of the population. But the lack of trust towards the state and a weak legal and institutional framework to prevent socio-environmental conflicts has contributed to a situation where it has become normal to have more than a

[55] See: Defensoría del Pueblo (January 2023) Reporte Mensual de Conflictos Sociales No. 227-Enero 2023. Defensoría del Pueblo, Lima.

[56] Ibid, p. 22.

[57] Defensoría del Pueblo (2012), p. 53.

100 socio-environmental conflicts at a time. This is not sustainable by any means and in this context, TNCs could have played a leading role in addressing their part of these conflicts.

Most of the preambles of IIAs recognize the importance of sustainable development and economic growth. But these goals cannot be achieved without the protection of human rights and the environment. In the Peruvian case, most of the regulations adopted in the context of social environmental conflicts have undermined the protection of these public goods. In the past years, the Constitutional Court has analyzed the constitutionality of laws extending state of emergency to areas of socio-environmental conflicts,[58] criminalizing social protests,[59] of laws limiting the scope of consultation of Indigenous Peoples[60] or of agreements between mining companies and the National Police,[61] where police officers agree to provide private security services to these companies.

These laws were adopted by the state to suppress protests against extractive projects and to foster a more "business-friendly" environment for businesses, particularly TNCs. The problem is that these laws are, for the most part, supported by TNCS, despite their pledge to support social responsibility and engagement with local stakeholders. In addition, most of the reforms adopted to "modernize the bureaucracy" or to "simplify permits for businesses" tend to focus on two issues:[62] to undermine the independence and autonomy of regulatory agencies and to reform criminal laws to limit the exercise of fundamental rights such as freedom of speech, freedom of movement or the right to peaceful protest.[63] Even if states are the primary responsible of these laws, these could not be adopted without the acquiesce of businesses, including TNCs.[64]

Similar to what was presented in Sect. 2 of this chapter, is a regime that is made to benefit TNCs, where the pursuit of economic growth is perceived as the only means to achieve progress, even if this comes at the expense of human rights of the population located in the area and the protection of the environment.[65] If the government were to adopt sanctions or other measures to demand stricter control from businesses, a state would face possible litigation before the ICISD.

---

[58] Tribunal Constitucional del Perú, Sentencia No. 945-2020-PHC/TC (24 November 2020).

[59] Tribunal Constitucional del Perú, Sentencia No. 0009-2018-PI/TC (2 June 2020).

[60] See: Sanborn et al. (2016).

[61] Tribunal Constitucional del Perú, Sentencia No. 437-2020-PI/TC (20 August 2020).

[62] Damonte et al. (2021).

[63] See: Paredes (2019), pp. 5–32.

[64] This is not only a problem in Peru but also in many countries in Latin America. See: Instituto Creer (2021), Análisis, sistematización y comparación de los mecanismos de acceso a reclamo en la región andina. Instituto CREER, GIZ, Bogotá.

[65] Escobal and Ponce (2007), pp. 67–100.

3.2 Peru, Regulation of Public Goods and ICSID: A Look at La Oroya and the Convinca Cases

The purpose of this section is not to formulate a critique on the ICSID but instead, to use two cases (one concluded and one pending) to illustrate how TNCs have used legitimate means to solve a controversy, like an arbitration tribunal, to undermine the regulation of public goods by the state.

Since it is a member of the ICSID, there has been 57 cases brought against Peru. According to the ICSID's database,[66] 24 cases are pending and 23 have been concluded. The first case against Peru was brought by a Paraguayan businessperson in August 1998,[67] and the latest case was filed in December 2021 by a Spanish TNC.[68]

The case of the *La Oroya* smelter is perhaps a case that brought to the public light environmental and health issues caused by smelters.[69] Located in the Central Valley of Peru, Doe Rue, a U.S. corporation, took control of the smelter in 1997, promising to operate the smelter following environmental standards. The TNC never fulfilled such commitment, despite receiving extensions by the government. In April 2011, Renco-Doe Run's parent company- filed a case before the ICSID against Peru, asking for compensation for breaching the provisions of the Free Trade Agreement between Peru and the United States.[70] In July 2016, the arbitration tribunal dismissed the case on jurisdictional grounds.[71] Despite the impact the smelter had on the health of the local population and the environment, the company attempted to use the FTA to receive financial compensation, without assuming its own responsibility to its stakeholders and Peruvian regulations at the time.[72]

Doe Run no longer controls the smelter but the health and environmental problems remain. For many years, local population considered that the Peruvian government never addressed their social situation.[73] In December 2006, a group of petitioners, in representation of the La Oroya community, filed before the Inter-American Commission on Human Rights (hereinafter, "IACHR) a case against the state of Peru for the alleged violation of the rights to life, security, health and judicial

---

[66] See: https://icsid.worldbank.org/cases/case-database?keyword=Peru.

[67] See: Eudoro A. Olguín v. Republic of Paraguay (ICSID Case No. ARB/98/5), https://icsid.worldbank.org/cases/case-database/case-detail?CaseNo=ARB/98/5.

[68] See: Enagás Internacional S.L.U. v. Republic of Peru (ICSID Case No. ARB/21/65), https://icsid.worldbank.org/cases/case-database/case-detail?CaseNo=ARB/21/65.

[69] See: Li (2015).

[70] See: The Renco Group, Inc. v. Republic of Peru (ICSID Case No. UNCT/13/1), https://icsid.worldbank.org/cases/case-database/case-detail?CaseNo=UNCT/13/1.

[71] See: The Renco Group, Inc. v. Republic of Peru (ICSID Case No. UNCT/13/1), Partial award on Jurisdiction (July 15, 2016), http://icsidfiles.worldbank.org/icsid/ICSIDBLOBS/OnlineAwards/C3004/DC8592_En.pdf.

[72] See: Valencia (2016).

[73] FIDH (2013).

protection. In September 2021, the IACHR filed this case before the Inter-American Court of Human Rights (hereinafter, "IACtHR), where the state will have to answer about its lack of action to protect the life and health of the members of the community, including children.[74]

The case of La Oroya is a perfect example of how the state has handled socio-environmental conflicts and how TNCs use FTA and IEL to evade its social and environmental responsibilities. Doe Run is a case of a TNC that abused its privileged position, the proven environmental and health damages to the local community without any action by the competent authorities. Unfortunately, this is not the only case.

In September 2021, a Peruvian-Colombian construction consortium presented a case against Peru before the ICSID.[75] The consortium, called Covinca, filed a case against the state for different measures, which includes the delay in the allocation of the terrains for the expansion of a highway. The request for arbitration is not yet available in the ICSID website, but a specialized media reports that another reason for Covinca to sue focuses on the economic impact suffered for the measures adopted by the country to address the coronavirus pandemic. The curfew and limitations to people and cars to circulate in the country, has impacted the toll booths of the highway under their administration,[76] causing significant financial damage to this consortium.

It is important to understand that, with a mortality of 6.9% per 100,000 habitants, Peru leads the world ranking with most coronavirus deaths proportionally to their population.[77] In second place is Mexico with 6.5% and Russia in a distant third place with 2.9%. As a Peruvian citizen, I have been a direct witness of the incapacity of the government to address the pandemic since March 2020 and I have seen, through social media and personal communications, the desperation of friends, family members and colleagues looking for an ICU bed or an oxygen tank for a member of their families.

In a country overwhelmed by the pandemic, any measure restricting mobility was valid under the norms for state of emergency to protect the population. The fact that a consortium is suing the state for attempting to keep its population alive, putting aside the possible impact of the measure, is disconcerting. This request, which is currently pending before the arbitration tribunal, goes beyond the purpose of the ICSID and any measure adopted in IEL to protect TNCs.

---

[74] IACHR (14 October 2021), IACHR Files Case Before IA Court on Peru's Responsibility for the Effects of Contamination in La Oroya Community, https://www.oas.org/en/iachr/jsForm/?File=/en/iachr/media_center/preleases/2021/274.asp.

[75] Concesionaria Peruana de Vías– COVINCA, S.A. v. Republic of Peru (ICSID Case No. ARB/21/45), https://icsid.worldbank.org/cases/case-database/case-detail?CaseNo=ARB/21/45.

[76] CIAR Global (27 September 2021), Concesionaria Vial Presenta Arbitraje De Inversiones Contra Perú En CIADI, https://ciarglobal.com/concesionaria-viaria-presenta-arbitraje-de-inversiones-contra-peru-en-ciadi/.

[77] See: John Hopkins Coronavirus Resource Centre, Mortality Analyses, https://coronavirus.jhu.edu/data/mortality.

As enraging as this measure might be, and my apologies to the editors and the readers for this personal testimony, businesses are using the tools IIAs provided them. In this way, the ultimate responsible is Peru and other Latin American countries that might be facing or about to face similar challenges. By prioritizing investment and fiscal regimes without adopting the necessary safeguards to protect public goods such as health, labour, human rights and the environment, these types of cases will continue. It is necessary for developing nations, like Peru, to include express clauses protecting their rights to protect these goods. Perhaps the Free Trade Agreement between Morocco and Nigeria could be a starting point for a new approach to these IIAs.[78]

4 Business and Human Rights: A Chance to Include the Protection of Public Goods in IIAs

As stated in the introduction to this chapter, the political uncertainty that Peru is experiencing complicates the adoption of binding standards to ensure that companies operating in the country develop responsible business conducts (RBC). However, this is not for lack of public policy, as in June 2021, the Peruvian government adopted its first National Action Plan on Business and Human Rights.[79]

This policy sets a framework of legal and institutional changes that must be met so that businesses operating in the country are in accordance with three leading instruments in the field of business & human rights (BHR): the UN Guiding Principles on Business and Human Rights,[80] the OECD Guidelines on Multinational Corporations[81] and the ILO Tripartite Declaration of Principles concerning Multinational Enterprises and Social Policy.[82]

The adoption of this National Action Plan is nothing short of remarkable, concluding a process that started with the adoption of the country's third National

---

[78] See: Reciprocal Investment, Promotion and Protection Agreement between the Government of the Kingdom of Morocco and the Government of the Federal Republic of Nigeria (3 December 2016), https://investmentpolicy.unctad.org/international-investment-agreements/treaty-files/5409/download.

[79] Ministerio de Justicia y Derechos Humanos (MINJUS) (11 June 2021) Plan Nacional de Acción sobre Empresas y Derechos Humanos 2021-2025, Decreto Supremo No. 009-2021-JUS. MINJUS, Lima.

[80] See: UN Guiding Principles, *supra* note 18.

[81] Organisation for Economic Co-operation and Development (OECD) (2011), OECD Guidelines for Multinational Corporations. OECD, Brussels.

[82] International Labour Organization (March 2017), ILO Tripartite Declaration of Principles concerning Multinational Enterprises and Social Policy. Adopted by the Governing Body of the International Labour Office at its 204th Session (Geneva, November 1977) and amended at its 279th (November 2000), 295th (March 2006) and 329th (March 2017) Sessions.

Human Rights Plan in 2018.[83] In the three years that the discussion, elaboration and approval of this National Action Plan on BHR lasted, the country had 3 Presidents, suffered an attempted *coup d'État* by Congress, faced harsh social protests due to corruption practices by senior politicians and held national elections while also being severely impacted by the Covid-19 pandemic.

One of the Plan's greatest achievements was the high degree of participation from different stakeholders throughout the process.[84] The private sector, the media, representatives of historically vulnerable groups, international organizations and various government agencies participated actively in the deliberations. The fact that the private sector accompanied the entire process is of utmost importance, since at the beginning of the process; its position was to reject the adoption of a BHR policy.

In the early discussions related to BHR in the country, the main consensus by businesses was that there was no need for state laws and that voluntary pledges or guiding principles were enough. To be fair, this has been the stand-by businesses in different parts of the world. Yet, in the Peruvian case, this narrow view of self-regulation was endorsed by major media outlets.

For example, soon after the government announced its intention to work on a national action plan on Business and Human Rights, the leading newspaper of the country, *El Comercio*, published an editorial questioning such decision,[85] calling it "a bureaucratic burden" that only targets established, regulated businesses instead of focusing on illegal mining activities in the Peruvian Amazon or to address the informality of the economy, among other social and economic problems.

The National Action Plan on BHR has five strategic objectives: i) to promote a culture of respect by businesses; (ii) to adopt policies to prevent adverse human rights impacts by businesses; (iii) to adopt policies related to accountability by businesses that negatively impact rights of individuals or groups; (iv) to promote due diligence procedures; and (v) to strengthen judicial and non-judicial grievance mechanisms.[86]

In October 2021, the UN Working Group on Business and Human Rights presented a report to the UN General Assembly on the impact that international investment agreements might have on human rights,[87] stressing the need for states to assure that these treaties do not undermine their capacity to adopt laws and policies to protect human rights or the environment.

---

[83] *Plan Nacional de Derechos Humanos 2018-2021*, Decreto Supremo No. 002-2018-JUS (31 January 2018).

[84] *Plan Nacional de Acción sobre Empresas y Derechos Humanos 2021-2025*, pp. 6–29.

[85] El Comercio, "*Editorial: Los derechos humanos y selectivos*" (1 de marzo de 2020). See: https://elcomercio.pe/opinion/editorial/editorial-los-derechos-humanos-y-selectivos-noticia/?ref=ecr.

[86] *Plan Nacional de Acción sobre Empresas y Derechos Humanos 2021-2025*, pp. 57–127.

[87] Working group on the issue of human rights and transnational corporations and other business enterprises, "*Human rights-compatible international investment agreements*", A/76/238 (27 July 2021).

In this report, the Working Group concludes that of the 25 National Action Plans on BHR adopted to date, only 4 have not included a section or a measure regarding international investment agreements and human rights: United States, Slovenia, Chile and Peru.[88] Considering the examples presented in this chapter about the Indigenous protest in Bagua and the case of La Oroya this absence is a significant omission showing that other actors could have a leading role in assuring the IIAs do not undermine public goods like health, labour, human rights or the environment.

4.1 OECD and Peru: Partnership Potential and a Chance for a New Approach to IIAs and IEL

Since 2011, Peru has been trying to become a member of the OECD. This is perhaps the only consistent foreign policy the country has had in the past decade. The great aspiration was to celebrate the country's 2021 bicentennial as a full member of the OECD but both the pandemic and the political instability of the past years have postponed this measure. Peru currently is a partner country. On January 2022, the OECD formally invited Peru, along with Argentina, Brazil, Bulgaria, Croatia, and Romania to begin formal open accession discussions.[89]

This does not mean that the OCDE has lost its impact or influence in the country. For example, the OCDE acknowledges that Peru has adopted, at least, 29 laws,[90] following a package of reforms in order to be accepted as a full member of this organization. Most of these laws focus on issues around competitiveness of the economy, procurement, anti-corruption, anti-money laundering provisions and the environment.[91] Moreover, the country has adopted or subscribed to 24 OECD legal instruments, going from Conventions to Codes of Conduct.[92]

It is telling that the protection of public goods is not as important as raising the competitiveness of the country. These measures are key for economic growth, as these attract foreign direct investment. But as it has been seen in this chapter, these reforms usually come at the expense of environmental, human rights, health and labour regulations.

[88] Working group on the issue of human rights and transnational corporations and other business enterprises, "*Human rights-compatible international investment agreements*", paras. 35–36.

[89] OECD, Resolution of the Council on the Opening of Accession Discussions, C(2017)92/FINAL, 25 January 2022. See: https://www.oecd.org/newsroom/Resolution-of-the-Council-on-the-Opening-of-Accession-Discussions-C-2017-92-final.pdf.

[90] OCDE, Programa País OCDE-Perú: Resúmenes ejecutivos y principales recomendaciones, OCDE, Lima, p. 4.

[91] OCDE, Programa País OCDE-Perú: Resúmenes ejecutivos y principales recomendaciones, OCDE, Lima, p. 4.

[92] OCDE, Programa País OCDE-Perú: Resúmenes ejecutivos y principales recomendaciones, OCDE, Lima, p. 5.

Under the flag of competitiveness reforms, the country has adopted a series of laws that are new to its legal tradition.[93] For example, Peru's Criminal Code has never recognized the criminal liability of legal persons. However, in 2016, the government passed a law establishing the administrative and criminal responsibility of a legal person for acts of international bribery.[94] This law was amended in 2018, expanding the responsibility for money laundering and organized crime, illegal mining and finance of terrorism.[95]

What is most telling is that these laws impose an additional burden on corporations and its administrators.[96] Yet this was not objected by business groups as it was seen as a small burden towards the bigger goal of becoming a part of the OECD. Yet, whenever different organizations recommend including specific human rights, environmental or labour provisions in these agreements, these are objected, and these organizations are called "anti-investment". It would be beneficial if the OCDE could work with the Peruvian towards the adoption of coherent policies to harmonize economic development with the protection of the environment or human rights.

Free trade agreements with the United States and Canada, as well as economic integration agreement with the European Union, have broad social provisions in their preambles or even specific environmental sections. However, none of these agreements have safeguards assuring that host states like Peru will not be taken to arbitration forums by TNCs for adopting laws or policies to protect the environment or human rights. As it has been seen in this chapter, the separation of fields has caused great problems in Peru, including the loss of people's lives.

So regardless of the outcome of the negotiations between the OECD and Peru, there is a chance for other bodies to work with government authorities in the adoption of measures that assure the integration of the country with the world, without sacrificing its Constitutional role to protect and respect human rights and the environment. The practice in the past decades is that state officials prioritize economic growth and economic integration, even if this increases the disenfranchisement and vulnerability of the population, particularly of marginalized groups.

---

[93] See: Carrión Zenteno (2021), pp. 201–218.

[94] Ley No. 30,424, Ley que Regula la Responsabilidad Adinistrativa de las Personas Jurídicas por el Delito de Cohecho Activo Transnacional, adopted on 1 April, 2016.

[95] Ley No. 30,835, Ley que Modifica la Denominación y los Artículos 1, 9 y 10 de la Ley 30,424, Ley que Regula la Responsabilidad Adinistrativa de las Personas Jurídicas por el Delito de Cohecho Activo Transnacional, adopted on 11 July 2018.

[96] Caro Coria (2021), pp. 245–271.

5 Conclusion

The purpose of this chapter was to show the impact that IEL and IIAs have had in Peru in the past three decades. The economic integration of the country has contributed to reduce poverty and increase the quality of life of most Peruvians, particularly those living in urban areas. Regardless of the political ideology of all governments that have ran the country, there is a common denominator: all laws and policies adopted to foster foreign direct investment and economic development have not considered or disregarded its impact on public goods like the environment, health, labour or human rights.

The new government has pledged to change the Constitution and to reinstate the role of the state as the central figure of the economy. It is uncertain if the current government will achieve this measure, as public opinion tends to be divided and there is no indication that it has the Congressional majority or legal venue to call for a new Constitutional Assembly. What is sure is that this political instability may affect the economic and social recovery of a country that is still in the middle of a coronavirus pandemic.

As I conclude the revision of this chapter, an oil spill in the coast of Lima has polluted the sea, affecting people, the fauna and the flora of the shore.[97] The oil spill was caused in the Pampilla oil refinery, operated by Spanish TNC Repsol.[98] It is estimated that approximately 6000 barrels of petroleum were spilled, and it is currently moving towards the Northern shoreline.[99]

In the aftermath of this human and environmental disaster, many of the problems highlighted in this chapter are: corporate negligence, weakness of the state to enforce its own rules, indifference towards victims or the environmental impact of business activities. These problems will continue to manifest if state officials continue to adopt norms and IIAs to attract foreign direct investment without protecting public goods.

The end doesn't justify the means and as seen in the case of La Oroya, TNCs will use every tool at their disposal to evade their responsibility. So, it wouldn't be a surprise that, when this book is published, to know that REPSOL has requested an arbitration against Peru before the ICSID. It relies on the state the duty to harmonize, or better yet, prioritize the protection of public goods over IIAs.

---

[97] The New York Times (21 January 2022), Oil Spill Triggered by Tsunami Devastates Coast of Peru, https://www.nytimes.com/2022/01/21/world/americas/peru-oil-spill-tonga-tsunami.html.

[98] Reuters (19 January 2022), Peru's Castillo decrees major oil spill an environmental emergency, https://www.reuters.com/business/environment/perus-castillo-decrees-major-oil-spill-an-environmental-emergency-2022-01-20/.

[99] The Guardian (19 January 2022), Peru demands compensation for disastrous oil spill caused by Tonga volcano, https://www.theguardian.com/world/2022/jan/19/peru-spain-repsol-disastrous-oil-spill.

References

Agüero A et al (2020) Análisis de políticas agropecuarias en Perú: 2014-2018. Banco Interamericano de Desarrollo, Washington

Aldana U et al (2020) Desigualdad y Pobreza en un Contexto de Crecimiento Económico. Instituto de Estudios Peruanos, Lima

Banco M (2021) Diagnóstico del Sector Minero Perú. Banco Mundial, Lima

Calvert J (2018) Civil society and investor-state dispute settlement: assessing the social dimensions of investment disputes in Latin America. New Polit Econ 23:1

Caro Coria D C (2021) Fundamento y Dogmática del Delito de Corrupción Privada. In: Ambos K, Malarino E, Fuchs M-C (eds) Corrupción y Derecho Penal: Prevención, Investigación y Sanción: Estudio Comparado, Tirant Lo Blanc & Fundación Konrad Adenauer, Bogotá

Carrión Zenteno A (2021) Responsabilidad Penal de la Persona Jurídica y Corrupción: La Ley 30424 entendida desde la Teoría de las Normas. In: Ambos K, Malarino E, Fuchs M-C (eds) Corrupción y Derecho Penal: Prevención, Investigación y Sanción: Estudio Comparado, Tirant Lo Blanc & Fundación Konrad Adenauer, Bogotá

Castilla L (2015) The Peruvian Success Story. Americas Quarterly. https://www.americasquarterly.org/fulltextarticle/the-peruvian-success-story/

Comisión Económica para América Latina (CEPAL) (2020) La Inversión Extranjera Directa en América Latina y el Caribe 2020. CEPAL, Santiago

Contreras C et al (2015) La desigualdad de la distribución de ingresos en el Perú: orígenes históricos y dinámica política y económica. Pontificia Universidad Católica del Perú, Lima

Crabtree J, Durand F (2017) Peru: elite power and political capture. Zed Books, London

Damonte G et al (eds) (2021) ¿Una oportunidad perdida? Boom extractivo y cambios institucionales en el Perú. Pontificia Universidad Católica del Perú, Lima

Defensoría del Pueblo (2012) Violencia en los Conflictos Sociales. Defensoría del Pueblo, Informe Defensorial No. 156, Lima Damonte G et al. (eds) (2021) ¿Una oportunidad perdida? Boom extractivo y cambios institucionales en el Perú. Pontificia Universidad Católica del Perú, Lima

Defensoría del Pueblo del Perú (2010) Actuaciones Defensoriales en el marco del conflicto de Bagua: Informe de la Defensora del Pueblo a la Comisión del Congreso de la República que investiga los sucesos de Bagua, aledaños y otros. Defensoría del Pueblo, Lima

Dupuy P-M et al (eds) (2009) Human rights in international investment law and arbitration. Oxford University Press, New York

Durand F (2021) Business and politics in Peru: the state and the National Bourgeoisie. Routledge, New York

Escobal J, Ponce C (2007) Liberalización comercial, tratados de libre comercio y pobreza rural. In: GRADE (ed) Investigación, políticas y desarrollo en el Perú. GRADE, Lima

FIDH (2013) Complejo Metalúrgico de La Oroya: Donde la inversión se protege por encima de los derechos humanos. FIDH, Lima

Human Rights Council (6 July 2011) Human rights and transnational corporations and other business enterprises, A/HRC/RES/17/4

Instituto Creer (2021) Análisis, sistematización y comparación de los mecanismos de acceso a reclamo en la región andina. Instituto CREER, GIZ, Bogotá

Instituto Nacional de Estadística e Informática (INEI) (2020) Producción y Empleo Informal en el Perú, Cuenta Satélite de la Economía Informal 2007-2019. INEI, Lima, p 101

Instituto Nacional de Estadística e Informática (INEI) (2021a) Informe Técnico Evolución de la Pobreza Monetaria 2009-2020. INEI, Lima. https://www.inei.gob.pe/cifras-de-pobreza/

Instituto Nacional de Estadística e Informática (INEI) (2021b) Perú: Comportamiento de los indicadores de mercado laboral a nivel nacional, Informe Técnico N° 03 Empleo Nacional. Trimestre: Abril-Mayo-Junio 2021. INEI, Lima, p 19

Lagunes P, Svejnar J (eds) (2020) Corruption and the Lava Jato Scandal in Latin America. Routledge, New York

Li F (2015) Unearthing conflict: corporate mining, activism, and expertise in Peru. Duke University Press, Durham

Metaxas T, Kechagia P (2016) Foreign direct investment in Latin America: the case of Peru. Theoret Pract Res Econ Fields 7:2(14)

Organismo Nacional de Procesos Electorales (ONPE) (2021) Presentación de Resultados: Elecciones Generales y Parlamento Andino 2021. https://resultadoshistorico.onpe.gob.pe/EG2021/EleccionesPresidenciales/RePres/T

Paredes M (2019) Conflictos mineros en el Perú: entre la protesta y la negociación. Debates En Sociología 45

Programa de las Naciones Unidas para el Desarrollo (PNUD) (2019) El Reto de la Igualdad Una lectura de las dinámicas territoriales en el Perú. PNUD, Lima

Radi Y (ed) (2018) Research handbook on human rights and investment. Edward Elgar, Cheltenham

Saco V (2016) El secreto del éxito del Perú en el Ciadi: destruyendo el paradigma de que el sistema de solución de diferencias inversionista-Estado es peligroso para los países en desarrollo. In: Tanzi A et al (eds) International Investment Law in Latin America: Problems and Prospects / Derecho Internacional de las Inversiones en América. Problemas y Perspectivas, Brill, Latina, pp 654–670

Sanborn A et al (2016) La Consulta Previa en el Perú : Avances y Retos. Universidad del Pacífico, Lima

Stanley L (2020) La regulación de la inversión extranjera directa: los casos de la Argentina, Colombia, el Perú. la República de Corea y Tailandia. CEPAL, Santiago

Steininger S (2021) The role of human rights in investment law and arbitration state obligations, corporate responsibility and community empowerment. In: Bantekas I, Stein M (eds) The Cambridge companion to business & human rights law. Cambridge University Press, Cambridge, pp 406–427

UN Working Group on Business and Human Rights (27 July 2021) Human rights-compatible international investment agreements, A/76/238

UNCITRAL Working Group III: Investor-State Settlement Reform., https://uncitral.un.org/en/working_groups/3/investor-state

United Nations Conference on Trade and Development (UNCTAD) (2012) World Investment Report 2012: Towards a New Generation of Investment Policies. UNCTAD, New York

Valencia A (2016) Human rights trade-offs in times of economic growth: the long-term capability impacts of extractive-led development. Springer

Zambrano G et al (eds) (2017) Bagua: Entendiendo el Derecho en un contexto culturalmente complejo. IDEHPUCP, Universidad Antonio Ruiz de Montoya, Fundación Konrad Adenauer, Lima

Salvador Herencia Carrasco Director of the Human Rights Clinic at the Human Rights Research and Education Centre and part-time professor of the Section de Droit Civil of the University of Ottawa. Board member of the Academia Latinoamericana de Derechos Humanos y Empresas.

Part IV
Trends in Regionalization

Mexico in International Investment Law: From NAFTA to USMCA

Virdzhiniya Petrova Georgieva

1 Introduction

Since the decade of 1940–1950 and until 1970, Mexico entered in a period of stable and sustained economic development, characterized by an annual GDP growth of 7.5%, 2.5% annual inflation level, low unemployment, and stable exchange rates.[1] As many other Latin American countries, it pursued a protectionist economic policy of import substitution and foreign investment controls, which aimed to shield domestic industries from foreign competition. The abandon of the Bretton Woods "par-value" system in 1971, and the sharp increase of oil prices during the Oil Shocks of 1973 and 1978, triggered the end of the "Mexican economic miracle" and provoked a deep recession, marked by a brusque devaluation of the peso *vis-à-vis* the dollar and a sudden elevation of the levels of inflation. The rise of oil costs and Mexico's huge oil reserves represented great incomes to the public budget, that, unfortunately, brought excessive public spending and unprecedented enlargement of public deficit and external debt during the presidencies of Luis Echeverría and José López Portillo.[2] In 1982, Mexico was facing a default of loans and told its creditors (mainly US commercial banks and other banks) that it was unable to make next payments. Mexico had to negotiate an emergency financial support from US banks and the International Monetary Fund (IMF). The "stand- by agreement" with the IMF was considered as "the first rendition of what would later be called the Washington Consensus", as its macroeconomic conditionality embraced a reduction on governmental spending, deregulation of economic activities, privatization of

[1] Cabral (1985), pp. 67–100.
[2] Aparicio Cabrera (2010), p. 2.

V. P. Georgieva (✉)
Universidad Nacional Autonóma de México (UNAM), Mexico City, Mexico

N. Monebhurrun et al. (eds.), *International Investment Law and Arbitration from a Latin American Perspective*, International Law and the Global South,
https://doi.org/10.1007/978-3-031-49382-9_11

public owned companies, higher taxes, policies to reduce inflation, elimination of capital controls and, generally, a more open domestic economy.[3] Thus, 1982, fastened the ultimate abandon of Mexico's import substitution model and marked the beginning of the neoliberal period of its politics and economy, which was coronated by the ratification of the General Agreement on Trade and Tariffs (GATT) in 1986 and the signature of the North American Free Trade Agreement (NAFTA) in 1992.

After the entry into force of Canada- United States Free Trade Agreement (CUSFTA) in 1989, Mexican President Carlos Salinas de Gortari offered to US President George Bush Sr. the negotiation of a regional free trade agreement between Mexico and the US to eliminate barriers to trade flows and to integrate and reinforce the complementarity of the two domestic economies. Canada joined the negotiation process later. US Congress ratified NAFTA in 1993 and it finally entered into force in 1994. According to its article 102- c), one of its main objectives was to "increase substantially investment opportunities in the territories of the Parties." This goal was based on the belief, shared by many developed and developing countries at that time, that the liberalization of foreign direct investment (FDI) cross-border movements would stimulate domestic economic growth and development. FDI were to bring foreign capitals, create new jobs, transfer technology and know-how to domestic companies, develop human resources and elevate the competitivity of national industries. In this sense, NAFTA's Chapter 11 promoted the elimination of barriers to FDI flows and established an objective international legal regime to protect foreign investors' rights and economic interests against political risks in host countries.[4] Hence, NAFTA's provisions recognized to foreign investors a "minimum standard of treatment", in "accordance with international law", including "fair and equitable treatment and full protection and security",[5] a "treatment no less favorable" than the one accorded to national investors,[6] as well as "most-favored-nation treatment",[7] free transfer of profits and capitals[8] and a payment of compensation for expropriation.[9] In cases of violations of one of these rights, investors were allowed to bring claims against NAFTA's member states before an independent and impartial international arbitral tribunal in order to recover damages. Investors' access to an international arbitral body was supposed to

[3] Gutner (2017), pp. 139–141.

[4] The political risks arise from the fact that the foreign investor is a private legal person which voluntarily enters in an unequal legal relationship with a sovereign legal person in both domestic and international law- the state. In the exercise of its sovereign powers, states can adopt all type of measures (legislative, administrative, judicial, etc.) that could interfere with foreign investors' economic activities and harm their private rights, such as the right to property, for example.

[5] Article 1105 of NAFTA.

[6] Article 1102 of NAFTA.

[7] Article 1103 of NAFTA.

[8] Article 1109 of NAFTA.

[9] Article 1110 of NAFTA.

preserve the neutrality of NAFTA's dispute settlement mechanism and to avoid the risks arising from the submission of investment lawsuits to state's domestic judiciaries.[10]

Before NAFTA's entry into force, Mexico had maintained state controls on investment flows for almost a century. These controls started after the adoption of the Mexican Constitution in 1917 and continued with the nationalization of oil and gas interests in 1937. Under Mexican domestic law, since 1940, many economic activities were reserved for state-owned companies and/or for companies owned by Mexicans, or with majority Mexican ownership. In every case, a FDI was to be submitted for approval to the National Foreign Investment Commission. NAFTA's adoption brought major changes in Mexican domestic law which culminated with the adoption of a new Law on Foreign Investment in 1993. The new law opened the economy to foreign investment flows and suppressed many of the preexisting state controls on their cross-border movement.[11]

In consequence, during its first 12 years of enforcement, NAFTA increased substantially the investment opportunities in Mexico. According to the World Bank, the investment flows to Mexico grew 20% after the entry into force of the agreement and the country received 106, 6 million dollars from investments from US and Canada, which represented 65.8% of the total of investment flows entries to Mexican territory.[12] However, 22 years after NAFTA's signature, some disenchantment appeared regarding its positive effects on FDI attraction to Mexico and its contribution to the country's economic development and social wellbeing. In fact, according to estimations of the Mexican government in 2014, it was expected that NAFTA's application would bring FDI up to 4% of the GDP, but it only constituted approximately 2–2.5%.[13] Additionally, the free cross-border movement of FDI flows did not reduce the asymmetries between the economies of NAFTA's member states and provoked the disarticulation of productive chains in detriment of some Mexican domestic industries. Mexico's low salaries continued to attract only specific types of FDI. Moreover, during this period, the growth of Mexican economy

[10] In all countries, domestic tribunals are, of course, independent from the executive branch. However, when the application of international norms by domestic courts is sought to constrain the activities of the executive branch, domestic judges might be timid and more reluctant regarding their potential in the international arena. (Benvenisti (1993), p. 159). The tendency for domestic judges to rule on international law issues in favor of the interests of their executive branch has been a driving force behind the creation of many international dispute settlement mechanisms. One of the main reasons for the success of international commercial and investment arbitration is the fact that arbitrators are not state agents and are supposed to be more independent than national judges when applying or interpreting international law.

[11] Folson (2014), p. 171.

[12] Secretaría de Economía de México (2012), *Con el TLCAN en 12 años se triplicó el comercio entre México, Estados Unidos y Canadá*, http://www.2006-2012.economia.gob.mx/eventos-noticias/sala-de-prensa/comunicados/5858-con-el-tlcan-en-12-anos-se-triplico-el-comercio-entre-mexico-estados-unidos-y-canada, 1.

[13] CANACINTRA (2014), Senado, Gobierno de México, *Una apreciación crítica sobre el TLCAN a 20 años*, https://www.senado.gob.mx/comisiones/relext_an/eventos/docs/RRM.pdf.

was stable, but insufficient, oscillating around 2% per year, and half of its population continued to live in poverty. Thus, even if NAFTA advanced the growth of FDI flows to Mexico, it did not stimulate substantial job creation,[14] increases of workers' salaries, transfers of technology to domestic industries and, in general, the development of sustainable conditions for the growth of the domestic market.

Additionally, during the last 10 years, NAFTA's international legal regime of investment protection became subject of severe criticism, inside and outside Mexico.

In fact, progressively, a shared view emerged on the global scale on the need to reform international investment agreements. Many developing countries, such as Ecuador, Bolivia, South Africa, and Indonesia, announced their intention to renegotiate and/or withdraw from treaties of this kind. Other states, such as India, the Czech Republic, and Netherlands, decided to go further and adopted new models of investment treaties.

Mexico first seemed to distance itself from this global crisis of the investment protection regime in international law. In addition to NAFTA's Chapter 11, Mexico has concluded 32 bilateral investment agreements (BITs, or *Acuerdos para la protección y promoción recíproca de inversiones*- APPRI) with countries from all over the world.[15] 30 of them are still in force and 21 are in their terminal phase of application, as they were signed for an initial period of 10 years; consequently, Mexico could renegotiate and/or withdraw from these treaties. However, Mexico not only did not announce its intention to modify the APPRI in force but it has recently signed some new bilateral agreements- two in 2015 with Brazil and Haiti, and the last one, in January 2020 with Hong Kong.[16] Additionally, Mexico has ratified 11 free trade agreements with investment chapters based on NAFTA's Chapter 11. Mexico did not request the modification of their provisions and has instead signed new similar agreements, such as the Comprehensive and Progressive Agreement for Trans-Pacific Partnership (CPTPP or TPP 11).[17]

NAFTA's Chapter 11 and the provisions of Mexico's other international investment agreements (APPRI and free trade agreements) have been invoked as legal basis of many claims brought by private companies before international arbitral tribunals. Mexico is the third country in Latin America and the fifth one in the world, with more demands against it in international investment arbitration. 53% of those cases were won by private companies and lost by the Mexican State. The compensations obtained by the investors ascended to approximately 243 million dollars,

[14] CANACINTRA (2014), Senado, Gobierno de México, *Una apreciación crítica sobre el TLCAN a 20 años*, https://www.senado.gob.mx/comisiones/relext_an/eventos/docs/RRM.pdf.

[15] In particular, with Germany, Argentina, Australia, Bahrein, Belorussia, China, Correa, Cuba, Denmark, United Arab Emirates, Slovakia, Spain, Finland, France, Greece, Haiti, India, Island, Italia, Kuwait, Netherlands, Panama, Portugal, United Kingdom, Czech Republic, Singapore, Sweden, Switzerland, Trinidad and Tobago and Turkey.

[16] Secretaría de Gobernación, Gobierno de México (2019), https://www.gob.mx/se/prensa/firman-mexico-y-hong-kong-acuerdo-para-promover-y-proteger-inversiones-232856.

[17] Secretaría de Relaciones Exteriores, Gobierno de México, Tratados en vigor, https://aplicaciones.sre.gob.mx/tratados/consulta_nva.php.

which were covered by Mexico's public budget. This amount did not include the overall cost of arbitral proceedings which, alone, exceeded approximately 5 million dollars, per each case.[18] Nevertheless, Mexico showed adherence to international investment arbitration, as demonstrated by its recent accession to the Washington Convention and its full submission to ICSID's jurisdiction in 2018.[19] This ratification followed some significant foreign investments in the country's energetic sector and was to bring legal certainty amidst a possible loss of confidence in Mexico's regulatory framework due the beginning of NAFTA's renegotiation and the near presidential elections, which were expected to be won by Andrés Manuel López Obrador: a politician with a leftist ideology.

Mexico's position in International Investment Law changed abruptly after the beginning of NAFTA's renegotiation process.

The re-negotiation of NAFTA took more than two years. In 2017, Mexico, the US and Canada celebrated five rounds of negotiations and in 2018- two. The climate of the negotiations took a new direction when Andrés Manuel López Obrador became the 65th President of Mexico. Shortly after his election, Jesús Seade- its chief negotiator- announced that Mexico, the US and Canada adopted a new free trade agreement called United States-Mexico-Canada Agreement (USMCA, or *Tratado entre México, Estados Unidos y Canadá- TMEC*), which was signed in 2018 and entered into force in 2020. USMCA's Chapter 14 is exclusively dedicated to the legal regulation of foreign investment flows in the North American region.

The entry into force of USMCA sealed Mexico's insertion in the global process of reform of international investment agreements. Mexico had been, traditionally, a fervent defender of the investment protection regime in international law, but, nowadays, it has shown its adherence to the proposals to rethink and re-equilibrate its legal design. In this sense, this article's main objective will be to analyze the causes of the renegotiation of NAFTA's Chapter 11, and the consequences of the entry into force of USMCA's Chapter 14 for Mexico's investment policy. The first part of the research will show that the reform of NAFTA's Chapter 11 is due to complex political and legal reasons surrounding the global crisis of international investment agreements. The second part of the article will study the changes introduced by UMSCA's Chapter 14 to some of NAFTA's Chapter 11 core substantial rules and principles and will evaluate their impact on the protection of foreign investors' rights in Mexico. The third part of the research will analyze the implications of USMCA's provisions on settlement of investment disputes for the future involvement of Mexico in international investment arbitration.

[18]ISDS (2020), *México profundiza derechos a los inversores extranjeros a pesar del alto número de demandas*, http://isds-americalatina.org/mexico/#notexi.

[19]ICSID (2018), *Mexico ratifies the ICSID Convention*, https://icsid.worldbank.org/news-and-events/news-releases/mexico-ratifies-icsid-convention.

2 The Causes of the Renegotiation of NAFTA's Chapter 11

Some of the main causes of the renegotiation of NAFTA's Chapter 11 are essentially political and related to the perception that NAFTA did not constitute an "engine of growth for all", as it created many "losers", not only between the three member states, but also between countries' own citizens. This vision appeared to be coincident with the opinion of large number of American and Mexican citizens, who felt disappointed by some of NAFTA's promises and brought to the presidencies of both countries two populist politicians, like Donald Trump and Andrés Manuel López Obrador, who were to defend the protection of the "pure people" against corrupt (transnational and neoliberal) "elites".

Since its arrival to the White House, US President Donald Trump promised to renegotiate NAFTA which it blamed for the job losses[20] of its principal voters- white men from the "Rust Belt" region.[21] In Trump's administration's point of view, NAFTA was " the worst trade deal in the history of the country";[22] because, "since it came into force in 1994, trade deficits have exploded, thousands of factories have closed, and millions of Americans have found themselves stranded, no longer able to utilize the skills for which they had been trained.(...)".[23] In many of his public statements, Trump denounced Mexico for "taking advantage" of the US by "huge trade deficits", depredatory and unfair trade practices. The American Union's "horrible deals" with states like Mexico that "are not paying their bills" would have transformed it, on its detriment, in the "world's major consumer". Using the neo-protectionist, mercantilist, and nationalist slogans "*America First*" and "*Make America Great Again*", Trump used NAFTA's renegotiation process to preserve the elimination of trade barriers to US products,[24] to stop the dislocation of productive activities and investment flows from the US, to reduce trade deficits with Mexico and Canada and to obtain a more reciprocal and secure access to their domestic markets.

In parallel, since its arrival at the Palace of Government (*Palacio de Gobierno*), Mexican President López Obrador promised the "end of the 36 years period of

[20]The de-location of many fabrics, which gave them, jobs for generations and their installation in developing countries, abundant in low-wage workers have been one of the principal subjects of Trump's presidential campaign. Since then, Trump promised to workers assembled in Indianapolis that "companies are not going to leave the United States anymore without consequences." After the elections, in his inauguration speech, he mentioned "the forgotten men and women of our country" and reassured them that they "will be forgotten no longer".

[21]The industrial "heart" of the United States, composed by the States of Pennsylvania, Michigan, Wisconsin, Ohio, and Minnesota.

[22]The Guardian (2018), *Nafta: what is it and why is Trump trying to renegotiate*?, https://www.theguardian.com/us-news/2018/aug/30/nafta-what-is-it-why-is-trump-trying-to-renegotiate.

[23]The Guardian (2018), *Nafta: what is it and why is Trump trying to renegotiate*?, https://www.theguardian.com/us-news/2018/aug/30/nafta-what-is-it-why-is-trump-trying-to-renegotiate.

[24]Office of the United States Trade Representative, Executive Office of the President, *Summary of Objectives for the NAFTA Re-negotiation,* https://ustr.gov/about-us/policy-offices/press-office/press-releases/2017/november/ustr-releases-updated-nafta.

neoliberalism" and the beginning of the "4th transformation" of the Mexican State. According to López Obrador, neoliberalism's "antipopular pillage" has been characterized by the adoption of public polices "that have promoted the wellbeing of the minorities and have marginalized most of our people". The new national strategy of its Government is based on the slogan "*For the good of all, the poor comes first*" and is seeking to promote the development of Mexican economy through a more equal repartition of its rents and resources and a stronger intervention of the state it the domestic market, as a way to guarantee social justice, peace and prosperity.[25] In this sense, President López Obrador's position toward NAFTA's renegotiation has been controversial. He agreed on the need to preserve its core objectives- the liberalization of trade and investment flows between the three North American countries- but he also emphasized that the agreement should be respectful for Mexico's sovereignty, particularly regarding the control of its energetic resources, which shall always "pertain to the Nation".[26] In the particular field of liberalization of FDI flows, President López Obrador has insisted that he will support a transparent regulatory framework for FDI, and, in this sense, has decided to suppress some administrative costs and controls for their register before governmental agencies.[27] However, he also ordered the cancellation of some important investment projects, such as the construction of a new airport for Mexico City[28] or the recently proposed reform on the electricity supply regime, which will benefit the state-owned electricity entity (*Comisión Federal de Electricidad*) "against the pillage of private companies" and foreign investors in Mexico's renewable energies sector.[29]

NAFTA's Chapter 11 renegotiation also obeys to the main legal reasons surrounding the global crisis of international investment agreements' regime.

These treaties have been perceived by governments and public opinion as unequal and disproportionate, too much in favor of foreign investors (mainly multinational companies) and completely against states' sovereignty and normative powers. As former Ecuadorian President Rafael Correa stated in 2009 after Ecuador's withdrawal from the ICSID Convention, for many developing countries they meant "colonialism and slavery towards multinational companies, Washington

---

[25] Gobierno de México, Presidencia de la República, *Presidente López Obrador declara formalmente fin del modelo neoliberal y su política económica*, https://www.gob.mx/presidencia/prensa/presidente-lopez-obrador-declara-formalmente-fin-del-modelo-neoliberal-y-su-politica-economica-lo-que-hagamos-sera-inspiracion-para-otros-pueblos.

[26] *Celebra AMLO que queda a salvo la soberanía de México durante la renegociación del TLCAN*, https://lopezobrador.org.mx/temas/tlc/.

[27] Milenio (2019), *Para atraer más Inversión Extranjera Directa, gobierno redujo costos en trámites*, https://www.milenio.com/negocios/atraer-inversion-extranjera-gobierno-redujo-costos-tramites.

[28] Gobierno de México, Presidencia de la República (2018), *Presidente López Obrador presenta proyecto de nuevo Sistema Aeroportuario de la Ciudad de México*, https://www.gob.mx/presidencia/prensa/presidente-lopez-obrador-presenta-proyecto-de-nuevo-sistema-aeroportuario-de-la-ciudad-de-mexico?idiom=es.

[29] BBC (2020), *México: la polémica reforma del sector eléctrico que enfrenta a AMLO con las compañías privadas*, https://www.bbc.com/mundo/noticias-america-latina-56270901.

and the World Bank".[30] The fact that investment treaties create duties only on behalf of States and rights only for foreign investors has been one of the mayor arguments for the renegotiation and re-equilibration of their legal design.

Another strong critique to NAFTA's Chapter 11, and to international investment agreements, in general, deals with the limits opposed to states' power to adopt domestic regulations pursuing general social interests. In fact, as mentioned above, NAFTA's Chapter 11 and all the other international investment agreements recognized the right of foreign investors to "fair and equitable treatment". The case law of international arbitral tribunals considered that this standard encompassed the protection of investors ``legitimate expectations", i.e. the expectations they had when deciding to make their investment in the host country.[31] According to this standard, if a state party to an international investment agreement, such as NAFTA, modify its domestic regulatory framework in a manner not expected or not anticipated by the investor at the moment of the investment establishment and this regulatory change produces economic costs for the investor, the state could be held internationally responsible for a violation of investor's "legitimate expectations", and, therefore, required to pay a compensation.[32] In the same sense, according to the case law of international arbitral tribunals, if states adopt new regulatory measures that negatively affect investor's economic rights and interests, they could be held internationally responsible for an "indirect expropriation" or a "measure tantamount to expropriation" and be obliged to make a reparation.[33] Many arbitral tribunals after the *Tecmed* case developed a very extensive interpretation of the concepts of "legitimate expectations"[34] and "indirect expropriation" that went far beyond the text of NAFTA and/or other particular investment agreements.

Mexico lost most of the cases brought against it by foreign investors before international arbitral tribunals precisely on the grounds of breaches of its obligations to respect investors' "legitimate expectations" and not to commit "indirect

---

[30] El Tiempo (2009), *Correa suscribe decreto que da por terminado convenio con el CIADI*, http://www.eltiempo.com.ec/noticias/economia/1/211881/correa-suscribe-decreto-que-da-por-terminado-convenio-con-el-ciadi.

[31] According to the arbitrators in the *Tecmed* case, the protection of investors legitimate expectations require "the Contracting Parties to provide to international investments treatment that does not affect the basic expectations that were taken into account by the foreign investor to make the investment. The foreign investor expects the host State to act in a consistent manner, free from ambiguity and totally transparently in its relations with the foreign investor, so that it may know beforehand any and all rules and regulations that will govern its investments." *(Técnicas Medioambientales Tecmed, S.A. v. United Mexican States, ICSID* Case No. ARB(AF)/00/2, para. 154.)

[32] *Sociedad General de Aguas de Barcelona S.A. and InterAgua Servicios Integrales del Agua S.A. v. Argentine Republic*, ICSID Case No. ARB/03/17, Decision on Liability, para. 207; *Total v. Argentina*, ICSID Case No. ARB/04/1, Decision on Liability, para. 122.

[33] Johnson and Volkov (2014).

[34] *Técnicas Medioambientales Tecmed, S.A v. The United Mexican States,* ICSID Case No. ARB (AF)/00/2; *PSEG Global et al. v. Republic of Turkey,* ICSID Case No. ARB/02/5; *Duke Energy v. Republic of Ecuador,* ICSID Case No. ARB/04/19.

expropriation". In the *Gemplus* case, for example, the arbitrators considered that Mexico's conduct towards the investor was "manifestly irrational, arbitrary and perverse, being also conducted in bad faith"[35] and was, therefore, constitutive of a violation of their "legitimate expectations". Consequently, Mexico had to pay compensations for more than 10 million dollars to both companies. In *Metalclad,* the arbitrators estimated that the adoption of a decree by the Governor of the state of San Luis Potosí declaring a protected environmental zone the place where was located a plant of treatment of dangerous residues, operated by a Spanish investor, was constitutive of an "indirect expropriation".[36] Other cases such as *Cargill,*[37] *Azinian,*[38] *Feldman,*[39] *Waste Management,*[40] *Tecmed*[41] and *Abengoa*[42] were also decided on the grounds of alleged "indirect expropriation" committed by the Mexican government.

On the global scale, the tobacco multinational company Philipp Morris instituted proceedings against Uruguay based on a BIT between Uruguay and Switzerland and invoked a violation of its "legitimate expectations" by the adoption of Uruguayan domestic legislation aimed to protect public health from tobacco's consume.[43] On the same basis, Veolia demanded Egypt for increases of the minimum salary[44] and Vattenfall protested against Germany's decision to abandon the use of nuclear energy.[45]

---

[35] ICSID Cases No. ARB(AF)/04/3 and No. ARB(AF)/04/4, para. 7–11.

[36] According to the arbitrators: "expropriation under NAFTA includes not only open, deliberate and acknowledged takings of property, such as outright seizure or formal or obligatory transfer of title in favor of the host State, but also covert or incidental interference with the use of property which has the effect of depriving the owner; in whole or in significant part, of the use or reasonably-to-be-expected economic benefit of property even if not necessarily to the obvious benefit of the host State". (*Metalclad Corporation v. The United Mexican States*, ICSID Case No. ARB(AF)/97/1, para. 10).

[37] *Cargill, Incorporated v. United Mexican States*, ICSID Case No. ARB(AF)/05/2, *Archer Daniels Midland Company and Tate & Lyle Ingredients Americas, Inc. v. The United Mexican States*, ICSID Case No. ARB (AF)/04/5.

[38] *Robert Azinian, Kenneth Davitian y Ellen Baca v. United Mexican States*, ICSID Case No. ARB (AF)/97/2.

[39] *Marvin Feldman v. United Mexican States,* ICSID Case No. ARB(AF)/99/l.

[40] *Waste Management, Inc. v. Estados Unidos Mexicanos*, ICSID Case No. ARB(AF)/ 00/3.

[41] ICSID Case No. ARB (AF)/00/2.

[42] *Abengoa S.A. y COFIDES S.A. v. United Mexican States*, ICSID Case No. ARB(AF)/09/2.

[43] The arbitral tribunal decided the case in favor of Uruguay's "discretional exercise of sovereign power". (*Philip Morris Brands Sàrl, Philip Morris Products S.A. and Abal Hermanos S.A. v. Oriental Republic of Uruguay*, ICSID Case No. ARB/10/7 (formerly *FTR Holding SA, Philip Morris Products S.A. and Abal Hermanos S.A. v. Oriental Republic of Uruguay*), para. 429 y ss.

[44] *Veolia Propreté v. Arab Republic of Egypt*, ICSID Case No. ARB/12/15.

[45] El Mundo (2016), *Jucio en Alemania al "cerrojazo" nuclear de Merkel*, http://www.elmundo.es/economia/2016/03/12/56e326fb22601dae268b45a5.html.

These important precedents have given to many the impression that international investment law's vague concepts of "legitimate expectations" and "indirect expropriation" grant investor companies with the "ability to contest any governmental line of actions that they do not like".[46] The extensive interpretation of the concept of "indirect expropriation", in particular, would have made international investment agreements look like some kind of "stabilization clauses", designed to guarantee the immutability of states' domestic legal systems *vis-à-vis* foreign investors.[47]

A third legal critique on the regime of international investment agreements concerns the lack of regulation of foreign investors' duties to protect the environment on the territory of host states and to respect the human (and social) rights of people that might be affected by the investment projects. Traditional international investment agreements did not include provisions on corporate social responsibility. In general, multinational companies are not endowed with international legal personality and have no binding duties arising from the norms and principles of international law. There have been many attempts to adopt binding instruments on transnational corporations and other business enterprises with respect to human rights. The last example is the ongoing negotiation of a UN Treaty on Business and Human Rights. However, the consensus necessary for its adoption has not been achieved yet.[48] In parallel, there are a lot of precedents where multinational companies, acting as foreign investors, caused irreparable environmental damages, and committed gross violations of human rights without assuming any negative legal consequences for their unlawful behavior.[49]

The lack of regulation of multinational companies' social and environmental responsibility in NAFTA's Chapter 11 resulted in many cases brought against Mexico before international arbitral tribunals where investors were developing business activities with potential negative impact on the environment; nevertheless, the arbitrators did not take into account any duty on their behalf to prevent, measure or repair this impact. In *Metalclad*,[50] for example, a US investor demanded Mexico for the cancellation of a building permit for a hazardous waste site in an ecological zone in the state of San Luis Potosí and claimed that this act constituted an "indirect expropriation". The arbitrators awarded 16.7 million dollars of compensation to *Metalclad* without evaluating the alleged negative impact of the waste site to the environment. In *Abengoa*[51] and *Tecmed*[52] cases, decided through the application of

---

[46] Dupré (2017).

[47] *El Paso Energy International Company v. The Argentine Republic*, ICSID Case No. ARB/03/15, para. 368.

[48] OCHR (2020), *OHCHR and business and human rights*, https://www.ohchr.org/EN/Issues/Business/Pages/WGHRandtransnationalcorporationsandotherbusiness.aspx.

[49] Monebhurrun (2017), p. 50.

[50] *Metalclad Corporation v. The United Mexican States*, ICSID Case No. ARB(AF)/97/1.

[51] *Abengoa S.A. y Cofides S.A. vs. Estados Unidos Mexicanos*, ICSID Case No. ARB(AF)/09/2.

[52] *Técnicas Medioambientales Tecmed, S.A. v. The United Mexican States*, ICSID Case No. ARB (AF)/00/2.

other international investment agreements, Mexico had adopted regulatory measures within the framework of environmental protection and public health and the arbitrators considered that they were tantamount to expropriation.

In addition to the critics on NAFTA's Chapter 11 and other international investment agreements' substantial provisions there are many contestations of their specialized dispute settlement mechanism.

In the first place, they concern some procedural aspects of international investment arbitration. In fact, its current regulation in international investment treaties, such as NAFTA, affords investors a complete "monopoly" regarding the initiation of arbitral proceedings. In other terms, investors are always the demandants and States-the respondents- before international arbitral bodies.[53] Furthermore, there is a perception that multinational companies always win, and States always lose in investment arbitration proceedings. According to UNCTAD, this happened in approximately 60% of the contentious cases brought to international arbitral tribunals in international investment law.[54] In many of these cases, states were required to pay exorbitant compensations to foreign investors. Thus, for example, in three joint cases, an arbitral tribunal established under the auspices of the Permanent Court of Arbitration, condemned Russia to pay 50 000 million of dollars to investor companies.[55] Additionally, the costs and fees of arbitral proceedings, *per se*, can exceed 3 million dollars for each case.[56] Other, more formal critics against international investment arbitration concern the lack of transparency of arbitral proceedings,[57] problems regarding the independence and impartiality of international arbitrators[58] and the absence of coherence and predictability in the case law of international arbitral tribunals.[59] These controversies raised an important debate on the need to create an international multilateral investment court- a permanent judicial

[53]Monebhurrún (2017).

[54]UNCTAD (2016), Review of Investor-State Arbitrations in 2016, http://investmentpolicyhub.unctad.org/News/Hub/Home/542.

[55]*Hulley Enterprises Ltd. c. Fédération de Russie (*Cour permanente d'arbitrage (CPA), affaire no AA 226), *Veteran Petroleum Ltd. c. Fédération de Russie* (Cour permanente d'arbitrage (CPA), affaire n° AA 228) et *Yukos Universal Ltd. c. Fédération de Russie* (Cour permanente d'arbitrage (CPA), affaire no AA 227).

[56]CNUCED (2014), *Transformation du régime des accords internationaux d'investissement*, https://unctad.org/system/files/official-document/ciiem4d2_fr.pdf, p. 5.

[57]CNUCED (2012), *Transparency: A Sequel*, Collection de la CNUCED consacrée aux problèmes relatifs aux accords internationaux d'investissement II, New York et Genève, publication des Nations Unies.

[58]Arbitrators' will to be designated in future cases and the frequent cumulation of functions (parties' legal counsels, for example, and after that arbitrators) have overshadowed their necessary impartiality. (CNUCED (2012), *Transformation du régime des accords internationaux d'investissement*, p. 5).

[59]The inexistence of appeal proceedings in international arbitration impedes the possibility to exam and reverse any possible errors in the interpretation and application of the legal rules and principles of international investment law.

body, with universal and/or regional jurisdiction, that could harmonize and unify the interpretation and application of international investment law.

The critics surrounding the substantial provisions of international investment agreements and their arbitral dispute settlement mechanism enhanced the adoption of diverse proposals for the reform of these treaties that have been discussed in many important international forums, such as the UNCTAD's World Investment Forum,[60] the OECD[61] and the EU.[62] However, the fragmentation of international investment law and the nonexistence of global multilateral organization with competence in this field pose obstacles to the adoption of a single overall reform; in consequence, states have opted for unilateral and selective modifications of their international investment agreements, such as the one pursued by NAFTA's parties.

NAFTA's renegotiation process, the reform of its Chapter 11 and the adoption of USMCA's Chapter 14 have taken into consideration the above-mentioned critics on the investment protection regime in international law and have translated them into important and sometimes radical normative changes. As it will be shown below, the general objective of all the modifications is to limit the legal protection offered by USMCA to foreign investors in Mexico and in the North American region.

3 The Reform of NAFTA's Chapter 11 substantial Provisions by the Adoption of USMCA's Chapter 14

The first major modification of USMCA's Chapter 14 in relation to NAFTA's Chapter 11 concerns the definition of investment. NAFTA's definition was particularly broad and permitted to include under the scope of the agreement many economic arrangements and entities.[63] The new definition of investment established

[60] http://unctad-worldinvestmentforum.org/.

[61] http://www.oecd.org/daf/inv/investment-policy/foi.htm.

[62] Comisión de la Unión Europea (2016), *Un futuro tribunal multilateral de inversiones*, Hoja Informativa, europa.eu/rapid/press-release_MEMO-16-4350_es.pdf.

[63] By virtue of NAFTA's Article 1139: "“(a) an enterprise; (b) an equity security of an enterprise; (c) a debt security of an enterprise (i) where the enterprise is an affiliate of the investor, or (ii) where the original maturity of the debt security is at least three years, but does not include a debt security, regardless of original maturity, of a state enterprise; (d) a loan to an enterprise (i) where the enterprise is an affiliate of the investor, or (ii) where the original maturity of the loan is at least three years, but does not include a loan, regardless of original maturity, to a state enterprise; (e) an interest in an enterprise that entitles the owner to share in income or profits of the enterprise; (f) an interest in an enterprise that entitles the owner to share in the assets of that enterprise on dissolution, other than a debt security or a loan excluded from subparagraph (c) or (d); (g) real estate or other property, tangible or intangible, acquired in the expectation or used for the purpose of economic benefit or other business purposes; and (h) interests arising from the commitment of capital or other resources in the territory of a Party to economic activity in such territory, such as under (i) contracts involving the presence of an investor's property in the territory of the Party, including turnkey or construction contracts, or concessions, or (ii) contracts where remuneration depends substantially

in USMCA's Article 14.1[64] is narrower and aimed to limit the protection offered to foreign investors under the agreement.

The same type of reform can be observed in other selective modifications of international investment agreements. Thus, for example, five years after the famous *White Industries Case* in 2011,[65] India adopted a new BIT model that included a definition of "investment" very similar to the one embraced in article 14.1 of USMCA, although even narrower.[66] In the same sense, Netherlands, being one of

on the production, revenues or profits of an enterprise;" According to the same article: "investment does not mean, (i) claims to money that arise solely from (i) commercial contracts for the sale of goods or services by a national or enterprise in the territory of a Party to an enterprise in the territory of another Party, or (ii) the extension of credit in connection with a commercial transaction, such as trade financing, other than a loan covered by subparagraph (d); or (j) any other claims to money, that do not involve the kinds of interests set out in subparagraphs (a) through (h);"

[64] According to this provision: "investment means every asset that an investor owns or controls, directly or indirectly, that has the characteristics of an investment, including such characteristics as the commitment of capital or other resources, the expectation of gain or profit, or the assumption of risk. An investment may include: (a) an enterprise; (b) shares, stock and other forms of equity participation in an enterprise; (c) bonds, debentures, other debt instruments, and loans; 1 (d) futures, options, and other derivatives; (e) turnkey, construction, management, production, concession, revenue-sharing, and other similar contracts; (f) intellectual property rights; (g) licenses, authorizations, permits, and similar rights conferred pursuant to a Party's law; 2 and (h) other tangible or intangible, movable or immovable property, and related property rights, such as liens, mortgages, pledges, and leases, but investment does not mean: (i) an order or judgment entered in a judicial or administrative action; (j) claims to money that arise solely from: (i) commercial contracts for the sale of goods or services by a natural person or enterprise in the territory of a Party to an enterprise in the territory of another Party, or (ii) the extension of credit in connection with a commercial contract referred to in subparagraph (j)(i);."

[65] *White Industries Australia Limited v. Republic of India,* UNCITRAL, Final Award (Nov. 30, 2011).

[66] According to article 1.4 of new Indian BIT Model: ""investment" means an enterprise constituted, organized and operated in good faith by an investor in accordance with the law of the Party in whose territory the investment is made, taken together with the assets of the enterprise, has the characteristics of an investment such as the commitment of capital or other resources, certain duration, the expectation of gain or profit, the assumption of risk and a significance for the development of the Party in whose territory the investment is made. An enterprise may possess the following assets: (a) shares, stocks and other forms of equity instruments of the enterprise or in another enterprise; (b) a debt instrument or security of another enterprise; (c) a loan to another enterprise (i) where the enterprise is an affiliate of the investor, or (ii) where the original maturity of the loan is at least three years; (d) licenses, permits, authorisations or similar rights conferred in accordance with the law of a Party; (e) rights conferred by contracts of a long-term nature such as those to cultivate, extract or exploit natural resources in accordance with the law of a Party, or (f) Copyrights, know-how and intellectual property rights such as patents, trademarks, industrial designs and trade names, to the extent they are recognized under the law of a Party; and (g) moveable or immovable property and related rights; (h) any other interests of the enterprise which involve substantial economic activity and out of which the enterprise derives significant financial value; For greater clarity, investment does not include the following assets of an enterprise: (i) portfolio investments of the enterprise or in another enterprise; (ii) debt securities issued by a government or government-owned or controlled enterprise, or loans to a government or government-owned or controlled enterprise; (iii) any pre-operational expenditure relating to

the main states of origin of companies that bring claims against developing states in international investment arbitration,[67] also adopted a new BIT model in 2019 with a reformed definition of investment. The first part of Article 1-a) of the agreement is identical to the first part of USMCA's article 14.1[68] and the established forms of investment cover almost the same categories.[69] The definition of investment in USMCA's article 14.1 is also very similar to the provisions of Mexico's last BIT with the United Arab Emirates.[70]

---

admission, establishment, acquisition or expansion of the enterprise incurred before the commencement of substantial business operations of the enterprise in the territory of the Party where the investment is made; (iv) claims to money that arise solely from commercial contracts for the sale of goods or services by a national or enterprise in the territory of a Party to an enterprise in the territory of another Party; (v) goodwill, brand value, market share or similar intangible rights; (vi) claims to money that arise solely from the extension of credit in connection with any commercial transaction; (vii) an order or judgment sought or entered in any judicial, administrative or arbitral proceeding; (viii) any other claims to money that do not involve the kind of interests or operations set out in the definition of investment in this Treaty."

[67] A recent study shows that, at least 12% of all the demands before international arbitral tribunals have been initiated by companies that pretended to have the nationality of Netherlands, under the 90 BITs that this country has concluded. (Verbeek and Knottneurus (2018)).

[68] According to this provision, "investment" means every kind of asset that has the characteristics of an investment, which includes a certain duration, the commitment of capital or other resources, the expectation of gain or profit, and the assumption of risk."

[69] In conformity with article 1-a) of Netherlands' new BIT model: "Forms that an investment may take include: (i) movable and immovable property as well as any other property rights in rem in respect of every kind of asset, such as mortgages, liens and pledges; (ii) rights derived from shares, bonds and other kinds of interests in companies and joint ventures; (iii) claims to money, to other assets or to any contractual performance having an economic value; (iv) rights in the field of intellectual property, technical processes, goodwill and know-how; (v) rights granted under public law or under contract, including rights to prospect, explore, extract and exploit natural resources. 'Claims to money' within the meaning of sub (iii) does not include claims to money that arise solely from commercial contracts for the sale of goods or services by a natural or legal in the territory of a Contracting Party to a natural or legal person in the territory of the other Contracting Party, the domestic financing of such contracts, or any related order, judgment, or arbitral award."

[70] Article 1-5 of Mexico- United Arab Emirates BIT states: "investment" means the following assets owned or controlled by investors of one Contracting Party and established or acquired in accordance with the laws and regulations of the other Contracting Party in whose territory the investment is made: (a) an enterprise; (b) shares, stocks and other forms of equity participation in an enterprise; (c) a debt security of an enterprise: (i) where the enterprise is an affiliate of the investor, or (ii) where the original maturity of the debt security is at least three (3) years, but does not include a debt security, regardless of original maturity. of a Contracting Party or of a State enterprise; I (d) a loan to an enterprise: (i) where the enterprise is an affiliate of the investor, or (ii) where the original maturity of the loan is at least three (3) years, but does not include a loan, regardless of original maturity, to a Contracting Party or to a State enterprise; (e) real estate or other property, tangible or intangible acquired in the expectation ~ '" or used for the purpose of economic benefit or other business purposes; (f) interests arising from the obligation to commit capital or other resources in the territory of a Contracting Party to economic activity in such territory, such as under: (i) contracts involving the presence of an investor's property in the territory of the other Contracting Party, including turnkey or construction contracts, or concessions; (ii) contracts where remuneration depends substantially on the production, revenues or profits of an enterprise, or (iii) business concessions

Another change of USMCA's Chapter 14 in relation to NAFTA's Chapter 11 concerns the definition of "investor". According to NAFTA's article 1139: "investor of a Party means a Party or state enterprise thereof, or a national or an enterprise of such Party, that seeks to make, is making or has made an investment;". In contrast, USMCA's article 14.1 states: "investor of a Party means a Party, or a national or an enterprise of a Party, that attempts to make, is making, or has made an investment in the territory of another Party, provided however that: (a) a natural person who is a dual citizen is deemed to be exclusively a national of the State of his or her dominant and effective citizenship; and (b) a natural person who is a citizen of a Party and a permanent resident of another Party is deemed to be exclusively a national of the Party of which that natural person is a citizen." The limitation in the scope of article 14.1 regarding investors with double nationality and/or residence encompass the protection offered by UMSCA to foreign investors only to private persons with effective citizenship.

It is also important to note that investors' protection in USMCA is not only for an enterprise that "has made an investment", but for the one that "has made an investment on the territory of another party". This is a very significant reform in the light of the lessons learned by Mexico from the *Cargill case*.[71] In this case, Cargill- United States corporation incorporated under the laws of the State of Delaware and headquartered in Wayzata, Minnesota- demanded Mexico on its own behalf and on behalf of its wholly owned enterprise in Mexico, Cargill de Mexico, S.A. de C. V, for losses suffered regarding an economic activity developed on the territory of the US. In that case, Mexico argued that: "NAFTA has a territorial basis. Chapter 11 is designed to afford protection to investments of persons of a Party in the territory of another Party (...)."[72] However, the arbitral tribunal considered that: "(...) the Article 1139 definition of "investment" is broad and inclusive (...)"[73] and concluded "there to be a violation of NAFTA Chapter 11 (...)".[74] The Tribunal fixed the damages to be paid by Mexico to Cargill to more

conferred by law or under contract, related to hydrocarbons, which shall be governed pursuant to the terms and conditions of such concession agreed upon between the investor and the Contracting Party or the constituent subdivision of the Contracting Party when applicable, in whose territory such concessions are made; (g) claims to money involving the kind of interests set out in (a) to (I) above, but no claims to money that arise solely from: (i) commercial contracts for the sale of goods or services by a national or enterprise in the territory of a Contracting Party to an enterprise in the territory of the other Contracting Party, or (ii)the extension of credit in connection with a commercial transaction, such as trade financing, other than a loan covered by subparagraph (d) above, and (h) Intellectual property rights. Including but not limited to copyrights and related rights, patents, industrial designs, know-how, trademarks, trade and business secrets, trade names, geographical indications, and layout-designs (topographies) of integrated circuits, and rights in plants varieties; as defined or referred in the Agreement on Trade Related Aspects of Intellectual Property Rights of the World Trade Organization."

[71] *Cargill vs. México*, ICSID Case No. ARB(AF)/05/2.

[72] *Cargill* case, para 136, p. 35.

[73] *Cargill* case, para. 147, p. 40.

[74] *Cargill* case para. 154, p. 42.

than 77 million dollars and ordered more than 2 million dollars for reimbursement of arbitral proceedings costs.[75] Nevertheless, USMCA's requirement of "an investment made in the "territory of a contracting party" might not be enough to avoid future cases like Cargill.[76]

Another relevant novelty of USMCA is the establishment of a definition of "investor of a no- Party", who is "an investor that attempts to make, is making, or has made an investment in the territory of that Party, that is not an investor of a Party". NAFTA's provisions were entitled to apply to businesses which were not owned or controlled by US, Mexican or Canadian nationals or enterprises. Thus, business owned by Europeans or Chinese nationals and/or companies, "which were constituted or organized" under NAFTA's member states laws could benefit from the rights recognized in Chapter 11. The inclusion of a definition of "investor of a no-Party" in USMCA is a clear intent to reintroduce more controls and to potentially exclude from the agreement's protection businesses owned or controlled by natural persons or companies of states no parties to the agreement. It must be interpreted in conformity with Article 1 of Annex 14-D of the USMCA,[77] which shows that this restriction is clearly directed to Chinese-owned or controlled investments in the US and Mexico.

---

[75] *Cargill* case, para. 5 and 561.

[76] The adoption of USMCA was a missed opportunity to include more precision about the location of the investment on the territory of host states and avoid the possibility for enterprises to deliver themselves to "treaty shopping" and to establish filial in their territory with the exclusive purpose to be treated as an "investor of that party". Other reforms of international investment agreements went further in this sense. Thus for example, article 1-b) of the new BIT model of Netherlands provides that ""investor" means with regard to either Contracting Party (...)", and article 1-6 states: " (c) Indications of having 'substantive business activities' in a Contracting Party may include: (i) the undertaking's registered office and/or administration is established in that Contracting Party; (ii) the undertaking's headquarters and/or management is established in that Contracting Party; (iii) the number of employees and their qualifications based in that Contracting Party; (iv) the turnover generated in that Contracting Party; and (v) an office, production facility and/or research laboratory is established in that Contracting Party;" According to its article 1.5: ""investor" means a natural or juridical person of a Party, other than a branch or representative office, that has made an investment in the territory of the other Party; For the purposes of this definition, a "juridical person" means: (a) a legal entity that is constituted, organised and operated under the law of that Party and that has substantial business activities in the territory of that Party; or (b) a legal entity that is constituted, organised and operated under the laws of that Party and that is directly or indirectly owned or controlled by a natural person of that Party or by a legal entity mentioned under subclause (a) herein." In the same sense, Mexico's last BIT with United Arab Emirates established in its article 1-6 that: ""investor of a Contracting Party" means an enterprise which is either constituted or otherwise organized under the law of a Contracting Party, and is engaged in substantive business operations in the territory of that Contracting Party, having made an investment in the territory of the other Contracting Party;"

[77] By virtue of this provision a "claimant" before an international arbitral tribunal is defined as "an investor of an Annex Party [i.e., the United States or Mexico], excluding an investor that is owned or controlled by a person of a non-Annex Party that the other Annex Party considers to be a non-market economy, that is a party to a qualifying investment dispute."

USMCA's provisions also follow the direction of other unilateral and selective modifications of international investment agreements concerning the scope of the standard of "fair and equitable treatment" and the contested concepts of "legitimate expectations" and "indirect expropriation".

As mentioned above, one of the strongest critics against the investment protection regime in international law focus on the vagueness of these concepts and the extensive way in which they have been interpreted in international arbitration case-law. Consequently, all the recent modifications of international investment agreements have embraced reforms in this sense. The most radical option has been to suppress completely any reference to the "fair and equitable treatment" standard in investment treaties' provisions. This option was undertaken by the new Indian BIT model.[78] Other reforms recognized states' obligation to afford to foreign investors "fair and equitable treatment" and full "physical security and protection"[79] but, at the same time, established a list of concrete measures that can be constitutive of an unfair and unequitable treatment.[80] Some unilateral modifications of international investment agreements also introduced radical reforms on the scope and meaning of the concept of "legitimate expectations"[81] and expressly limited and even excluded states liability for an alleged "indirect expropriation".[82]

---

[78]In fact, the new model agreement's article 3.1 only introduces a reference to parties' obligation not to subject "investments made by investors of the other Party to measures which constitute a violation of customary international law". Furthermore, the provision establishes an exhaustive list of state conducts that might infringe with this duty through "(i) Denial of justice in any judicial or administrative proceedings; or (ii) fundamental breach of due process; or (iii) targeted discrimination on manifestly unjustified grounds, such as gender, race or religious belief; or (iv)manifestly abusive treatment, such as coercion, duress and harassment."

[79]According to article 9-1 of the Netherlands new BIT model: "Each Contracting Party shall ensure fair and equitable treatment of the investments of investors of the other Contracting Party. In addition, each Contracting Party shall accord to such investments full physical security and protection."

[80]In conformity with article 9-2 of the new BIT model of Netherlands: "A Contracting Party breaches the aforementioned obligation of fair and equitable treatment where a measure or series of measures constitutes: a) Denial of justice in criminal, civil or administrative proceedings; b) Fundamental breach of due process, including a fundamental breach of transparency, in judicial and administrative proceedings; c) Manifest arbitrariness; d) Direct or targeted indirect discrimination on wrongful grounds, such as gender, race, nationality, sexual orientation or religious belief; e) Abusive treatment of investors such as harassment, coercion, abuse of power, corrupt practices or similar bad faith conduct; or f) A breach of any further elements of the fair and equitable treatment obligation adopted by the Contracting Parties in accordance with paragraph 3 of this Article."

[81]India's new BIT model doesn't mention the protection of investors' legitimate expectations" in the content of the "fair and equitable treatment" standard. Thus, even if India creates expectations on behalf of the investors and does not act in consistency with them, investors will not be able to invoke a violation of the agreement.

[82]By virtue of article 2.2 of the Netherlands new BIT model: "The provisions of this Agreement shall not affect the right of the Contracting Parties to regulate within their territories necessary to achieve legitimate policy objectives such as the protection of public health, safety, environment, public morals, labor rights, animal welfare, social or consumer protection or for prudential financial reasons. The mere fact that a Contracting Party regulates, including through a modification to its

USMCA's new provisions on investors right to a "fair and equitable treatment" are consistent with the global intents to restrict its scope and to re-balance states' obligations and investors rights under the agreement. NAFTA's article 1105 established the so called "minimum standard of treatment (. . .) in accordance with international law, including fair and equitable treatment and full protection and security." An official NAFTA interpretative ruling stated that: "Article 1105-(1) prescribes the customary international law minimum standard of treatment of aliens as the minimum standard of treatment to be afforded to investments of investors of another Party. The concepts of "fair and equitable treatment" and "full protection and security" do not require treatment in addition to or beyond that which is required by the customary international law minimum standard of treatment of aliens. A determination that there has been a breach of another provision of the NAFTA, or of a separate international agreement, does not establish that there has been a breach of Article 1105(1)."[83] Post- NAFTA US free trade agreements also endorsed a limitation of the scope of the terms "fair and equitable treatment" and "full protection and security".[84] Mexico has traditionally considered that the standard of "fair and equitable treatment" cannot go further than the minimum standard of treatment to aliens according to customary international law, first developed since the decision *Neer* in 1926.[85] NAFTA tribunals have established that: "acts that would give rise to a breach of the minimum standard of treatment prescribed by the NAFTA and customary international law as those that, weighed against the given factual context, amount to a gross denial of justice or manifest arbitrariness falling

laws, in a manner which negatively affects an investment or interferes with an investor's expectations, including its expectation of profits, is not a breach of an obligation under this Agreement." India's new model BIT goes further and expressly distinguish between direct and indirect expropriation, stating that: " the economic impact of the measure or series of measures, although the sole fact that a measure or series of measures of a Party has an adverse effect on the economic value of an investment does not establish that an indirect expropriation has occurred;" (article 5.3-i) and reaffirming states' normative sovereignty in the following terms: "Non-discriminatory regulatory measures by a Party or measures or awards by judicial bodies of a Party that are designed and applied to protect legitimate public interest or public purpose objectives such as public health, safety and the environment shall not constitute expropriation under this Article" (article 5.5).

[83] North American Free Trade Agreement, Notes of Interpretation of Certain Chapter 11 Provisions, NAFTA Free Trade Commission, July 31, 2001, http://www.sice.oas.org/tpd/nafta/commission/ch11understanding_e.asp.

[84] They inserted the word "customary" before "international law" when describing the "minimum standard of treatment" and introduced lists of measures that could violate the "fair and equitable treatment" standard, such as: the denial of justice in criminal, civil and administrative adjudicatory proceedings in accordance with the principle of due process embodied in the principal legal systems of the world; in addition, "full protection and security" was meant to require the provision of a level of police protection under customary international law. (Folson (2014), p. 281).

[85] *USA (L.F. Neer) v. Mexico* (1926), 4 R.I.A.A. 60 (Gen. Cl. Comm'n 1926).

below acceptable international standards."[86] This conception is introduced, as well, in Mexico's last BIT with the United Arab Emirates.[87]

Article 14.6-1 of the USMCA is almost identical to NAFTA's article 1105 and reaffirms the obligation for Contracting Parties to "accord to covered investments treatment in accordance with customary international law,[88] including fair and equitable treatment and full protection and security." However, article 14.6- 2 incorporates NAFTA's interpretative rulings regarding article 1105 and includes direct references to US and Mexico's post NAFTA investment agreements.[89] Therefore, it redefines and restrains the scope of the concept of "fair and equitable treatment" in line with the general evolution of international investment law in this field.

Article 14.6-4 went in the same direction regarding the protection of investors' "legitimate expectations". In fact, USMCA's article 14.6-4 restrains substantially the possibility for investors to invoke a violation of their "legitimate expectations". According to this provision: "4. For greater certainty, the mere fact that a Party takes or fails to take an action that may be inconsistent with an investor's expectations does not constitute a breach of this Article, even if there is loss or damage to the covered investment as a result." This reform will further constrain the interpretation of the scope of the minimum standard of treatment according to international customary law.

---

[86] *International Thunderbird Gaming Corporation v. United Mexican States*, UNCITRAL (January 26, 2006), para. 194.

[87] According to article 4 of the treaty: "1. Each Contracting Party shall accord to investments of investors of the Contracting Party treatment in accordance with customary international including fair and equitable treatment and full protection and security. 2. For greater certainty: (a) the concepts of "fair and equitable treatment" and "full protection and security" do not require treatment in addition to or beyond that which is required by the customary international law minimum standard of treatment of aliens, and;'(b) a determination that there has been a breach of another provision of this Agreement, or of a separate international agreement, does not establish that there has been a breach of this Article."

[88] Customary international law is defined in Annex 14-A of USMCA in the following terms: "The Parties confirm their shared understanding that "customary international law" generally and as specifically referenced in Article 14.6 (Minimum Standard of Treatment) results from a general and consistent practice of States that they follow from a sense of legal obligation. The customary international law minimum standard of treatment of aliens refers to all customary international law principles that protect the investments of aliens."

[89] Article14-6 2 states: "2. For greater certainty, paragraph 1 prescribes the customary international law minimum standard of treatment of aliens as the standard of treatment to be afforded to covered investments. The concepts of "fair and equitable treatment" and "full protection and security" do not require treatment in addition to or beyond that which is required by that standard, and do not create additional substantive rights. The obligations in paragraph 1 to provide: (a) "fair and equitable treatment" includes the obligation not to deny justice in criminal, civil, or administrative adjudicatory proceedings in accordance with the principle of due process embodied in the principal legal systems of the world; and (b) "full protection and security" requires each Party to provide the level of police protection required under customary international law. 3. A determination that there has been a breach of another provision of this Agreement, or of a separate international agreement, does not establish that there has been a breach of this Article."

Following the example of the recent reforms of other international investment agreements, USMCA embraced very important modifications on the regulation of "indirect expropriation". Even if the text of article 14.8 is almost identical to NAFTA's article 1110, the annex 14- B of USMC's Chapter 14 redefines and substantially limits the scope of investor's protection against this type of measures.[90] The new formula is similar to the one adopted in the Restatement Third of Foreign Relations Law of the US.[91] Additionally, states' normative sovereignty is reaffirmed in Article 14. 16. According to this provision: "Nothing in this Chapter shall be construed to prevent a Party from adopting, maintaining, or enforcing any measure otherwise consistent with this Chapter that it considers appropriate to ensure that investment activity in its territory is undertaken in a manner sensitive to environmental, health, safety, or other regulatory objectives." Therefore, in future arbitrations initiated under UMSCA, investors will have to pass a very high threshold when trying to demonstrate that an action taken by Mexico (or the US) is equivalent to a direct expropriation. Mexico's exercise of public power will be sheltered from demands by foreign investor if the actions are not arbitrary nor discriminatory and aim to protect public welfare objectives.

USMCA also addresses the question of investors' corporate social responsibility. As mentioned above the impact of business activities on the environment and on human rights protection is one of the causes of the current crisis of the investment protection regime in international law. All the proposals of reform have considered the necessity to establish some duties on behalf of investors in these fields. Netherlands new BIT model, for example, has introduced in its provisions a special Chapter intitled "Sustainable development".[92] However, even this progressive

[90] Article 14. 8 states:" 3. The second situation addressed by Article 14.8.1 (Expropriation and Compensation) is indirect expropriation, in which an action or series of actions by a Party has an effect equivalent to direct expropriation without formal transfer of title or outright seizure. (a) The determination of whether an action or series of actions by a Party, in a specific fact situation, constitutes an indirect expropriation, requires a case-by-case, fact based inquiry that considers, among other factors: (i) the economic impact of the government action, although the fact that an action or series of actions by a Party has an adverse effect on the economic value of an investment, standing alone, does not establish that an indirect expropriation has occurred, (ii) the extent to which the government action interferes with distinct, reasonable investment-backed expectations, 19 and (iii) the character of the government action, including its object, context, and intent. (b) Non-discriminatory regulatory actions by a Party that are designed and applied to protect legitimate public welfare objectives, such as health, safety and the environment, do not constitute indirect expropriations, except in rare circumstances."

[91] According to its provisions: "A state is responsible as for an expropriation of property when it subjects alien property to taxation, regulation, or other action that is confiscatory, or that prevents, unreasonably interferes with, or unduly delays, effective enjoyment of an alien's property or its removal from the state's territory... A state is not responsible for loss of property or for other economic disadvantage resulting from bona fide general taxation, regulation, forfeiture for crime, or other action of the kind that is commonly accepted as within the police power of states, if it is not discriminatory..."

[92] This article emphasizes states' parties' commitments to "to promote the development of international investment in such a way as to contribute to the objective of sustainable development".

model of investment agreement failed to establish direct duties on multination companies under international law.[93] India's new BIT model only included a single article concerning corporate social responsibility which is very similar to article 7 of the Netherlands' model.[94]

As mentioned above, NAFTA was silent on problems referred to corporate social responsibility. Its article 1114 was intitled "environmental concerns" and was aimed to prevent "legal dumping" in the social and environmental field; it also allowed states to adopt measures to ensure that investment activities in their territories were developed in "a manner consistent with environmental concern". UMSCA does not establish direct and enforceable duties on behalf of investors to protect human rights and the environment in host countries. However, following the example of Netherlands new model BIT, Chapter 14 last article 14.17 is a reminder of states' direct obligations to monitor business activities impact on human rights and the environment.[95] The wording of this article even suggests that there is no binding obligation

---

Article 6 also prohibits "legal dumping" by lowing the standards of environmental and social protection in order to attract foreign investments and proscribes the adoption and application of domestic "laws contributing to the objective of sustainable development in a manner that would constitute unjustifiable discrimination or a disguised restriction on trade and investment." Finally, it reaffirms states' obligations under other multilateral agreements and soft law instruments. According to article 7-5: "The Contracting Parties express their commitment to the international framework on Business and Human Rights, such as the United Nations Guiding Principles on Business and Human Rights and the OECD Guidelines for Multinational Enterprises, and commit to strengthen this framework." The provision is only related to treaties that states have already ratified, by does not establish any further obligation to become party of those agreements. Article 6-6 states: "Within the scope and application of this Agreement, the Contracting Parties reaffirm their obligations under the multilateral agreements in the field of environmental protection, labor standards and the protection of human rights to which they are party, such as the Paris Agreement, the fundamental ILO Conventions and the Universal Declaration of Human Rights. Furthermore, each Contracting Party shall continue to make sustained efforts towards ratifying the fundamental ILO Conventions that it has not yet ratified."

[93] Article 7 related to corporate social responsibility only establishes their obligation to respect domestic laws of host states on environmental, social and human rights protection and reaffirms the importance of the investors conducting "due diligence process to identify, prevent, mitigate and account for the environmental and social risks and impacts of its investment. Finally, it urges contracting parties to "to encourage investors operating within its territory or subject to its jurisdiction to voluntarily incorporate into their internal policies those internationally recognized Netherlands model Investment Agreement 22 March 2019 standards, guidelines and principles of corporate social responsibility that have been endorsed or are supported by that Party, such as the OECD Guidelines for Multinational Enterprises, the United Nations Guiding Principles on Business and Human Rights, and the Recommendation CM/REC(2016) of the Committee of Ministers to Member States on human rights and business."

[94] Article 12 of the Indian BIT model states: "Investors and their enterprises operating within its territory of each Party shall endeavor to voluntarily incorporate internationally recognized standards of corporate social responsibility in their practices and internal policies, such as statements of principle that have been endorsed or are supported by the Parties. These principles may address issues such as labor, the environment, human rights, community relations and anti-corruption."

[95] Article 14.17 states: "The Parties reaffirm the importance of each Party encouraging enterprises operating within its territory or subject to its jurisdiction to voluntarily incorporate into their internal

on states to ensure that companies will respect and subject their activities to internationally recognized standard on business, human rights and the environment. The provision does not establish that states "shall" "ensure", but only reaffirms the "importance of each party encouraging" investors to "voluntary incorporate" these standards in their practices. Thus, UMSCA creates duties for states but not for private persons. However, this provision could produce mayor future implications. Law, in general, and international (investment) law only advances little by little. The reform of USMCA is a "sand grain" in the growing awareness of the international community on the need to advance social corporate responsibility. The existing soft law standards are now referred in hard international law, which, of course, does not render them binding, *per se*, but might be the first step of the future recognition of their binding character.[96]

4 The Reforms to NAFTA's Provisions Regarding the Settlement of Investment Disputes

As mentioned above, the critics against international investment arbitration's current regime conduced to the adoption of selective unilateral reforms to international investment agreements which include important and sometimes radical modifications to the rules governing this specialized dispute settlement mechanism. Therefore, for example, in a clear attempt to limit at maximum investor's right to initiate international arbitral proceedings, India's new model BIT re-introduced the rule of exhaustion of local remedies. Under this agreement, investors must first bring their claims before domestic tribunals or administrative bodies[97] and only after that can they initiate international arbitral proceedings against the state. In addition, the model treaty provided strict procedural limitations on the timeframe for the beginning of arbitral proceedings[98] that created an almost "impenetrable" barrier to investors' access to international arbitration. Many other new investment agreements also reaffirmed the need to reach an overall and multilateral reform of international investment arbitration, to create a multilateral investment court,[99] to give priority to

policies those internationally recognized standards, guidelines, and principles of corporate social responsibility that have been endorsed or are supported by that Party, which may include the OECD Guidelines for Multinational Enterprises. These standards, guidelines, and principles may address areas such as labor, environment, gender equality, human rights, indigenous and aboriginal peoples' rights, and corruption."

[96] This recognition could also serve as a proof of a consistent state practice (*inveterata consuetudo*) required to transform soft law standards in customary international law.

[97] Articles 15.4 and 15.5 of India's new model BIT.

[98] Articles 15.4 and 15.5 of India's new model BIT.

[99] Articles 3.10 and 13.2 of the UE-Singapore BIT.

alternative dispute resolution mechanisms[100] and to approve new regulations on the constitution of arbitral tribunals and on the conduct of the proceedings.[101]

NAFTA's s system of arbitration allowed foreign investors to challenge governmental acts if they were taken in violation of the rights established in its Chapter 11. Those disputes were subject to a binding international arbitration. During the negotiation of the agreement Mexico had to make a great concession and renounce to the invocation of the Calvo Doctrine that was a traditional part of its investment policy. According to this doctrine, common to many Latin American countries, foreign investors had to forego the diplomatic protection of their national states, be treated as Mexican nationals, and seek legal remedies before domestic judicial bodies.[102] Thus, according to article 27-I of the Constitution of the United Mexican States: "(. . .) The State may grant the same right to foreigners, provided that they agree before the Ministry of Foreign Affairs to consider themselves as Mexicans regarding such property and not to invoke the protection of their governments in reference to said property, under penalty of forfeiting the property in favor of the country." In contrast, according to NAFTA's provisions, foreign investors were granted the right to initiate arbitral proceedings under the ICSID Convention if both State members to the dispute had ratified this agreement. As mentioned above, Mexico became party of the treaty in 2018. So, most of the investor claims under NAFTA in cases brought against Mexico or by Mexican investors against another state party were submitted according to the ICSID Additional Facility Rules or the UNCITRAL Arbitration Rules.[103]

As stated above, due to a general crisis of the investment protection regime, USMCA's negotiation served as an opportunity to improve and reform the rules governing the arbitral settlement of disputes arising from its Chapter 14. In this sense, USMCA gave path to some important normative changes that limit investors' opportunities to submit claims against states before international arbitral tribunals.

One of the most significant changes is that Canada did not sign USMCA's Annexes 14-C, D and E. Consequently, Canada is not party to the reformed rules on dispute settlement; Mexican and US investors cannot bring claims against Canada under USMCA's Chapter 14 and, inversely, Canadian investors cannot initiate proceedings against Mexico or the US, unless for the so called "legacy claims".[104]

A second important modification of USMCA's Chapter 14 dispute settlement mechanism concerns the material scope of the claims that can be submitted to international arbitration. Under NAFTA's Chapter 11 investors were able to initiate

[100] Articles 17 and 19 of the new BIT model of Netherlands.

[101] Article 20 of the new BIT model of Netherlands.

[102] Folson (2014), p. 181.

[103] Folson (2014), p. 185.

[104] I. e. claims brought under NAFTA in relation to "legacy investments" (investments "established or acquired between January 1, 1994, and the date of termination of NAFTA 1994, and in existence on the date of entry into force of this Agreement." (USMCA Annex 14- C, 6 a)).

arbitral proceedings against member states for violations of all the rights recognized in its provisions. USMCA's Chapter 14 incorporates important exceptions in this sense. According to article 14 D. 3. 1 a) and b): "(a) the claimant, (. . .) may submit to arbitration under this Annex a claim: (i) that the respondent has breached: (A) Article 14.4 (National Treatment) or Article 14.5 (Most-Favored Nation Treatment), except with respect to the establishment or acquisition of an investment, or (B) Article 14.8 (Expropriation and Compensation), except with respect to indirect expropriation, and (ii) that the claimant has incurred loss or damage by reason of, or arising out of, that breach." The "national treatment" claims cannot encompass questions related to the establishment or acquisition of the investment; consequently, they can only refer to "expansion, management, conduct, operation, and sale or other disposition of investments" (Articles 14.4 and 14.5). Additionally, claims based on the most-favored nation clause "excludes provisions in other international trade or investment agreements that establish international dispute resolution procedures or impose substantive obligations; and (ii) the "treatment" referred to in Article 14.5 only encompasses measures adopted or maintained by the other Annex Party, which for greater clarity may include measures adopted in connection with the implementation of substantive obligations in other international trade or investment agreements." (footnote 22 of Annex 14-D). Consequently, investors cannot bring claims for breaches of article 14. 6 regarding the minimum standard of treatment.

These changes dramatically narrow the scope of arbitral proceedings under USMCA and substantially limit investors rights to bring claims against states based on the new agreement. If Mexico (or the US) infringes its duties to afford to investors a minimum standard of treatment or not to commit an indirect expropriation, investors could only obtain reparation for breaches of USMCA's related provisions bringing cases before its domestic tribunals. By closing the door of international arbitration for the most invoked category of claims under NAFTA, the USMCA seems to be privileging local remedies over international arbitration.

This fact is confirmed by the further procedural restrictions on investors access to international arbitration. According to article 14. D. 5: "1. No claim shall be submitted to arbitration under this Annex unless: (a) the claimant (for claims brought under Article 14.D.3.1(a) (Submission of a Claim to Arbitration)) and the claimant or the enterprise (for claims brought under Article 14.D.3.1(b)) first initiated a proceeding before a competent court or administrative tribunal of the respondent with respect to the measures alleged to constitute a breach referred to in Article 14. D.3; (b) the claimant or the enterprise obtained a final decision from a court of last resort of the respondent or 30 months have elapsed from the date the proceeding in subparagraph (a) was initiated;25 (c) no more than four years have elapsed from the date on which the claimant first acquired, or should have first acquired, knowledge of the breach alleged under Article 14.D.3.1 (Submission of a Claim to Arbitration) and knowledge that the claimant (for claims brought under Article 14.D.3.1(a)) or the enterprise (for claims brought under Article 14.D.3.1(b)) has incurred loss or damage;" By virtue of footnote 25: "The provisions in subparagraphs (a) and (b) do not apply to the extent recourse to domestic remedies was obviously futile." According to Appendix 3 of USMCA: "An investor of the United States may not submit to arbitration a claim that Mexico has breached an obligation under this Chapter: (. . .) if the investor or the enterprise, respectively, has alleged that breach of an obligation under this Chapter, as distinguished from breach of other obligations under Mexican law, in proceedings before a court or administrative tribunal of Mexico." This footnote not only reestablishes the rule of exhaustion of local remedies, but also conceives Mexican local remedies as the unique and exclusive remedy for some claims under USMCA, as it expressly precludes the possibility to bring claims before Mexican domestic tribunals and then relitigate the same claims before international arbitral bodies.

As other new international investment agreements, UMSCA's Chapter 14 provisions contain some modifications regarding the regulation of international arbitral proceedings. Thus, for example, NAFTA did not ascertain specific requirements on arbitrators independence, impartiality and ethics and USMCA imposes to arbitrators the duty to "comply with the International Bar Association Guidelines on Conflicts of Interest in International Arbitration, including guidelines regarding direct or indirect conflicts of interest, or any supplemental guidelines or rules adopted by the Annex Parties; not take instructions from any organization or government regarding the dispute; and 14-D-7 (c) not, for the duration of the proceedings, act as counsel or as party-appointed expert or witness in any pending arbitration under the annexes to this Chapter."[105] USMCA's text also founds some innovations regarding the transparency of arbitral proceedings, such as the public disclosure of documents and the conduct of open hearings by the arbitral tribunal.[106]

It is worthy to mention that the limitation of the protection afforded to investors under USMCA also encompassed the establishment of state controls on the fulfillment of the international arbitral function by the tribunals constituted according to its Chapter 14. In fact, by virtue of article 14. D. 7: "12. In any arbitration conducted under this Annex, at the request of a disputing party, a tribunal shall, before issuing a decision or award on liability, transmit its proposed decision or award to the disputing parties. Within 60 days after the tribunal transmits its proposed decision or award, the disputing parties may submit written comments to the tribunal concerning any aspect of its proposed decision or award. The tribunal shall consider any comments and issue its decision or award no later than 45 days after the expiration of the 60 days comment period." The possibility of the disputing parties to make "any comments" that an international arbitral body "shall consider" before adopting a final binding award is a direct attack on the intrinsic character of international arbitration as a "third-party" dispute settlement mechanism. The general principle of law *Nemo iudex in causa sua* has its origins in the roman maxims *Nemo debet esse iudex in propria causa sua, quia no potest case iudex et pars* (Nobody can judge its own cause, as it is impossible to be, at the same time, a judge and a party), *Ne quis in sua causa iudicet vel sibi ius dicat* (Nobody can examine its own cause as a judge or make justice to himself) and *Nemo potest ese simul actor et*

[105] Article 14.D.6. 5 a), b and c).

[106] Article 14. D. 8.

iudex (Nobody can be a judge and a party at the same time). According to this principle, judges or arbitrators must be free from external interferences that might disrupt the neutral and independent character of their jurisdictional function. By permitting to the disputing parties to control "any aspect" of arbitration awards and, consequently, to act as arbitrators of their own conflict, USMCA's article 14.D 7 poses a real threat for the effective functioning of international investment arbitration.

5 Conclusion

USMCA's Chapter 14 drastically limited the international legal protection of foreign investors' rights in Mexico. Its provisions restricted the definition of "investment" and restrained the scope of the concepts of "fair and equitable treatment", "legitimate expectations" and "indirect expropriation". Additionally, the agreement closed investors' door to international arbitration for claims related to the violation of some of these rights. By keeping out from international arbitration the most invoked category of claims under NAFTA, the USMCA is privileging local remedies over international dispute settlement mechanisms. The agreement reintroduced the rule of exhaustion of local remedies and precluded investors to invoke a claim based on USMCA's Chapter 14 before an international arbitral tribunal if that claim was first submitted to a Mexican court or tribunal. Mexico was also allowed to submit written comments on the projects of awards in cases brought against it before international arbitral bodies.

Consequently, USMCA's Chapter 14 rebalanced investors' international legal protection with Mexico's sovereignty regarding the control and regulation of FDI transborder flows in accordance with its own domestic law and policy objectives. The new Chapter is clearly designed to preserve Mexico's regulatory space and its capacity to promote objectives that might negatively interfere with investment protection, without being internationally liable toward foreign investors. Mexico's ratification of USMCA also reveals its rejection of the vagueness of some of the standards of investment protection in NAFTA and its will to avoid their unpredictable and extensive interpretations in the case law of international arbitral tribunals. In many future cases brought against Mexico before international arbitral tribunals, foreign investors will have to pass a very high threshold when trying to demonstrate a violation of their internationally recognized rights by measures adopted by the state in the exercise of its sovereign powers. Thus, USMCA's Chapter 14 rebalances the rights and duties arising from the agreement in favor of Mexico. If we admit that NAFTA was an unequal treaty where everything was in favor of foreign investors and against Mexico, USMCA could turn to be an unequal treaty with an exactly inverse equilibrium, which could create huge gaps in investment protection and give to Mexico more grounds to compromise this protection with limited checks and balances and without objective international controls. The guarantee of investors' rights to receive no-discriminatory and no-arbitrary treatment after the establishment of their investment in Mexico will depend much more on state's good faith and on the effectiveness of the legal protection afforded to them by Mexican domestic law and by Mexican domestic tribunals.

In this sense, the normative changes brought by USMCA's Chapter 11 could also re-awake Mexico's historical and constitutional affinity with the Calvo doctrine, with the principles of non-intervention and sovereign equality between states and with legal nationalism, in general. The expression of the Calvo doctrine in article 27 of the Mexican Constitution is only one aspect of its general sovereign, dualist and auto-protective spirit,[107] which is a product of many centuries of Mexican social and political history, characterized by foreign invasions, US imperialism and foreign interferences of all types in Mexico's internal affairs. Mexico's domestic legal order harbor an innate instinct to preserve its autonomy and to reaffirm its own superiority in the face of foreign elements, including foreign investors. In the legal nationalism of Mexico's, and Latin American countries' domestic legal systems, in general, any loss of sovereignty is mixed with the fear and rejection of aliens and legal "otherness". The present political context in Mexico under the Presidency of Andrés Manuel López could strengthen the patterns of a return to the Calvo doctrine in the name of the nation's welfare.

USMCA's Chapter 14 implications for Mexican future investment policy might "scary" foreign investors and affect Mexico's capacity to attract and retain these economic flows. However, the decision of an investor to establish its activities in Mexico does not depend only on the content of its international investment agreements, but on many other no legal domestic conditions, such as the political stability, the regulation of the bank sector, the domestic consumers' behavior, the tax framework, the inflation levels, the exchange rates, the currency convertibility, the unemployment rates, etc. In this sense, Mexico's domestic market could continue to be attractive for foreign investors, despite USMCA's Chapter 14 bleak legal design.

References

Aparicio Cabrera A (2010) Economía Mexicana 1910-2010: Balance de un Siglo, ponencia presentada durante la Conmemoración de la Independencia y del Centenario de la Revolución, Facultad de Economía de la UNAM: 2

BBC (2020) México: la polémica reforma del sector eléctrico que enfrenta a AMLO con las compañías privadas. https://www.bbc.com/mundo/noticias-america-latina-56270901

[107] Thus, for example, according to article 33 of the Mexican Constitution: "The President of the Republic shall have the power to expel from national territory any foreigner, according to the law and after a hearing. The law shall establish the administrative procedure for this purpose, as well as the place where the foreigner should be detained and the time that the detention lasts." By virtue of article 89, by conduction the foreign policy, Mexican President "shall observe the following principles: the right to self-determination; non-intervention; peaceful solution of controversies; outlawing the use of force or threat in international relations; equal rights of States..."

Benvenisti E (1993) Judicial misgivings regarding the application of international law: an analysis of attitudes of international courts. EJIL 4:159
Cabral R (1985) "Industrialización y política económica", en Desarrollo y Crisis de la economía mexicana, Selección de Rolando Cordera, lecturas No. 39. Fondo de Cultura Económica, pp 67–100
CANACINTRA (2014) Senado, Gobierno de México, Una apreciación crítica sobre el TLCAN a 20 años, https://www.senado.gob.mx/comisiones/relext_an/eventos/docs/RRM.pdf
Comisión de la Unión Europea (2016) Un futuro tribunal multilateral de inversiones, Hoja Informativa, europa.eu/rapid/press-release_MEMO-16-4350_es.pdf
Dupré M (2017) L'arbitrage d'investissement à la croisée des chemins. Alternatives Économiques, http://www.veblen-institute.org/L-arbitrage-d-investissement-a-la-croisee-des-chemins.html
El Mundo (2016) Jucio en Alemania al "cerrojazo" nuclear de Merkel, http://www.elmundo.es/economia/2016/03/12/56e326fb22601dae268b45a5.html
El Tiempo (2009) Correa suscribe decreto que da por terminado convenio con el CIADI, http://www.eltiempo.com.ec/noticias/economia/1/211881/correa-suscribe-decreto-que-da-por-terminado-convenio-con-el-ciadi
Folson R (2014) NAFTA in a Nutshell. West Academics Publishing, p 171
Gobierno de México., Presidencia de la República, Presidente López Obrador declara formalmente fin del modelo neoliberal y su política económica, https://www.gob.mx/presidencia/prensa/presidente-lopez-obrador-declara-formalmente-fin-del-modelo-neoliberal-y-su-politica-economica-lo-que-hagamos-sera-inspiracion-para-otros-pueblos
Gobierno de México, Presidencia de la República (2018) Presidente López Obrador presenta proyecto de nuevo Sistema Aeroportuario de la Ciudad de México, https://www.gob.mx/presidencia/prensa/presidente-lopez-obrador-presenta-proyecto-de-nuevo-sistema-aeroportuario-de-la-ciudad-de-mexico?idiom=es
Gutner T (2017) The politics of international organizations. SAGE Publications, pp 139–141
ICSID (2018) Mexico ratifies the ICSID Convention. https://icsid.worldbank.org/news-and-events/news-releases/mexico-ratifies-icsid-convention
ISDS (2020) México profundiza derechos a los inversores extranjeros a pesar del alto número de demandas. http://isds-americalatina.org/mexico/#notexi
Johnson L, Volkov O (2014) State Liability for Regulatory Change: How International Investment Rules are Overriding Domestic Law. https://www.iisd.org/itn/2014/01/06/state-liability-for-regulatory-change-how-international-investment-rules-are-overriding-domestic-law/#_ftn3
Milenio (2019) Para atraer más Inversión Extranjera Directa, gobierno redujo costos en trámites. https://www.milenio.com/negocios/atraer-inversion-extranjera-gobierno-redujo-costos-tramites
Monebhurrun N (2017) Mapping the duties of private companies in international investment law. Braz J Int Law 14:5
OCHR (2020) OHCHR and business and human rights, https://www.ohchr.org/EN/Issues/Business/Pages/WGHRandtransnationalcorporationsandotherbusiness.aspx
Office of the United States Trade Representative, Executive Office of the President., Summary of Objectives for the NAFTA Re-negotiation, https://ustr.gov/about-us/policy-offices/press-office/press-releases/2017/november/ustr-releases-updated-nafta
Secretaría de Economía de México (2012) Con el TLCAN en 12 años se triplicó el comercio entre México, Estados Unidos y Canadá. http://www.2006-2012.economia.gob.mx/eventos-noticias/sala-de-prensa/comunicados/5858-con-el-tlcan-en-12-anos-se-triplico-el-comercio-entre-mexico-estados-unidos-y-canada
Secretaría de Gobernación, Gobierno de México (2019). https://www.gob.mx/se/prensa/firman-mexico-y-hong-kong-acuerdo-para-promover-y-proteger-inversiones-232856
Secretaría de Relaciones Exteriores., Gobierno de México, Tratados en vigor, https://aplicaciones.sre.gob.mx/tratados/consulta_nva.php
The Guardian (2018) Nafta: what is it and why is Trump trying to renegotiate? https://www.theguardian.com/us-news/2018/aug/30/nafta-what-is-it-why-is-trump-trying-to-renegotiate

UNCTAD (2012) Transparency: A Sequel, Collection de la CNUCED consacrée aux problèmes relatifs aux accords internationaux d'investissement II, New York et Genève, publication des Nations Unies

UNCTAD (2014) Transformation du régime des accords internationaux d'investissement. https://unctad.org/system/files/official-document/ciiem4d2_fr.pdf, p. 5

UNCTAD (2016) Review of Investor-State Arbitrations in 2016, http://investmentpolicyhub.unctad.org/News/Hub/Home/542

Verbeek B-J, Knottneurus R (2018) Le projet 2018 de TBI néerlandais: évaluation critique. https://www.iisd.org/itn/fr/2018/07/30/the-2018-draft-dutch-model-bit-a-critical-assessment-bart-jaap-verbeek-and-roeline-knottnerus/

Virdzhiniya Petrova Georgieva holds a Licence Degree in Law from the *Sorbonne Law School*, a Master 1 Degree in European Law, a Master II Degree in International Economic Law from the same University. She also has a Master and PhD degree in Law from the *National Autonomous University of Mexico*. She currently acts as Associate Professor at the *National Autonomous University of Mexico.*

Correction to: International Investment Law in Chile: Recent Developments in Times of Reform

Pablo Nilo Donoso

Correction to:
Chapter 3 in: N. Monebhurrun et al. (eds.), *International Investment Law and Arbitration from a Latin American Perspective*, International Law and the Global South, https://doi.org/10.1007/978-3-031-49382-9_3

The original version of this chapter was inadvertently published without a few final corrections. The chapter has been updated with the following important changes:

- An article note has been included on page 1.
- In the first line on page 52, the text "(also "the Program")" has been included.
- In section 5.3.3, the last two paragraphs have been replaced with a new content.

The updated original version for this chapter can be found at https://doi.org/10.1007/978-3-031-49382-9_3

N. Monebhurrun et al. (eds.), *International Investment Law and Arbitration from a Latin American Perspective*, International Law and the Global South,
https://doi.org/10.1007/978-3-031-49382-9_12

MIX
Papier aus verantwortungsvollen Quellen
Paper from responsible sources
FSC® C105338
FSC
www.fsc.org

If you have any concerns about our products,
you can contact us on
ProductSafety@springernature.com

In case Publisher is established outside the EU,
the EU authorized representative is:
Springer Nature Customer Service Center GmbH
Europaplatz 3, 69115 Heidelberg, Germany

Printed by Libri Plureos GmbH
in Hamburg, Germany